Family Law

'That something named as "family law" is a veritable minefield. Here remains in constant collision the endless desire for domination of women confronted by the aspirations for accelerated social change for securing equality and justice for all women as human beings and as citizens. With a characteristically lucid combination of scholarly analysis and activist insight, Flavia Agnes brings to us a fuller understanding of these contending politics of desire juxtaposing coequally the diverse elements in religious traditions and customary social/cultural practices with some progressive accidents of legislative and judicial decisions. But 'more' is also needed in the hyperglobalizing Indian conjuncture. Agnes suggests the imperatives of retooling and recrafting activist critique in the service of a better future for women's rights as human rights.'

Upendra Baxi
Emeritus Professor, Universities of Warwick and Delhi

'This book is an outstanding contribution to the understanding of the jurisprudential foundations and constitutional underpinnings of family law. This work fulfills an important gap in the existing literature by providing an interdisciplinary and critical analysis of family law relating to a number of religions in contemporary India.'

C. Raj Kumar
Vice Chancellor, O.P. Jindal Global University and Dean, Jindal Global Law School

'Flavia's book is a very timely one and one that will be welcomed by law schools and more importantly law students. This work is an invaluable resource to law students, legal researchers and those engaged in feminist legal advocacy.'

Ratna Kapur
Director, Centre for Feminist Legal Research, New Delhi

'This work is thorough and exhaustive and has the potential of becoming a source book on women's rights and law for jurists, teachers, students and activists.'

Kalpana Kannabiran
Senior Fellow and Director, Chityala Ailamma Centre for Interdisciplinary Research, Secunderabad

'The much needed analysis of family law in India based on the practical experience of lawyers and women litigants is finally here. The two volumes instead of focussing on what the law is or even what it ought to be have rather focussed on "the impact of varied legal processes upon the lives of women". Flavia Agnes has not shied away from using the tools of feminist legal theory to examine the law and the legal system and challenge its basic concepts and theoretical footing. The volumes thus fill the huge gap in the research and writing on family law, and will be a much valued possession for students and teachers of family law and provide a useful perspective for practitioners as well.'

Elizabeth V.S.
Additional Professor, NLSUI Bangalore

Family Law

Volume 1

Family Laws and Constitutional Claims

Flavia Agnes

OXFORD
UNIVERSITY PRESS

OXFORD
UNIVERSITY PRESS

Oxford University Press is a department of the University of Oxford.
It furthers the University's objective of excellence in research, scholarship,
and education by publishing worldwide. Oxford is a registered trademark of
Oxford University Press in the UK and in certain other countries

Published in India by
Oxford University Press
22 Workspace, 2nd Floor, 1/22 Asaf Ali Road, New Delhi 110002, India

First published 2011
Third impression 2021
Digitally Printed in 2024

ISBN-13 (print edition): 978-0-19-806790-0
ISBN-10 (print edition): 0-19-806790-9

ISBN-13 (eBook): 978-0-19-908826-3
ISBN-10 (eBook): 0-19-908826-8

Typeset in Arno Pro 11/13
by BeSpoke Integrated Solutions, Puducherry, India 605 008
Printed in India by Manipal Technologies Limited, Manipal

To the women from whom I learnt the interface between life and law

Contents

Section B

Section C

Boxes and Figures

Abbreviations

AC	Appeal Cases	DPSP	Directive Principles of State Policy
AIDWA	All India Democratic Women's Association	FB	Full Bench
		GLR	Gauhati Law Reporter
AIMPLB	All India Muslim Personal Law Board	Guj	Gujarat High Court
AIR	All India Reporter	GWA	Guardians and Wards Act
AIWC	All India Women's Conference	HAMA	Hindu Adoption and Maintenance Act
All	Allahabad High Court		
AP	Andhra Pradesh High Court	HGMA	Hindu Guardinanship and Minority Act
Art.	Article		
AWAG	Ahmedabad Women's Action Group	HMA	Hindu Marriage Act
BHCR	Bombay High Court Reporter	HP	Himachal Pradesh High Court
BLR	Bombay Law Reporter	HSA	Hindu Succession Act
BMRA	Bombay Marriage Registration Act	HUF	Hindu Undivided family
Bom	Bombay High Court	IA	Indian Appeals
Bom.CR	Bombay Case Reporter	ICMA	Indian Christian Marriage Act
Cal	Calcutta High Court	IDA	Indian Divorce Act
CEDAW	Convention on the Elimination of All Forms of Discrimination against Women	ILR	Indian Law Reporter
		ILS	Indian Law Society
		IPC	Indian Penal Code
CMRA	Child Marriage Restraint Act	J&K	Jammu and Kashmir High Court
CNI	Church of North India	JT	Judgement Today
Co. Ltd.	Company Limited	Kar	Karnataka High Court
Col.	Collectively	Ker	Kerala High Court
CPI(M)	Communist Party of India (Marxist)	KLT	Kerala Law Times
Cr.PC	Criminal Procedure Code	L.R.	Legal Representatives
Cri.LJ	Criminal Law Journal	Lah	Lahore High Court
CSI	Church of South India	LSD	Lok Sabha Debates
DA	Divorce Act	Lt. Col	Lieutenant Colonel
Del	Delhi High Court	Mad	Madras High Court
DMC	Divorce and Matrimonial Cases	Mh.LJ	Maharashtra Law Journal
DNA	Deoxy Ribonucleic Acid	MIA	Moore's Indian Appeals

ML	Muslim Law	r/w	Read With
MP	Madhya Pradesh High Court	RCR	Restitution of Conjugal Rights
MWA	Muslim Women's Act	RSD	Rajya Sabha Debates
Nag	Nagpur High Court	SB	Special Bench
NCW	National Commission for Women	SC	Supreme Court
NFIW	National Federation of Indian Women	SCC	Supreme Court Cases
NGO	Non-governmental Organization	SCW	Supreme Court Weekly
NPC	National Planning Committee	SDA	Sadar Diwani Adalat
Ori	Orissa High Court	Supp	Supplement
Ors.	Others	TLLS	Tagore Law Lecture Series
P&H	Punjab and Haryana High Court	UCC	Uniform Civil Code
Pat	Patna High Court	UP	Uttar Pradesh High Court
PC	Privy Council	WIA	Women's Indian Association
PMDA	Parsi Marriage and Divorce Act	WP	Writ Petition
POC	Perry's Oriental Cases	WR	Weekly Reporter
Punj	Punjab High Court	WRAG	Women's Research and Action Group

Foreword

It is indeed a matter of great privilege for me to have been entrusted with the task of writing the Foreword to the two volumes of *Family Law*. Despite the size of the volumes, when taken together, there is an unwavering clarity of thought in both the volumes. The author stays true to her image of a person whose primary aim behind writing the present book (as also the ones previously written by her) is to bring a number of problems in the society to the fore, and not merely to enter into an academic exercise of compilation of information.

There is no gainsaying that India has undergone an unprecedented transformation in last few decades. However, other than the changes in the economic and political spheres, the Indian society has also changed exponentially, leading to an upheaval in human relations. Since India is being observed and scrutinized at the world stage more than ever before, there is an impending duty upon the legislature to do away with some of the draconian and exceedingly conservative personal laws that are considered to be unequal and biased against women and, thereby, present a more liberal face before the world. In the march towards becoming an economic superpower, an equally important need to create a balanced society can certainly not be underplayed.

Personal laws have witnessed rapid advances due to the constantly changing nature of human relations. Therefore, to keep pace with such changes is a great challenge for both, the legislature and the judiciary. However, the courts have shown a positive and a fair amount of pro-activeness, combined with judicial creativity in meeting with the demands of a dynamic society. At the same time, in keeping pace with the changing trends in the society, the courts have taken utmost care to preserve the social fabric.

These volumes greatly emphasize the idea that 'justice' in its true sense, can never be achieved without bringing about a sense of fairness and parity in the society. It is in this light that the author delves into the real idea of a truly participative democracy and the need to accord an equal place to women in the society. The uniqueness of these books lies in the fact that they have tried to view the idea of fairness and justice from the point of view of women, particularly those who have hitherto been marginalized as to what is their idea of a fair social order. The books cover vast contours of the society, thereby making it a multi-dimensional work.

In volume 1, chapter 1 elaborately examines the various personal laws of the Hindus, Muslims, Christians, Parsis, and Jews and states that the personal laws of each religious community is a cumulative result of the social, economic, and political factors prevalent in the society. Therefore, the concept of justice differs in each religion depending upon such factors. However, the common thread running through all these religions is the underlying and impending need for a change in the personal laws and to increasingly bring it in conformity with the modern advances in the society.

Chapter 2 of the same volume studies the constitutional provisions which have a bearing on the field of personal laws and the role of the judiciary in reconciling the personal laws of each community with the supreme constitutional provisions. The author also intellectually enters into areas which are currently mired in political debates, such as the comparison of personal laws of the minority communities with that of the majority, Uniform Civil Code and so on.

In volume 2, chapter 1 scrutinizes the institution of marriage and its evolution from olden times to its swiftly changing nature in today's society owing to various social, moral, and economic factors. The author further examines the legislative changes brought about to maintain harmony and preservation of this institution, such as the Protection of Women from Domestic Violence Act. This chapter also highlights several problems that have perennially plagued the society, such as child marriage, registration of marriages, and traditional notions of heterosexual marriages.

In volume 2, chapter 2 provides a broad perspective on the rights and duties of spouses, not only towards each other, but also in relation to other family members, especially children. In addition, the author has also discussed the various legal mechanisms in place for enforcement of these rights and duties.

Chapter 3 in volume 2 is a detailed study of the procedural aspects of matrimonial laws and whether such procedural mechanisms are in consonance with the idea of justice. However, inspite of the present legal mechanisms, the author has also given due importance to conciliatory measures as an alternative means to avoid litigation.

Personal laws occupy a unique position in today's age and play a pivotal role in keeping the society within the moral and civil bounds. It is trite to say that every person is covered under the ambit of such personal laws, and is greatly affected by changes that are brought about in this field. Therefore, there is an indispensable need to educate, not only the lawyers, but also the citizenry about the importance and impact of personal laws. It is informative books such as these that help in positively shaping the public opinion.

The legislative and judicial decisions mentioned on every subject are a result of extensive collection from a number of sources and have been carefully edited to cover each realm of the subject. Legal principles have been succinctly extracted from these decisions and lucidly interpreted. The books are, therefore, an exhaustive amalgamation of legal principles, decisions, and opinions. However, apart from reliance on legal texts and case laws, the author has not lost sight of the ground realities and the practicalities that exist in the society as well as the operation of law. Further, an extensive subject index has been provided for an uncomplicated search of the point under reference, keeping in mind the wide nature of the laws that these books cover.

It would not be incorrect to say that going through the entire two volumes has been a highly enriching experience for me. I am of the sincere belief that this educative work is highly useful and will be well received by the members of the Bench, Bar, students of law, and academics.

NEW DELHI   Justice Ajit Prakash Shah
10 November 2010   (Former Chief Justice of
                                  the High Court of Delhi)

Acknowledgements

Two volumes of Family Law that have spanned over five years gather a lot of debt. They have evolved through innumerable contributions from friends and colleagues involved with the women's movement and from the legal fraternity to whom I remain indebted. My ideology of legal feminism and feminist lawyering is grounded within two seemingly diverse disciplines—the domain of formal law and litigation with its own grammar and set of rules, and a counter perspective of women's rights which challenges the notions of 'neutrality' and 'formal equality' within law, while bringing isolated experiences of individual women who venture out to claim their rights, into the precincts of formal courts. These volumes are an attempt to bridge the gap between the two.

There are many, who have constructively contributed to these works. At the top of this list are students, too numerous to list, from various law universities and colleges, who have interned with *Majlis* in Mumbai over the past few years. Their enthusiasm and reassurance that both the books would be extremely useful to students of family law helped boost my confidence and sustain my interest in this project. Thanks are also due to Prof. Vijay Ghormade, Principal, G.J. Advani Law College, Mumbai, who urged me to embark on this journey.

Without his assurance, I could not have ventured into the project.

I deeply appreciate the invaluable contribution of Aparna Ray who assisted me during the initial phase of this project and scanned through reams of unruly material that I sent her and reworked it into a comprehensive framework of a textbook. I am grateful to my colleague Nausheen Yousuf for pointing out the gaps in the sections on Muslim law and for her assistance in filling these gaps. I am also grateful to Persis Sidhva, a fifth year student of Government Law College, Mumbai, for her unstinting support and help in sourcing material and checking references.

The entire team of lawyers and researchers at *Majlis* has patiently stood by me through these years and shared my concerns. My special thanks to Pooja Kute, Audrey D'Mello, Dolly Mendonca, and Anisha Gopi as well as my ex-colleagues, Veena Gowda, Sumangala Biradar, and Apurva Parsekar. The insights gained while strategizing for women's rights and litigating on their behalf have helped me grasp the complex interface between life, law, and litigation and have enriched these works.

My friends, Vasudha Nagaraj, Monica Sakhrani, Mitra sharafi Chaitanya Lakkimsetti, and Shoba Ghosh read some of the chapters as they evolved and made valuable suggestions. Madhusree Dutta has been an integral part of this project and has shared my anxieties, frustrations, and fatigue. The books evolved while responding to her critical comments and to probing questions from someone who stands outside the realm of formal law and litigation but who has a great impulse for the culture of rights. I sincerely appreciate her valuable contribution to the books.

I thank Justice, A.P. Shah, former Chief Justice of the Delhi High Court for writing the Foreword which has added value to both the volumes. I would also like to mention the contributions of Prof. Upendra Baxi, whose legal engagements have been a constant source of inspiration.

I also owe a debt to Prof. Werner Mensky and Prof. Marc Galantar whose engagements with legal pluralism and people's law have influenced my own writings.

Special thanks are also due to Justice A.K. Ganguly of the Supreme Court with whom I have shared a platform on a number of occasions on issues of gender sensitization for the judiciary. I also thank Justice D. Y. Chandrachud of the Bombay High Court and Director, Maharashtra Judicial Academy, for providing me with an opportunity to interact with the lower judiciary in Maharashtra on concerns of women's rights. Special thanks are also due to Prof. Mohan Gopal, Director, National Judicial Academy, for involving me in various programmes of the Academy as a visiting faculty. These interactions have helped me frame women's rights within a formal legal discourse and to contribute, in a modest way, to the evolution of feminist jurisprudence in the Indian context.

I gratefully acknowledge the initial grant from Christian Aid which helped me take up this project.

I wish to extend my sincere appreciation to the editors at Oxford University Press for goading me on and for constantly setting new deadlines as I kept lapsing. The comments from the anonymous reviewer and the queries raised by editors at OUP have helped in sharpening some of the arguments and removing some of the inconsistencies and ambivalence.

My family, particularly my daughters, Audrey and Odile has patiently awaited the completion of these books. However, they now share with me the joy of completion of both the works.

Flavia Agnes
November 2010

Law, Justice, and Gender

THE THEORY AND PRACTICE OF LAW

The primary concern while setting out to write this book *Family Law* (brought to you in two volumes), has been to weave women's rights into legal theory. Law, justice, and gender have been its three major concerns. The book examines the interface between life and law, between meta-narratives of justice and the lived experiences of women, and provides in-depth exposé of the complex realm of family laws while exploring the overlaps and contradictions within them.

The vibrancy of law, as it evolves through litigation, is examined in this context. It is within this dynamic space that judges, lawyers, and litigants interact to challenge or validate the lived-in practices or people's law against the grain of formal law, which leads to multiple interpretations and varied negotiations. Hence the book does not confine itself to a discussion on formal law enshrined within statutes, codes, sections, and articles.

Writing this book has provided me with an opportunity to test legal premises and skills of litigation against the rigour of academic discourse. The thread that binds the five chapters

in the two volumes is the concern about the impact of varied legal processes upon the lives of women. This is a question lawyers defending women's rights are constantly confronted with. The book reflects this concern and places these contestations beyond the immediacy of legal practice, in an attempt to translate them into legal academics and legal pedagogy. While negotiating the boundaries of formal law, the book contextualizes social realities, legal campaigns, and judicial discretions. Hence, from the formal terrain of law, the discussion often spills on to historical and sociological processes as well contemporary concerns. The title *Family Law* is located within this wider framework.

The term 'law' is not reflective of legal positivism[1] but conceptualizes law as a social mediator of relationships between people within the broader spectrum of legal realism. The theory of legal realism asserts that law should

---

[1] Legal theorists Jeremy Bentham, John Austin and later Hans Kelsen and H.L.A. Hart, among others, subscribed to the philosophy of legal positivism or 'law's autonomy' and viewed law as 'natural law and natural rights', a sovereign command or a 'set of rules usually enforced by a set of institutions'.

be understood and determined by the actual practices of courts, law offices, and police stations, rather than as rules and doctrines set forth in statutes or learned treatises.[2] This premise contested the autonomy of law by affirming that judges made law through discretionary acts of interpretation. It served to usher in a series of 'critical movements' in law, such as law and society, the critical legal studies, legal anthropology, legal pluralism, and feminist legal theory, to name a few. However, despite these multiple and innovative interventions, it is widely accepted that inter-disciplinarity, as a pedagogic approach to law, continues to remain at the margins.

It is imperative that legal theory is embedded within sociological, historical, and economic contexts, in what Roger Cotterrell (1989) refers to as 'politics of jurisprudence'. Cotterrell argues that there is a need to study both the doctrine and the social, economic, and political contexts of the doctrine, in order to be able to explain how legal change takes place. An understanding of social effects of laws and of the sociological factors that shape it, requires a theory which attempts to systematically explain the nature of law. Cotterrell argues that since all theories are partial and contextual, theories generated in the North American or European contexts may not achieve universality, despite their claims.

Reflecting similar concerns, this book is an attempt to fill the void within the rubric of a contemporary and evolving discipline, 'gender and law', which, by its very formulation, is inter-disciplinary in its approach. In this context, this book attempts to bridge the gap between the theory and practice of law, between the

'doctrinal' and 'non-doctrinal', between the 'ideal' and the 'technical' and hopes to blur these binaries through a comprehensive and inclusive approach.

Within these trajectories in the realm of legal theory, the book explores a wide range of topics. The history and development of personal laws and their textual and customary sources, the impact of statutory codes, evolution of the institution of marriage and its dissolution, rights and obligations which accrue through the contract of marriage, state recognition of informal sexual relationships—these are some of the issues which are explored from the perspective of both legal theory and legal practice. Extraneous influences of other socio-political and historical developments, such as Anglo-Saxon legal traditions and their impact upon pre-colonial non-state adjudication, women's entry into the political domain and their role in framing the Indian Constitution, the manner in which assurances of equality and freedom allude women, the notion of honour in the context of citizenship, the determination of morality in the context of women's economic rights, tribunalization of formal court structures and its impact upon women—these diverse strands become important scripts in this exploration. Contestations, negotiations, and subversions by women with their families, communities and state structures through which a women-oriented legal theory is evolved is the recurring theme of the book.

THE 'JUSTICE' CLAIMS OF WOMEN

Moving away from grand theories and master narratives of law, the notion of 'justice' is explored in the context of legal interpretations of women's claims. While tracking diverse strands, the challenge has been to examine what constitutes 'justice' for women within the normative patriarchal social structures of both

---

[2] The theory of legal realism had a great impact in the United States. Oliver Wendell Holmes, Jr. J., Roscoe Pound, Benjamin Cardozo J., and Karl Llewellyn were some of the renowned proponents of this theory.

formal and informal laws. Law is always presumed to 'do justice' and it is believed that if law is unjust today, it can be reformed to do justice. However, a consensus on what exactly 'justice' and 'equity' mean is hard to attain. As a consequence, it is always the notion of justice held by dominant groups that is reflected in the laws of the region, which invariably causes injustice to the weaker and marginalized sections of society.

'Justice' is the key concern of law or in other words, law is centrally implicated in the project of justice. Philosophers and social thinkers down the ages have called law to account in the name of justice and demanded that law provide a language for justice. But Sarat and Kearns (1998) argue that running through the history of jurisprudence and legal theory is a recurring concern about the ways in which law is implicated in injustice. Theories of law and theories of justice often work in tandem.

Interpreting justice as fairness and equality, John Rawls (1971) advanced a distributive model of justice which has been critiqued by several later theorists.[3] Iris Young (1990) argues that Rawls' distributive model based on impartiality, formal equality and the unitary model of subjectivity, fails to consider institutional arrangements of exclusions of people of other cultural traditions such as non-Western and non-white. She urges social theorists to define and assess the distributive paradigm and emphasizes the need for affirmation rather than suppression of social group differences, concluding that the concept of justice coincides with the concept of the political.

Several feminist theorists have argued that the instrumental characterization of law as a tool for the potential transformation of society is far too simplistic. They hold that law is a crude and limited device and is circumscribed by the dominant ideologies of the society in which it is produced. Existing beliefs and assumptions shape the context of a legal provision. Even when changes are successfully made on a doctrinal level, they can and will fail if judges or others charged with the application of new laws revert to interpretations that merely replicate old results. The impact of dominant ideologies on the shape and content of law and the legal process makes the idea of 'progress' through legal reforms problematic (MacKinnon 1989; Fineman 1995; Sunder Rajan 2003; Menon 2004). Since legal, moral, and social codes are determined by hegemonic claims of patriarchy, an exploration into the notion of justice and fairness to women can be embarked upon only after piercing the veil of 'neutrality', 'impartiality' and 'formal equality' within law.

The core which runs through this volume is women's rights, hence it becomes imperative for me to address the doctrinal concern—whether a woman-centric legal doctrine can be termed as 'biased' and lacking a 'neutral' perspective?[4] Can the lens of feminism or concern for women's rights be labeled as 'biased'? Further, is there a framework of neutrality that prevails beyond it, which a legal scholar must adhere to? These questions have been addressed by several feminist legal scholars, too numerous to list here, both Western and non-Western. I have merely followed their footsteps and have

---

[3] See Amartya Sen's critique of this theory in *The Idea of Justice* (2009), where he argues that justice as relational and a process of challenging injustice.

[4] This is usually formulated as '*the woman question*' a phrase first used by Simone De Beauvoir, in her path breaking treatise, *The Second Sex* in 1949 (English translation Penguin: 1972). Since then, several feminists have explored this theme in various disciplines such as philosophy, political theory, literature, etc. See Bartlett 1990: 829–8.

contextualized this premise within the context of concerns raised in this book.

While challenging the premise of 'neutrality of law', I ground my arguments within feminist legal theory, posited as 'perspective scholarship', which challenges the traditional notion that law is a neutral, objective, relational set of rules, unaffected in content and form by the passions and perspectives of those who possess and wield the power inherent in law and legal institutions. Perspective scholarship adds the explicit consideration of diverse perspectives to the realist, law-in-society tradition and is based on the premise that certain groups historically have been unrepresented (or under-represented) in law and that their exclusion has led to biases and an incompleteness or deficit in contemporary legal analysis and legal institutions. Perspective scholars argue the corresponding contention that historically excluded groups have different, perhaps unique, views and experiences that are relevant to the issues and circumstances regulated and controlled by law. This scholarship adds nuance to the traditional and rather monotone canvas of law. It makes more complete and more complex our consideration of the questions, 'what is law?' and 'what are the roles and function of law in our society?' (Fineman 1995: 24–5) Within the realm of perspective scholarship, feminist legal theory has helped redefine the prevailing notions of justice within both the private domain of the family and the public domain of the civil society.

Within this perspective, the concern of this book is to assess how women perceive justice, how they pursue and access it, and what are the measures of determining the success of these pursuits. These complex questions need to be addressed in order to evolve a women-centric theory of justice, based on the experiences of women who seek it. The book attempts to

capture these contests and provides new critical frames to engage with justice. It documents the narratives of women's successes and failures in challenging injustice in their lives, through an exploration of legal precedents, relying extensively on the 'case law' methodology.

While theorizing about women's rights, 'gender' becomes a useful term to signify a deeply entrenched institutionalization of sexual difference which permeates our society. It has now become evident that much of what has traditionally been thought of as inherent sexual differences are socially produced. Many injustices are experienced by women by virtue of the fact that they are women. This is primarily due to the gendered nature of the family and society, which adversely affects women. Susan Okin (1989) terms this as a major 'justice crisis' in contemporary Western societies arising from concerns of gender. The term 'gender' and 'justice' is used here in a similar context, to examine the 'justice crisis' within family laws in India.

Substantive law is enmeshed within procedural technicalities and hinders the process of accessing justice. As Katharine Bartlett (1990: 829–88) has argued there has not been sufficient theorization about methodological aspects of what 'doing' of law should entail and what true status should be given to contesting legal claims. Procedures and methodological aspects are important because the claims of law's legitimacy are based on what constitutes 'truth' and moulds our views about the possibilities of legal practice and reform. The process of determining 'truth' is critical while examining the procedures under criminal law, but it also has a bearing on civil law while examining issues such as validity of marriage, sexual conduct of women, determination of paternity, etc. These aspects which affect women's rights, depend on the legal appreciation of 'truth' (and credibility), legal 'presumptions' and popular notions of legality.

Within the rights discourse, the domain of the law is entwined within the domain of the courts. The space within which the rights claims are located become important symbols of 'justice' in popular perceptions. It is within this 'sacrosanct' space that the magisterial power of law is experienced, claims are secured and rights are protected. The family courts are the terrain where law, justice, and gender interlock within a contested frame. The conceptual framework of these courts, their functioning, the sensitivity of the judges and court officials, and the infrastructure provided to women litigants from vulnerable and marginalized groups are important yardsticks for measuring the notions of procedural justice.

In the interface between life and law, the isolated experiences of individual women who venture out to claim their rights become central to the enquiry. In this interface, the mundane and the ordinariness of life gets intermingled with lofty jurisprudential concepts and gets transformed into a 'legal narrative'. The manner in which women negotiate their claims and entitlements within the realm of law is an important indicator for testing out our notions of 'law', 'justice' and 'legality'. Marc Galanter (1989) has pointed out, a case law centered methodology, though popular among legal scholars, is extremely constraining. To get a more rounded perspective, the exploration must extend beyond legal texts to the workings of the lawyers' chambers and proceedings in trial courts. Here the pre-litigation legal strategies, interim orders, and timely negotiations play a more vital role in securing rights than alluring legal principles and theories of justice. In an attempt to bring these negotiations into the realm of formal legal pedagogy, the interface

of life and law is examined through legal narratives from a lawyer's perspective.

EXAMINING THE CONTOURS OF FEMINIST LEGAL THEORY

Within the broad canvas of 'gender and law', the two volumes of this book on family law problematize three specific themes in contemporary feminist legal theory in India:

i. The notion of 'equality' or 'sameness' between men and women within marriage and implications of using a gender neutral term 'spouse';

ii. The use of a generic term 'women', devoid of its specific socio-cultural context and location and its implications for women from minority communities, in the context of the demand for a uniform civil code; and

iii. The notion of 'universal' human rights values as evolved in the West and the desirability of applying them within specific local contexts of the non-West.

The following is a further elaboration of these three themes.

i. *The notion of 'equality' or 'sameness' between men and women within marriage and implications of using a gender neutral term 'spouse'.*

Principles of 'equality' and 'sameness' can be applied only to those situated equally. Applying the standard of equality to those who are situated unequally serves only to widen the gulf of inequality. Marriage and family are inherently gendered institutions with clearly defined gender roles. I argue that since women are judged as 'women' according to gendered expectations, gender-specific terms such as 'husband' and 'wife' help us grasp the implications of these terms within matrimonial relationships. The gender neutral term 'spouse' tends to gloss over the inequality inherent within the institution of marriage where gender roles are clearly defined.

To elaborate further, though 'adultery' is a ground for divorce for both men and women, the social and legal implications for the husband and the wife differ widely. Historically, Hindu husbands had sanctions of polygamy and institutions such as concubinage and prostitution served to cater to men's polygamous and extra-marital sexual desires. Hence as per popular perceptions of legality, adultery by men tends to be condoned, by community, law and even by wives themselves as their own social status and economic rights depend upon their marriage. But in the context of the high premium awarded to women's chastity, any lapse on the part of women seem to be viewed far more stringently, leading to denial of maintenance and may even hamper rights to custody of children.[5]

Even innocuous terms such as 'cruelty' or 'desertion' which may superficially appear to be devoid of a gendered context, when used as grounds for divorce acquire a specific gendered meaning. The problem gets exaggerated in proceedings for maintenance, where economic claims are pitted against women's sexual morality. Chapters 1 and 2 of the next volume address this concern.

To draw out the way in which the meaning of 'men' and 'women' has served to structure major social institutions is not to fall back on purely 'natural' categories. Women are disadvantaged not only by the fact of gender differences but also by rules that ignore the difference

While campaigning for rights in the public domain, such as the right to vote, the right to hold public office, and for the right to equal remuneration, liberal feminists in the West evolved the equality paradigm, emphasizing

sameness of treatment. Hesitant to accommodate differences, they demanded that gender-neutral terms (e.g., person) should replace gender specific terms (e.g., men). There was a fear among some feminist scholars that a reference to 'men' and 'women' may reinforce the patriarchal claim that 'woman' is a natural and timeless category defined by certain innate, biological characteristics (Pateman 1988: 17).

The 'sameness' model feminists emphasize that the way for women to achieve legal recognition of their equal status to men is to deny the legal relevance of their differences and insist that women should be recognized as gender-neutral legal persons. But Fineman (1991) counters this with the argument that while there are powerful symbolic reasons for applying the sameness model, symbolism cannot be a primary concern if application of formal equality (or rule equality) standards perpetuates status inequality. Feminist legal theory must take the unequal position of women as a present given and must incorporate gendered differences as an explicit part of its analysis of family law.

ii. *The use of a generic term 'women', devoid of its specific socio-cultural context and locations and its implications for women from minority communities, in the context of the demand for a uniform civil code (UCC).*

While examining the demand for a uniform set of family laws applicable to all communities, a question that needs to be interrogated is whether the term 'women' is a universal category, devoid of specific socio-cultural contexts and locations and whether personal laws can be examined ahistorically, stripped of their colonial and post-colonial groundings? The concerns of Chapter 1 of this volume is to trace the historical developments of the various personal laws.

The demand for a UCC places gender as a neutral terrain, distanced from contemporary

---

[5] *Dwarakabai v. Prof. Mainam Mathews*, AIR 1953 Mad 792.

political processes. The demand projects minority women as lacking a voice and an agency either in their own communities or through the process of litigation, to claim their rights within existing structures. It projects legislative intervention in the form of an enactment of a uniform code as the only option to attain gender justice for minority women.

The claims of women from minority communities cannot be formulated merely within the narrow context of a progression from community control to state control and needs to be contextualized within the multiple hierarchies and complex negotiations between community, nation-state and the female subject, and the dynamics of contemporary majority-minority politics. In the wake of increasing hostilities towards minority communities, 'personal laws' have become important markers of community/religious identity for minority groups. Women are an integral part of this identity and get marked as prime targets during communal riots and are subjected to gruesome sexual violence, as was evident during the communal violence which took place in Gujarat in 2002 (Agnes forthcoming).

Faced with this painful reality, I have argued that a process of reform within personal laws is better suited to protect women from these communities against their own internal patriarchies, rather than endorsing a majoritarian Hindu agenda of enforcing a uniform civil code as a feminist project. Such a project, which would inadvertently situate minority women in an antagonist relationship against their own communities, and hence may not receive the support of women from these communities, who have been subjected to extreme violence and humiliation, as Muslims, during communal violence. The solution to the problem cannot lie within separate registers of 'gender' and 'minority identity' and feminism needs to develop an

intersectional approach which would factor in the multiple layers of discriminations which Muslim women are subjected to. This issue is discussed in Chapter 2 of this volume.

While using the generic term 'women', it cannot be denied that there are many important differences amongst women. Since all women are not similarly situated, there is a need to contextualize the specificities of women belonging to marginalized communities. Since women's oppression is not homogenous in content and since it is not determined by one root, underlying cause, there cannot be one 'feminist method', or 'feminist epistemology' (Fraser and Nicholson 1988).

While examining the rights of minority women in the Indian context, the formulations of critical race theorists in the United States, specifically the term 'intersectionality of race and gender', coined by Kimberlé Crenshaw (1989: 139–67) to contextualize black women's situation, is an important analytical tool.[6] Crenshaw argues that the experiences of black women cannot be subsumed within the traditional boundaries of either race or gender discrimination and the intersection of racism and sexism factors into black women's lives in ways that cannot be captured wholly by looking at the race or gender dimensions of those experiences separately.

iii. *The notion of 'universal' human rights values as evolved in the West and the desirability of applying them within specific local contexts of the non-West.*

---

[6] The term was first coined in the context of 'feminist thought and critical race theory' and refers to the manner in which various socially and culturally constructed categories of discrimination interact on multiple and often simultaneous levels, contributing to systematic social inequality. Also see Crenshaw (1991: 1241–99).

The legitimacy of pluralistic and non-state customary laws has been subjected to criticism within the international human rights discourse under the coinage, 'women's rights are human rights'. Issues such as violence against women and trafficking of women for sex work have also been prominent concerns in this discourse. But alongside, there have been other issues such as polygamous marriages, child marriages, etc. I argue against the demand for universal application of human rights as articulated by international women's groups from the West (and endorsed by some women's groups and feminist scholars in India) in favour of a more nuanced and culture specific theory of women's rights.

Here I find Chandra Mohanty's (2003) critique of euro-centrism within Western developmental discourses of modernity through the lens of racial, sexual, and class-based assumptions, useful. Mohanty points out that gender essentialism, i.e., over generalized claims about women, assumes that women have a coherent group identity within different cultures prior to their entry into social relations. Such generalizations are hegemonic in that they represent the problems of privileged women who are often (though not exclusively) white, Western, and middle class. These generalizations, based on some abstract notion of strategic sisterhood, efface the problems, perspective, and political concerns of women, marginalized because of class, race, religion, ethnicity, and/or sexual orientation.

The demand for compulsory registration of marriage and for declaring all unregistered marriages as well as all child marriages as void needs to be examined in the context of increasing state control and raises a concern whether such control will be beneficial to women or, on the contrary, serve to defeat their existing

rights. Law-making cannot be a narrow and short-sighted venture at the instance of some pressure groups, acting upon certain international mandates of human rights. It carries very deep implications for a vast majority of people.

The question of Muslim polygamy also needs to be examined in the context of Hindu polygamy and the implications of imposing monogamy through the enactment of the Hindu Marriage Act, 1955. Women in culturally accepted polygamous or marriage-like relationships are denied their right to maintenance due to these hegemonic claims.

These concerns become critical while we examine the issues of child marriages and registration of marriages and maintenance to women in polygamous marriages which are discussed in Chapters 1 and 2 of the second volume. I have argued that the contemporary feminist discourse needs to be far more nuanced while addressing these issues. Rather than blindly advocating a 'universally' accepted position framed by a First world feminist discourse, women's rights groups need to advance a position which is rooted within Third world realities. A feminist voice must lend credence to the claims of the weaker against the might of the *status quo*-ists institutional authorities.

Fine tuning this delicate balance is a challenging task, but this precisely has been the aspiration while setting out to write this book. Often, the positions taken here may seem contrary to the well-trodden feminist path or even ambiguous and contradictory to the positions advocated elsewhere within this book itself. I have tried to examine each issue within its own contours to provide the reader a diverse and complex view of the manner in which legal dictums unfold upon the lives of women. The overall attempt has been to address the debates within the contemporary women's movement in India and bring them within the domain of legal pedagogy.

OVERVIEW OF CHAPTERS

Chapter 1 discusses the history of laws governing various religious denominations, from their scriptural sources to contemporary applications. The colonial norm of labeling community practices as 'religious' personal laws served to create mutually exclusive and hostile communities. Within the post-colonial nation-state, personal laws have become markers of cultural identity. Despite this, I argue that the progression within these laws has been towards uniformity, when tested against the constitutional paradigms, despite the claims of divinity and diversity.

A sketch of the legal structure within which the 'personal law regime' was situated during the early period of colonial rule is provided by way of introductory comments. The adversarial adjudication and hierarchical court system influenced all family laws in India, including the customary and religious. Contestations over community-based rights were framed through principles of 'justice, equity, and good conscience'. The adversarial contests and legal rules governing them transformed the fluid realm of community-based customs into rigid codes by invoking the principle of legal precedent. This drastically curtailed the process of evolution of laws at the local level.

Against this backdrop of a newly evolving colonial legal edifice, personal laws of five different religious denominations—Hindu, Muslim, Christian, Parsi, and Jewish—are examined. This serves to widen the discourse over personal laws beyond the binaries of Hindu-Muslim, which usually gets framed as a majority-minority conflict. The historical origins, community interfaces, progression from non-state customary practices to state regulated legal rules, the process of codification, and the constitutional validity of these laws are explored. To broaden the discussion, the civil law of marriage, i.e., the Special Marriage Act and customary laws are also examined. The civil law of marriage provides an optional secular code for all Indians and is a step towards uniformity and secularization of laws of marriage and divorce. But it has failed to make a dent within community-based customary practices. The scope of the book precludes an elaborate discussion on the rich tradition of customs which are prevalent among various tribes and castes in India. Hence the discussion is confined to the margins and intersections of state law and customary law, within the purview of family law.

The core argument of this chapter is that despite the claim of divine revelation, religious laws, in effect, are people's laws which are moulded through community practices, which in turn are influenced by the prevailing socio-economic and political forces. They are susceptible to human interventions by way of legal interpretations. Further, since socio-economic and political realities of a region influence its personal laws, it can be argued that any change in this broader realm will, in turn, bring changes within the personal laws. Hence personal laws are not static but dynamic. A gradual change takes place within them through a cumulative process of change in community customs and practices, legal interpretations, and codifications. Though at first sight the process of codification appears to be a sudden rupture in community practices, internalization of the new principles introduced by it is a gradual process and gets transfixed only through a contentious, litigation process or internal changes within community beliefs and practices.

Within this prevailing social reality, the concern of this chapter is to examine whether women's rights have been adequately protected within an overarching patriarchy, both historical (feudal) and contemporary (capitalist). The process of attaining gender justice has not been linear and both community and state laws continue to function from an inherent patriarchal bias against women. Further, the domains of formal state law and community-based non-state law are not mutually exclusive. Though apparently in conflict, statutory law, which is deemed to be uniform and certain, but also formal and alien, coexists alongside pluralistic community practices, which are fluid and ridden with internal contradictions, but also accessible. Most women live with these contradictions in a sort of middle ground and negotiate their rights within both, the formal and alien court structures and the informal and accessible community spaces.

Chapter 2 examines the provisions of a modern constitution and its assurances of freedom and equality to its female citizens. Three different concerns are addressed here:

1. Providing an overview and examining the mandate of social transformation;
2. Examining the theoretical framework of Article 44: the enactment of a uniform civil code for all communities and its political implications for minorities;
3. Examining the notion of citizenship and the manner in which women get excluded from the citizenship project.

The role of the judiciary for protecting the citizens against arbitrary state actions and denial of basic rights of equality, liberty, and freedom enshrined in this basic document is critical. The judiciary has played in ensuring that these assurances do not remain hollow promises by invoking them to defend the rights of either individual or a class of women, through its power of judicial review.

Beyond the domain of law, rights, and litigation, this section also explores the various struggles in which women have attempted to intersect the binaries of the private and public domains of traditional notions of citizenship, defined according to masculine norms of propertied men. Their struggle for acquiring basic literacy, formal education, and professional skills and formation of women's organizations and associations and their participation in the national movements are etched out.

In the second section, the political debate around Article 44 (enactment of a uniform civil code), is examined within a complex rubric of contesting claims located within the majority-minority dichotomy. The rights of Muslim women, which were entangled within claims of modernity and national integration at one end and the protection of minority culture and religious freedoms at the other, are explored at length. Of equal concern are the communally-tinted media projections of Muslim women, which have caused extensive harm to their cause. The third section examines, from a purely academic point of view, the drafts of the uniform civil code prepared by various sections—legal academia, state functionaries, and women's groups—from the perspective of gender justice.

In its conclusions, the chapter attempts to take the argument further into the domain of citizenship claims within a broader political context. In a stratified and hierarchical social order, women's claims to citizenship are not only framed through a relationship with the state but are constantly negotiated through other social units such as the community and the family. The implications and outcomes of these negotiations and the manner in which several segments of poor and marginalized women are excluded from the claim of citizenship are examined. The manner in which issues of sexuality and sexual ownership of women and claims of poor women beyond national boundaries are important concerns in this conclusion.

The second volume of the book addresses three distinct concerns—women's rights within the law of marriage and divorce, matrimonial rights, and obligations and the procedural aspect of the functioning of family courts in India. The concluding chapter of the second volume explores the interface between life and law and argues that the life experiences do not neatly correspond to formal institutional locations and that the law gets constituted in a 'bottom up' manner as opposed to the top down process of law making by legislators and judges.

Law is a dynamic and evolving process and one is inundated with material generated through reported cases. The book contains only a glimpse of legal trends and selective leading cases. But hopefully, it will prove to be a comprehensive resource for teaching family law in India.

A word of caution: There is no certainty in judicial verdicts, and through a stroke of pen a judgment can undo several earlier rulings which had laboriously carved out a space for women's rights. The recent ruling of Justice Markandey Katju and Justice T.S. Thakur in *D. Velusamy v. D. Patchaiammal* is a case in point. This judgment has constrained the scope of the Domestic Violence Act, which had provided a safety net for women trapped in informal and bigamous marriages. Several rulings of various high courts and the Supreme Court had also attempted to expand the scope of maintenance under Section 125 of the Cr.PC to secure the rights of women in this category. A reference made in *Chanmuniya v. Virendra Kumar Singh Kushwaha* by Justice G.S. Singhvi and Justice A.K. Ganguly (also of the Supreme Court), on 7 October 2010 to a larger bench, which is pending, will hopefully undo the harm caused by this ruling and place the rights of women in informal relationships on a firmer footing.

1

Personal Laws and Women's Rights

AN OVERVIEW OF THE PERSONAL LAW REGIME
An exploration into gender concerns within family laws in India must begin with the history of personal laws. With its rich and diverse cultural heritage, religious beliefs, and customary practices, India provides a vast, complex, and at times contradictory, field of personal laws where the traditional coexists with the modern. State-enacted statutory law and court-evolved case law have reconciled with non-state 'people's law'. The contradictions and confusions which are inevitable in this co-existence make personal laws a challenging field of study, both in terms of legal history as well as contemporary social and legal practices. This chapter attempts to trace this rich and diverse pluralistic legal tradition.

A comprehensive account of personal laws under seven major systems that exist in India—Hindu, Islamic, Christian, Parsi, Jewish, Civil, and Customary—is explored in this chapter. Encompassing debates spanning the colonial and post-colonial periods, it provides an intersectional reading of customary, religious/textual, and civil law while examining the jurisprudential negotiations between community and state and between codified laws and fluid customs, within the framework of legal pluralism. It examines the specific ways in which personal laws represent the blurring of boundaries between textual, interpretive and customary traditions. The state enacted civil law of marriage and divorce, The Special Marriage Act, which is applicable to people across religious denominations and functions as an 'optional' civil code is included to take the discussion beyond the realm of 'religious laws'. The discussion on customary law is confined to the margins and intersections of state law and customary law which comes under the purview of 'family law'. Due to the limited scope of this book, it does not extend into the vast and dynamic field of customary law in India.

While examining the realm of personal laws, it becomes necessary to expose the reader to the legal system introduced during the early part of the colonial rule within which the regime of personal laws came to be located. This process drastically changed the non-state customary practices into state regulated 'personal laws'. Hence an overview of this system and the manner in which it impacted the realm of family laws and family relations in India is provided by way of introduction.

The primary concern of this chapter is to dispel the misconceptions which plague the domain of personal laws and to explore the spaces which protect women's rights. The aim here is also to widen the debate over 'personal laws' beyond the narrow confines of Hindu (progressive) versus Muslim (regressive-fundamentalist) and explore the different ways in which various communities have dealt with their personal laws. Each realm of law is examined within its own internal processes and dynamics rather than attempting to fit them into a predetermined structure.

Family Laws: Customary Usages rather than Scriptural Dictates

A popular misconception which shrouds the issue of 'personal laws' is that these laws are based on religious texts which lay a claim to 'divine revelations' and are hence, pre-ordained, infallible, sanctimonious, and static. While 'divine revelations' can at best be termed as a source of law, they do not contain 'law' as we understand the term today. Divine law-making cannot be termed as a legal system in its own right. It needs human interventions by way of interpretation, application, and lived-in experiences of people to transform it into the law of the land. Hence it would be accurate to state that the diverse laws regulating family relationships are rooted either in customary practices or in interpretations of the divine law by scholars which were later modified through colonial interventions. Some parts of personal laws were subsequently codified into statutes during the colonial and the post-colonial period.

There is also a tendency to project all customary laws as anti-women and state enactments or official laws as pro-women. Contrary to popular belief, the history of women's rights is not linear, with scriptural and customary laws forming one end of the scale and statutory reforms slowly and steadily progressing towards the other. The history is complex with various interactive forces constantly at play. Women's rights are not only constrained by certain patriarchal norms, but are also shaped and moulded by several social, economic, and political underpinnings.

We also need to acknowledge that despite codification, a large segment of the Hindu (this applies to other communities as well) population lives and manages its affairs outside the pale of state laws and regulations. In fact, a Hindu need never interact with state authorities, neither for the solemnization of marriage nor for its dissolution, as these can be carried out through customary practices within the non-state mediation fora. It is within this sphere that the rights of poor and marginalized women, to whom the formal court structures seem too distant and alien, are constantly contested and negotiated.

To trace the antecedents of the non-state dispute resolution mechanisms within Hindu law, we need to examine the ancient Hindu *dharmashastras* (or the Brahminical *smriti* law), upon which the modern Hindu law of marriage and divorce is based. These scriptures do not contain legal principles in the strict sense that we understand the term today. The smritis preached *dharma*, denoting ethics, morality, and good behaviour (*sadachara*). Custom was recognized as an important source of law. A custom which contravenes a smriti rule could be perfectly valid and could be given effect to, not only in informal dispute settlement processes but even in a formal court of law. The accepted legal maxim was that a clear proof of custom outweighs a written text (Diwan and Diwan 1997: 24).

Some scholars have extended this legal maxim even further by emphasizing that the smritis were a mere recording of accepted local customs (Bhattacharjee 1994:12–39). Even the oft cited *Manusmriti*, which is projected as a 'divine code' or as 'Laws of Manu' (akin to the Laws of Moses), is a compilation of ancient customs and usages (Desai 1998:19). Since the smritis were based on local customs, there was great diversity within them. Practices which were contradictory to each other could be termed as 'Hindu' traditions. In addition, the lower castes (Shudras) and various tribes were not governed by the smriti codes. Their practices differed a great deal from the brahminical smriti dictates.

Similarly, though Islamic law claims its origins to the 'revealed law' or the Holy Quran, the Islamic *Fiqh* (or jurisprudential law) is based on the knowledge derived from the four sources of Islamic law—the Quran (divine revelation), *Sunna* (tradition of the prophet), *Ijma* (scholarly agreement), and *Qiyas* (reasoning by analogy) (Fyzee 1974: 16–18). In the Indian context, until the enactment of the Application of Shariat Act in 1937, many Muslim communities continued to follow the local pre-conversion community practices and some of these practices were upheld by colonial courts.[1] Mensky affirms that the internal diversity of Muslim understandings of law almost matches that of pluralist Hindu conceptualizations. Both legal systems have had to rely on human processes to ensure that their law does not remain static in the rapidly changing socio cultural environments over many centuries and to develop their normative orders in harmony with what their respective societies considered to be in line with dharma or *sharia* (Mensky 2003: 47).

Even the statutes governing Christian marriages do not have claims of 'divine origin'. These were enacted during the colonial period (the Indian Divorce Act, 1869 and the Indian Christian Marriage Act, 1872) and were based on the then prevailing English matrimonial law of the Anglican Church (a Protestant denomination). Further, the Christian converts continued to practice the local customary practices of property inheritance of their pre-conversion days. One of the earliest judgments of the Privy Council in 1863, *Abraham* v. *Abraham*,[2] held as follows:

The profession of Christianity releases the convert from the trammels of the Hindu law but it does not of necessity involve any change of the rights or relations of the convert in matters with which Christianity has no concern such as his rights and interests in and his powers over property.

This principle was applied to various Christian communities even after the enactment of the egalitarian Indian Succession Act, 1865.[3] The practice continued well into the post-Independence period.[4]

Although Parsis and Jews carried their own personal laws into India and continued to practice them as a marker of their separate identity, they too mingled with local communities and adopted local languages and customary practices. The Parsis adopted the local practice of dispute resolution (*panchayats*) and were able to incorporate this system even into their

---

[1] See the decision in *Hirbae* v. *Sonbae*, POC (1853) pp. 110 (also referred to as the Khoja's and Memon's case), which is discussed in a subsequent section of this book titled 'Evolution of Indo-Islamic Law'.

[2] (1863) 9 MIA 195

[3] See the decisions in *Francis Ghosal* v. *Gabri Ghosal*, (1907) 31 Bom 25.

[4] See the ruling in *Premchand* v. *Lilavathi*, AIR 1956 HP 17 and *Mary Roy* v. *State of Kerala*, AIR 1986 SC 1011 discussed in a subsequent section of this book which discusses the Christian law of succession.

statutory law of marriage and divorce.[5] Similarly, though the Jewish law lays a claim to 'divine revelations' or the ancient Mosaic law, this law has been considerably modernized. Further, the courts have held that the Jewish law as practiced by Jewish people elsewhere cannot be applied to the Jewish people in India as their law would have been modified as per local customs.[6]

So, as we embark on this exploration of personal laws, it needs to be emphasized that the investigation is not of 'religious texts' or 'religious tenets' but of colonial interventions and subsequent legislative enactments. Within the dynamic terrain of contested claims, statutory stipulations are constantly shaped by judicial interpretations hence land mark rulings which have brought substantial changes within personal laws have been highlighted.

Anglo-Saxon Jurisprudence and Ascendance of 'Scriptural Law'

The development of personal laws is intrinsically linked to the history of colonialism. According to Derrett, the oddity of the personal law system stems from two sources: the history of India and the juridical presupposition of the European rulers of the eighteenth century.[7] To categorize the diverse and pluralistic population along religious identities in order to apply to them 'their' personal laws and to evolve a judicial system in response to the then prevailing social conditions was not an easy task for the British administrators of the early colonial period. It was a process of trial and error, a balancing act which needed astute political maneuvering. The extent of legal interference in local practices depended on a variety of factors, both political and economic.

At the advent of colonial rule, the Company officers who were engaged in setting up trading establishments were often called upon to adjudicate over family and civil disputes. Later, they acquired the Diwani rights to arbitrate in civil disputes under the authority of the Mughal ruler in parts of Bengal, Bihar, and Orissa.[8] The first seed of Anglo-Saxon jurisprudence was sown at this juncture. Since the Company officers did not have a legal background, they relied either upon the local *pundits* and *qazis* or the principles of English law in an *ad hoc* manner. To provide legal validity to such arbitrations, after the Company established its rule, various charters of the British Parliament bestowed upon it the jurisdiction over the natives and

---

[5] See Part III, Parsi Matrimonial Courts of the Parsi Marriage and Divorce Act, 1936, particularly Section 24 which stipulates that only Parsis can be appointed as delegates (jury) in a Parsi Matrimonial Court. For a detailed discussion regarding the Parsi family laws see subsequent section of this book titled 'Parsi Law of Marriage and Succession'.

[6] See the ruling of Justice Crump in *Rachel Benjamin v. Benjamin Soloman Benjamin*, (1926) Vol.28 Bom.LR 328. This judgment also mentions the Jewish Benevolent Society, a body elected by the community, which had the power to arbitrate in family disputes. For a detailed discussion see subsequent section of this book titled 'Jewish Law of Marriage and Divorce'.

[7] The Britishers knew that such a system operated in the Ottoman Empire and they viewed the Mughals as a variety of 'Moors' or Muhammadan sovereigns with whom the Christian world had various dealings. Derrett also mentions that some jurists may have remembered the system of personal laws which prevailed in the Middle Ages in Continental Europe, whereby citizens of various towns and provinces of the Empire were entitled to have their laws administered to them. (Derrett 1999: 53)

[8] The legal system in existence then was Islamic, but the courts set up by Mughuls were *Fauzdari* (criminal). The *Diwani* (or civil) courts administering civil law applied the custom of the people in dispute resolution.

also deputed lawyers to adjudicate over these disputes (Jain 1966: 24).

The term 'personal laws' was first introduced in the Presidencies of Calcutta, Bombay, and Madras during the late eighteenth century, when the pre-colonial, non-state arbitration fora were transformed into state-regulated and state-controlled adjudicative systems. The transformation was at two levels: (i) through the introduction of a legal structure modelled on English courts which were adversarial in nature (that is, Anglo-Saxon jurisprudence); and (ii) through principles of substantive law which were evolved and administered in these courts (that is, Anglo-Hindu and Anglo-Mohammedan laws).

The Charter of George I in 1726 authorized the establishment of Mayor's Courts (courts of the King of England) at Calcutta, Bombay, and Madras. These courts started applying the principles of English courts. But it was felt that this scheme would not work well in the hinterlands of the Presidencies. This hesitation prevented the English administrators from introducing English law as the law of the land. There was the wariness of a colonial power to intrude in sensitive areas of group morality (Baxi 1986: 42).

The Warren Hastings' Plan of 1772 provided for the establishment of civil and criminal courts in each district (the so-called *mofussil* courts or *mufassils*) and explicitly saved the right of Hindus and Muslims to apply their own personal laws in civil matters. Article XXIII of the Plan stipulated that the laws of Quran with respect to the Mohammedans and those of *Shastra*s with respect to the 'Gentoos'.[9] At this juncture, it became imperative to categorise the pluralistic communities along religious lines in order to apply to them their specific 'personal'

laws. This set in motion a gradual process of homogenising the local customs and practices which could be regulated through the state machinery. The religious identities of various communities became rigid in the course of litigation over property disputes.[10]

The practice of saving personal laws of the natives which started at this juncture, continued through all subsequent British Regulations. But the Charters were not clear whether the native laws of Hindus and Muslims referred to their religious laws or to the customary usages, or to both. When the Company officers stepped in to arbitrate in civil and criminal disputes, due to their limited understanding of local traditions and customs, they relied on Hindu pundits and Muslim qazis to ascertain their respective laws. This set in motion the process of Brahminisation and Islamisation of laws.

In 1774, the Mayor's Court of Calcutta was converted into a Supreme Court and in 1781, it was granted original civil jurisdiction over 'natives'. It was laid down that in matters of inheritance, succession, land rent, goods, and all matters of contract, their respective 'personal' laws should be applied.

It was believed that the source of Hindu and Muslim laws were their religious texts. Hence, a wide range of customs which had no scriptural authority, met with the disapproval of the administrators. The plurality of customs often led to the pundits expressing contradictory opinions which resulted in a distrust of the opinions of the pundits. The administrators were of the view that if the 'original' texts were made available, they could adjudicate directly, without the help of partisan and corrupt pundits

---

[9] 'Gentoos' was the Portuguese term for Hindus. The term has its origin in the Biblical term 'Gentiles', meaning heathens or non-believers.

[10] See *Raj Bahadur* v. *Bishen Dayal*, (1882) ILR 4 All 343 and *Ma Yait* v. *Maung Chit Maung*, (1921) ILR 49 Cal 310.

and qazis, who were referred to as the 'native officers of the court'.

Since scriptures were unequivocally accepted as the source of both Hindu and Muslim laws (in the mould of the Roman Canon law), translation of scriptures became the first priority for the political scheme of English administrators. The task of translating the ancient texts was viewed as an essential pre-condition to good governance. The process was initiated by Hastings in eighteenth century and was facilitated by Jones, Halhed, Colebrooke, and Macnaghten. These translated texts became the basis of Anglo-Hindu and Anglo-Mohammedan laws in India.

The activity of translation of the texts was based primarily in the Bengal region and hence incorporated the practices prevalent in this region. In 1772, Hastings hired a group of eleven pundits for the purpose of creating a digest of Hindu law, which brought a heavy Anglo-Brahminical bias into the law. This was translated into Persian and later into English and was published in 1776 by the title, *A Code of Gentoo Laws or Ordinations of Pundits*. The translation of the *Manu Smriti* by Sir William Jones became one of the most favoured texts of the British. It influenced oriental studies far more profoundly than it had ever influenced the administration of law in pre-British India (Derrett 1999: 250). Colebrooke's translation of *Dayabhaga* and *Mitakshara* became the two most frequently quoted sources of Hindu law in court judgments. In 1791, Charles Hamilton translated the Arabic text, the *Hedaya* (the Guide). Jones translated *Al Sirajiyyah*, the Mohammedan law of inheritance.

During this time, several Sanskrit scholars wrote treatises to meet the British demand. But the work of European authors came to be trusted and used in preference even to genuine *shastric* works (Kishwar 1994: 2145). The translated codes, backed by the authority of British courts, began to make alterations in custom. In their attempt to make the shastric injunctions precise and definite to suit the structure of the Anglicised adversarial court system, the British forced it towards a straight jacketed mould, which led to a loss of complexities and localised contexts. This also provided the scope for the biases of the English scholars to creep into the translated texts.

The administrators of Bengal, in their fervour to trace the correct and original sources, totally disregarded local customs. But the Bombay Presidency Regulations of the same period, especially the 1799 Regulation (under John Duncan), did not follow the legal scheme devised by Hastings in Bengal. Here, the English distinction between 'King's law' and 'Common law' was applied instead of the Roman categorization of 'Canon Law' (church law) and 'Civil Law', and custom was granted due recognition as an important source of law.

But Mountstuart Elphinstone, who was the Governor of Bombay Presidency from 1819–27, was of the opinion that the Bengal model of categorizing laws as 'Canon' and 'Civil' would not work in the Bombay Presidency (Shodhan 2001: 5). In his scheme, codification of common law was essential to guide the European judges in their administration of the native law to the natives. The common law had to be based on customary practices of the people rather than the archaic religious texts. To concretise this scheme, he set up a Regulation Committee and brought about the Regulation Code, 1827 (also known as Elphinstone's Code). Two officers appointed by Elphinstone, Harry Borradaile and Arthur Steele, were assigned the task of recording the customs of the Deccan and Gujarat regions. The reports they compiled, though not systematic, provided some useful insights into the customs and practices of the various castes in the region. These texts became the guiding force for the colonial judiciary while validating or discarding customary practices.[11]

Matrimonial Law: From the Ecclesiastical to the Civil Law Regime

In 1823, the Recorder's Court, which was set up under the King's Charter, was converted into a Supreme Court and was awarded original jurisdiction within the town and island of Bombay under the following four heads— common law, equity, ecclesiastical, and admiralty. The *Sadar Diwani Adalat*, which was set up in 1799, had appellate jurisdiction over local courts established by the Company in the interiors of the Bombay Presidency.

All disputes between Hindus and Muslims were decided by the courts under the civil law by applying to them their own 'personal' laws or the laws of the defendant in case of dispute. The term 'personal', at this stage, was broader than 'family law', and included matters concerning caste, religious institutions, land rent, contract, etc., which were decided under the category—civil law.

But there was no mention as to how matrimonial disputes of other communities, for example, Parsis and Jews would be decided. Hence, sometime in 1850, when a Parsi lady sued her husband for a decree of restitution of conjugal rights before the Supreme Court at Bombay, the case was heard on the Ecclesiastical side of the Supreme Court. The Privy Council overruled this decision and held that it was impossible to apply the law of the Diocese of London, a Christian law, to persons professing the Zoroastrian religion and the Supreme Court, in the exercise of its Ecclesiastical jurisdiction,

could not entertain a suit between Parsis for restitution of conjugal rights.[12]

To clear the ambiguity, in 1862, when the high courts of Calcutta, Bombay, and Madras were set up, the Letters Patent which were issued entrusted the courts with the widest of civil powers. Clause 35 of the Letters Patent awarded the high courts matrimonial jurisdiction, but this was confined to Christian marriages. The jurisdiction to adjudicate over matrimonial disputes of other communities was awarded under Clause 12—civil jurisdiction. This clause provided the widest scope to adjudicate over matrimonial disputes of all communities.

Search for Uniformity and Certainty: Legal Precedents and Statutory Codification

After the political upheaval of 1857, the administration of India shifted from the Company to the British Crown. The Government of India Act of 1858 transformed every aspect of Indian administration. The legal structure went through a major change. The Supreme Courts in the Presidency towns of Calcutta, Bombay, and Madras which operated with relative autonomy, were replaced by integrated high courts with the Privy Council as the final Court of Appeal. The Presidencies lost their autonomy and were joined into a unified imperial rule. The features of administration as developed in Bengal were made the basis for new forms of unified administration for all the three Presidencies. The Bombay Presidency's treatment of self-governing groups and its acceptance of customary law gave way to the Bengal practice of viewing all groups as possessing of a unified Hindu and Muslim legal entity.

---

[11] Borradaile's Report of Civil Cases 1820–24 and Arthur Steele's *Hindu Caste, Their Law, Religion and Customs* (1827).

[12] *Ardaseer Gursetjee* v. *Perozeboye*, (1856) MIA 348. The case is discussed in detail later in 'Parsi Law of Marriage and Succession'.

The new legal structure, based on the model of the English courts, necessitated the enactment of statutes. But the realm of the 'personal' was spared from the process of codification as per the assurance given in the Queen's Proclamation. Despite this, the Hindu and Muslim family laws went through great transformation during this period. The establishment of courts based on rules and procedures of English courts, with a clear hierarchy of courts, was meant to make the arbitration fora certain along the model of English courts. While at the initial stage, scriptural law was awarded judicial recognition, after 1864, the British attempted to curtail the use of scriptural law. The British interpretations of the ancient texts became binding legal principles and made the law certain, rigid, and uniform. The impact of the emerging judge-made law and its precedent-focused methodology as *stare decisis*, was eventually experienced as oppressive and was characterized by 'unprecedented rigidity' (Desai 1994: 63). Cohn argues that the process of publishing authoritative decisions in English transformed 'Hindu law' into a form of 'English case law' and brought in colonial supremacy into Indian law (Cohn 1997: 75).

'Justice, Equity, and Good Conscience' and 'Public Morality'

With the introduction of matrimonial statutes for Christians and Parsis and certain statutes of common application, English legal principles were introduced within the Indian matrimonial jurisprudence. In addition, English principles of justice, equity, and good conscience were used as direct channels for introducing English laws and practices into areas reserved as 'personal laws'. This principle was first introduced in 1887 in *Waghela Rajsanji* v. *Shekh Masluddin*,[13]

[13] (1887) 14 IA 89

while deciding an issue of guardianship, the Privy Council held: 'If there was no rule of Indian law which could be applied to a particular case, then it should be decided by equity and good conscience, and they interpreted equity and good conscience to mean the rules of English law if found applicable to Indian society and circumstances.' In subsequent years, this principle could be used as a direct channel for introducing English legal principles into Indian laws. This principle along with the principle of 'public morality' was relied upon while curtailing the rights of women in various situations.

In *Visvanathan* v. *Saminathan*[14] the Madras High Court had held that the custom of bride price cannot, in every case, be held as immoral and against public policy. But a later decision of the Bombay High Court in *Dholidas* v. *Fulchand*[15] held that the custom of bride price is against public policy and hence an agreement to pay the bride price could not be enforced. In 1908, in *Kalavagunta Venkata Kristnayya* v. *Kalavagunta Venkatachalam*,[16] the Madras High Court dissented from its own earlier ruling. While invalidating a contract to pay bride price, held that bride price should be regarded by court as immoral and opposed to public policy. But agreements to pay dowry to the groom's family were held to be valid.[17]

There were many instances of Hindu, Parsi, Christian, and Jewish women converting to Islam and marrying Muslim men, without first dissolving their earlier marriages, under the mistaken notion that conversion dissolves their earlier marriage. But applying the principle of justice, equity, and good conscience, the women

[14] (1890) ILR 13 Mad 83
[15] (1898) ILR 22 Bom 658
[16] (1908) 32 Mad 185
[17] See the ruling in *Jagdishwar Prasad* v. *Sheo Baksh Rai*, AIR 1919 All 248.

were convicted for bigamy.[18] In *Rabasa Khanum* v. *Khodadad Bomanji Irani*[19] where a Parsi wife had converted to Islam was convicted, the court held that since there was no law which could be applied to her, the case must be decided on principles of justice and right or equity and good conscience.

In order to protect their rights several women from various Dravidian communities claimed a Sudra status and pleaded that they are outside the purview of Brahminical smriti code. In *Subaratha Mudali* v. *Balakrishna Swami Naidu*[20] the Madras High Court held that the dancing girls are sudras and hence smriti law cannot be applied to them. As per their custom, daughters were entitled to inherit in preference to sons. The court also recognized the right of women to adopt girls. But in several other cases decided by the Bombay and Calcutta High Courts, it was ruled that the custom of adopting daughters by dancing girls was immoral and against public policy (Kuppuswami 1993: 51).

In this context, a ruling of V.R. Krishna Iyer J. in *Rattan Lal* v. *Vardesh Chander*[21] eloquently articulates the concern:

We have to part company with the precedents of the British-Indian period tying our non-statutory areas of law to vintage English law, christening it, 'justice, equity and good conscience'. After all, conscience is the finer texture of norms woven from the ethos and life-style of a community, and since British and Indian ways of life vary so much, the validity of an Anglophilic bias in Bharat's justice, equity and good conscience is questionable today. The great values that bind law to life spell out the text of justice, equity and good conscience ... Free India has to find

its conscience in our rugged realities – and no more in alien legal thought. In a larger sense, the insignia of creativity in law, as in life, is freedom from subtle alien bondage, not a silent spring nor a hothouse flower. (Para 21, p.597)

From Uniformity to a Culture-specific Legal Plurality

The reforms of the post-Independence period further privileged modernization, codification, and unification as key elements of progressive development. The nationalist leaders trained in British law had imbibed the colonial biases. They had contempt for 'tradition' and a desire to 'modernise' through statutory enactments. But even the codified laws continued to reflect anti-women ideology and biases.

The reforms did not introduce any principle which had not already existed somewhere in India (Kishwar 1994: 2147). Despite this, they were projected as a vehicle for ushering in Western modernity. There were, however, several liberal customary practices which were discarded by the Hindu code for the sake of uniformity (Derrett 1999: 107). In their stated determination to put an end to the growth of custom, the reformers were in fact putting an end to the essence of Hindu law, and yet persisted in calling the codification 'Hindu'.

The reformed, modern Hindu law of the 1950s finally seemed to emerge as a beacon of light for a better, secular future, in which the so-called 'religious' norm is eventually rendered as legally irrelevant. But according to Mensky:

In social reality, all that happened was that the official Indian law changed, while more and more of Hindu law went underground, populating the realm of the unofficial law. What was abolished by the formal law was manifestly only a fragment of the field, not the entire social reality of Hindu law. The conceptual framework

---

[18] See the rulings in *Ram Kumari* (*In the matter of*) (1895) 18 Cal 264, *Budansa Rowther* v. *Fatima Bibi*, AIR 1914 Mad. 192 and *Emperor* v. *Mt. Ruri*, AIR 1919 Lah 389.

[19] AIR 1947 Bom 272

[20] (1917) 33 MLJ. 207

[21] AIR 1976 SC 588

and ideologies underpinning multiple ways of life, and hence the entire customary social edifice of Hindu culture, remained largely immune to the powerful wonder drug of legal modernization which had been administered in measured doses before and after 1947. (Mensky 2003: 24)

Mensky argues further that Hindu law has always been a people's law, whether or not the state wished to see it that way. Hence, something as complex as Hindu personal law could not be reformed away and abolished by a statute, nor could its influence as a legal normative order that permeates the entire socio-legal Indian field be legislated into oblivion (Mensky 2003: 25).

It is within the framework of the contemporary concerns indicated above that the site of personal laws needs to be revisited. But while flagging the various complexities and nuances, the scope of this chapter is confined only to providing an overview of contesting legal theories, premises, and postulates that govern the field of personal laws in contemporary legal and political discourses, from a perspective of women's rights.

Section A

HINDU LAW OF MARRIAGE AND PROPERTY
Origin and Development of Hindu Law

'Hindu': An Amorphous Community

The preliminary question, as we approach the subject of Hindu law, is: To whom does it apply? Even more basic: Who is a Hindu? The answers to these seemingly simple questions lead us to an extremely difficult and complex legal sphere.

A precise meaning of the word 'Hindu' has defied all efforts at definition through statutes or judicial pronouncements. Under the present day statutes governing Hindus, any definition of 'Hindu' in terms of religion will be inadequate. A person who practices or professes Hinduism is a Hindu. But a person does not cease to be a

Hindu nor become less of a Hindu merely because a person has ceased to have faith in the 'Hindu' religion or philosophy and does not practice or profess it. Even when a Hindu starts practicing, professing, or having faith in a non-Hindu religion, he/she will not cease to be a Hindu unless it is conclusively established that he/she has formally converted to that faith. Even an atheist does not cease to be a Hindu.[22] An attempt to define the term was made in 1966 by the Supreme Court in *Shastri Yagnapurushadasji v. Muldas Vaishya*[23] (popularly referred to as the *Satsanghi case*) in the following words:

Acceptance of the Vedas with reverence, recognition of the fact that the means of ways to salvation are diverse and realisation of the truth that the number of gods to be worshipped is large, are the distinguishing features of Hindu religion.

Relying upon this definition, the Court held that the Satsanghis are Hindus. The issue before the Court was one of social justice, that is, entry of Harijans to a temple belonging to Satsanghis of Swaminarayan sampradaya (sect). The Satsanghis pleaded that they were not Hindus and hence were not governed by the pre-Constitution temple entry legislation of the Bombay Presidency through which Harijans were granted the right to worship in a Hindu temple. By the time the judgment was pronounced, the courts were under the constitutional mandate of equality, non-discrimination, and social justice. And hence the question whether the Satsanghis are Hindus had become irrelevant and was only of academic interest.

In the broad context in which the terms Hindu and Hindu law are used, this definition by the Supreme Court is highly inadequate. According to Paras Diwan, instead of a religious

---

[22] See Derett (1957) for the difficulties of defining who is a Hindu.

[23] AIR 1966 SC 1119

sect, had it been argued that Chamars were not Hindus, the Court would have faced an uphill task. It would be problematic to define a community like the Chamars, who apparently know little of the Hindu religion and less of Hindu philosophy, as Hindus (Diwan 1995: 4).

The test of whether a person is a Hindu for legal purposes starts with ethnic and geographical tests, which raise a presumption that can be rebutted not by proof of absence of belief or presence of disbelief, but only by proof of exclusive adherence (or conversion) to a foreign (non-Hindu) faith.

Mensky defines Hindu law as a family of laws rather than one single unit. Hindu law has always been a collection of socio-legal systems of parallel complexity, fluidity, and diversity, evading codification. Hence the label 'Hindu law' must be taken to cover a large variety of quite different legal systems (Mensky 2003: xvi). Many of its rules are contradictory, incorporating not only high-caste Sanskritic elements, but also innumerable subaltern, local, and often less prestigious perspectives. The diversity of the communities to whom the Hindu law was made applicable, led Derrett to comment as follows: 'The Hindus are as diverse in race, psychology, habitat, employment and way of life as any collection of human beings that might be gathered from the ends of earth' (Derrett 1957: 1).

Scriptural Sources of Hindu Law

The scriptural sources of Hindu law are diverse. The original texts were of Aryan origin but the assimilation between Aryan and non-Aryan tribes led to an amalgamation of customs and practices.

The scriptural law, like in most ancient legal systems, traces its origin to divine revelations. During the early period, there was no distinction between religion, law, and morality. They were cumulatively referred to as 'dharma'. The

three sources of dharma are *shruti* (the divine revelations or utterances, primarily the Vedas), *smriti* (the memorized word—the *dharmasutras* and the *dharmashastras*), and *sadachara* (good custom) (Desai 1994: 3). Although the Vedas were treated as the fountainhead of Hindu law by jurists, they do not contain positive law (or lawyer's law) (Shastri 1933: 12). Hence the codified laws governing Hindu marriage and family relationships derive their roots from the smritis and *nibandhas* (commentaries and digests).[24]

From about eighth century BC to AD fifth century, elaborate guidelines governing all aspects of social relations were laid down in the smritis. The *smritikars* (the authors of smritis) were not kings, religious heads, or legislators (Bhattacharjee 1994: 19). They were philosophers, social thinkers, and teachers. They preached dharma, a code of conduct governing all aspects of life, from the spiritual to the temporal. The dharmashastras covered all aspects of law, ethics, and morality. These were works of encyclopedic scope and covered a wide range of topics. While some fifty-five rules were mandatory, others were directory and hence were not binding and could be treated as mere guidelines.

Initially, the texts were not written and knowledge was passed down, generation to generation, by an oral tradition through the institution of Brahminical priesthood or *guru-shishya parampara*. So each generation could have re-interpreted the guidelines incorporating their contemporary contexts. In this tradition, the same smriti could have been evolved by several philosophers and at different historical times. Hence it is not surprising to find

[24] Bhattacharjee has argued that nibandhas had already replaced the smritis at the time of colonial intervention and hence smritis could no longer be considered as the 'source' of Hindu law (Bhattacharjee 1994: 17).

Box 1.1 Enactments Strengthening the Rights of Individual Men against the Family/Community

- The Caste Disabilities Removal Act, 1850 set aside the provisions of Hindu law which penalised the renunciation of religion by depriving a convert of his right in the joint family property.
- The Hindu Inheritance (Removal of Disabilities) Act, 1928 prohibited the exclusion from inheritance of certain disqualified heirs.
- The Hindu Gains of Learning Act, 1930 stipulated that all gains of learning (income earned through professional qualifications) would be the exclusive and separate property of a Hindu male even if he had been supported to acquire professional qualifications from the funds of the joint family.

contradictory statements regarding a controversial issue attributed to the same smritikar.

The nibandhas, which were detailed commentaries on the earlier smritis, were of a later period (AD fifth to eighteenth century). Here too, authors had sufficient scope to re-interpret the original precepts as per the social organisations of their times. Many a time, while laying down a new principle, the commentators used the ploy of interpretation or explanation of an old dictum for greater validity.

The two distinct and dominant schools, validated under the Anglo-Hindu law (a colonial construction), were Mitakshara of Vijnaneshwar (eleventh century) and Dayabhaga of Jimmutavahana (twelfth century). While the latter was the leading authority in Bengal, the former was recognised as an authority in the rest of British India. But there were also several regional deviations which were categorised as sub-schools of Mitakshara. Significant among these were Mithila, Benaras, Bombay, and Dravida schools.[25]

Colonial Legal Interventions

As the East India Company shifted its interest from a trading power to a political power, establishment of courts modeled on Anglo-Saxon jurisprudence became a political expediency. Gradually, hegemonic imperial claims influenced every aspect of Indian life—economic, political, and legal. This clear marker of modernity was welcomed by the newly evolving English-educated middle class of Bengal and provided the British a moral justification for ruling India as harbingers of enlightenment.[26] Through their interventions, the Hindu society could rid itself of its 'barbarism' and enter an era of 'civilization'. An image of the cruel and superstitious natives who needed Christian salvation was deliberately constructed by the Evangelists. The entry of Hindu social reformers into the campaign against Sati at the advent of nineteenth century strengthened the process of interventions not only by judicial decisions but also by legislative reforms.

The significant legislation introduced during this period were the Sati Regulation Act, 1829, followed by the Widow Remarriage Act, 1856, and the Age of Consent Acts of 1860 and 1891.[27] The legislation, focusing on the 'barbaric' customs of the natives, resulting in extreme cruelty against women within the domestic sphere,

---

[25] Raghavachariar provides a comprehensive list of various schools and the relevant authorities [Raghavachariar (Vol. I) 1980: 5]. ·

[26] Radha Kumar argues that this intimacy with the British also later resulted in most social movements of the nineteenth century being located in the Calcutta Presidency (Kumar 1993: 9).

[27] See subsequent section of this book titled 'Social Reform Movements and Legislative Reforms', where the legal reforms have been discussed in detail.

convey an impression that the exception to the rule of non-interference in the realm of personal laws was for the benefit of women. There is a presumption that by incorporating the concepts of modernity into native jurisprudence, the status of women in India was elevated.

However, the British intervention did not stop at the level of welfare legislation for women, but extended into two other spheres which has not received due attention. One set of legislation carved out a space for men's individual property rights into a system based on joint family property and rigid caste affiliations and laid the ground for the introduction of a capital mode of production in an urban setting.

What is even more disturbing for our purpose here, simultaneously, through a series of judicial decisions, the scope of women's rights was constrained beyond all recognition. As pluralistic communities became characterised as 'Hindu', women's right to property ownership was curtailed. Gradually, this notion of a constrained and limited *stridhana* became the accepted principle of Hindu law for the whole of British India. Women lost the right to will or gift away their stridhana and it acquired the character of a limited estate.[28] Any transaction by a widow in respect of the property inherited by her had to be justified on two grounds—legal necessity or religious or charitable purposes—and upon her death, the property reverted to the husband's male heirs. The introduction of the notion of 'reversioners', which was borrowed from English law, into Hindu law, bestowed upon the male relatives the right to challenge all property dealings by Hindu widows. To set right this distortion of Hindu law, the Hindu Women's Rights to

Property Act, 1937 (or the Deshmukh Act, as it is popularly referred to) was enacted. The campaign was led by social reformer G.V. Deshmukh, who introduced the bill to set right the problems created by the judicial decisions of English courts which had constrained the scope of stridhana. But the bill met with a great deal of hostility and Deshmukh was ridiculed for introducing this bill. After much debate, only a watered down version of the original bill could be enacted.[29]

A Moment of Defiance: The Rukhmabai Case

A discussion on the subversion of women's rights would remain incomplete without a detailed discussion of the *Rukhmabai case*. The struggle of a young woman, Rukhmabai, who defied tradition and the colonial legal dictates by refusing to be bound to a marriage contracted when she was barely eleven, is of special relevance. The social drama which unfolded around her legal case has been described as 'a unique event in colonial India' by some historians (Chandra 1998: 1). Her legal battle can easily be termed as one of the 'glorious events played out in the theatre of a great court' and 'a moment of defiance to the colonial legal order'. Questioning what was assumed to be natural, she offered a subversive model of assertion by women of their desire as individuals, in a terrain dominated by family, community, and imperial notions of justice and governance. The case also provides a concrete example of how alien and anti-women notions of English law came to be introduced within the Hindu law to subvert women's rights.

The social drama was triggered off when Dadaji Bhikaji filed a case against Rukhmabai in

---

[28] See subsequent section of this book titled 'Stridhan Property and its Subversion' for a more detailed discussion.

[29] See subsequent section of this book, 'Codified Law and Illusory Inheritance Rights', for a detailed discussion.

the Bombay High Court in 1884 for restitution of conjugal rights. It reached its peak in 1885, when Pinhey J. in a historical verdict, declined to pass a decree of restitution of conjugal rights in favour of the husband. In a bold and fearless verdict, he declared that since conjugality had not been instituted, the question of granting the relief of 'restoring conjugality', did not apply to this case. The judge proclaimed:

It is a misnomer to call this 'a suit for the restitution of conjugal rights'. Restitution of conjugal rights can only apply to a situation when a married couple, after cohabitation, separate and live apart. Here, the husband has asked the court to compel the wife to go to his house, so that he may complete his contract with her by consummating the marriage. It seems to me that it would be a barbarous, cruel and revolting thing to do, to compel a young lady under those circumstances to go to a man whom she dislikes, in order that he may cohabit with her against her will. No law or practice justifies such an order. I am not obliged to grant the plaintiff the relief which he seeks, and to compel this young lady of twenty two to go to the house of her husband in order that he may consummate the marriage arranged for her during her helpless infancy...the practice of allowing suits for the restitution of conjugal rights originated in England under peculiar circumstances, and was transplanted from England into India. It has no foundation in Hindu law ... For many years after I came to India such suits were not allowed. It is only of late years the practice of allowing such suits has been introduced into this country from England (I think only since the amalgamation of the old Supreme and Sadar Courts in the present high courts which has brought English lawyers more into contact with the mofussil). It is, in my opinion, a matter for regret that the remedy of restitution of conjugal rights was ever introduced into this country.[30]

Ironically, the revivalists interpreted this judgment as interference in the sacrosanct arena of Hindu conjugality by the British courts (and a breach of the assurance of non interference). For the reformers like Behramji Malabari, an ardent supporter of Rukhmabai, the intervention of the English courts was an armour in their campaign against the upper caste Hindu custom of child marriage.[31]

The litigation, the judgment, and the controversy which followed were all laden with ironies. The husband's case was trumpeted by the revivalists and it is with their support he had approached the English courts, rather than the caste panchayat, for the remedy of restoring his 'Hindu' conjugality. Within customary law, the relief of restoring conjugality was non-existent and the husband could not obtain any relief in this sphere. Also, the parties belonged to a lower caste among whom custom recognised the right of the wife to dissolve her marriage. And most important, Pinhey J. had declined the relief on the ground that it was an outdated medieval Christian remedy under English law and further that the Hindu law did not recognize such a barbaric custom!

However, in the highly politicized climate, these subtle legal points were lost. Within this politically surcharged atmosphere, the husband filed an appeal and the colonial courts succumbed to the political pressure. In 1886, the division bench presided over by Sir Charles Sargent CJ. and Bayley J. rejected the argument that there is no authority for a decree for 'institution' of conjugal rights under Hindu law and decreed:

The gist of the action for restitution of conjugal rights is that married persons are bound to live together. Whether the withdrawal is before or after consummation, there has been a violation of conjugal duty which entitles the injured party to the relief prayed.[32]

---

[31] See subsequent section of this book titled 'The Age of Consent Act of 1891' for further discussion on this issue

[30] *Dadaji Bhikaji v. Rukhmabai*, (1885) ILR 9 Bom 529.

[32] *Dadaji Bhikaji v. Rukhmabai*, (1885) ILR 9 Bom 529.

The court ruled in favour of the husband and granted him the decree of 'restitution of conjugal rights'. In a moment of pride and glory for Indian women for centuries to come, Rukhmabai declared that she would willingly undergo imprisonment rather than let a man she detested enforce conjugality! Fortunately for all concerned, the matter was finally 'settled' by payment of compensation by Rukhmabai to her husband. What was crucial for this debate is the fact that Rukhmabai owned property and had a separate income from which she was in a position to pay her husband a 'compensation' for her refusal to live with him. Only through payment of compensation, the dispute could finally be settled.

Thereafter, Rukhmabai went abroad to study medicine, became a doctor, and came back to serve fellow women of her country. She lived a very long life and passed away at the ripe old age of 91 years.

The motif of Rukhmabai's defiance of both, the verdict of the alien English judges and the patriarchal dictates couched in nationalist pride, in defense of her right over her personhood, at a time when English women were waging a battle for their right to own separate property as wives, would indeed serve to shift the rigid and fixed binaries of First World feminists / Third World victims.[33]

Social Reform Movements and Legislative Reforms

The legal discourse around the Deshmukh Act, which was aimed at undoing the harm caused by the British judges while denying Hindu women their right of stridhan, and the challenge to the colonial legal order posed by a

Box 1.2 Important Legislation during the 19th Century Social Reform Movements Period

- The Bengal Sati Regulation Act, 1829
- The Widow Remarriage Act, 1856
- The Age of Consent Acts, 1861, 1891
- The Child Marriage Restraint Act, 1929

defiant Rukhmabai, are important markers of history. They serve to counter the premise that the British rule was necessary to redeem the Hindu society of its barbarism, usher India into modernity, and bring in gender justice. But for the Hindu social reformers of the nineteenth century, who sought the intervention of the British rulers, legislative reforms became an important tool to set right the wrongs suffered by Hindu women within the conjugal sphere. These statutory reforms which attempted to transform marriage and family relationships were precursors of the Hindu family law reforms of the post-Independence period. They served to challenge the Brahminical patriarchy of the orthodox segments of Bengal and later, Maharashtra. The reformist agenda was built around issues of extreme violence perpetrated upon women as child brides and widows, particularly among Kulin Brahmins and the unbridled polygamy among them.[34]

The campaigns served to bring the sacred and private realm of Hindu conjugality into the public domain for critical scrutiny and challenged the scriptural validity of such inhuman practices. While this was the most positive aspect of the campaigns, the enactments themselves did not have the desired impact upon the lives of Hindu women.

---

[33] I have borrowed this phrase from Ratna Kapur who has explored this theme in her essay (See Kapur, 2002).

[34] In 1871, it was found that thirty-three Kulin Brahmins of Hooghly district were married to two thousand and fifty-one women. (Basu 2001: 9)

The Bengal Sati Regulation Act, 1829

The movement for abolition of sati had begun with European religious reaction taking the direction of condemnation, declaring it to be a heathen practice. The missionaries began to mould public opinion, both in India and Britain, by recording and highlighting incidents of sati. Later, Raja Rammohun Roy, a social reformer, started condemning this practice in his journalistic writing. This provided a boost to the campaign initiated by the missionaries. But since the practice was perceived to be based on scriptural dictates, there was a hesitation to ban it completely. So in 1813, the government banned only the 'bad' satis, that is, where women were forced to commit sati, but declared as legal voluntary satis performed as per scriptural dictates (Mani 1989: 94). But after the British rule was firmly established, the government felt more confident to bring in a total ban and enacted the Regulation of 1829. The Act was challenged in the Privy Council by pro-sati religious factions on the ground of freedom of religion. This was countered by the argument that there could not be freedom of religion that could go beyond what was compatible with the paramount claims of humanity and justice.

Interestingly, the debate over sati was not around ushering modernity. It was more on accurate interpretations of ancient texts. Lata Mani has argued that the discourse was more on 'authentic' culture and tradition and Brahmanic scriptures were increasingly seen to be the locus of this authenticity so that, for example, the legislative prohibition of sati became a question of scriptural interpretation (Mani 1989: 88–126). The discourse was not merely about women, but there were also instances in which the moral claim of colonial rule was confronted and negotiated. Tradition was thus not the ground on which the status of woman was being contested. Rather the reverse was true—women, in fact, became the site on which tradition was debated and reformulated. What was at stake was not women but tradition.

Despite the ban, the practice prevailed in many regions. The issue hit the headlines again a century and a half later, in 1987, with the much publicized incident of sati at Deorala, a village in Rajasthan, where a young eighteen year old Roop Kanwar had committed sati.[35] Subsequently, the government brought yet another ordinance to ban sati and made forcing, abetting, committing, and glorifying sati, a criminal offence.[36]

The Hindu Widow Remarriage Act, 1856

The aim of the Act was to redeem upper caste child widows of a deplorable plight which would drive them to destitution and prostitution.[37] The controversy was set within contesting claims—the revivalists claiming that the bill, if enacted, would affect a vital part of the Hindu shastras and widows marrying under it would be regarded as social outcastes. The reformers, at the other hand, led by Ishwar Chandra Vidyasagar, claimed that the custom prohibiting widow remarriage was a modern innovation which was unknown in Vedic times.[38] He pointed out that *Parasara Samhita* (an ancient scriptural authority) had clearly indicated a widow's right of remarriage (Basu 2001: 68).

---

[35] For a detailed account of the Deorala incident, see Sen, 2001.

[36] The Commission of Sati (Prevention) Act, 1987.

[37] As per a survey conducted in Calcutta in 1890, there were around ten thousand widows under the age of four. Further, 90 per cent of the prostitutes were widows (Basu 2001: 6–7).

[38] *Mayne's Treatise on Hindu Law and Usage* also affirms that widow remarriage was accepted in Vedic times (Kuppuswami 1993: 93).

These contentions are overlaid by another reality—that of caste hierarchies. The remarriage of widows needs to be contextualized within the social reality of these hierarchies. The prohibition of widow-remarriage was seen as a badge of respectability. Castes which did not allow it, ranked higher in social estimation (Basu 2001: 72). This was carried to the extent that castes were sometimes divided into two sections, one following and the other forbidding the practice.

The enactment legitimizing widow remarriage was a boost to the reformist campaign. But at the ground level, the campaign was a failure as few upper caste widows ventured out to defy tradition and contract remarriages. While tradition proved to be one barrier, the economics of the Act proved to be yet another. While scrutinizing cases reported in law journals of this period, it is evident that any woman marrying under this Act lost the right to her husband's property. The property reverted back to the male relatives of the husband.

The adverse impact of the statute was felt most by women from the lower castes. These women had a right of divorce and remarriage (including widow remarriage) prior to the enactment under the customs of their caste. Despite this, upon remarriage, through the application of the Act, they were deprived of this right due to adverse rulings of the colonial courts. So a beneficial legislation, meant to bring in social transformation and alleviate the sufferings of women from the upper castes (Kulin Brahmin), served to usher in notions of Brahminical patriarchy among the lower castes.[39]

The Age of Consent Acts of 1860 and 1891

These enactments addressed the issue of child marriage and more specifically, violent sexual

[39] For a detailed discussion, see Introduction to *Women and Law in India* (Agnes, et al. 2004: xiii–xx).

intercourse by adult men upon their child brides. The first Act, which was enacted in 1861, stipulated ten years as the minimum age at which consent to sexual intercourse could be given. A sexual intercourse, even with the consent of a girl below this age, was deemed as statutory rape under the newly enacted Indian Penal Code of 1861. But despite the stipulation, infants and children continued to be married off to elderly men, as per the norms of the higher castes, to ensure ritualistic purity. On the other hand, social reformers considered the age of ten too low and campaigned for raising it to twelve years.

The revivalist Hindu intelligentsia of Bengal opposed the raising of the age to twelve on the ground that it violated a fundamental ritual observance, the *garbhadhan* ceremony or the obligatory cohabitation between husband and wife, which should take place immediately after the wife attains puberty. Since puberty was quite likely to occur before a girl reached the age of twelve years in the hot climate of Bengal, the new legislation meant that the ritual of garbhadhan could not be performed and this would violate scriptural dictates (Sarkar 1993: 1899–78).

On the other side, the public pressure that built around the Rukhmabai case gave a boost to the campaign led by the Parsi social reformer, Behramji Merwanji Malabari. Others, like M.G. Ranade J. also supported this campaign. The turning point was the gruesome death of Phulmonee, a girl who was about ten years old, in 1890. She died due to the violent sexual intercourse during which she suffered rupture of her vagina and had bled to death. Though her thirty-five year old husband, Hari Maity, was charged with murder, he was exonerated of the charge as the child bride was held to be above ten years and as a husband, he had a legal right of sexual intercourse (Sarkar 1993: 1873–4).

Gradually, from the possible effects of child marriage on the health of future generations, the debate shifted to the life and safety of Hindu wives. Forty-four women doctors brought out long lists of cases where child-wives had been maimed or killed because of rape (Ibid.). Finally, amidst a raging controversy, the Act was amended in 1891 and the age of consent for sexual intercourse was raised to twelve years. The Act sought to protect married as well as unmarried girls from premature prostitution as well as premature marital cohabitation.

The Child Marriage Restraint Act, 1929

Despite the two enactments, the bane of child marriage continued. To tackle the problem further, the social reformer, Rai Saheb Harbilas Gour Sarda introduced the Child Marriage Restraint Bill in 1927. The Bill initially sought to ban marriages of girls below the age of twelve. By this time, several women's associations had been formed and a call was given for the All India Women's Conference (AIWC) to boost women's education. Though the agenda of the AIWC was not political at this stage, it passed a resolution at its very first conference held in Poona in 1927 calling for a ban on child marriages and suggested that the age of marriage should be raised to fourteen years and marriages below this age should be banned. The Bill was referred to the Select Committee and was kept in abeyance for two years. Finally, it was enacted in 1929. This act came to be known as the Sarda Act, as a tribute to the sustained efforts of Rai Saheb Harbilas Gour Sarda in bringing in this statute.

The issue of child marriage continued to haunt social reformers in the post-Independence period and during the enactment of the Hindu Code Bill. Concerns over child marriage have continued even in the twenty-first century. The more recent efforts culminated in a new statute titled, Prevention of Child Marriage Act, 2006. The entire debate and the complex issues

concerning child marriage are discussed in Section 'Marriage of Minors' in Chapter 1 of the second volume.

Post-Independence Hindu Law Reforms

The history of Hindu law reform spans a period of fifteen years, from 1941 to 1956. It was discussed in three Parliaments of historical significance—the Federal Parliament, the Provisional Parliament, and the first Parliament of the newly independent nation. During the Constituent Assembly period, a committee was set up under B.N. Rau, which solicited a wide spectrum of opinions and finally, in 1946, presented a draft of the personal law code that was to apply to all Hindus. In 1948, a Select Committee, chaired by B. R. Ambedkar, examined the draft. However, each phase that the draft went through saw a dilution of women's rights till finally the political interest of the ruling party became the primary consideration. In a nutshell, the contentious issues which were debated during this period were—equal inheritance rights of daughters, the absolute and inalienable rights of widows, the right of upper caste Hindu women for divorce and remarriage, and the imposition of monogamy upon Hindu males. Within a rigid Hindu patriarchy, it was presumed that granting wives the right of divorce along with equal property rights in parental property would spell doom for the Hindu society and destroy the sacred institution of marriage and family.

The three important factors which need to be examined in the context of Hindu law reform are discussed below.

The Opposition within the Congress Leadership

The tension that was prevalent during the nineteenth century social reform movements between traditionalists and modernists continued to dominate the parliamentary debates

Box 1.3   Salient Features of the Hindu Law Reforms of the 1950s

The Hindu Marriage Act, 1955
- Hindu marriages became dissoluble contracts
- Free consent became an important ingredient of marriage
- Women (and men) were granted the right of divorce and remarriage
- Hindu marriages became monogamous

The Hindu Succession Act, 1956
- Equal inheritance rights were granted to daughters in the separate/self acquired property of their father
- A large number of female relatives became Class I heirs—mothers, widows, daughters, wives of pre-deceased son, grandson, and great grandson
- A widow could not be divested of the inherited property upon remarriage. The property inherited by her became her absolute property

The Hindu Minority and Guardianship Act, 1956
- Mother was deemed natural guardian of the child, after father
- Women acquired a right to appoint a guardian

The Hindu Adoption and Maintenance Act, 1956
- Girls could be taken in adoption (Earlier only boys could be taken in adoption)
- Consent of the wife became mandatory for adoption
- Right of Separate Residence and Maintenance to wives/widows

around the Hindu Code Bill. Several provisions, including the provisions of Hindu monogamy, right of divorce, abolition of coparcenary, and inheritance to daughters, were opposed. It was felt that the Hindu society will suffer a moral setback if women were to be granted the right to divorce along with a right to inherit property. According to Derrett, every argument that could be mustered against the project was garnered, including many that cancelled each other out (Derrett 1957: 69). The reforms were opposed by the then President and Constitutional head, Rajendra Prasad, senior Congressmen like Pattabhi Sitaramayya, the architect of the united Indian nation, Sardar Patel, and the President of the ruling Congress, P.D. Tandon, among others. Among its ardent supporters was B.R. Ambedkar. In 1952, when Jawaharlal Nehru vacillated due to pressure

from his colleagues within the party, Ambedkar resigned in protest from his post as the first Law Minister of the independent nation.

In addition, there was also severe opposition from representatives of Hindu fundamentalist parties. They termed the reforms as anti-Hindu and anti-Indian and, as a delaying tactic, raised the demand for a uniform code. They claimed that the reforms were drastic and harmful and that it would be like an 'atom bomb on Hindu society', which would destroy the Hindu community. They also compared it to the draconian Rowlatt Act of the Britishers. Outside the Parliament, the All Indian Anti Hindu Code Bill Committee was formed in March 1949, including in its fold strange bedfellows like the Delhi Bar Association, the Shankaracharya of Dwaraka, and the Rashtriya Swayamsewak Sangh and was led by a little known Swami

Karpatriji Maharaj (Guha 2007: 231). At this point, the women Parliamentarians who had initially demanded a uniform family code changed their position and supported the Hindu law reform. It was the upper caste Hindu women alone, of all religious sects and castes, who lagged behind even in the most basic of all rights, the right of divorce and property inheritance. Hence there was immediacy in bringing in the reforms. This was a significant political move, since an uncompromising demand for a uniform code would have meant an alliance with the most reactionary and anti-women lobby and would have caused a further set back to women's rights (Karat 1993).

The Political Compulsions Beneath the Reforms

The primary concern of the reforms was homogenizing the pluralistic Hindu society. They set the final seal on the process of homogenizing of the Hindu society initiated by the British administration during the colonial rule. The integration of the Hindus from three different political regimes, that is, British India, the princely states, and the tribal regions, into one nation could best be done by bringing them under one law. Hence, the primary concern was to define the term 'Hindu' in its widest sense and to encompass all sects, castes, and religious denominations within it. The Hindu Law Committee had defined a 'Hindu' as anyone professing the Hindu religion. But later, the word 'professes' was deleted to broaden its scope (Parashar 1992: 103).

Examining the motive for Hindu law reform, Archana Parashar argues that the hidden agenda was unification of the nation through uniformity in law. National integration was of paramount importance. Establishing the supremacy of the state over religious institutions was another important consideration. This could be best achieved by re-defining the rights given to women. Through the re-orientation of female roles, the State could replace the claim of religion and religious institutions over people's lives. While bringing in reforms, the State relied on the two conflicting claims of tradition and modernity. While professing that it was bound by the Constitution, it projected the image of a continuity with the past (by preserving the provisions from the ancient sacred law) to bring in selective reforms (Parashar 1992: 140).

For the State, the unifying potential of the Hindu code became more important than its potential for ensuring legal equality for women. Hence, several customary rights of women, particularly from the lower castes and the Southern regions, were sacrificed in the interest of uniformity. Local customs of matrilineal inheritance and other customary safeguards were not incorporated into the new code.

The Congress party was dominated by lawyers trained in British law or those who studied

---

Box 1.4 Excerpts of Section 2 of the Hindu Marriage Act, 1955

... the Act applies to

(a) anyone who is a Hindu by religion in any of its forms or developments, including a Virashaiva, a Lingayat or a follower of Brahmo, Prarthana or Arya Samaj;

(b) to any person who is a Buddhist, Jaina or Sikh by religion; and

(c) to any other person domiciled in the territories to which this Act extends, who is not a Muslim, Christian, Parsi or Jew by religion, ...

law in England. Consequently, they had imbibed the colonial biases regarding the functioning of a pluralistic Indian society and were convinced that there was a need to modernise it. There was a fascination among social reformers with uniformity as a vehicle of national unity. The State, as an instrument of social reform to be imposed upon the people without creating a social consensus, derives essentially from the norms of functioning inherent in the colonialist state machinery and ideology. The English-educated elite had faithfully imbibed the colonial state's ideology, projecting itself as the most progressive instrument of social reform (Kishwar 1994: 2145). Hunt and Wickham argue: 'Law is not and never has been, a unitary phenomenon, but the assumption that it is, has played a central role in most legal discourses and theories of law. Within a plurality of legal forms, 'state law' persistently, but never with complete success, seeks to impose a unity (1998: 39)'.

The Veracity of its Claim of Liberating Women
There is a general presumption that Hindus are governed by a secular, egalitarian, and gender-just code and that this code should now be extended to Muslims in order to liberate Muslim women. The judiciary has contributed to this myth by reiterating that Hindus have forsaken their personal laws and are governed by a common code.[40] This misconception forms the basis of the demand for the uniform civil code. Hence the veracity of this demand needs to be closely scrutinized.

Since the political impediment to reform Hindu law was grave, several balancing acts had to be performed by the State while reforming the Hindu law. Crucial provisions empowering women had to be constantly watered down to

reach the level of minimum consensus. While projecting it to be pro-women, male privileges had to be protected. While introducing modernity, archaic Brahminical rituals had to be retained.[41] While usurping the power exercised by religious heads, the needs of emerging capitalism had to be safe-guarded. Only through such balancing acts could the agenda of law reform be achieved.

Unfortunately, the anomalies and anti-women bias within the Hindu code were not discussed widely in public fora. They remained hidden in statute books and legal manuals. There seemed to be almost a conspiracy of silence beneath which these inadequacies were crouched. This led to a fiction that the Hindu code is sufficiently modernised and hence it is the perfect family code which ought to be extended to other religious denominations in order to liberate women. The acts were neither Hindu in character nor based on modern principles of equality, but reflected the worst tendencies of both.

The Law of Marriage and Divorce

Hindu Marriage: A Sanskara *and a Contract*
The smritis regarded marriage as an essential *sanskara* (religious obligation). Marriage was mandatory to discharge the debt to one's ancestors—the debt of begetting offsprings. It was also essential for the performance of religious and spiritual duties. So a wife was not just a *patni* (wife) or *grihapatni* (housewife), but a *dharmapatni* (the term denoting a sacred union). She was also the *ardhangini* (half of

---

[40] See the comments of the Supreme Court in *Sarla Mudgal* v. *Union of India*, (1995) 3 SCC 635.

[41] Section 7 (2) of the Hindu Marriage Act specifically mentions *saptapadi* which is a Brahminical ritual. Most lower castes were not permitted the ritual of saptapadi. Among some castes five steps were permitted and among others only four. Further the ritual for the marriage of virgin brides differed from that of the second marriage of widows and divorcees.

him) and without her, he was not complete (Diwan & Diwan 1997: 17). In this context, performance of certain religious rituals and ceremonies was mandatory. The sacrosanct marital bond was indissoluble and eternal. It was a relationship not merely defined by this life, but by the several lives an individual would have to endure, and was enshrined in the Hindu philosophy of rebirth. Virginity and chastity of a woman was highly priced, and was praised by the smritis.

But until the enactment of the Hindu Marriage Act in 1955, Hindu marriages were not monogamous and the strict code of sexual purity was applicable only to women. Since progeny was the most important factor, a husband could procure numerous wives for this purpose. During the early pastoral stage and vedic period, the husband could also appropriate the children born to these wives out of other alliances through the institution of 'sonship', to fulfill spiritual obligations or for temporal objectives such as property devolution.[42] Children could also be begotten through concubines, slaves, and other informal alliances, and these children were conferred recognition under a legal premise called *dasiputra*.

Although marriages were deemed indissoluble, under certain exceptional situations, the wife or the husband was permitted to dissolve the matrimonial union. Narada (who relied upon an earlier version of *Manusmriti*) laid down five situations in which a woman could take another husband—her first husband having perished, died naturally, gone abroad, impotent, or lost caste.[43] Kautilya's *Arthashastra* also stipulated certain situations in which either the husband or the wife could divorce the other—mutual enmity, apprehension of danger, and desertion for justifiable reasons. According to scholars, the stipulation in *Manusmriti* against remarriage of wives and widows appears to be a later insertion (Kuppuswami 1993: 146). The lower castes were not governed by this code of sexual purity and divorce and remarriage of women was permitted among many castes.[44] For instance, in the Deccan region, widows and divorcees could remarry and these marriages were referred to as *pat* or *natra* marriages.[45]

But over time, the institution of marriage acquired a rigidity and women, who were often married off in their childhood or early teens, felt trapped within the bondage of sexual slavery. When the concept of divorce was introduced under the English law and Christian marriages were transformed from sacrament to dissoluable contracts, women leaders from the All India Women's Conference (AIWC) and other women's associations waged a sustained campaign to acquire a statutory right of divorce. The credit for framing and introducing the Hindu Women's Right to Divorce Bill in Parliament must be given to the social reformer, G. V. Deshmukh. The bill was introduced in 1938, soon after another important bill on women's rights, Hindu Women's Property Rights Bill, that he had introduced had been enacted in 1937.[46]

[42]   The epics Ramayana and Mahabharata contain several illustrations of this prevailing social norm.
[43]   Raghavachariar provides a comprehensive list of various schools and the relevant authorities (Raghavachariar, (Vol.I) 1980: 5).

[44]   See subsequent section, titled 'Customary Law and Women's Rights' for a detailed discussion.
[45]   Though these unions did not have the sanctity of a marriage with a virgin bride, they were legally recognized unions and women acquired customary rights of maintenance. See subsequent section, titled 'Validity of Customary Laws' where the conflict between customary practices and codified law is discussed.
[46]   See section titled 'Codified Law and Illusory Inheritance Rights' later in this chapter.

The Hindu Marriage Act, (HMA) enacted in 1955 was the culmination of this sustained struggle, where upper caste Hindu women acquired an equal right of divorce, on the same footing as their husbands. Though the act retained the sacramental aspects and ritualistic solemnization of Hindu marriage, it rendered Hindu marriages a contractual and dissoluble union between two consenting adults, following the developments under the English law. It provided for dissolution of marriage under certain stipulated conditions through a judicial decree. Capacity to marry (Section 5) and essential ceremonies of marriage (Section 7) became necessary ingredients of a valid Hindu marriage. A marriage which did not meet the requirements of Section 5 and Section 7 could be declared as void (Section 11) or voidable (Section 12). The validity of a Hindu marriage in the post-codification period was bound by these legal provisions. This was a clear departure from a Hindu marriage which was an essential 'sanskara' or religious sacrament.[47]

Several scholars have commented on the ambiguity of the reforms that were introduced in the 1950s. Derrett expressed his anxiety as to whether the reforms have destroyed the essential character of the ancient Hindu law by introducing a Western model of family law within the tradition bound Hindu society (Derrett 1978). Some others have questioned the claim of a 'contractual' Hindu marriage which has retained several sacramental aspects of the Hindu marriage (Uberoi 1996: 319–46). Some of these ambiguities within the statute as well as in judicial pronouncements are examined below from the perspective of women's rights.

The Legal Loopholes

Maintenance: Implications of Formal Equality

The Hindu Marriage Act of 1955 brought in the concept of equality between the husband and the wife. It was presumed that this notion of equality would enhance the status of women within the family. But despite the notion of formal equality in the statute, on the ground level, marriages continued to be based on unequal status between the spouses. (One concrete indication of the low status of the bride is the requirement of dowry, which the bride's parents are obligated to pay to the bridegroom at the time of marriage as a consideration of marriage.) At another level, within the notion of formal equality, the spouses were deemed equal and had equal rights and obligations towards each other.

So, while a basic inequality between men and women persisted, both within marriage and inheritance rights, under the perverse logic of equality, the Hindu woman was under a legal obligation to maintain her husband.[48] The concept did not exist under any prevalent notion of marriage under the Indian context—Hindu law, either scriptural or customary, Muslim law, or even in the modern and secular Special Marriage Act, 1954. The concept was introduced for the first time under the Hindu Marriage Act and was based on the western notion of formal equality.[49]

It is pertinent to note that the enactment of 1955 did not grant Hindu women the right of divorce by mutual consent which had already been introduced under the Special Marriage Act in 1954, as it was considered too radical for

---

[47] For a detailed discussion on Hindu woman's right to divorce see section titled 'Hindu Women and Right to Divorce' in chapter 'Marriage and its Dissolution' in the second volume of this book.

[48] Sections 24 and 25 of the Hindu Marriage Act, 1955. Also see Khanna 1992: 25.

[49] This concept has subsequently been incorporated into the Parsi Marriage & Divorce Act, 1936 by the 1988 amendments (Sections 39 and 40 of the Act).

the conservative Hindu Society.[50] Since the notion of a Hindu Undivided Family (HUF) property was retained, women were denied the right to ancestral property as daughters. Yet, despite the basic economic as well as status inequality that prevailed, under a strange notion of equality, women were considered as equal partners, possessing equal capacity to provide maintenance to their husbands. In *Lalit Mohan* v. *Tripta Devi*,[51] while granting permanent alimony and expenses of the proceedings to the husband, the court termed the stipulation of awarding maintenance to the husband a 'revolutionary' provision.[52]

Restitution of Conjugal Rights and the 'Lord and Master' Concept

Ironically, while women were burdened with the responsibility of maintaining the husband under a perverse notion of equality, the courts continued to undermine a woman's right to retain her job against her husband's wishes under the ancient notion of 'the Lord and Master'. Adopting this concept into modernized law, the courts granted the husbands the privilege of determining the choice of matrimonial home. If the woman was employed at a place away from the matrimonial home, the husband could claim restitution of conjugal rights against the wife.[53]

For decades after the enactment, in a series of decisions, the courts held that Hindu marriage is a sacrament and it is the sacred duty of the wife to follow her husband and reside with him wherever he chooses to reside. In all these cases, the women were working and supporting the family. The husbands had approached the courts for restoring conjugality just to spite the women. The courts upheld the husband's rights and granted them a decree of restitution. The decisions are summarised below.

In 1958, in *Ram Prakash* v. *Savitri Devi*,[54] the court held that 'According to Hindu law, marriage is a holy union for the performance of marital duties with her husband where he may choose to reside and to fulfill her duties in her husband's home.'

In 1964, in *Tirath Kaur* v. *Kirpal Singh*,[55] the wife pleaded that she was willing to carry on with the marriage but was not prepared to give up the job. But the Punjab High Court disallowed her plea and ruled in favour of the husband, stating that 'The wife's refusal to give up the job amounts to desertion. This would entitle the husband for a decree of restitution of conjugal rights.'

In 1966, the Madhya Pradesh High Court, in *Gaya Prasad* v. *Bhagwat*,[56] held that 'A wife's first duty to her husband is to submit herself obediently to his authority and to remain under his roof and protection.'

In 1973, the Punjab and Haryana High Court, in *Surinder Kāur* v. *Gardeep Singh*,[57] held that 'The Hindu law imposes on the wife the duty of attendance, obedience to and veneration for the husband to live with him wherever he chooses to reside.'

In 1977, the issue came up before the full bench of the Punjab and Haryana High Court in the case of *Kailash Wati* v. *Ayodhia Parkash*.[58] The wife was employed prior to the marriage.

---

[50] The remedy of divorce by mutual consent was introduced into the Hindu Marriage Act in 1976 through Section 13 B of the Act. Cruelty and desertion as grounds of divorce were also introduced in 1976.

[51] AIR 1990 J&K 7

[52] This issue is discussed further at chapter titled 'Matrimonial Rights and Obligations' in the second volume of this book.

[53] Section 9 of the Hindu Marriage Act.

[54] AIR 1958 Punj 87

[55] AIR 1964 Punj 28

[56] AIR 1966 MP 212

[57] AIR 1973 P&H 134

[58] ILR (1977) 1 P&H 642 FB

Seven years after the marriage, the husband asked the wife to resign her job. Upon her on her refusal to do so, he filed for restitution of conjugal rights. The wife stated that she was prepared to honour her matrimonial obligations but was not prepared to resign her job. The Full Bench of Punjab and Haryana High Court held:

According to Hindu Law, marriage is a holy union for the performance of marital duties with her husband where he may choose to reside and to fulfill her duties in her husband's home. The court reaffirmed that the wife's refusal to resign her job amounts to withdrawal from the husband's society, and granted the decree in favour of the husband.

So while under the modern concept of equality the husbands had the right to be maintained by their wives, under the concept of a sacramental marriage, they could restrain them from gainful employment. The right was based on a plea that it was the sacred duty of a Hindu wife to reside under the care and protection of her husband, her lord and master. While the husbands' plea is not surprising, the judicial affirmation of this plea under a modern statute is disturbing.

It is only around 1975 that the courts began to recognise the woman's right to hold on to a job away from her husband's residence. There are three important judgments of this time, which secured for women their right of holding a job away from their husband's residence.

The Gujarat High Court, in 1975, in the case of *Praveenben* v. *Sureshbhai*,[59] while denying the husband the relief, declared:

In the modern outlook, the husband and wife are equally free to take up a job and retain it. Since there had been a mutual arrangement, it was not a case where it could be said that the wife had withdrawn from the society of the husband.

The Madras High Court, also in 1975, while deciding a case in which the wife's income was used to sustain herself and her child, *N.R. Radhakrishna* v. *Dhanalakshmi*,[60] ruled that 'Under the modern law, the concept of the wife's obedience to her husband and her duty to live under his roof under all circumstances does not apply.'

The Delhi High Court, in 1978, in the leading case, *Swaraj Garg* v. *R.M. Garg*,[61] dissented from the Full Bench decision in Kailash Wati (discussed above) and held:

In the absence of a pre-marital agreement between the parties, it cannot be said that the wife who had a permanent job with good income had to live at a place determined by the husband when the husband did not earn enough to maintain the family.

Providing constitutional validity to the wife's right to hold on to the job, Deshpande J. ruled that an exclusive right to the husband to decide the matrimonial home would be violative of the equality of sexes clause under Article 14 of the Constitution.

In all the cases, the fact that the wives were earning more than their husbands and were substantially contributing towards household expenditure seems to have influenced the judges while denying husbands the decree of restitution of conjugal rights.

Despite these rulings, the practice of filing a suit for restitution of conjugal rights every time the wife files for maintenance continues. In a study of family courts in four states—Maharashtra, Karnataka, Andhra Pradesh, and West Bengal—carried out by the author between 2003–5, it was revealed that while more women file for divorce, judicial separation, and annulment of marriage, the ratio is reversed where restitution of conjugal rights is concerned with

---

[59] AIR 1975 Guj 69

[60] AIR 1975 Mad 331
[61] AIR 1978 Del 296

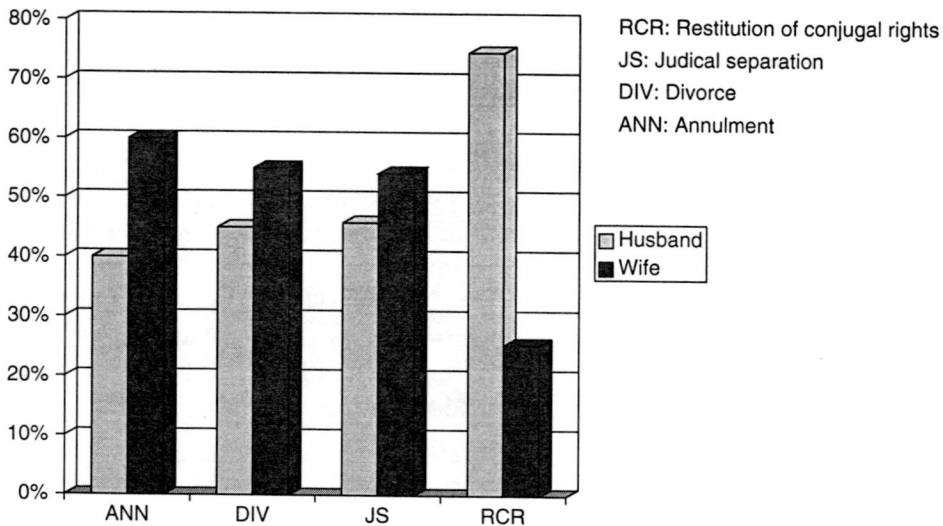

Figure 1.1 Category of Cases Filed in the Family Courts of Maharashtra and Karnataka

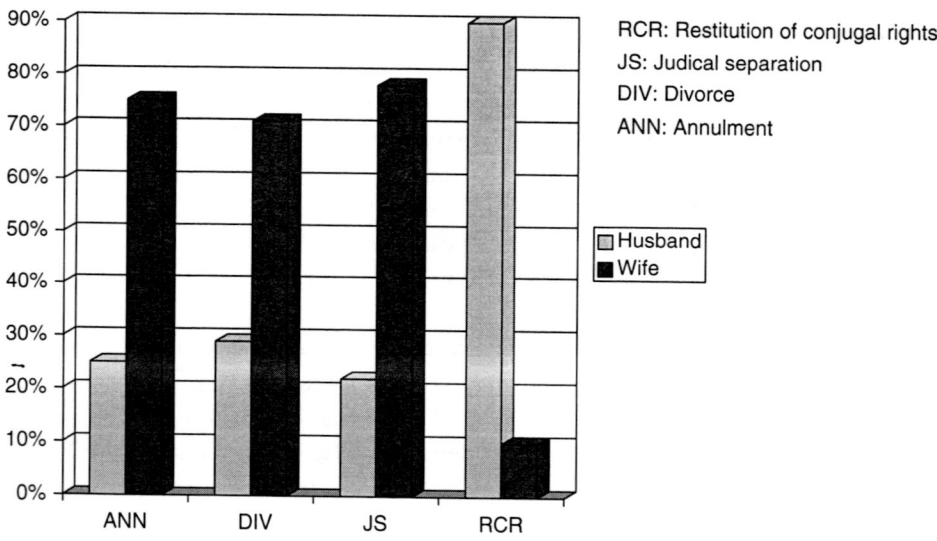

Figure 1.2 Category of Cases Filed in the Family Courts in Kolkata, West Bengal

far more husbands filing against their wives. The following table reflects this trend (Agnes 2006).

During the interviews with judges presiding over the family courts, many acknowledged the fact that it is a usual practice adopted by lawyers defending husbands to file a suit for restitution of conjugal rights to defeat the women's claim for maintenance[62] (Agnes 2006: 27).

---

[62] The remedy of RCR in contemporary matrimonial litigation is discussed in Chapter 1 of the second volume.

Consequences of Monogamy

The Hindu Marriage Act introduced the Christian concept of monogamy into the Hindu marriage. The provision of monogamy was introduced ostensibly to elevate the status of Hindu women and it was a demand raised by women in the nationalist movement. During parliamentary debates, it was claimed that Hinduism is not a religion, but a conglomeration of culture. But while the Act transformed the Hindu marriage from a status to a dissoluble contract, the form of solemnizing the contract remained Brahminical and scriptural, with *vivaha homa* (the sacred fire) and *saptapadi* (seven steps round the sacred fire) as its core components. Further, within a pluralistic society, the Act also had to validate diverse customary practices.[63] However, a 'valid custom' as accepted under the Act, had to meet the standards stipulated under the English law – ancient and existing continuously since time immemorial. This mingling of Brahminical rituals and customary practices, with English principles thrown in for good measure, has resulted in absurd and ridiculous rulings regarding the validity of Hindu marriages and women have been the worst sufferers of these legal absurdities.

In the process of urbanization, most customary practices have been modified and urban communities, living in close proximity, have adopted a synthesis of marriage rituals. The forms range from exchange of garlands to applying *sindoor* (vermilion) on the bride's forehead, from declaring themselves married by signing on a stamp paper in a lawyers chamber to performing some rituals before a deity in a particular temple (for instance, marriages contracted at the Kalighat temple in Kolkata). The media, especially Hindi films, have contributed to the confusion by projecting these practices as valid forms of Hindu marriage.[64]

This ambiguity regarding the valid form of marriage is not found under any law governing minority communities. Under other laws, formalities of solemnizing marriage are strictly prescribed and the officiating priest has to either provide the necessary documents by way of a marriage certificate or is required to register the marriage with the Registrar of births, deaths, and marriages. Since Muslim, Christian, and Parsi religions are more institutionalised, the rules and procedures for contracting marriage are definite and unambiguous and are strictly controlled by the religious hierarchies. But Hindu marriages (as well as the Hindu law), which were based more on community practices, are relatively less institutionalised and hence its legality is more ambiguous. Due to the breakdown of traditional communities within which these marriages were performed, the situation has further deteriorated.

This ambiguity has provided a Hindu male ample scope to contract bigamous marriages. Since the law recognizes only monogamous marriages, women in polygamous relationships are placed in a vulnerable situation. In the absence of any clear proof, the man has the choice of admitting either his first or subsequent relationship as a valid marriage and escaping from financial responsibility towards the other woman. When the man refuses to validate the marriage, the woman loses not only her right to maintenance but also faces humiliation and social stigma as a mistress.[65] An examination of

---

[63]   Section 7 (1) & (2) of Hindu Marriage Act, 1955.

[64]   See subsequent chapter in the second volume of this book, 'Marriage and Its Dissolution', for a further discussion on this issue.

[65]   See subsequent chapter 'Matrimonial Rights and Obligations', for contemporary trends regarding the rights of second wife to maintenance and for the legal premise of 'presumption of valid marriage'. The cases

law journals would reveal how widely prevalent this ploy of refusing to validate the marriage is in maintenance proceedings by Hindu husbands.[66]

The flip side of this predicament in maintenance proceedings is the dilemma faced by women in criminal proceedings in cases of bigamy. Here, years of litigation failed to end in conviction for the errant male due to the courts adopting a rigid view that saptapadi, vivaha homa, *kanyadan*, etc., are essential for solemnizing a Hindu marriage. If the first wife is not able to prove these ceremonies in respect of her husband's second marriage, the husband could wriggle out of conviction. This, despite the fact that he had cohabited with the second wife, the community had accepted the man and the woman as husband and wife, or even if he had fathered children through the second wife.[67]

So, the progressive sounding provision of monogamy not only turned out to be a mockery, but in fact is even more detrimental to women than the uncodified Hindu law which recognized rights of wives in polygamous marriages. For instance, in a case for maintenance where the husband pleaded that since the woman was his second wife, he was not entitled to pay her maintenance, the court took recourse to the uncodified Hindu law and held that since the couple is governed by the ancient Hindu law (which permits bigamy) and not by the reformed code, the second wife is entitled to maintenance.[68] This judgment speaks much for a law which was ushered in with great fanfare as an instrument of empowering Hindu women.

Constitutional Challenges

The statutory as well as customary laws which were in existence prior to the coming into force of the Constitution have to confirm to the constitutional mandate. But a question which confronts the judiciary is whether the personal laws which were in existence prior to the enactment of the Constitution come within the purview of Article 13 which stipulates that all laws and customs must adhere to the constitutional mandate. This issue was raised in the context of monogamy. The question whether the stipulation of equality can be applied to the private domain of family life has been another concern that was addressed by the judiciary.

On Monogamy

The first constitutional challenge to the provisions of the Hindu Marriage Act came from the Hindu male challenging the provision of monogamy before the Bombay High Court, in *State of Bombay* v. *Narasu Appa Mali.*[69] A petition was filed in the Bombay High Court challenging the monogamy imposed by the Bombay Hindu Marriage Act, 1946. A Hindu husband pleaded that the stipulation of monogamy violates his personal freedom and hinders the practice of his religion. He also argued that this dictate is discriminatory against Hindu men, since Muslim men are permitted to contract

---

discussed in these sections are startlingly revealing as to the large number of husbands who challenge the validity of their marriage on the ground that their marriages are bigamous, when their wives file applications for maintenance.

[66] In a popular matrimonial law journal, *Divorce and Matrimonial Cases* (DMC) in Volume I of 1994, of all the reported cases where validity of marriages was an issue while claiming maintenance are as follows:

Reported cases relating to maintenance: 40–100%
Cases where validity of marriage was an issue: 9–36%
Cases where the husband's plea was upheld: 4–16%
Admittedly polygamous marriages: 6–24%
(Agnes 2000: 132)

[67] For a detailed discussion on this issue see Agnes 1995: 3238.

[68] *Anupama Pradhan* v. *Sultan Pradhan*, 1991 Cri. LJ 3216 Ori.

[69] AIR 1952 Bom 84

polygamous marriages. Rejecting these contentions, the high court held that personal laws are not 'laws in force' as per the stipulation of Article 13 of the Constitution and hence they are not void even when they come into conflict with the provision of equality under the Constitution, because Fundamental Rights cannot be applied to personal laws.

The subsequent case, *Srinivasa Aiyar* v. *Saraswati Ammal,*[70] also advanced similar arguments. It was argued that prohibiting polygamy denied Hindu men equality before the law and equal protection of law, and further, that it discriminated against Hindu men on the grounds of religion as it restricted the right to freely profess, practice, and propagate religion. The Madras High Court did not address the core issue—whether the term laws in force includes personal laws. Instead, it was held that even assuming that the term 'laws in force' under Article 13 includes personal laws, the Act does not offend Article 15 which stipulates non-discrimination on the basis of sex.

However, subsequently, in *C. Masilamani Mudaliar* v. *Idol of Sri Swaminathaswami Thirukoil,*[71] the Supreme Court, while not referring specifically to the principle laid down in *Narasu Appa Mali* (discussed above), has implicitly overruled the same and held that personal laws come within the purview of Article 13 and hence are subject to the application of Fundamental Rights. This case concerned the rights of a Hindu woman to execute a will in respect of the property acquired or possessed by her, under S.14 of the Hindu Succession Act, 1956.

Restitution of Conjugal Rights
The second issue which came up for judicial scrutiny was the provision of Restitution of Conjugal Rights (RCR) under Section 9 of the Hindu Marriage Act. Choudhary J. of Andhra Pradesh High Court, in July 1983, struck down this provision as unconstitutional on the ground that it constitutes the grossest form of violation of an individual's right to privacy. The court held that it denies the woman her free choice of whether, when, and how her body is to become the vehicle for the procreation of another human being and hence is violative of the right to privacy guaranteed by Article 21 of the Constitution.[72]

Although Section 9 of the Hindu Marriage Act is based on formal equality and there is no distinction between the rights of husband and wife, the court held that treating equally persons who are unequally situated, is neither just nor equal. By treating husband and wife, who are inherently unequal, as equal, the judge held that this section offends the rule of equal protection under the laws ensured by Article 14 of the Constitution. He further added that in actual fact, the remedy works only for the benefit of husbands and is oppressive to women.

The case concerned the marriage of a screen actress, T. Sareetha, who had left her matrimonial home. Her husband, Venkatasubbiah, tried to curb her freedom by filing a suit for RCR and obtained a favourable order. When Sareetha appealed to the Andhra Pradesh High Court, P.A. Choudhury J. delivered the historical judgment and held that the remedy is savage and barbaric. He struck down the concerned section and redeemed Sareetha and all women of Andhra Pradesh, from the oppressive yoke of Hindu conjugality.[73]

[70] AIR 1952 Mad 193

[71] (1996) 8 SCC 525, decided by K. Ramaswamy, S. Saghir Ahmad, and G.B. Pattanaik JJ.

[72] *T. Sareetha* v. *T. Venkatasubbiah,* AIR 1983 AP 356.

[73] Ibid.

However, in the following year, the Delhi High Court examined the same issue in *Harvinder Kaur* v. *Harminder Singh*[74] and held to the contrary. The wife, Harvinder Kaur, had challenged the decree of restitution of conjugal rights granted in favour of her husband, Harminder Singh, by the lower court. The Delhi High Court dismissed her appeal and upheld the husband's right to restore conjugality and declared that Section 9 of the Hindu Marriage Act is constitutionally valid. The court further explained:

The object of a decree of restitution of conjugal rights is to bring about cohabitation between the estranged parties so that they can live together in amity. It is a two in one provision. On the one hand, it enables the court to coax and cajole the parties to resume marital life and is designed to encourage reconciliation.

Introduction of constitutional law in home is most inappropriate. It is like introducing a bull in a china shop. It will prove to be a ruthless destroyer of the marriage institution. In the privacy of the home neither Article 21 nor Article 14 have any place. In a sensitive sphere which is most intimate and delicate, the introduction of the cold principles of constitutional law will have the effect of weakening the marriage bond. The introduction of constitutional law into the ordinary domestic relationship of husband and wife will strike at its very root and will be a fruitful source of dissent and quarreling. The 'domestic community' does not rest on contracts sealed with seals and sealing wax, nor on constitutional law. It rests on that kind of moral cement which unites and produces 'two-in-oneship'.[75]

The controversy created by these two diagonally opposite viewpoints was reconciled by the Supreme Court in *Saroj Rani* v. *Sudarshan Kumar Chaddha*,[76] by overruling the verdict of the Andhra Pradesh High Court. The Apex Court held:

---

74 AIR 1984 Del 66.
75 Ibid
76 AIR 1984 SC 1562

In India conjugal rights i.e. right of the husband or the wife to the society of the other spouse is not only a creation of the statute. Such a right is inherent in the very institution of marriage itself. There are sufficient safe guards in Section 9 to prevent it from becoming a tyranny. It is significant to note that the decree can be executed by attachment of property. A decree of restitution of conjugal rights offers inducement for the husband and wife to live together. It serves a social purpose as an aid to the prevention of break-up of marriage.

The Law of Property
Historical Misconceptions

It is generally believed that ancient Hindu law was particularly harsh towards women and denied them sexual and economic freedom. In support of this premise, it is emphasized that Manu, the arch lawgiver stipulated, 'A woman must be dependent upon her father in childhood, upon her husband in youth and upon her sons in old age. She should never be free.'[77] It is also believed that the modernity ushered in during the colonial era helped loosen out this strict sexual control by granting women the right of property ownership.

But rather curiously, very few people are aware that Manu is the first lawgiver who laid down comprehensive principles concerning women's separate property, approximately 2,000 years prior to the English legal system accepting this principle and issued a warning, 'friends or relations of a woman, who, out of folly or avarice, live upon the property belonging to her, or the wicked ones who deprive her of the enjoyment of her own belongings go to hell.'[78] Similarly, Narada's dictate that the husband must give one-third of his property to the

---

77 Manu VIII: 416 as cited in Kuppuswami 1993: 874.
78 Manu's dictate is reaffirmed by later smritikars like Katyayana.

first wife at his second marriage[79] is obscure knowledge.

The smritis and commentaries, with their roots in a feudal society of agrarian landholdings, prescribed a patriarchal family structure within which women's right to property was constrained. Under the Mitakshara law, the property of a Hindu male devolved through survivorship jointly upon four generations of male heirs. The ownership was by birth and not by succession. Upon his birth, the male member acquired the right to property.

Although the male members owned property, this ownership cannot be equated with the modern notion of ownership which essentially confers the right of alienation. The basic characteristic of joint property was its inalienability. The property could not be easily disposed of by way of sale, gift, or will.[80] Hence the joint ownership of males was more notional than actual. The property was managed by the head of the family, the *karta*, for the benefit of the entire family, including its female members. So, in effect, until the property was partitioned, the right of male members was essentially the right of maintenance. Even after partition, the property in the hands of each of the coparceners, continued to be joint property, held in trust along with his male progeny for the benefit of the next line of descendants.

Since women did not form part of the traditional joint family property or coparcenary,

they did not have even the notional right of joint ownership. Hence they could not demand partition. But women had the right to be maintained from the joint property and this right included the right of residence. Women also had the right to claim marriage expenses from the joint property in their natal home.

The husband was bound to maintain the wife despite all her faults, including 'quarrelsome nature', 'neglect of household', 'barrenness' and 'adultery'. He could marry again, but he was under a legal obligation to continue to maintain the first wife. In addition, the wife was entitled to 'supercession fee' or '*sulka*'—an equal share of property which the husband gifted to the new wife.

Since divorce was not commonly prevalent, after marriage, women could not easily be deprived of their right of residence and maintenance. Further, under certain situations like cruelty or adultery, the woman had the right to claim separate residence and maintenance and this provision was given statutory recognition through the Hindu Woman's Separate Residence and Maintenance Act, 1946.

Stridhan Property and its Subversion

The early smritikars, Gautama and Manu, enumerated six categories of stridhan property (or *stridhana*—literal meaning—woman's property). Vishnu, a later smritikar, added four more categories to this enumeration. The later sages Yagnavalkya, Katyayana, Narada, Devala, etc., widened the scope further. Yagnavalkya (around AD second century) expanded the scope of stridhana by adding the word *adhya* (meaning 'and the rest') to the enumerations of Manu and Vishnu.

The *Katyayana Smriti* lays great emphasis on stridhana and discusses the concept elaborately. Katyayana emphasised exclusive ownership, both in terms of sale and gift, and stipulated,

[79] Narada's dictate is based on Manu who laid down: 'To a woman whose husband marries a second wife, let him give an equal sum as a compensation for the supersession, provided no stridhana has been bestowed on her but if she has been allotted let him allot half.' (*Manusmriti* III: 52) (Translation by Georg Buhler (1975) *The Laws of Manu* (Reprint).

[80] The property could be alienated (sold) only under two conditions: to fulfill religious obligations or for the benefit of the estate.

'Neither the husband nor the son, nor the father, nor the brother have authority over stridhana to take it or to give it away.' This injunction is almost in the nature of a warning to male members to lay their hands off the woman's property. If the husband borrowed the woman's stridhan money, he was under a legal obligation to repay it with interest.

Sir Henry Maine, in his *Early History of Institutions* (1875), while describing the institution of stridhana commented, 'It is certainly remarkable that the institution seems to have been developed among the Hindus at a period relatively much earlier than among the Romans.'[81] But he seemed to be under the erroneous impression that it gradually deteriorated to an insignificant position.

Mitakshara (Vijnaneshwara, AD eleventh century), the most widely recognized source of Anglo-Hindu law, expanded the scope of the term *adhya* mentioned by Yagnavalkya and laid that property obtained by a woman through inheritance, purchase, partition, seizure (adverse possession), and finding is her stridhana. Through this expansion, every category of property was brought under the scope of stridhana and the woman was granted exclusive ownership over it.

Dayabhaga (Jimmutavahana, AD twelfth century), the accepted authority of the Bengal school, did not adopt the notion of joint male ownership or coparcenary. In the absence of a coparcenary spreading over four generations, the need to prescribe a wide interpretation to the term was absent here. So under the Dayabhaga system, stridhana was restricted to gifts and movables. Under all other schools, stridhana included movable as well as immovable property. Property acquired by a woman by her own exertions was her stridhana

---

[81] As cited by Kuppuswami 1993: 875.   ·

according to Bombay, Benaras, and Dravida schools (Desai 1994: 163–9).

The most distinguishing feature of stridhan property was its line of descent. Under Mitakshara, after the woman's death, it devolved firstly on an unmarried daughter and then on a married daughter who is not provided for, followed by a married daughter who is provided for. Next in line was the daughter's daughter followed by the daughter's son. The woman's own son could inherit it only in the absence of heirs in the female line.

As can be observed, a system of property ownership by women seems to have been an integral and significant part of the ancient moral, ethical, and legal social norms. It does appear that patriarchal collusions constantly undermined the scriptural dictates of the 'dharma of stridhana'. At each time, the smritikars, with great effort, brought the emphasis back to women's ownership of property and in the process also expanded its scope. There seems to be a constant tussle between the smriti dictates and patriarchal subversions within the family.

During the colonial rule, several judicial decisions constrained the scope of stridhan property. As already mentioned, the Mitakshara had expanded the scope of stridhana to include property acquired by a woman through every source, including inheritance and partition. But the judicial decisions changed this concept and lay down that inherited property is not stridhana. A new legal principle was gradually introduced through court decisions that whether the property is inherited by a woman through her male relatives (father, son, husband) or through her female relatives (mother, mother's mother, daughter), it is not her stridhana and that it would devolve on the heirs of her husband or father. Women lost the right to will or gift away their stridhan and it acquired the character of a limited estate. Upon the widow's death, the property reverted back to the husband's male relatives named as 'reversioners'. The introduction of this concept borrowed from English law, bestowed upon the male relatives the right to challenge all property dealings by Hindu widows.

To provide concrete examples of this trend, some decisions are examined below. These judgments have several commonalities. The litigations against the widows were initiated by their husbands' heirs. In a significant number of cases, following local customs, the lower courts upheld the women's rights. These were reversed by the higher judiciary and then became binding principles of law. Significantly, in all these cases the decisions were from property disputes within the Bengal Presidency, but under the consolidated scheme of hierarchy of courts, they became the binding principles of law for the other Presidencies as well.

In 1868, in *Srinath Gangopadhya* v. *Sarbamangala Debi*,[82] the Calcutta High Court held that as per the Benaras school, once a stridhan property devolves upon a heir, it loses its character as stridhan and devolves as per ordinary rules of Hindu law.

In 1874, in *Gonda Kooer* v. *Kooer Gody Singh*,[83] the widow had purchased the property out of the accumulated income from her stridhana and pleaded that it should be considered as her stridhana. But following the rule laid down by the Privy Council, the Calcutta High Court held that the property was not stridhana and hence she does not have the right to dispose of it by will and upon her death, it would devolve on her husband's heirs.

In 1873, in *Deo Prashad* v. *Lujoo Roy*,[84] the court ruled that the property inherited by a daughter from her father is not stridhana.

In 1874, in *Dowlut Kooer* v. *Burma Deo Sahoy*,[85] the principle was extended to the property inherited by an unmarried daughter from her mother.

Later, the courts stretched this principle to include the property inherited from all female relatives, thus sealing all avenues for the continuation of property devolution in the female line. The substantial case law which had piled up made it impossible to retract from this position.

In 1879, in the case of *Chotay Lal* v. *Chunno Lall*,[86] while holding that the property inherited from the father is not stridhana, the Privy Council expressly stated that since this rule has been established by a series of decisions, a different interpretation of the old and obscure texts can not be followed. The Privy Council further stated that the courts ought not to unsettle a rule of inheritance affirmed by a long course of decisions, unless it is manifestly opposed to law and reason. It was explained that the rule has been laid down by Sir William Macnaghten in his *Treatise on Hindu Law* as follows:

'Under no circumstances can a daughter's son, daughter, husband or other descendants inherit the property which devolved on her at her father's death. Such property is not stridhana and will devolve on her father's heirs.'

The court further held that this rule is not opposed to the spirit and principles of *Mitakshara*. It is interesting to note that while during the early years of administration, contemporary practices were discarded in favour of

---

[82] (1868) 10 WR 488
[83] (1874) 14 BLR 159

[84] (1873) 20 WR 102
[85] (1874) 22 WR 54
[86] (1879) ILR 4 Cal 744

ancient texts, during the later period, after the establishment of Anglicised courts, the court decisions and translated texts were granted greater validity than the ancient texts which were now labeled as old and obscure.

The facts of two subsequent cases decided by the Privy Council on the issue of women's right to property, which were later validated as land mark decisions, are set out in detail below.

Mussammat Thakoor Deyhee v. Rai Baluk Ram was a case decided by the Privy Council in 1886.[87] A childless widow Choteh Babee, gifted the property she inherited from her husband to her niece. It is reported in the judgment that Choteh Babee, despite being a *purdahnishin*, was an excellent business woman who managed her property well. The husband's heirs challenged the deed on the ground that it was fraudulent and that she had no power of alienation over immovable property inherited from her husband. The lower court at Banaras held that the widow was competent to gift the property. The appellate court at Agra reversed the decision on the ground that the deed of gift was a forged document. At this point, the right of the widow to gift her property was not in dispute. The court only examined whether the gift deed was an authentic or a forged document. In appeal the Privy Council ruled: 'The widow has no power to dispose immovable property inherited from her husband, whether ancestral or acquired.'

Sheo Shankar v. Debi Sahai, a case decided in 1903,[88] provides yet another illustration of the judicial trend. The woman had inherited the property from her mother. After her death, her sons claimed the property as heirs of the mother and grandmother and deprived their sister. The

subordinate judge of Gorakhpur held that the property inherited through the female line was the woman's stridhana and hence her sons had no right over it. On appeal, the Allahabad High Court reversed the decision. This resulted in an appeal to the Privy Council. In 1903, the Privy Council upheld the decision of the high court and laid down that the property inherited by a woman from her mother is not her stridhana and hence it will not devolve on her daughter who is her stridhana heir, but will devolve upon her son.

These judgments reveal how gradually the notion of stridhan property was subverted through patriarchal collusions aided by colonial judicial decisions. This right did not find a mention in the codified Hindu Marriage Act of 1956. Much later this customary right was re-introduced into legal texts through a provision of the criminal law, Section 406 of IPC, criminal breach of trust, in the case of *Pratibha Rani v. Suraj Kumar* where the woman had initiated criminal proceedings for reclaiming her stridhan. [89]

Codified Law and Illusory Inheritance Rights

As already discussed, the smritis and commentaries, with their roots in a feudal society of agrarian landholdings, prescribed a patriarchal family structure, within which women's right to property was constrained. Under the Mitakshara law, the property of a Hindu male devolved through survivorship jointly upon four generations of male heirs. The ownership was by birth and not by succession. Upon his birth, the male member acquired the right to property. This was the unique feature of the Hindu Joint Family or HUF property. This system was meant to safeguard agrarian landholdings from fragmentation and ensured that the property

---

[87]   (1886) 11 MIA 139
[88]   (1903) 30 IA 202

[89]   AIR 1985 SC 658: 1985 Cri.LJ 817

remained within a particular clan from generation to generation. Inalienability of immovable property was an essential feature of HUF property.

With the subversion of the institution of stridhana which was meant to protect women's right to property during the colonial period and with the consolidation of property rights in the hands of individual men, through certain legislative measures,[90] women's condition had become deplorable. Their rights had corroded beyond recognition and women were left with no rights whatsoever, except the limited right of maintenance from the HUF property.

To set right the problems created by the judicial decisions of the English courts which had constrained the scope of stridhana, during the later phase of the nineteenth century, the social reformer, G.V. Deshmukh, introduced the Hindu Women's Rights to Property Bill (Gill 1986: 485).

While introducing the Bill in the Legislative Assembly on 4 February 1937, Deshmukh stated:

The British concepts like 'reversioner' 'surrender' etc. had caused a great loss to women's right to property. The word 'reversioner' reflected an English notion peculiar to their own country. From that moment, the widow began to be infested by those pests called 'reversioners'. In fact, a majority of the litigation in connection with the property of widows was by and on account of the reversioners. The reversioner could harass the widow by challenging every act of hers in dealing with the property (Gill 1986: 104).

Deshmukh added that due to the prevailing social conditions, the English judges had arrived at an erroneous conclusion that the temperament of the Hindu society was such that it did not want Hindu women to have absolute right in the property (Gill 1986: 104–7). Through

[90] See preceding section titled 'Colonial Legal Interventions'.

this Bill, Deshmukh hoped to achieve equality between Hindu men and women in respect of their property.

The Bill met with a great deal of hostility and Deshmukh was ridiculed for introducing it. After much debate, a watered down version of the original Bill was finally enacted. The provisions of the Bill granting women absolute right to property were mutilated and widows were granted only a limited right of inheritance by introducing an English concept called 'widow's estate'. The provision granting daughters a share in the parental property was excluded. The right of married women to separate property under the scriptural notion of stridhana, which the Bill originally set to restore, was subverted. The women's right to property was confined within the limited sphere of inheritance rights of widows. The Act created more problems than it solved. In order to bring in clarity in this Act, the first Hindu Law Committee was set up in 1941 which recommended enactment of a comprehensive code of marriage and succession. This led to the setting up of the second Hindu Law Committee in 1944.

The main opposition to the enactment of the Hindu Code Bill was around the issue of property rights to women as daughters in parental property (both ancestral and self acquired). This opposition stalled Hindu law reforms right up to mid-1950s, with certain Congress leaders remaining rigid and uncompromising in their opposition to granting women property rights in HUF property. There was a general fear that this move will lead to fragmentation of agricultural property. The extent of opposition within the Congress to daughters inheriting property was such that even the then Law Minister, C. C. Biswas, in 1954, on the floor of the house, publicly expressed his disagreement with this provision

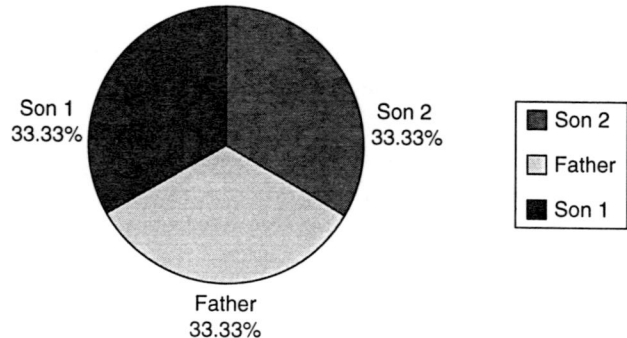

Figure 1.3 Share of the Father and Two Sons as Coparceners in the HUF Property

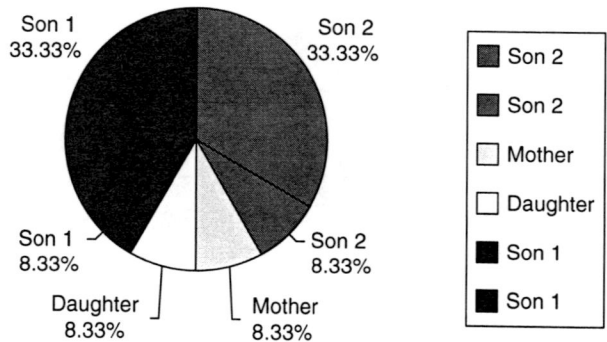

Figure 1.4 Share of the Male and Female Heirs in the HUF Property upon the Death of the Father

(Kishwar 1994: 2154). Due to severe opposition from the then President, Rajendra Prasad, who expressed his unwillingness to give his assent to the Bill if coparcenary was abolished, the system of coparcenary had to be retained. This resulted in the denial of equal rights to women in the ancestral home and property. Though superficially, it did seem that the daughters were awarded equal rights to property, when compared to the rights of the brother, the sister's share was dismal.

As per the provisions of Section 6 of the Hindu Succession Act, 1956, in a family where there are two sons and one daughter, upon the death of the father each of the sons would inherit one-third of the property as coparceners. The remaining one-third is the father's

separate property which would be divided in four parts, one for the wife, one for the daughter, and one each for the sons. So while the sons would be entitled to one-third plus one-fourth of the father's share of one-third, the daughter's share would only be one-fourth of the father's share of the property. In actual terms, it would be one-twelfth of the entire property, whereas the share of each son would be five-twelfth of the entire property. This dismal share came to be projected as gender equality.

Further, daughters were granted equal rights only in the separate or self-acquired property of their father. But even this right could be throttled by throwing the property back into the common stock using the 'Doctrine of Blending' or by forming new coparcenaries. An incentive for such a move was provided by the State by conferring tax reliefs for coparcenaries under the Income Tax Act.[91]

Since the earlier safeguard provided by the ancient law givers to women by way of stridhana, a necessary concomitant to male coparcenaries, had been corroded, denial of equal rights to daughters only served to widen the gender divide. While at one level, coparcenary was retained, the necessary safeguards within it for the protection of women's rights were abrogated. The main feature of the traditional Hindu joint family was its inalienability. But the new right bestowed upon the male members to sell, gift, or will away the property further weakened the position of female members. In this context, the daughters' right to be maintained from the family property or to claim marriage expenses out of this property became illusory. The property inherited by the son from the father now became his separate property and the female members could not lay any claims to it.[92]

While the English concept of alienation through testamentary succession was incorporated into the Hindu Succession Act, the protection granted to the family members under the English law did not find a mention here.[93]

So, individual men could will away both their share in the joint family property as well as the whole of their separate property with absolute abundance. During the Parliamentary debates, these loopholes were specifically pointed out to the members who were opposing the provision granting property rights to daughters to indicate how they could circumvent the provisions of the Act (Kishwar 1994: 2155).

While there were no safeguards to protect the right of daughters in their natal family, the capitalist, consumerist forces transformed the ancient custom of stridhana into a modern distortion called dowry.[94] Under its modern guise, the daughters lost control on this property, which was presumably given on her behalf to secure her happiness in her matrimonial home. In subsequent decades, the demand for dowry became an instrument of violence and subjugation of the newly married brides and several penal provisions had to be enacted to safeguard women from the menace of dowry related violence in their matrimonial home.

The Hindu law of property and succession has been challenged on grounds of sex discrimination by both men and women. When the

[91] Under Section 10 (2) of the Income Tax Act, an exemption is granted to income from the Hindu Undivided Family (HUF). Under Sections 20 & 20A of the Wealth Tax Act, certain tax concessions are granted to members of HUF at the time of partition.

[92] See the decisions in *Commissioner of Wealth Tax v. Chandre Sen*, AIR 1986 SC 1753 and *Yudhishter v. Ashok Kumar*, AIR 1987 SC 558, where the court held that the property inherited by the son is his separate property.

[93] The English statute, Inheritance (Family Provision) Act of 1938 provided for a legal remedy, if the husband failed to make reasonable provisions for his wife and children. The right of a former wife who is entitled to receive maintenance was protected through the Matrimonial Causes (Property and Maintenance) Act of 1958 (subsequently re-enacted in the Matrimonial Causes Act 1965). Since this enactment placed a divorced wife in a superior position than the surviving spouse, a further statute was enacted entitled, Inheritance (Provision for Family and Dependents) Act 1975 through which the surviving spouse could claim not only maintenance but also a share in the capital.

[94] M.N. Srinivas has argued that modern dowry is entirely the product of the forces let loose by British rule such as monetization, education and the introduction of the 'organised sector'. To equate it with *dakshina* is only an attempt to legitimize a modern monstrosity by linking it up with an ancient and respected custom (Srinivas 1984: 11–13).

provision of the Hindu Succession Act which awarded a Hindu woman the right of absolute ownership over her property was challenged, the courts, invoking Article 15 (3) of the Constitution, held that special provisions for women do not amount to discrimination against men. The courts explained that the provision is an attempt to remedy the historical disadvantages suffered by Hindu women, more specifically, widows, under the ancient (smriti) law of succession.[95]

However several patriarchal presumptions still dominate the Hindu law of succession. For instance, the provision that when a female Hindu dies intestate, any property she has inherited from her husband will pass to the husband's heirs prevails, while there is no such rule in respect of men who die intestate. When this provision was challenged, it was upheld on the ground that the intent of the law was to ensure the continuity of property in the male line.[96]

There are a few judgments which have struck down restrictions on women's ownership of land on the ground of unconstitutionality, discrimination, and violation of Article 15 of the Constitution.[97] But traditional distinctions between sons and daughters have been upheld in *Sucha Singh Biswas* v. *The State of Punjab*,[98] on the basis that a daughter will leave her parental home to join another family after her marriage.

Another glaring discrimination was highlighted in the recent controversial ruling of the Supreme Court, delivered in May 2009, which held that even when a woman has been treated with cruelty and driven out of her matrimonial home soon after her marriage, the property would go to her husband's male relatives and not the members of her natal family. The woman, Narayani Devi, was married at a very young age of fifteen years. Within three months of the marriage, when her husband died of snake bite, she was accused of bringing bad luck to the family and was driven out of the matrimonial home. She returned to her parental home, educated herself, and a decade later, secured employment as a teacher in a Government school. When she expired in 1996, at the age of fifty six, without leaving a will, she left behind rupees twenty lakh (Rs 20,00,000) by way of bank deposits and provident fund dues. When members of her natal family filed for succession, they were shocked to find that Narayani Devi's husband's nephew had also made a claim for this money. The litigation over this went on for well over a decade. The final ruling of the Supreme Court was delivered in this context.[99] The Court reasoned that it was a difficult case where sentiments or sympathy alone could not be the guiding factor. The blatantly sexist judgment was highlighted in the media and has been criticized by women's groups.[100] The apex Court seems to have adopted a formalistic approach of law and followed the letter of the law and not the spirit of the Hindu Succession Act. If the courts had adopted the legal dictum that no one is allowed to take advantage of one's own wrong, perhaps it was possible to reach a different conclusion. The courts also had the power under Article 142 to reinterpret this provision in the interest of justice. But the apex Court lost this great opportunity.

The issue of denial of property rights has been brought into focus by Bina Agarwal's near-encyclopedic volume, *A Field of One's*

---

[95] *Kaur Sing* v. *Jaggar Singh*, AIR 1961 Punj 489 and *Pratap Singh* v. *Union of India*, AIR 1985 SC 1695.

[96] *Sonubai Yeshwant Jadhan* v. *Bala Govinda Yadav*, AIR 1983 Bom 156.

[97] *Pritam Kaur* v. *State of PEPSU*, AIR 1963 Punj 9.

[98] AIR 1974 P&H 162.

[99] *Omprakash* v. *Radhacharan* 2009 (7) SCALES 1.

[100] *Unfair Deal* by Kumara V. Swamy, *The Telegraph*, Calcutta, 20 May 2009.

Own: Gender and Land Rights in South Asia (1994), which uses economic, legal, and anthropological analyses. It underlines the need for women to get land or property, and examines the ways in which notions of 'family' and 'tradition' are used to deprive them of it.

In another comprehensive study of all property and succession cases with a gender aspect from across the country between 1988 and 1991, Srimati Basu (2001) has concluded that in litigation around property claims, women emerged victorious in 66.4 per cent of the 119 cases and were clear losers in only 29.4 per cent of the cases. But a closer inspection revealed that many of these victories were only superficial as in some of these cases, traditional notions of the patriarchal family intervene to block some problematic aspects of the law from scrutiny.

Recent Amendments to the Hindu Succession Act
With the illusory inheritance rights, the struggle for equality continued well into the new millennium. Denial of property rights in their natal home, along with dowry related violence in their matrimonial home, led to the murder and suicide of several young married women in all metro cities and even in smaller towns in India during the fifty years since the enactment of the Hindu Succession Act of 1956.

Property laws also continued to retain certain anomalies concerning agricultural land, widow's rights, and the dwelling house. Agricultural land was a state subject, hence beyond the scope of the Hindu Succession Act, and through state-made laws, women could be denied a share in ancestral as well as separate property which was marked as 'agricultural land'. Land fragmentation continued to be the concern here and this became a whip to deny women their rights in parental property. Blatantly discriminatory aspects of the various Land Ceiling Acts enacted by state governments were declared as constitutionally valid.[101] The acts provide for two additional hectares of land for each adult son, but no such benefits are provided for adult daughters who form part of the domestic unit. The acts presume that women are either not capable of owning and administering property or that property is of no concern to adult females. So neither as unmarried daughters nor as married wives do they have an additional entitlement. Their status is confined to that of dependents.

Under Section 23 of the Hindu Succession Act, women's right to claim partition of the dwelling house was restrained. Only when male heirs decided to partition the property could female heirs claim their share. Further, married women were not given the right even to reside in the parental home.

There was a sustained campaign by women's groups who were demanding an amendment in the above mentioned discriminatory aspects of the Hindu Succession Act. Some southern states brought in certain changes through state amendments. In 1976, in the state of Kerala under the leftist scheme of land reforms, the concept of joint family holdings was abolished.[102] In 1986, women in Andhra Pradesh were granted the right of coparcenary. The states of Tamil Nadu and Karnataka introduced the provisions of the Andhra Pradesh amendments in 1989 and 1994 respectively. In 1994, women in Maharashtra were granted the right

---

[101] *Ambika Prasad Mishra* v. *State of UP*, 1980 (3) SCC 719.

[102] Though this was a progressive move, ironically, it resulted in the abolition of matriliny among several caste groups in Kerala and a large number of women lost control over their lands. See Saradamoni, K. (1994) 'Progressive Land Legislations and Subordination of Women' in Lotika Sarkar and B. Sivaramayya (ed.), *Women and Law: Contemporary Problems*, pp.155–67.

to be recognised as coparceners.[103] Since the southern states had a culture of granting women rights to property under customary law, the state amendments did not cause a major stir. In contrast, none of the northern states enacted such provisions and there was also resistance for a central amendment. At the other extreme the state of Haryana unanimously passed an amendment in 1987 for the abolition of Hindu women's rights in the self acquired property of a Hindu male under the plea that it leads to fragmentation of agricultural land.

Finally, after a long and arduous campaign, under the UPA government, in 2005, the Hindu Succession Act was amended and women were granted rights in the HUF property. Section 6 of the amended Act reads that the 'daughter of the coparcener' will now receive the same rights as the other coparceners. She will have the same rights, duties and will be treated in a manner similar to that of a son. In other words, the daughter now does not have to receive a share as a member of the Class I heirs, but will receive her share as a coparcener. She can sue for partition of the property and can be made karta or the manager of the Hindu Joint Family. Section 23 of the pre-amendment Act has also been deleted, whereby all daughters, married or unmarried, now have the right to claim partition of the dwelling house and married women have acquired the right to reside in the parental home.

Another achievement of the amendment is the deletion of Section 4(2). This section exempted interests in agricultural land, the inheritance of which was subject to state tenurial laws. This naturally disallowed women from claiming a share in agricultural land. The amended Act now brings such agricultural lands at par with other kinds of property. This is linked to the newly awarded coparcenary rights to the woman, who can use her rights to benefit from agricultural land, which has now been brought under the ambit of the Hindu Succession Act.

The implications of this amendment are clear. At the most basic level, by bringing agricultural land under the ambit of the Hindu Succession Act, there is an active effort to address the issue of poverty and women's control over the family's resources. Both economically and symbolically, the Act has the potentiality of enhancing the woman's status within her natal family. Research indicates that there is a correlation between women's access to economic resources and physical abuse perpetrated against them. It is their economic vulnerability that exposes them to the dangers of extreme physical abuse (Agarwal 1994: 39). It is hoped that the amendments will have a positive impact and reduce the extent of domestic violence prevalent in the country.

Doubts and apprehensions about the feasibility and its ground level impact persist. Primary among them is the question whether it is possible for a daughter to ever be able to fulfill all the duties and religious obligations which are prescribed to a son under the traditional Hindu law. At the other level, there are doubts as to whether the amendment will lead to a change in the mind set to the extent that a married daughter will be treated as much a part of her natal family (and not as 'paraya dhan', denoting that she is the property of an outsider) in her own natal family and be given the status awarded to a son in the family. Will the legislation help to bring in social and attitudinal change regarding the role, status, and rights of women as daughter, is the moot question.

The impact of the amendment is yet to be seen. And it must be noted that despite such an amendment, it is impossible for any concrete changes to take place, with reference to the

---

[103] See 174th Report of the Law Commission of India, May 2000 for details of the state amendments in these five states.

status of women in society, in the absence of legal awareness and easy and affordable access to justice delivery systems. This is particularly relevant to women from smaller cities and far flung rural areas. The full impact of the amendments depends largely on these collateral concerns and efficacy of legal institutions.

Section B

ISLAMIC LAW OF MARRIAGE AND SUCCESSION

'Islam' means peace and submission.[104] The *Sharia* is the central core of Islam and is considered to be an infallible guide to ethics. But it is not 'law' in the modern sense. The Islamic jurisprudential law is called *Fiqh*. According to Fyzee, this is the name given to the whole science of jurisprudence. It is the knowledge and obligation derived from the four sources of Islamic law—the Quran, Sunna, Ijma, and Qiyas (Fyzee 1974: 16–18; Hidayatullah and Hidayatullah 1990: xix–xxiv). 'Muhammadan (or Mohammedan) law', to this day, means the appropriate school of law, modified by customs where legally applicable (Derret 1999: 53). According to Mensky (2003) the internal diversity of Muslim law almost matches that of pluralist Hindu conceptualizations as both legal systems had to rely on human processes to evolve their religious laws.

There is a great similarity between 'Anglo-Hindu' and the 'Anglo-Mohammedan' law as it evolved during the colonial period through judicial interventions which were based on the translated religious texts or the opinions given by religious experts—Qazis and Pundits. While a large part of Muslim law is uncodified, there have been some specific statutes, such as the Dissolution of Muslim Marriages Act of 1939 and the Muslim Women (Protection of Rights upon Divorce) Act 1986. But overall, contemporary law has evolved more on a case to case basis through judicial interventions. A large section of the Muslim community is outside the purview of official law and disputes are resolved within the community (*Jamat*) with the help of community leaders as per the customs of a particular community. The following section contains a brief sketch of Muslim law from the perspective of women's rights.

Origin and Development of Islamic Law

Sources of Islamic Law

The Quran, which is said to be the divine revelation (the word of God), is considered to be the highest source of law. The Quran, or revealed law, is often translated as 'reading' or 'recital'. It represents the Will of God communicated to the Prophet through Angel Gabriel. Compiled from memory after the Prophet's death from the version of Osman, the third Caliph, it contains about six thousand verses, but not more than two hundred verses deal with legal principles and only eighty verses deal with issues of family relations. The Caliphs, as the Prophet's successors, took up the responsibility of adjudicating disputes among the people and while drawing upon the Quran, they continued the application of the ancient Arab system of arbitration and customary law. But the Quran cannot be construed as 'law'; it is the source of law. Divine law cannot become a legal system in its own right. It requires human intervention by way of interpretation or application. It is in this context that the other sources of law become important.

The second source of Islamic law is 'Sunna' or tradition. The word Sunna means 'trodden

---

[104] In its religious sense, it denotes submission to the Will of God and in its secular sense, the establishment of peace. In English, the word 'Muslim' is used both as a noun and as an adjective and denotes both the person professing the faith and something specific to Muslims, such as law, culture, art, etc. See Hidayatullah and Hidayatullah (1990: xix).

path'. Initially the term was applied to customs and practices of pre-Islamic tribes and the early Muslims of AD seventh century. But later, the word came to denote the practice and precedents of the Prophet, that is, the Hadis. As a source of law, the Hadis is as binding as the principles of the Quran. By eighth century, it became the ideal and established doctrine of the ancient schools, expounded by its representatives. Hence, in the present context, 'Sunna' could mean either the living tradition of the schools or the traditions of the Prophet.

The third and equally binding source is Ijma, which is an agreement among legal scholars of any generation. This was supported by the Hanafi doctrine that the provisions of law must change with the changing times and of the Maliki doctrine that new facts require new decisions. In developing Islamic law by consensus, the doctrine of *Ijtihad,* which means using one's own reasoning to deduce a rule of Shariat law, was developed. With the passage of time, however, this liberty to reason was restricted and by the ninth century, Ijtihad was considered as the privilege of great scholars of the past.

The last source of Islamic law is Qiyas, which means reasoning by analogy. It does not involve laying down new principles, but is merely a rule of interpretation. A principle laid down in the text can be applied to another situation, if it can be demonstrated, by applying logic and reasoning, that the rule laid down in the text governs the situation at hand though the language of the text and the situation at hand are not strictly the same. It became a source of law as a sort of compromise by the Shafii and Maliki schools. There is also a concept of 'blending' desirable rules from a variety of sources, which is known as *talfiq* (patching), within Islamic jurisprudence (Derrett 1978: 8 as cited by Mensky 2003: 217). The *Fatwa*s (legal opinions of scholars and judges), though not a source of law, have been instrumental in the development and enrichment of legal principles (Hidayatullah and Hidayatullah 1990: xxiv).

The Shia and Sunni Schools

There are two broad sects of Islam, the Sunnis and the Shias. The four recognized schools of Sunni law are: Hanafi, Maliki, Shafii, and Hanbali. The Hanafi school, founded by Abu Hanifa (AD 699–767), has a wide following. It is also known as the Kufa school. Originating in Iraq, the doctrine spread to Syria, Afghanistan, Turkish Central Asia, and the Indian subcontinent.

The founder of the Shia school is Imam Jafar. Most important among the Shia schools of law are Ithna Ashari, Jaffariya and Ismaili. The Ismaili sect of the Shia school is the dominant majority in Persia. Elsewhere they are generally in a minority. In India, the Bohras and Khojas (Agha Khani) are Shias belonging to the Ismaili sect.

The main difference between the Shia and Sunni sects is the doctrine of *Imamat.* According to the Sunnis, the leader of Muslims is the Khalifa, the successor of the Prophet, who is a temporal and political ruler rather than a religious chief. For religious matters, they must follow the Shariat. The institution of the *Khalifat* was abolished in 1924. According to the Shias, the Imam is the final interpreter of the law on earth. He is a leader not by suffrage of the people but by divine right as descendant of the Prophet. Some Shia sects like the Dawoodi Bohras originated as the outcome of a rebellion against the oppressive Sunni theology in around eighth century AD, and were considered to be reformative and emancipatory (Fyzee 1974: 39–40).

The laws of the two main sects and their subsects vary a great deal from each other. Among the various schools, the Maliki school is the most favourable to women and the Shafii school comes next. North Africa mainly follows Maliki law and women enjoy greater rights. Under this doctrine, a wife has an option to dissolve her marriage on the following grounds: cruelty, non-payment of maintenance, absence of husband, insanity, leprosy, castration, and sexual malformation (Fyzee 1974: 169).

Rights of Women under Islam: Clearing the Misconceptions

It is important to contextualise the principles of Shariat law within tribal Arabia. The Arabs were traders and had mastered the law of contract.[105] The basic principle of contract was applied to other social relationships, including marriage. Although the Shariat is premised upon a patriarchal family structure, it is not based on a feudal economic structure. The matrimonial principles differ from the principles evolved within European feudalism reflected in the Canon law. The principal of indissolubility of marriage, which is intrinsically linked to inalienability of feudal land, did not govern Islamic law of marriage and divorce. The principles governing marriage transactions were similar to trade contracts, with offer, acceptance, and consideration forming its base. The principles of a contractual marriage provided better scope for defining women's rights than marriages under the Christian laws of feudal Europe during the corresponding period.

In an era of unlimited polygamy, the Prophet restricted the number of wives to four, with an injunction that each wife be treated with equal dignity and affection. The Prophet also converted the custom of bride price of tribal Arabia to *mehr*, which would be a future security to a married woman (Diwan 1993: 52–3). Islam

was also the first legal system to grant women the right of inheritance and stipulated fixed shares to women. Some positive provisions of the Islamic law of marriage and succession are discussed below.

Marriage is a civil and dissoluble contract: This is in sharp contrast to the principles of Christianity and Hinduism where marriage was traditionally viewed as an indissoluble sacrament. Later, at the advent of nineteenth century, when Europe made a shift from feudalism to capitalism, marriage was transformed from status to contract.[106] This concept was later introduced into the English law of marriage in the later part of the nineteenth century (Matrimonial Causes Act, 1857), and a century later, in 1955, it was incorporated into codified Hindu law.

The right of mehr: The stipulation of mehr at the time of marriage is an important aspect of a Muslim marriage. This is meant as a safeguard to the woman. The high amount of mehr stipulated in the *nikahnama* (contract of marriage) or *kabin-nama* (agreement of marriage) was meant to act as a deterrent to unilateral divorce.[107] Under the Shariat law, the woman

---

[105] According to Paras Diwan, Hindus perfected the concept of *dan* (gift) and applied it to marriage alliances, that is, *kanyadan*. Muslims perfected the concept of sale and found it convenient to express many transactions, including marriage, in the language of sale (Diwan 1993: 52–3).

[106] I am referring to the celebrated statement of Henry Sumner Maine in *Ancient Laws* (1972: 100) that 'the movement of the progressive societies has hitherto been a movement from *status to contract*' According to this thesis, in the ancient world individuals were bound by status to traditional groups, while in modern times, individuals are viewed as autonomous agents, and are free to make contracts and form associations. Hence the institution of marriage also evolved from 'status' marriages which were permanent and indissoluble to dissoluble contract marriages.

[107] The Hindu and English systems rely upon the concept of maintenance to safeguard women's economic right within marriage. Maintenance presumes a state of dependency. The concept of stipulating mehr is based on a more noble principle (a mark of respect for the woman) than maintenance and eternal dependency. Further, under all matrimonial laws, maintenance is

has a charge over her husband's property for the payment of her mehr, even after his death.

The right to enter into a pre-marriage (pre-nuptial) agreement (*qarar-nama* or *kabin-nama*): These agreements relate mainly to two aspects: (i) regulation of matrimonial life, and (ii) stipulations regarding dissolution of marriage. This can be an effective way of controlling polygamy. The woman can stipulate that in the event of the husband entering into a second marriage, he should provide her a separate residence. If the husband violates the agreement, the wife is entitled to divorce herself, without the intervention of the court.[108] Such agreements can be entered into either prior to marriage or even thereafter.

The right to maintenance or for personal allowances: This is referred to as *mewa khori* (literally, 'for eating fruit'), *guzara,* or *kharch-e-pandan* (literally, 'betel nut expenses') are similar in character (Fyzee 1974: 129).

The one third rule regarding testamentary succession: As per this rule, a Muslim cannot will away more than one-third of his property. Wills also cannot be made in favour of legal heirs. The heirs have to inherit according to the rules of succession as laid down in the Shariat. Women are granted defined shares under the scheme of succession[109] (Hidayatullah and Hidayatullah 1990: 104).

The woman's share under the Islamic law of inheritance is not equal to that of her male counterpart. She is entitled to half the share of the male counterpart.[110] Although the stipulation falls short of the present concept of gender equality, it was a radical measure for its time and was based on a principle of equity. The man had to provide the mehr for the wife and bear the marriage expenses of his unmarried daughters and sisters from his share of inheritance. The women were excluded from such encumbrances.

Reform within Islam

Although Islamic law is stated to be theocratic, several countries (Islamic as well as others) have modified the law to meet the demands of the changing social conditions and values. Furqan Ahmad maintains that a major portion of statutory personal law enacted in most Muslim countries represents a mere codification of the traditional law and is, at best, a unification of divergent legal principles. But it cannot be denied that these changes have brought about significant reform in classical Islamic law.

---

linked to a woman's chastity and hence becomes a way of controlling the woman's sexuality. An unchaste woman is not entitled to maintenance. A semblance of the tradition of mehr as future security is also found in Jewish law, discussed later in the book, and was known as 'Kethuba'.

[108] Before the enactment of the Dissolution of Muslim Marriages Act, a Muslim reformist, Mrs Hamida Ali, on behalf of some of the leading women's organizations in India, had prepared a specimen form of such an agreement which was published in the *Bombay Law Journal* in the year 1936. See Fyzee (1936: 113).

[109] Under the Indian Succession Act and the Hindu Succession Act, there is no restraint regarding testamentary succession and a person can will away all the property and disinherit his legal heirs.

[110] Although there are wide differences in the laws of various sects and sub-sects, the inheritance rights of women under the Islamic law can be broadly categorized as follows: (i) the daughter inherits half the share inherited by the son. For example, when there are no other heirs, the daughter inherits one third and the son inherits two thirds of the property; (ii) the mother inherits one sixth of the property while the father inherits one third; and (iii) the wife (or if there is more than one wife then all of them jointly) inherits one eight of the husband's property (Fyzee 1974: 48–62).

The reforms have been either approved by the *Ullamas* or have been modified according to their suggestions (Ahmad 1994: 113).

The process of change within the Muslim world has not been linear. Countries where Islam is the state/predominant religion, particularly the Arab world, have continued to preserve the uncodified Muslim law which has incorporated local customs. On the other hand, countries like Turkey and Albania have opted for a complete abandonment of traditional Islamic family law and have replaced it with secular systems. Lebanon and Israel have incorporated the provisions of Turkish family code and have made them applicable to the Muslim population (Mahmood 1972: 3).

Many countries have adopted a moderate course—retaining the fundamental structure of the traditional family law of Islam, but adapting its various locally prevalent versions to suit contemporary social requirements. Around twenty countries have enacted either substantive or regulatory reforms to change matrimonial law, either partly or wholly, by relying upon the principle of ijtihad within the broad framework of Islam itself (Mahmood 1972: 270–2). Crossing the barriers of officially adopted or dominant schools, laws have been codified on the basis of a selection of legal rules derived from various schools of Islamic law.

For example, although the dominant school in India and Pakistan is Hanafi, the Dissolution of Muslim Marriages Act of 1939 incorporated principles of Maliki law and granted women the right of divorce. According to Hanafi authorities, rules of other Sunni schools may be applied by command of the sovereign power. Through this principle, in 1931, the ruler of Bhopal enacted a code, *Dabita Tahaffuzi Huquqai Zawjain* (Law for the Protection of Rights of Spouses), incorporating Maliki rules. The same principle was later relied upon while granting

Muslim women in British India the right of divorce through the enactment of the Dissolution of Muslim Marriages Act. Similarly, on the basis of a doctrine of the Hanbali school of Islamic law, several countries have granted women the right to stipulate a restraint against bigamous marriages of their husbands.

Several countries have also regulated the husband's right to polygamy through statutory and regulatory provisions. Turkey and Tunisia have abolished polygamy altogether. In many countries, prior permission of the court is required for a bigamous marriage. Indonesia, Sri Lanka, and Pakistan have imposed various restrictions on polygamy (Ahmad 1994). For instance, during the regime of Ayub Khan, the Muslim Family Laws Ordinance of 1961 was promulgated in Pakistan. Through this ordinance, the husband's right to bigamy was sought to be regulated. It was made mandatory for the husband to obtain prior permission of an Arbitration council. These reforms are meant to mould classical Islamic law according to changing social needs.

Evolution of Indo-Islamic Law

Islam came to India through the trade routes of Arabs, via the Arabian Sea. Some of these traders settled down along the Malabar coast in the eighth century and adopted local customs and practices. For instance, the Mopillahs of Kerala and Lakshadweep did not follow the Shariat.[111] Instead, they adopted the matrilineal tradition prevalent in this region.[112]

---

[111] According to Mayne, *Marummakkathayam* was practised by Warriers, Unnis, Padvals, Chakkiars, Thiyas, Nambiars (Brahmin), and Mopillahs (Muslim). The Aliyasanthana was prevalent in South Kanara among the Billavas, Bunts, Maraveers, etc (Kuppuswami 1993: 1209 and Dube 1994: 1273).

[112] A concrete example of this can still be found in Lakshadweep Islands where the population is

The Shariat was first introduced in the Sultanates of Afghan and Turk and entered India around twelfth or thirteenth century. The Muslim sultans who invaded India were Hanafis. They relied on the Ullama to be the religious and legal arbitrators. The new Sultanates followed the basic law of Islam, the Shariat, as interpreted by the Ullama in the royal courts. It is through this channel that the Shariat was established in India. The text books of Hanafi law are based on *Fatawa-e-Alamgiri*, which is a collection of Fatawas compiled during Aurangzeb's reign and the *Hedaya* (the guide).

The Muslim society, as it evolved in India, could be categorized into three broad sections—the nobility, the peasantry, and the artisans. The Muslim population of the towns consisted of artisans and traders. Among the artisan classes, there was great assimilation between Hindu and Muslim rituals, ceremonies, and customs.

There were many instances of converted Muslims following their earlier non-Islamic norms and practices (for instance, the caste system or the joint family property system, that is, coparcenary).[113] The Islamic law of pre-emption crept into Hindu customs and practices and came to be accepted as a part of Hindu law. The population in the villages, both Hindus as well as Muslims, followed their own local laws and customs. The *Bhakti* and the *Sufi* movements, from the fourteenth to the sixteenth century, which were based on egalitarian principles of equality and love in opposition to the stronghold of religious orthodoxy and caste hierarchy, helped in bringing further assimilation between the lower strata of the Hindu and Muslim communities (Thapar 1992: 298–312). At the advent of colonial rule there were several amphibious communities which could not clearly be distinguished as either wholly Hindu or wholly Muslim due to the intermingling of their laws, customs, and practices.[114] Many a times, the religion of a community was 'fixed' during litigation over property rights.[115]

While there are various schools of Islamic theology, the courts have been an important source of advancing Islamic jurisprudence. After the East India Company acquired the *diwani* rights under the Mughul emperors in parts of Bengal, Bihar, and Orissa, they acquired the power to settle disputes between the 'natives'.[116] In order to find the genuine and authentic law of the natives, several scriptures were translated into English and were relied upon while adjudicating over matters which were categorized as 'personal laws' of the native communities. In 1791, under directions from Hastings, Charles Hamilton translated the Arabic text, the Hedaya, into English. Sir William Jones translated *Al Sirajiyyah*, the Mohammedan law of inheritance. Neil Baillie's *Digest of Moohammudan Law* was based on *Fatwa-e-Alamgiri*. Colonial courts relied on these translated texts in the evolution of Anglo-Mohammedan law.

---

overwhelmingly Muslim and follows the pre-conversion matrilineal patterns of property inheritance, which resemble the matrilineal traditions of some Hindu communities of Kerala (Dube: 1994).

[113] There were several cases concerning the Bohras, Khojas, and Kutchi Memons of Gujarat and the Muslim Ghirasias of Bharuch, where, during litigation, Hindu law of coparcenary was applied.   •

[114] This confusion prevails among some communities even in contemporary times. See Mayaram (1997).

[115] See the rulings in *Raj Bahadur* v. *Bishen Dayal* (1882) ILR 4 All 343 and *Ma Yait* v. *Maung Chit Maung* (1921) 48 IA 553.

[116] For a detailed discussion see Introduction to this chapter.

Later, several Islamic jurists contributed to the process through their scholarly works—Ameer Ali, Badruddin Tyabji, and Asif Ali Fyzee, to name just a few. It is through the wisdom and guidance of these legal luminaries that the Islamic jurisprudential law—Islamic *Fiqh*—was developed in later years.

The process of advancing the law through judicial pronouncements continued in the post-Independence period and is now referred to as the 'Indo-Muslim Law' or 'Indo-Islamic Law'. So, though much of the Islamic law has remained uncodified, the 'official law' has been advanced through judicial interpretations by the Supreme Court and various high courts on a case to case basis.

The Muslim law has also evolved through the legal opinions of ullamas, muftis and qazis. The fatwa of a mufti is a legal opinion while a qaza (judgment) of a qazi (judge) is a binding judgment.

Superior Status of Muslim Women during the pre-Independence Period

It is interesting to note that at the time of Independence, women's rights under Muslim law were far superior to both Brahminical Hindu law and Christian matrimonial law. Many a times, Quranic rights were defeated by upholding anti-Muslim customary practices as the following case illustrates.

The Muslim trading communities of Gujarat, the Khojas and Kutchi Memons, followed the local custom of coparcenary or joint family property.[117] These male-headed coparcenaries denied women their right to a stipulated share

in the property as per the Shariat. (Under the rules of the Shariat, coparcenary is not recognized.) On 11 October 1847, by a common judgment, Erskine Perry J. decided three cases filed by women claiming inheritance right to parental property.[118] In the first case, two daughters of a rich merchant, Mir Ali, who did not leave behind a male heir, filed a suit to claim their father's property worth three lakhs. On their behalf, it was argued that the Hindu custom of disinheriting daughters, which has been adopted by Mohammedans, is most unreasonable. Hence public policy would dictate the adoption of the wiser rule laid down by the Quran by which daughters are awarded a fixed share. A contrast was drawn between the relative position which females held in Hindu and Muslim systems. On behalf of the women, it was further argued that since the Muslim system was more beneficial to women, in larger interest of women's welfare, it was the duty of the court to give it effect when the two diverse practices are examined.

The comments by Erskine Perry J. while disallowing the woman's claim, makes for interesting reading:

A custom for females to take no share in the inheritance is not unreasonable in the eyes of the English law for it accords in great part with the universal custom, as to real estates where there are any male issues and with some local customs mentioned by Blackstone through which in certain manors females are excluded in all cases.[119]

---

[117] The Kutchi Memons are originally from Sindh or Kutch and speak the Kutchi language. They are believed to have been converted to Islam by *Sadr Din*. Although they practice Islam, their manners and customs continued to be Hindu. They believed in the ten incarnations of Lord Vishnu and at the time of the litigation, as per

the comments of the judge, not a single person knew Arabic or Persian.

[118] The first two cases concerned Khoja women, *Hirbae v. Sonbae* and *Gungbae v. Sonabae*. The third case was by a Kutchi Memon, *Rahimatbae v. Hadji Jussa*. The three cases were heard together and are reported at POC (1853) 110.

[119] *Hirbae v. Sonbae*, (1853) POC 110 (also referred to as the Khoja's and Memon's case).

The judge commented further that since the attempt of the young women to disturb the course of succession which has prevailed among their ancestors for many hundreds of years has failed, they must now pay the price of this unsuccessful experiment by paying the cost to the defendants.[120]

Another interesting case, decided by the Privy Council in 1898, *Skinner v. Skinner*,[121] reveals that the succession rights of a Muslim widow were even superior to those granted under the Indian Succession Act. The case concerned a couple who were Muslims but who had, at the time of their marriage, converted to Christianity and performed the wedding ceremonies as per Christian rites. Subsequently, however, they reconverted to Islam and performed a nikah ceremony. An amount of Rs 50,000 was settled as mehr at the time of the nikah. Within a few years, the couple was estranged and the spouses cohabited with other partners. The husband, prior to his death, drew up a will and disinherited the wife of her share in property and bestowed the property upon the children from the subsequent alliance.

After the death of the husband, the widow claimed her mehr and her share in the property and challenged the validity of the will under Muslim law. The issue before the court was whether the couple was governed by the Indian Succession Act or the Islamic law. If the couple was governed by the Indian Succession Act, disinheritance through a will was valid. But the wife pleaded that she had never been divorced and both the parties were followers of Islam until the death of her husband and hence were governed by the Muslim law of succession. The trial court as well as the appellate courts, including the Privy Council, held that since a valid divorce could not be proved and the parties had continued to follow Islam, Islamic law would apply and the widow could not be disinherited of her rightful share in property through a will.

Although Muslim law contains several positive provisions which would safeguard women's rights, these provisions have deteriorated due to socio-cultural reasons and patriarchal subversions. Practices like seclusion (*purdah*) and child marriage have rendered women vulnerable and dependent on their male relatives. The Quaranic right of mehr has been reduced to a mere token and exorbitant demands for dowry have become the norm among various Muslim communities. Poverty and illiteracy have further contributed to the subordination of women. From the 1980s, and specifically after the controversy over the Shah Bano judgment,[122] Muslim law has been projected as obscurantist, patriarchal, and anti-women by Hindu communal forces and this issue has been sensationalized by the media. Even women's organizations have contributed to this myth-making process.

The Law of Marriage and Divorce

Nikah: A Contractual Union

According to the Muslim notion of marriage, marital union is contractual in nature. Inspite of being solemnized by reciting verses from the Quran, it is considered as a civil contract, meant to legitimize sexual relations for procreation. Since marriage is contractual in nature, it is imperative that the parties agree to get married out of their own volition. Free consent is pivotal, and is understood by the term '*qabul*'. The offer or proposal of marriage is known as '*ijab*'

---

[120]   Ibid., at pp.121.
[121]   (1898) ILR 25 Cal 537 PC

[122]   *Mohd. Ahmad Khan v. Shahbano Begum*, AIR 1985 SC 945. The judgment and its aftermath are discussed in detail at 'Communalizing the demand for UCC' in Chapter 2 of this book.

(Fyzee 1974: 91). Thus, the nikah is contracted by a declaration of offer by one party, followed by acceptance. It is necessary for the parties to declare their offer and acceptance in the presence of witnesses. Minors may also enter into contractual relations with the help of their guardians, *wali*, who will act on behalf of their wards. The words must indicate clearly the fact that a marriage has been contracted. The document which records the contractual agreement of marriage is termed as *nikahnama* (Fyzee 1974: 125).

A unique feature of the contract of marriage under Islamic law is that conditions can be stipulated within this contract. This is termed as *aqd-e-nikah* (conditions of marriage). The right to stipulate conditions in a marriage contract is a quaranic right bestowed upon women. The nikahnama, with conditional stipulations, can be arrived at during the time of marriage and the husband is bound by the conditions. During the British period, the courts in India upheld various conditions stipulated in the nikahnama.

There is also a scope for drawing up pre-nuptial agreements or kabin-nama. Pre-nuptial agreements are invalid under Anglo-Saxon jurisprudence, upon which the Hindu, Christian, and Parsi laws in India are based. Since these civil laws derive from the scriptural notion of marriage as a sacramental union, individual contractual obligations are not awarded validity. The British courts also upheld a Muslim woman's right to impose conditions upon her husband through a pre-nuptial agreement, though such agreements were deemed to be against public policy under the English law.[123] Some illustrations of conditional restrains upon the husband are: restraint on polygamy, right to matrimonial home/residence, right of prompt *mehr*, fixed quantum of maintenance, acceptance

of children of wife's former marriage, right to visit parents, etc. According to Ameer Ali, a renowned Islamic scholar, the following agreements can be enforced in a court of law.

1. The husband will not contract a second marriage during the subsistence of the first;
2. The husband will not remove the wife from the conjugal domicile (matrimonial home) without her consent;
3. The husband will not absent himself from the conjugal domicile beyond a certain period;
4. The husband and wife will live in a specified place;
5. A certain amount of *dower*[124] will be payable immediately after marriage or within a stipulated period;
6. The husband will pay the wife a fixed sum of maintenance;
7. The husband will maintain the children of the wife from her former husband;
8. The husband will not prevent her from receiving visits from her relations whenever she likes.[125]

The right to enter into a pre-marriage agreement is not available under any other matrimonial statute (except\under the Goan law modelled on the French code). Since marriage under the Anglo-Saxon law was indissoluble, pre-marriage and post-marriage contracts stipulating conditions were held to be against public policy under the English law.

The delegated right of divorce (*talaq-e-tawfeez*) is also made a part of the nikahnama in several countries, including Pakistan and

---

[123] See cases discussed ahead.

[124] The Britishers who were familiar with the term '*dower*' which was used in the context of a widow's estate, applied the same term to mehr. Ameer Ali also uses it and hence I have retained it though 'mehr' is used elsewhere in this section.

[125] Ameer Ali, *Muslim Law*, Vol.II, pp.321–2 (as cited by Diwan and Diwan (1997: 67).

Bangladesh. By mandatory incorporation of this legal provision, women acquire the delegated right to divorce themselves from their husbands.

The nikahnama is usually drawn by the qazi who performs the marriage and varies from community to community and region to region. Recently, Muslim women's groups who have been demanding the abolition of polygamy, arbitrary triple talaq, etc., campaigned for a 'model nikahnama' which could provide a safeguard to Muslim women through community-based initiatives. It was felt that such nikahnamas would also protect Muslim women's rights to fair and adequate amounts of mehr as well as ensure that women are granted the delegated right of divorce, that is, *talaq-e-tawfeez*, by incorporating a clause to this effect. Some groups in Mumbai also drew up model nikahnamas and organized public events to release them.[126] Responding to these campaigns, in December 2004, the All India Muslim Personal Law Board (AIMPLB),[127] and later the Shia Law Board,[128] released model nikahnamas which would better protect Muslim women. Some issues like tawfeez-e-talaq have been controversial in this debate. But inspite of the controversy, as discussed above, a Muslim woman has the right to include stipulations within the nikahnama or draw up a pre-nuptial agreement to secure her rights. The acceptance by the AIMPLB of a 'model nikahnama' with certain conditional stipulations will not bestow any new right upon Muslim women which she does not already have under the Quaranic law. But presumably, the stamp of approval from the Board will serve to popularize nikahnamas with mandatory stipulations, as the Board is considered as a representative body of various Islamic sects, theologicians, and authorities on Islamic jurisprudence. It is held in high esteem as an arbitrator of Muslim interests by a large section of the community, though not all sects and schools or secular Muslims in public life recognize or accept its authority.

Mehr: An Economic Safeguard

Mehr is a quranic right.[129] A specific mention of this right is made in all subsequent legal texts. It is a mark of respect to the wife and is meant to set off the disability suffered by women under the law of inheritance. Hence the amount stipulated has to be substantial. While as per Hanafi law, a minimum of ten dirhams is mandatory,[130] legal texts routinely mention amounts of one thousand and two thousand dirhams by way of examples which indicate that the amounts settled were meant to be far above the lowest stipulated. Additions to the amount stipulated at the time of marriage can be made at any time during the marriage (Fyzee 1974: 140). The high amounts stipulated in the nikahnama were meant to act as a deterrent to unilateral divorce.

Several theorists are of the opinion that mehr forms the consideration in the contract of nikah. The Prophet converted the custom of bride

---

[126] 'Nikahnama draft allows couples to opt for arbitration' in *Times of India* (Bombay) 27 September 2004.

[127] Ziauddin Sardar, 'Change is coming to Islam' in *Times of India* (Bombay) 26 December 2004.

[128] 'Law Board makes it official: Shia women get divorce rights' in *Indian Express* (Bombay) 27 November 2006.

[129] It is also referred to as '*dower*' in various legal texts. But dower is the right of a widow under English law and this term was brought in by the British and later incorporated into various texts of Anglo-Mohammadan law.

[130] Dirham is a Persian term which is derived from Greek (Fyzee 1974: 135) and is used in Anglo-Muhammadan legal texts in the context of mehr or dower. It refers to a silver coin of 2.97 grammes of weight (Fyzee 1974: 135). The current value of ten dirhams is around Rs 128.

price of tribal Arabia to mehr which would be a future security to a married woman.

The stipulation of mehr at the time of marriage is an integral part of a Muslim marriage. It can be stipulated as either prompt (*Mu'ajjal*) or deferred (*Mu'wajjal*). If it is prompt, it is payable at the time of marriage. If it is deferred, it must be paid subsequently and in any case, upon the dissolution of marriage either by death or divorce. If the mehr dues are unpaid at the time of the dissolution of marriage, the woman is entitled to retain possession of her deceased husband's property. This right is usually discussed in legal texts as 'widow's right of dower', but the same principle would apply if the marriage is dissolved in any other manner.

Mehr need not be paid only in cash. Gold ornaments, valuables, and other movable and immovable property can also be given as mehr. The husband could also settle his share of family property or a particular house as mehr. The woman would then be entitled to this property or its monetary value. If the woman claimed that the matrimonial residence has been given to her in lieu of her mehr debt, it was for the husband to rebut the presumption.

The cases reported in law journals of the pre-Independence era shed light on some significant aspects of women's rights under Muslim law.[131] The legal precedents also indicate that the rights of mehr and pre-marriage agreements were not illusory but secured women viable economic safeguards. They signify that a large number of Muslim women approached the colonial courts for enforcement of their monetary claims.

In *Badarannissa Bibi's case*, decided by the Calcutta High Court in 1871,[132] the husband had entered into a pre-marriage agreement (kabin-nama) with his wife, authorizing her to divorce him if he remarried without her consent. Subsequently, the husband did remarry and the wife approached the court for redress. The court dismissed the wife's plea on the ground that Mohammedan law does not permit a wife to divorce upon a private agreement. In appeal, an Islamic jurist, Moulvi Mahamat Hossein, represented the wife and pointed out relevant sections from the legal texts which specifically mention the delegated power of the wife to divorce and pleaded that such a provision is not repugnant to Mohammedan law. The court concurred with this view and ruled in the woman's favour.

In *Sultan Begam's case*,[133] the widow claimed Rs 50,000 out of the stipulated amount of Rs 1,50,000 since the assets of her deceased husband were not sufficient to satisfy the entire amount. The husband's relatives alleged that the mehr which had been publicly announced was not intended to be paid and only a smaller amount, agreed in private, was payable. But the Privy Council validated the kabin-nama of 1877 where a sum of Rs 1,25,000 was stipulated. The document was signed by the husband and attested and witnessed by twenty-five persons. The court held that the fact that the husband did not have the means or expectations to pay the amount was no reason to decree a smaller sum.

Under the English law of contracts, a person who is not a party to a contract cannot enforce it even when she/he is a beneficiary. Hence the Privy Council ruling of 1910 in *Khwaja Mohammed v. Husseini Begum*[134] became an important point of departure from these established norms of English law which took into account the cultural reality of India. The Privy

---

[131] For a detailed discussion on this issue, see Agnes 1996: 2832–8.

[132] *Badarannissa Bibi v. Mafiattala*, (1871) 7 BLR 442.

[133] *Sultana Begam v. Sarajuddin*, AIR 1936 Lah 183.

[134] (1910) 37 IA 152

Council laid down a new precedent by upholding a minor girl's right to enforce a contract against her father-in-law, even though she was not a party to it. The facts of the case make interesting reading. In 1877, on the occasion of the marriage of his son, the father-in-law executed an agreement that he would pay the daughter-in-law Rs 500 per month as kharch-i-pandan (an allowance for personal expenses) in perpetuity. Thirteen years later, the couple was separated. Thereafter, the wife sued her father-in-law for arrears. The trial court refused to enforce the agreement and held: 'It is unreasonable to suppose that the wife can enforce her contract against her father-in-law even when she refuses to live with her husband. To hold so would be repulsive to conscience and common sense.' The court also cast aspersions on the woman's character. In appeal, the Allahabad High Court decreed in the wife's favour and held that no condition had been attached to the payment of the annuity and the chastity of the wife was not an issue under the agreement. The matter went up to the Privy Council which made very pertinent comments:

Kharch-i-pandan, which literally means "betel box expenses", is a personal allowance to the wife customary among Mohammedan families of rank, especially in Upper India, fixed either before or after the marriage. When they are minors, as is frequently the case, the arrangement is made between the respective parents and guardians on behalf of minors. Hence serious injustice will be caused if the common law doctrine (read English law doctrine) is applied to agreements entered into in connection with such contracts.

In a case decided by the Allahabad High Court in the 1921, *Muhammad Muin-ud-din* v. *Jamal Fatima*,[135] the husband had married twice and had treated both wives with cruelty. The father of the third wife entered into an agreement with the husband and his father prior to the marriage, binding the husband to pay a sum of

Rs 15 per month for life, in addition to the mehr, in case of divorce. The wife was subsequently divorced and she approached the court for the enforcement of her contract. The court held that the agreement was enforceable as it was meant to secure the wife against ill-treatment. The court rejected the plea that pre-nuptial agreements are against public policy and held that agreements protecting a woman's future rights are valid under Islamic law.

In *Mansur* v. *Azizul*,[136] the Oudh High Court laid down an important principle regarding Muslim women's right to shelter or formulated, as we refer to it today, the right to matrimonial home. At the time of the second marriage, the husband entered into an agreement granting the first wife an option to live separately and claim maintenance of Rs 5 per month in the event of disagreement between the two wives. Subsequently, the first wife sued for arrears of maintenance amounting to Rs 58-7-0.[137] Upholding her right of separate residence and maintenance, the court observed:

If a Muslim marries two wives and if the wives are not able to get along, and if the husband is not able to provide separate apartments, agreement in favour of one wife granting her maintenance (guzara) is not against public policy.

In *Shummsoonnisa Begam's case*[138], one of the earliest cases decided by the Privy Council, the superior position of a Muslim wife over her separate property has been commented upon. The plaintiff was a rich widow with five children and had inherited a large share of her father's property in November 1847. A few months prior to this, in May 1847, she married

---

[135] AIR 1921 All 152

[136] AIR 1928 Oudh 303

[137] The figures indicate the then prevailing currency - rupees, annas and paise. Sixteen annas amounted to one rupee. Each anna comprised four paise.

[138] *Moonshee Buzloor Ruheem* v. *Shumsoonisa Begum* (1867) 11 MIA 551.

Moonshee Buzloor Ruheem. Due to ill treatment, in December 1855, she left her husband. But the husband retained the government securities which she had inherited from her father. So, in April 1856, she filed for recovery of her property. In retaliation, the husband filed for restitution of conjugal rights. The husband's suit for restitution was dismissed and the wife obtained a decree in her favour regarding the property detained by her husband, valued at Rs 2,34,800. The husband appealed against both the orders to the Privy Council. He claimed that he had purchased the securities from the wife and she had spent the amount for the marriages of her children from her previous marriage. But documents concerning the securities were traced in the hands of the husband's creditors. The Privy Council, while upholding the wife's claim of property, held as follows:

The wife came to her husband's house as a wealthy woman and left as a destitute. As a Muslim woman of rank, she was in Zenanah and had passed the securities to her husband who was supposed to have managed them for her for the purpose of collecting interest. Instead he had transferred them to his creditors. Her communication to the outside world was from behind the *purdah*. Due to her state of seclusion (i.e. *Purdah-nusheen*) her husband, who managed her affairs for her, was in a position to use undue influence on her.

Regarding the right of Muslim women upon marriage, the Privy Council commented:

Distinction must be drawn between the rights of a Mohammedan and a Hindu woman and in all that concerns her power over her property, the former is, by law, far more independent, in fact even more independent than an English woman. There is no doubt that a Mussulman woman when married retains her dominion over her own property and is free from the control of her husband in its disposition. The Mohammedan law is more favourable than the Hindu law to women and their rights and does not insist on their dependence upon and subject to the stronger sex.

The amounts mentioned in the judgments cited above need to be viewed in the context of the living standards of this period. Only then will it be possible for us to grasp the security which the high amounts stipulated as mehr provided for women. The salaries for clerical posts in government jobs during this period ranged from Rs 40 to Rs 100. A sum of Rs 10 to Rs 20 was deemed an adequate amount as maintenance.

Although it is possible to argue that the cases discussed above concern women of affluent families, the decisions are a reflection of the prevalent social norms and hence it can reasonably be assumed that mehr was a right which provided the Muslim woman substantial economic protection. The case law also provides concrete evidence that even lower class women did enter into agreements with their husbands to protect their economic rights as the low amounts settled as maintenance indicate. To give an example, in *Poonoo Bibi's case*,[139] the monthly maintenance amount was Rs 10. The husband entered into the following agreement with his wife:

I shall never give you trouble in feeding and clothing you; I shall make over to you and nobody else besides you whatever I shall draw from employment; I shall never exercise any violence on you; I shall not take you anywhere else away from your home; I shall not marry or make nikah without your permission; I shall do nothing without your permission; if I do anything without your permission you will be at liberty to divorce me and realize from me the amount of *dynmohur* forthwith and this nikah will then be null and void.

Subsequently, he deserted Poonoo Bibi and she filed for the enforcement of the agreement regarding his savings. He was employed in a clerical post and was drawing a salary of Rs 40 and had savings of Rs 568. His advocate argued that the agreement is against public policy as it amounts to reducing the husband to a slave.

[139] *Poonoo Bibi v. Puex Puksh* (1875) 15 BLR App. 5.

The court overruled this objection. Later, there was a compromise and the wife agreed to a monthly maintenance of Rs 10.

In recent times, the amount of mehr which is fixed at the time of marriage has been reduced to a mere token and has ceased to be a safeguard against arbitrary divorce. The Brahminical custom of dowry has crept into most lower castes and Muslim communities. Recent studies indicate that among several Muslim communities the amount of dowry is substantially higher than the amount of mehr.[140]

Since the source of judicial interpretation of Islamic law in India and Pakistan is the same, it is interesting to note the development of case law in respect of mehr through judicial decisions of courts in Pakistan. Some of the legal points which were disputed during litigation and were settled in favour of women are summarized below for easy reference:

1. Various amounts paid by the husband to the wife during the marriage should not be presumed to be in lieu of dower;

2. The dower can be fixed or raised by the husband at any point during the continuance of the marriage. A declaration by him to this effect is sufficient;

3. Even after consumption has taken place, the wife may refuse to live with her husband unless he pays her prompt dower. Non-payment of mehr is a complete defence to a suit for restitution of conjugal rights and the wife is competent to refuse herself to her husband;

4. A woman can claim dower upon divorce if none had been fixed initially. This is applicable even in case of Muslim male and Christian female contracting a registered marriage abroad (Balchin 1994: 52).

In the judgments discussed below, it was ruled that if, at the time of the husband's death, the widow is in possession of the property and her mehr dues are unpaid, she has the right to retain possession. The husband's relatives do not have the right to dispossess her until her claim is satisfied. This is a substantial safeguard against destitution.

In 1868 in *Ahmed Hossein* v. *Mst. Khodeja*,[141] the Bombay High Court held that the right of the widow who is in possession of property to hold on to the same until her dower debt is satisfied is a lien in the strictest sense of the term.

In 1871, in *Mt. Bebee Bachun* v. *Sheikh Hossein*,[142] the Privy Council held that a widow was entitled to retain possession of the estate until her dower is satisfied.

In 1885, in *Azizullah Khan* v. *Ahmedullah Khan*,[143] the Allahabad High Court held that a widow who is in possession of her husband's estate occupied a position analogous to a mortgagee and her possession could not be disturbed till her debt was paid.

In 1916, in *Hamira Bibi* v. *Zubaida Bibi*,[144] it was held:

---

[140] In a study of Muslim women conducted by Women's Research and Action Group, Bombay (WRAG) during 1994–6, most communities confirmed that they still follow the custom of mehr but it has been reduced to a mere token. The communities have now adopted the practice of dowry. They further confirmed that the amount of dowry is always higher than mehr. For details, see the following newsletters of the organization: Vol. I/2 (September 1994); Vol.II/1 (February 1995); Vol. II/2–3 (August 1995) and Vol. II/4 (October 1995).

[141] (1868) 10 WR 368
[142] (1871) 14 MIA 377
[143] 1885 ICR 7 All 353
[144] AIR 1916 PC 46

The dower ranks as a debt and the wife is entitled, along with other creditors, to have it satisfied on the death of the husband out of his estate. If she is lawfully in possession of the property, she is entitled to retain it till the dower debt is paid. This is called the widow's lien for dower.

In 1925, in *Maina Bibi* v. *Vakil Ahmad*, [145] the Privy Council held:

The position of a widow in possession of her husband's estate is not analogous to that of a mortgagee in possession. The mortgagee takes and retains possession under an agreement or arrangement made between him and the mortgager. In the present case, neither the possession of the property nor the right to retain that possession when acquired is conferred upon the widow by an agreement or the bounty of her deceased husband. The possession of the property being once lawfully acquired, the right of the widow to retain it till her dower debt is paid is conferred upon her by Mahomedan law.

In 1937, in *Nawab Begum* v. *Hussain Ali Khan*,[146] the Lahore High Court held that the widow has first charge on the property of her deceased husband so long as the dower debt is not paid.

In addition the Courts have also ruled that that mehr cannot be absolved in distress.[147]

Forms of Dissolving Muslim Marriages[148]
Since the Islamic law of marriage is based on the contractual theory, the law from its inception provided for its dissolution and prescribed elaborate rules. The dissolution can be brought about by the death of a spouse, by an act of the parties, or by judicial verdict.

[145] AIR 1925 PC 63
[146] AIR 1937 Lah 589
[147] See the decisions in *Nurannessa Khanum* v. *Khaje Muhammad Sakru*, AIR 1920 Cal 463 and *Hasnumiya Dadamiya* v. *Halimunnisa Hafizullah*, AIR 1942 Bom 128.
[148] Fyzee 1974: 148–64

By Death of a Spouse: The death of the husband or wife dissolves the marital bond. While the husband is permitted to marry soon after the death of his wife, the widow is mandated to wait for the completion of her *Iddat* period (4 months and 10 days) and, if she is pregnant, until she delivers.

By an Act of the Parties: Both the husband and the wife are empowered to dissolve the marriage and rules regarding the same are clearly laid out.

(i) Divorce by the husband: a) *Talaq*, b) *Ila* and c) *Zihar*.

a. Talaq: When dissolution of marriage proceeds from the husband, it is called 'talaq'. The word derives its origins from the root word, *Talaqqa*, which means 'to release', and signifies the repudiation of the marriage by the husband (Fyzee 1974: 150). Talaq is a broad term and includes within it various modes of dissolving the marriage, the two major modes are *talaq-al-Sunna* and *talaq-al-Bida'a*. The major difference between the two modes is that the first mode provides for repentance, retraction and reconciliation, while in the other form talaq becomes irrevocable when it is uttered and does not allow for a period of retraction and reconciliation. If this difference is kept in mind, it is easy to understand the two different forms of talaq (Fyzee: 1974).

Talaq-al-Sunna is the approved form which is considered to be in conformity with the norms as laid down by Prophet Mohammad. This mode provides for reconciliation after the pronouncement which can either be in the *Ahsan* or the *Hasan* mode. The Ahsan mode is considered to be the better of the two and comprises a single pronouncement of talaq in a period of *tuhr* (menstrual purity) which must be followed by sexual abstinence during the period of iddat (three months or until her delivery, if she is pregnant). The Hasan form consists of three successive pronouncements during three consecutive periods of tuhr and the talaq becomes binding on the third pronouncement. The rule of final bar and irrevocability was provided for by the Prophet to put an end to a barbarious pre-Islamic practice of pronouncing talaq several times and taking the wife back each time and demanding sexual relationship in order to humiliate her. 'This rule follows the Quranic injunction: Then when they have reached their term, take them back in kindness or part from then in kindness' (Fyzee 1974: 154). Thereafter if the parties wish to reconcile they need to perform a fresh nikah with fresh mehr.

Talaq-al-Bida'a (an innovation) is the mode in which talaq is pronounced thrice in one sitting. This is also referred to as *talaq-al-bain* or irrevocable divorce. This is the disapproved form, considered to be sinful by the Prophet but is accepted by some Sunni (Hanafi) sects. Hence the expression—bad in theology but good in law—is often used to describe it. The right of unilateral divorce given to Muslim husbands renders the wives extremely vulnerable and insecure regarding their marital status. Hence it is condemned as one of the main flaws of Muslim law and there is a constant demand from women's organisations for its ban. Another disapproved form refers to the single irrevocable declaration, which is made during the period of *tuhr* and may also be given in writing (through a talaqnama), and comes into effect immediately, severing the marital tie. While the wife is required to undergo iddat, reconciliation is not possible during the iddat period.

Commencement of the legal effects of talaq: In the Ahsan mode, the talaq becomes effective at the expiry of three months of its pronouncement. In the Hasan mode, it becomes effective

when the third talaq is pronounced. The talaq-ul-bida'a becomes effective from the moment it is pronouncement or when the deed of talaq (talaqnama) is executed and served on the wife.[149]

b. Ila: A vow of abstinence taken by the husband that he would restrain from having sexual intercourse with his wife for a certain period of time, repudiates the marriage. A minimum of four months is prescribed and a vow taken for a period of less than four months has no effect. After the lapse of this time period, the husband loses all his conjugal rights over his wife. The wife becomes entitled to claim dissolution of her marriage by the decree of the court.

c. Zihar: A form wherein the husband swears that his wife is like his mother, sister, or any other female relative within the prohibited degrees. If he intends to revoke his declaration, he has to pay money by way of expiation or fast for certain time period. After the oath is taken, the wife has a right to go to court and obtain a decree of dissolution of marriage.

(ii) Divorce by the Wife (*talaq-e-tawfeez* or delegated divorce): The husband may delegate the power of pronouncing divorce to a third person or to the wife herself. In Pakistan and Bangladesh, this power is given to the wife through a mandatory clause which is included in the standard nikahnama. Through this, the wife acquires the power to dissolve her marriage without judicial intervention. The delegated power can be conditional or unconditional.

(iii) Additional Modes of Dissolving the Marriage:

---

[149] For restraints upon such talaqs and for essential legal requirements, see Validity of Triple Talaq, discussed later in this sub-section at pp. 60–4

(a) *Khul* (or *khoola*): The literal meaning of this word is 'to untie' or 'to disrobe' and within the law of marriage, the words indicate 'to lay down one's authority over one's wife'. When a wife, owing to her unwillingness, is desirous of obtaining a divorce, she may obtain release from the marital contract by giving up either her settled dower or any other property.

(b) *Mubaraa*: This is a form of divorce by mutual agreement.

3. **By Judicial Process:** (i) *Lian*, or (ii) *Faskh*

(i) Lian: Where the husband accuses his wife of adultery (*zina*) but cannot prove it, the wife is entitled to file a suit for dissolution of marriage. If the husband retracts the charge of adultery during court proceedings, the wife will not be awarded the decree of divorce.

(ii) Faskh: This refers to a decree of dissolution issued by a court or, in other words, a judicial divorce. In India, Muslim women can approach the courts for a judicial divorce under the provisions of the Dissolution of Muslim Marriage Act, 1939, which is discussed in detail later in this section.

Among Muslims in India talaq is the popular form and the other two forms are of mere academic interest. While a Muslim husband can dissolve his marriage only under the uncodified Muslim law through the pronouncement of talaq, the Muslim wife has several options— delegated right of talaq, divorce by consent– mubara'a, divorce at her own initiative–khula, and judicial divorce. The right of the wife to khula is on power with the right of the husband for talaq. Fyzee comments that there is no general presumption that the husband has been released of his obligation to pay the wife her mehr and each case would have to be decided

on its own merits and further, some legal texts unduly stretch the law in fvour of husband and release him of his responsibility of paying mehr to the wife (Fyzee 1974: 165).

A renowned jurist, Syed Abdul A'la Maududi in *Huquq-uz-Zaujain* has commented as follows:[150]

> It is indeed a mockery of the Shariat that we regard khula as something depending either on the consent of the husband or on the verdict of the qazi. The law of Islam is not responsible for the way Muslim women are being denied their right in this respect.

The Mandatory Stipulation of Halala

After the irrevocable form of divorce, a husband cannot remarry the wife until she performs *halala*. This was meant to be a restraint upon the husband from pronouncing the dreaded triple talaq in a callous or flippant manner. It was also introduced to reduce the hardship caused to women in Hasan mode of talaq, where in pre-Islamic times, the husband would prevent the wife from remarrying and keep her in perpetual bondage by pretending to take her back after repeated divorces. However, this rule causes great hardships to women as it prescribes that after her talaq, she should marry another person, consummate the marriage, subsequently obtain a divorce, observe the period of iddat and only after the entire process is complete, enter into a remarriage with her former husband. However, it is also stated that the process of halala cannot be used as a device to re-marry the former spouse. It must happen in the natural course of events.

[150] Syed Abdul A'la Maududi, in Huquq-uz-Zaujain, 9th ed., Lahore 1964 (p. 61), translated from Urdu by Tahir Mahmood, *The Muslim Law of India*, 3rd ed., New Delhi: Lexis Nexis Butterworths: New Delhi, p. 99.

A question before the Bombay High Court in 2010, in *Sabah Khan* v. *Adnan Sami Khan*,[151] was whether halala needs to be performed in a case of a divorce by khula, mubara'a or *talaq-e-ahsan* (approved form of talaq). The couple had married in 2001 and the marriage was dissolved through a mutual divorce agreement in 2004 at the instance of the wife. At the time of drawing up the divorce agreement, the husband had also pronounced a single talaq which fact was recorded in the agreement. Subsequently the couple remarried in 2007. In 2009, the wife filed for dissolution of her second marriage under Section 2(viii) of the Dissolution of Muslim Marriages Act, 1939 in the family court at Mumbai and claimed her rights of matrimonial home and property. At this time, the husband contended that the wife had not performed the mandatory halala before the second marriage and hence the second marriage was a nullity and the wife was not entitled to claim any rights.

The family court upheld the husband's contentions that the dissolution of marriage was by mutual consent, mubara'a and it was mandatory for the wife to perform halala before her remarriage. Hence, this second marriage was invalid. In appeal the high court ruled in favour of the wife and held that the second marriage was valid since the divorce agreement was in the mode of 'talaq-e-ahsan' through just one pronouncement of talaq as reflected in the agreement and not a triple pronouncement and hence the wife would not be required to undergo halala. The high court also commented that the rule of halala is not applicable when the marriage is dissolved through khula or mubara'a. The court further explained that in every case where the marriage is dissolved, halala is not required to be performed. It is mandatory only in cases of triple talaq. If this judgment is read along with the Delhi High Court ruling in *Masroor Ahmed* v. *State (NCT of Delhi)*[152] where it was held that triple talaq in one sitting is to be considered as a revocable talaq, then it would be correct to presume that halala would not be mandatory even in cases of triple talaq.

Dissolution of Muslim Marriages Act, 1939

This statutory enactment, which bestows the right of judicial divorce upon Muslim woman, was enacted two decades before the Hindu woman acquired a similar right. Two renowned Islamic jurists, Asif Ali Fyzee and Maulana Ashraf Ali Thanavi, had spearheaded the campaign to obtain for women governed by Hanafi law, the right bestowed upon women governed by Maliki law, through a state enactment. The grounds available are: husband's polygamy, adultery, imprisonment, impotency, cruelty, and non-maintenance for two years.

The leading judgment on this issue was given by Krishna Iyer J. in *A. Yousuf Rawther* v. *Sowramma*,[153] while he was presiding over the Kerala High Court in 1971. The renowned jurist held that if a wife is able to prove that her husband has failed to maintain her for a period of two years, irrespective of the circumstances under which she was living separately, she is entitled to a decree of divorce. Contextualizing the stipulation, Krishna Iyer J. had commented:

The interpretation of a legislation, obviously intended to protect a weaker section i.e., women, must be informed by the social perspective and purpose and,

---

[151] *Sabah Khan* v. *Adnan Sami Khan*, 2010 (112) Bom. LR 1409.

[152] MANU/DE/9441/2007
[153] AIR 1971 Ker 261

within its grammatical flexibility, must further the beneficent object. And so we must appreciate the Islamic ethos and the general sociological background which inspired the enactment of the law before locating the precise connotation of the words used in the statute.[154]

The court based its interpretations on an earlier judgment by the Islamic jurist and Chief Justice of Sindh High Court, Tyabji J. in *Noor Bibi* v. *Pir Bux*.[155] The learned Chief Justice had proclaimed:

Irrespective of the question as to whether a wife was entitled for maintenance or not, relief should be given to the wife, the moment it is shown that she was living separately from her husband for a period of two years and that maintenance had not been paid to her during this period.

This judgment is an important legal milestone as it explains the position of a Muslim wife, under the act in the following words:

The Muslim marriage differs from the Hindu marriage in that it is not a sacrament. A Muslim marriage is a covenant by which the parties enter the state of marriage. The parties are permitted to stipulate the conditions upon which they will do so, provided the conditions are not illegal according to Muslim law. The subsistence of the marriage confers certain essential rights and imposes certain duties upon the parties. When a husband and a wife have been living apart, and the wife is not being maintained by the husband, a dissolution is not permitted as a punishment for the husband who had failed to fulfil one of the obligations of marriage, or allowed as a means of enforcing the wife's rights to maintenance. In the Muslim law of dissolution, the failure to maintain when it had continued for a prolonged period, is regarded as an instance where a cessation has occurred. It will be seen therefore that the wife's disobedience or refusal to live with her husband does not affect the principle on which the dissolution is allowed.

Tyabji, C J. had proclaimed this judgment in 1950 when the Hindu marriage was deemed sacramental and indissoluble and the Hindu wife was not entitled to a divorce. Later, Hindu women were awarded the right of divorce, but only to the limited extent of a matrimonial fault. Subsequently, consent divorces were also permitted. But a Hindu wife does not have a right to dissolve her marriage on the premise of 'breakdown of marriage'. Similar is the position of Christian and Parsi women. Hence, even though, desertion is a ground, if the husband is able to prove that the wife has been living separately 'without a reasonable cause', she would not be entitled to a divorce. The significance of Islamic law must be viewed in the context of the constraints which bind women from other religious communities.

In 2004, the Karnataka High Court reaffirmed this position in *Mehafoz Alam Dastagirsab Killedar* v. *Shagufta*.[156] The husband challenged the decree of dissolution granted to the wife by the family court at Belgaum, on the premise that neither had the wife claimed maintenance, nor was she entitled to it and hence, the court could not dissolve the marriage on the ground of non-payment of maintenance for two years. The high court dismissed the appeal and held:

We are of the view that the stipulation of non-maintenance for two years cannot be made conditional or subjected to qualifications. Such an interpretation would amount to re-enacting the law. The law was enacted to provide relief to a needy Mohammedan wife. Hence it must be interpreted in such a manner as to further the object and intention of the statute and not to curtail its scope and ambit.

In *Abdurahiman* v. *Khairunneesa*,[157] in an application filed by the wife on the ground of

---

[154] The same quote is also cited in *Shamim Ara's case* which was discussed earlier.
[155] AIR 1950 Sindh 8

[156] I (2004) DMC 76 Kar
[157] I (2010) DMC 707 Ker

her husband's remarriage, rejecting the plea that he is treating both the wives equally, the Kerala High Court held that the mandate was not only 'equal treatment' but 'equitable' treatment. The court further clarified that equitable treatment should be 'in accordance with injunctions of Quran'. In a claim for divorce under Section 2(viii)(f) of the Act, it is the assertion of the woman that matters as she is the best judge to decide whether she has been treated equitably or not. The husband has a right to unilaterally walk out of marriage, even a monogamous marriage. Though polygamous marriage by itself is not recognized as a ground under Section 2(viii)(f) of DMMA for divorce, provision concedes to wife a right to walk out of marriage if she is satisfied that she has not been treated equitably in such marriage.

Rather unfortunately, many Muslim wives and even community organizations and counselling centres providing support to Muslim women are unaware that the Muslim women have the same right to approach the Court for divorce on the grounds of cruelty, desertion (non-maintenance), or even adultery as the Hindu women. There is a general belief that the only way a Muslim woman can dissolve her marriage is by approaching the qazi for a khula and further, if she obtains khula, she would be forced to relinquish her claim to her mehr. This misconception, serves to curtail women's right to dissolve the marriage through judicial pronouncements and undermines the right of Muslim women under Islamic law and has a communal tint to it.[158]

Validity of Triple Talaq

The husband's power of divorce in a manner considered to be 'sinful' or 'unapproved' by

Prophet himself, has become the most popular form of dissolution of marriage. The entire discourse on Muslim women's rights revolves around this issue. The wife's right of dissolving her marriage often gets subsumed under this overarching power of the husband to pronounce unilateral talaq in public imagination. Muslim wives live under the constant fear that their husbands may pronounce these dreaded words in a moment of anger or marital discord and once pronounced, it is irrevocable and the wives would lose all their rights arising from the contract of marriage. The media projections have only served to strengthen these misconceptions and have caused severe harm to Muslim women's rights. Hence the issue of validity of triple talaq assumes great importance in a discussion on Muslim family law.

This form of divorce received validity during the British period, as the Britishers considered Muslim marriages as mere civil contracts or 'loose unions', which could easily be dissolved by mere pronouncement of the word 'talaq'. Once the casual utterance of triple talaq by the husband was given legal recognition, the safeguards of mandatory arbitration provided under Islamic law prior to the pronouncement of talaq was held to be irrelevant. The talaqs pronounced in extreme anger or in a state of intoxication, where the husband had lost control of himself were held to be valid. This attitude of the judiciary seriously impaired the rights of Muslim women during colonial period. But in recent times, a re-interpretation of the husband's right to pronounce talaq has taken place through court verdicts and the courts have invalidated such arbitrary modes of triple talaq without first complying with the Quranic stipulations in this regard.

The following rulings trace the history of the manner in which this law was evolved through

---

[158] See 'Framing the Muslim Woman' in Chapter 2 of this book.

judicial interpretations over a period of three decades. Interestingly all these rulings were in the context of the wife's claim of maintenance under Section 125 of Cr.PC and the husband in his reply to this claim had submitted that he had divorced the wife and hence the wife was not entitled to maintenance.

The first in this series was the judgment of Baharul Islam J. of the Gauhati High Court in 1981, in a case under Section 125 of the Cr.PC for maintenance by the wife in *Sri Jiauddin v. Anwara Begum*.[159] The husband pleaded that he had pronounced talaq and that Anwara Begum was no longer his wife. No evidence of the pronouncement of talaq was produced before the court. In appeal, the high court held that while the Muslim marriage is a civil contract, a high degree of sanctity is attached to it. The law recognized the necessity of dissolution of marriage but, only under exceptional circumstances and for a reasonable cause. An attempt at reconciliation by two relatives—one each of the parties, is an essential condition precedent to 'talaq'. This ruling was followed by the division bench of Baharul Islam CJ. and D. Pathak J.) of the Gauhati High Court in the same year, in the case of *Rukia Khatun v. Abdul Khalique Laskar*.[160] In 1993, in *Zeenat Fatema Rashid v. Mohd. Iqbal*,[161] the Gauhati High Court reiterated this principle and held that Mohammedan husband cannot divorce his wife at his whim and caprice and arbitration prior to divorce is mandatory. The court commented that if talaq is pronounced arbitrarily, it must be treated as a special offence.

These rulings were soon followed by other high courts.

In 1998, in *Saleem Basha v. Mumtaz Begum*,[162] the Madras High Court held that among Muslims, divorce must be preceded by attempts of reconciliation between the husband and wife, in the presence of two mediators, one chosen by the wife and the other by the husband and that a Mohammedan husband cannot divorce his wife at his whims and caprice. Divorce must be for a reasonable cause, preceded by a pre-divorce conference to arrive at a settlement.

In 2000, in *Zulekha Begum v. Abdul Rehman*,[163] the wife was constantly harassed and driven out of the house in her fifth month pregnancy, in 1986. Thereafter, the husband remarried. When the family court entertained the wife's petition for maintenance, the husband appealed on the ground that he had divorced the wife and hence was not liable to maintain her. The Karnataka High Court rejected the plea on the ground that the fact of divorce was not proved and emphasised on the mandatory provision of pre-divorce arbitration to settle the dispute and that a divorce without such attempts is not valid. The husband must also prove that there was a valid ground for divorcing the wife. The case was remitted back to the family court for ascertaining the amount of maintenance.

Dagdu Pathan v. Rahimbi,[164] is a full bench ruling of the Bombay High Court of 2002. The court was examining the issue that if a Muslim husband pleads in his written statement that his marriage had been dissolved by talaq at an earlier date, whether the filing of the written statement containing the plea of divorce amounts to dissolution of marriage, from the date on which

---

[159] (1981) 1 GLR 358
[160] (1981) 1 GLR 375
[161] II (1993) DMC 49 Gau

[162] 1998 Cri.LJ 4782 Mad
[163] II (2000) DMC 99 Kar
[164] II (2002) DMC 315 Bom FB

such a statement was made. The court relied upon the following words of the Holy Quran,

To divorce the wife without reason, only to harm her or revengeful due to the husband's unlawful demands and to divorce her in violation of the procedure prescribed by the Shariat is *Haram*.

The court ruled that all the stages of conveying the reasons for divorce, appointment of arbitrators, conciliation proceedings between the parties by the arbitrators, and the failure of such proceedings are required to be proved when the wife disputes the factum of talaq before a court of law. A mere statement made in writing or oral disposition before the court regarding talaq in the past is not sufficient to prove the fact of divorce.

Shamim Ara v. *State of U.P.*[165] is the leading case on this issue which declared the law of the land. This landmark judgment delivered by the Supreme Court in 2002 needs to be discussed in detail. In 1979, Shamim Ara filed an application under Section 125 of the Cr.PC against her husband Abrar Ahmed for maintenance. Her case was transferred to the family courts after its institution in the state. In a written statement filed in 1990, her husband claimed that he had divorced Shamim in 1987. However, no particulars of divorce were stated. Strangely, the family court relied on an affidavit filed by her husband in a civil suit to which the wife Shamim was not a party. He claimed that in this affidavit, he had stated that he had divorced his wife. The family court held that the affidavit corroborated the plea taken by the husband in his written statement that he had divorced his wife. On this basis, the court concluded that in view of her being divorced, she was not entitled to any maintenance. Curiously, the details of this affidavit were not available from the records.

In an appeal filed by the wife, the Allahabad High Court ruled that the divorce was not given in the presence of the wife and that it was not communicated to her. But since through his written statement, the husband had communicated the fact of divorce to her, the court held that the requirement of communication of the divorce stood completed and hence, she was not entitled to maintenance thereafter.

The issue before the Supreme Court was whether the statement contained in a written statement regarding divorce can be construed as a valid communication of the divorce. Chiding the subordinate courts for the gross error committed, the Supreme Court commented:

None of the ancient holy books or scriptures of Muslims mentions such form of divorce as being accepted by the high court and the family court. No such text has been brought to our notice which provides that a recital in any document, whether a pleading or an affidavit, incorporating a statement by the husband that he has already divorced his wife on a specified or unspecified date, even if not communicated to the wife, could become an effective divorce on the date on which the wife happens to learn of such statement contained in the copy of the affidavit or pleading served on her.

The Court was of the firm opinion that if talaq was to be effective, it had to be pronounced. The term 'pronounce' was explained as: 'to proclaim, to utter formally, to declare, to articulate'. The Court referred to various high court decisions to highlight an interpretation of talaq which was in conformity with Quranic injunctions and held that a mere plea in the written statement submitted to the court that talaq was given cannot be treated as a pronouncement of talaq by the husband on the wife.

Accordingly, it was held that neither did the marriage between the parties stand dissolved, nor had the liability of the husband to pay maintenance come to an end. The husband was

[165] 2002 (7) SCC 518

to continue to remain liable for maintenance till the obligation came to an end in accordance with law. The Court relied upon the comments of Krishna Iyer J. in Sowramma's case,[166] decided by the Kerala High Court in 1971, which had held that the interpretation of a legislation which is intended to protect a weaker section of the community, like women, must further the beneficent object. The Court concluded that this is the governing principle of Islamic law which must guide the courts in India.

Since the Supreme Court ruling in *Shamim Ara* (discussed above), several high courts have ruled on this issue and have held that triple talaq is not valid. A sampling of these rulings are listed below:

In 2004 in *Najmunbee v. Sk Sikander Sk Rehman,*[167] the Bombay High Court, in 2005, in *Mustari Begum v. Mirza Mustaque Baig,*[168] the Orissa High Court, in 2006 in *Shahzad v. Anisa Bee*[169] and *Farida Bano v. Kamruddin,*[170] the Madhya Pradesh High Court, in *Gama Nisha v. Chottu Mian,*[171] the Jharkhand High Court have followed the Shamim Ara ruling and have held that a Muslim husband cannot repudiate the marriage at will. They emphasised the requirement of pre-divorce arbitration and further that the divorce must be pronounced and a mere plea of divorce taken in a written statement cannot in itself be treated as effecting talaq on the date of delivery of the copy of the written statement. A written statement cannot be treated as a talaq. Further, in oral divorce, the word *talaq* must be articulated and there should be a reasonable cause for pronouncing the

divorce. A fatwa of talaq is also a question of fact which is required to be proved with evidence.

Riaz Fatima v. Mohd. Sharif,[172] illustrates the validity of a fatwa. In this case, while pleading divorce, the husband produced the copy of a fatwa obtained by him in this respect. He also disputed paternity of the minor child. Rejecting the husband's contentions, the trial court had awarded Rs 400 to the wife and Rs 225 to the minor daughter. But the Sessions Court had overruled this decision. In appeal, the Delhi High Court, set aside the judgment of the sessions court and held that unless all the necessary conditions of divorce are fulfilled, even the fatwa of talaq obtained by the husband lacks legal validity.

The *Dilshad Begaum*[173] case elaborates further the requirements for proving divorce. In this case, the Sessions Judge had accepted the contention of the husband that he had pronounced talaq on his wife in the presence of witnesses in a masjid. This was duly proven by his subsequent actions. Hence, the order of maintenance of Rs 400 awarded to the wife by the trial court was quashed. In an appeal, the Bombay High Court held that though the husband had proven that he had pronounced talaq on his wife, it was not a valid and legal talaq as the additional requirements had not been satisfied. A compromise was arranged through a written document in which the husband had agreed to transfer one third of his land to his wife if he failed to cohabit with her or failed to maintain her as his wife. The court held that this document was not acted upon by the husband. Since the husband had not complied with the conditions, the high court set

---

[166] *A. Yousuf Rawther v. Sowramma,* AIR 1971 Ker 261, discussed later
[167] I (2004) DMC 211 Bom
[168] II (2005) DMC 94 Ori
[169] II (2006) DMC 229 MP
[170] II (2006) DMC 698 MP
[171] II (2008) DMC 472 Jha

[172] I (2007) DMC 26 Del
[173] *Dilshad Begum Ahmadkhan Pathan v. Ahmadkhan Hanifkhan Pathan,* II (2007) DMC 738 Bom.

aside the judgment of the Sessions Court on the ground that the talaq pronounced by the husband was not valid and legal.

It needs to be emphasized that each of these judgments came about while the court was deciding the maintenance application filed by the wife in a lower court under Section 125 of the Cr.PC and the plea of talaq was contained in the written statement in reply to the application. It is evident that this was a legal ploy adopted on behalf of the husband by his lawyer. After the ruling in the *Shahbano case*[174] and the enactment of the Muslim Women's Act in 1986,[175] a misconception prevailed that a Muslim husband is not liable to pay maintenance to his deserted wife if he pleads that he has divorced her. Most trial court rulings which denied the wife's right to maintenance did not reach the higher courts.[176] The reported judgments are in the context of the very few cases which could reach the higher courts.

It is in this context, that the higher courts came to the rescue of Muslim women and set right the harm that was being caused to them. Rather unfortunately, despite the plethora of judgments cited here, many lawyers and some trial court judges continue to endorse the view that after the pronouncement of triple talaq or a document containing the plea of talaq, Muslim women can be deprived of their legal right of maintenance from their husbands. Ironically instead of highlighting these judgments, the media has sensationalized the issue of triple talaq which has led to the demand by human

rights and women's rights groups that triple talaq should be banned. Such demands serve only to reinforce the popular misconceptions regarding the rights of Muslim women. Examining the demand in the context of a series of judgments the demand seems to be based on ignorance of law. At times the media augments its argument about triple talaq by an opinion of a mufti or a *maulana*. But whether a particular mufti or maulana endorses the position laid down by the Apex Court or dissents from it is an irrelevant issue. When a Muslim woman seeks court intervention to protect her rights, the trial court is bound to examine her rights only in the context of established legal dictates.

Law of Succession

Islamic laws of inheritance are distinct from the Hindu law of succession. There is no distinction between ancestral and self-acquired property or even movable and immovable property. No Muslim can inherit during the lifetime of his ancestors. In other words, he/she only inherits as a heir on the death of his ancestor. It is also interesting to note that in Islamic law, there is no legal construct like the Hindu joint family. Unlike in Hindu law, there is no presumption of jointness among family members, even if they do live, eat, and worship together. Rights are individual. Even upon marriage, the person and property of the wife do not merge with that of her husband, as was the case under English law.

The Islamic laws of inheritance are often treated as an area of great complexity. However, they are complex because they are precise. There is a category of inheritors known as 'Sharers' who are entitled to inherit a fixed share and their shares do not fluctuate as under the Hindu law. Their shares are prescribed in the Quran and they are the Quranic Sharers and cannot be deprived of their share in the property. The second category of inheritors are known as 'Residuaries', who are not entitled to

---

[174] *Mohd. Ahmed Khan* v. *Shah Bano Begam*, AIR 1985 SC 945 discussed in detail in the next chapter in the section on Uniform Civil Code.

[175] See Chapter 2 of the next volume for a detailed discussion on Muslim women's right to maintenance.

[176] For a useful discussion about the communal biases which a Muslim woman faces when she approaches the trial court for her right of maintenance, see Mukhopadhyay (2003: 84–93).

a prescribed share but they are entitled to the residual property after the fixed Sharers have been awarded their shares. The third category are the 'Distant Kindred' who comprise of the blood relatives who are not awarded a share either as Sharers or Residuaries. Homicide tends to be a prohibition on inheriting.

Though women are awarded a share, their entitlement is half that of the male heirs in the same category. For example, the daughter's share is half that of the son's share. This prescription does not meet the norm of equality but is based on equity. It was introduced at a time when women were not independent and were not capable of looking after their own financial needs. Men were considered to be the guardians of their wives, mothers, and daughters. It was also perceived that the principles governing inheritance must keep in view the additional liability imposed upon men of paying mehr to their wives. But this rule has been criticised in the context of awarding equal inheritance rights to women.

Another unique feature of Muslim law is the restraint on bequeaths or the capacity to dispose of the property through a will. Only one-third of the property can be willed away and the rest must devolve upon the legal heirs. Hence a Muslim man cannot deprive his wife or daughter of their rightful share either by forming an HUF or through a will which will deprive women of their share in property. This is viewed as a positive feature unique to Muslim law.

Section C

CHRISTIAN LAW OF MARRIAGE AND SUCCESSION

Development of Christian Law in India

The laws governing the Christian community in India are ridden with contradictions and their progression has not been linear. At one level, Christians are governed by pioneering statutes which revolutionized the scheme of personal laws in India and set the parameters of reform for all communities. These laws were based on the then prevailing English laws. On the other, these statutes remained static for well over a century and had become archaic and redundant, while other communities strived to keep abreast with the changing trends in matrimonial laws in the western world. Two other factors of historical significance have also contributed to the complexity.

The laws governing Christians are shaped by two distinct colonial influences—the Anglo-Saxon jurisprudence introduced by the British and the Continental system introduced by the French and the Portuguese within their respective territories.

The post-Independence attempts of reform are marked by conflict between the conservative Roman Catholic doctrine and the reformist Protestant theology, which are rooted in European politics.

As per the 2001 census figures, Christians constitute 2.3 per cent of the total Indian population. These various sects among the Christians in India follow diverse rituals and cultural practices, but broadly they belong to three different traditions:

1. The orthodox Churches of West Asian traditions, that is, Syro-Malabar, Syro-Malankara, the Mar Thoma Church, etc.

2. The Roman Catholic Church of Latin rites.

3. The various reformist churches of Protestant tradition, now consolidated into the Church of South India (CSI) and the Church of North India (CNI).[177]

There is also a large population of Christians among various tribes, particularly in the north-eastern states. These tribes are granted protection

[177] Formation of these federations is a post-Independence phenomenon. CSI was formed on 7 September 1947, within a month of India attaining Independence. The formation of CNI is a more recent development of the seventies.

under the Constitution in respect of their culture, tradition, customs, and laws[178] and hence are not governed by Christian personal laws.

Until the nineteenth century, converted Christians generally followed pre-conversion local customary practices in respect of property inheritance and marriage rituals. The concept of a distinct Christian personal law evolved much later, during the later half of the nineteenth century, with the statutory enactments introduced by the British and the Portuguese. Thus, while being shaped by the European philosophies of the conservative and highly institutionalized Roman Catholic Church and the liberal and loosely structured Protestant theology, the indigenous Christian community also incorporated local customs, traditions, and languages, resulting in wide regional diversities. The converted Christians also retained their pre-conversion caste hierarchies (Grafe 1982: 98 and Thekkedath 1982: 23).

The laws governing the Christian communities have three distinct sources:

1. The statutes enacted by the British in the nineteenth century;
2. The Civil Code introduced by the Portuguese and the French within their colonies;
3. The local customary laws.

In addition, Roman Catholics are governed by a dual system of civil law—the (Indian) Divorce Act, 1869[179] and Canon law (Church law).

Although Christian marriages are solemnized in church, they are simultaneously registered with a civil authority, the Registrar of Births, Marriages and Deaths,[180] which transforms them into civil contracts. These contracts can only be dissolved through a court decree under the provisions of the Indian Divorce Act.[181]

In 1995, in *Molly Joseph* v. *George Sebastian*,[182] the Supreme Court undermined the authority of the Ecclesiastical tribunal by holding that annulments granted by the tribunal are not valid under civil law and a couple who has gone through such annulment cannot contract a valid remarriage. In the case before the Supreme Court, the woman had remarried after a church annulment. When marital discord arose, the husband approached the Court for an annulment on two grounds—(i) the wife is insane, and (ii) the annulment granted by the church in her earlier marriage is not valid under civil law and hence her subsequent marriage to him is not valid.

In the proceedings before the trial court, the wife admitted her previous marriage and pleaded that it was annulled by the Ecclesiastical Tribunal and that this fact was known to the husband. Based on her admission of the earlier marriage and disregarding her plea of the church annulment, the trial court granted a decree in the husband's favour. The woman approached the high court and not satisfied with its ruling, approached the Supreme Court. Dismissing her appeal, the Supreme Court declared:

---

[178] See Articles 371A, 371B, and 371C of the Constitution of India, which relate to Nagaland, Assam, and Manipur respectively.

[179] After the amendment of 2001, the word 'Indian' has been deleted from the title of the Act. But throughout this chapter, I have retained the old title to avoid confusion.

[180] Under the provisions of Sections 36, 55, and 62 of the Indian Christian Marriage Act, 1872, every person authorized to solemnize Christian marriages is bound to send a copy of all the marriage certificates of the marriages solemnized by him to the Registrar General of Births, Deaths, and Marriages at monthly or periodical intervals. Any marriage which is not solemnized as per the provisions of the Act is void as per Section 4 of the Act.

[181] Here it is necessary to emphasize that although Christian marriages are solemnized in the church, they are governed purely by civil statutes—the Indian Christian Marriage Act, 1872 and the Indian Divorce Act, 1869. The title of the Indian Divorce Act was amended in 2001 and the word 'Indian' was deleted.

[182] 1996 AIR SCW 4267

A marriage cannot be dissolved by a declaration granted by the Ecclesiastical Tribunal. Such annulments are not binding on the district court or the high court. The Ecclesiastical Tribunal cannot exercise a power parallel to the power which has been vested in the District Court or the high court by the provisions of the Indian Divorce Act. The Church Authorities would continue to be under disability to perform or solemnize a second marriage for any of the parties until the marriage is dissolved or annulled in accordance with the statutory law in force.

Through these decisions, the state has established its sovereignty over its Christian subjects, subordinating the procedures laid down by the colonial state as well as the religious hierarchy to its laws. Though this could be interpreted as a welcome move as it distanced Christian law from its colonial baggage, the ground level implications of the decision was that it rendered Christian marriages even more stringent and blocked all avenues of any progressive intervention, even by church authorities.

Most Christians are unaware of these dual procedures and believe that an annulment granted by the tribunal qualifies them for remarriage. Since the church will not remarry the couple without a canonical annulment, generally a couple facing problems is encouraged to file a petition with the church tribunal. This leads to a misconception that the annulment granted by the tribunal constitutes a final dissolution of their marriage.

Law of Marriage and Divorce

Christian Marriage: An Indissoluble Sacrament[183]

Under pre-Christian Roman law, though women did not have an independent identity, they had some degree of autonomy with respect to the dissolution of their marriages. This was because marriages could be entered into as private contracts. But with the advent of Christianity into Europe and a gradual increase of state power, the church acquired exclusive control over marriages and declared marriages as holy unions.

By twelfth century, the power of the Roman Church over marriages was well established. The Church of Rome became the supreme ecclesiastical authority in matrimonial matters. Though the Canon law (or Church law) of marriage, was based partly on Roman law and partly on Jewish law, it advanced the doctrine of indissolubility. The church proclaimed that by marriage, the husband and wife were made of one flesh by the act of God, marriage being a holy tie, a sacrament (Diwan and Diwan 1997: 21). The concept of holy wedlock gave a sacramental character to marriages.

The church insisted on a public religious ceremony for solemnization of marriage. It was also mandatory to seek permission from the church before a marriage could be solemnized. This was done to prevent informal relationships or 'loose living' and concubinage or mere 'fornications'. But the pre-Christian practice of private marriage contracts between consenting individuals continued and these 'clandestine' marriages were tolerated by the church. But in AD 802, celebration of marriage in the absence of a bishop, priest, and elders was forbidden. A public announcement of the intention to wed was made compulsory.[184]

A decree of the Council of Trent in 1563 laid down that for a valid marriage, consent of both parties should be declared in the presence of three witnesses and a priest (Diwan and Diwan 1997: 22). A contractual union was not spiritually complete without the blessings of the

---

[183] Also see further discussion on this issue in 'Material Basis for the Notion of Sacramental Indissolubility' in Chapter 1 in the second volume of this book where this issue is discussed further.

[184] This is also known as 'publishing of marriage banns'. This is a mandatory stipulation under the Christian law in India even today.

church. Gradually, through these stipulations, marriages came under the exclusive domain of the church. The formalities served to render an air of solemnity to Christian marriages, which were seen as an earthly manifestation of a divine contract.

The doctrine that was advocated was: 'What God hath joined together, no man shall put as under.' With this, the authority to dissolve a marriage was taken out of human power and was inscribed with divinity or heavenly powers. It now became almost impossible to invoke earthly interventions to dissolve a marriage. Although marriages continued to be contractual with consent as an essential ingredient, it also became a holy and hallowed institution—a mystic union of body and soul. Only through the death of one of the spouses could the sacred union be dissolved and the surviving spouse could acquire the right of remarriage (Diwan and Diwan 1997: 21).

Cannon law declared that consent and consummation are essential for a valid marriage. From this premise, two theories began to emerge—annulment and separation. The doctrine of annulment was evolved to circumvent the premise of indissolubility of a marriage. It was made possible to obtain a decree of annulment from the Ecclesiastical Court, which was the supreme upholder of religion and dispenser of justice. The doctrine of annulment was based on a fictional notion that either the marriage was valid forever or never. This premise awarded retrospective effect to a decree of nullity (Diwan and Diwan 1997: 23). It was laid down that mere performance of ceremonies does not render a marriage valid. Consummation became an essential ingredient of marriage. Where a marriage had not been consummated, it could be dissolved through a papal dispensation if the parties declared on oath that it was not consummated.

Gradually, a theory of separation, *a Mensa et Toro*, was evolved to resolve the issue of conflict marriages. This Roman phrase literally meant 'separation from bed and board', and this theory permitted the parties trapped within incompatible marriages to live separately from each other during the subsistence of the marriage, but did not permit them to marry during the lifetime of the other. However, once the spouse obtained the decree of separation, the other spouse could not enforce conjugality upon the separated spouse. This provided a breather to women who could save themselves from enforced 'conjugality' by their husbands against their wishes.

Evolution of the Concept of Divorce[185]

The Continental legal system changed its character after 1800 under the French code, *Code Civilii*, also known as the Code of Napoleon. Under this, marriage assumed the characteristics of a civil and dissoluble contract.

In England the change was more gradual. The turning point was the progressive and revolutionary English statute, the Matrimonial Causes Act of 1857. This statute transferred the power over family matters from the Ecclesiastical courts to civil courts and introduced the concept of dissolution of marriage for the first time. This move was historical because it made a dent in the Christian doctrine, 'what God has put together, no man shall put as under'. For the first time, divorce was within the reach of commoners. But divorce was not to be treated lightly, hence the grounds for obtaining it were stringent for women—adultery coupled with either cruelty or desertion. Men could obtain divorce on the sole ground of adultery. The remedy of 'legal separation' was less stringent and legally separated women could hold separate property.

---

[185] Also see Chapter 1 of the second volume for more on this issue.

The Indian Divorce Act of 1869 was introduced in India by the British rulers and was based on the Matrimonial Causes Act of 1857. The later enactment—the Indian Christian Marriage Act of 1872 (ICMA)—provided for the solemnization and regulation of Christian marriages. The enactment was meant primarily for the use of British residents in India so that they could avail of the remedies which were prevalent in England. The inclusions of indigenous Christians was only incidental, as a careful reading of the ICMA reveals.[186]

Over the years, the parent statute, that is, the Matrimonial Causes Act of 1857 went through several modifications, keeping abreast with the winds of change blowing across Europe. In 1923, the stipulation of proving additional grounds of cruelty or desertion was removed and adultery *simpliciter* was made a ground of divorce. In 1937, three new grounds, cruelty, desertion, and insanity were introduced as independent grounds of divorce. These trends initiated in England are reflected in all matrimonial statutes in India—the Parsi Marriage and Divorce Act of 1936, the Special Marriage Act of 1954, and the Hindu Marriage Act of 1955.

These changes were incorporated into the Indian Divorce Act governing Christians. Section 7 of the Act provided for automatic incorporation of all the changes under the parent statute, the Matrimonial Causes Act into this Act. However, after Independence, when this issue was argued, the courts in India held that the statute of a sovereign state could not be made subordinate to the developments in a foreign country.[187] So the mantle of reform fell squarely on the Indian state. Unfortunately, the Indian state did not meet the challenge and Christian women continued to suffer.

Discriminatory Grounds of Divorce

The Act stipulated stringent and near impossible grounds under which a Christian woman could obtain a divorce. Section 10 of the Act stipulated that while a husband could get divorce only on the ground of adultery, the wife had to prove additional grounds such as cruelty or desertion. Cruelty and desertion were not independent grounds of divorce. Men and women under other matrimonial laws could obtain divorce by pleading the sole grounds of either cruelty, desertion or adultery. Adultery was a mandatory but not a sufficient ground of divorce. Since adultery is extremely difficult to prove, and not all husbands who treat their wives with cruelty or desertion, also commit adultery, Christian women faced great hardships while obtaining divorce. Since the penal provisions of Section 498A of the IPC came into existence in 1983, a Christian woman could initiate criminal proceedings against her husband for cruelty, but she could not use the same ground for obtaining a divorce.

One of the first instances when the blatantly discriminatory provision of Section 10 of the IDA was challenged was in 1953.[188] The woman concerned, Dwarakabai, challenged the constitutional validity of the Indian Divorce Act before the Madras High Court and pleaded that the stipulation violates the constitutional guarantee of equality under Article 14. The court declared that the discrimination is based on sensible and reasonable classification which took into consideration the ability of men and

---

[186] For instance, Part IV of the ICMA lays down special procedure for registering the marriages of native Christians.

[187] *T. M. Bashiam* v. *M. Victor*, AIR 1970 Mad 12 SB.

[188] *Dwarakabai* v. *Prof. Mainam Mathews*, AIR 1953 Mad 792.

women and the results of their acts of adultery, and was not merely based on sex.

Adultery by a man is different from adultery by wife. A husband cannot bear a child and make it legitimate to be maintained by the wife. But if the wife bears a child, the husband is bound to maintain it.

Later judgments departed from this extremely sexist premise, but the courts refrained from striking down the offensive provisions as unconstitutional.

In 1968, the Madras High Court in *Solomon Devasahayam* v. *Chandirah Mary*[189] held that the Indian Divorce Act is wholly out of date.

In 1989 a special bench of the Calcutta High Court in *Swapna Ghosh* v. *Sadananda Ghosh*[190] ruled that the offensive provision smacks of sex-discrimination. The judgment also quoted with approval the recommendations of the Law Commission and observed that if the Parliament does not amend the offensive provision, the courts will be compelled to strike it down as unconstitutional. However, it stopped short of striking down the section.

In 1990, in an interim application, in *Mary Sonia Zachariah* v. *Union of India*,[191] the Kerala High Court set a time limit and directed the Government of India to give effect to the recommendations of the Law Commission within six months of the order. But the government ignored these directions.

Finally, in February, 1995, in a landmark judgment, *Ammini* v. *Union of India*,[192] the Full Bench of the Kerala High Court stuck down the offensive provisions as arbitrary and violative of Articles 14 and 21 of Constitution. The Court held:

The legal effect of the provisions of Section 10 of the Indian Divorce Act is to compel the wife who is deserted or cruelly treated to continue a life as the wife of a man she hates. Such a life will be a sub-human life without dignity and personal liberty. It will be humiliating and oppressive without the freedom to remarry and enjoy life in the normal course. Such a life can legitimately be treated only as a life imposed by a tyrannical or authoritarian law on a helpless, deserted or cruelly treated Christian wife quite against her will and will be a life without dignity and liberty ensured by the Constitution. Hence the provisions which require the Christian wives to prove adultery along with desertion and cruelty are violative of Article 21 of the Constitution of India.

Since it was a high court ruling, its effects were confined only to the State of Kerala. So, in 1995–96, three Christian women filed similar petitions in the Bombay High Court, which, in a combined judgment of the Full Bench delivered in April 1997, also struck down the discriminatory provisions.[193] In subsequent years the Delhi and Karnataka High Courts also struck down the discriminatory provisions.[194]

While these judgments brought some respite to Christian women in these states, Christian women in other states could not avail of these progressive measures since none of the cases reached the Supreme Court. The rights could only be decided on a case to case basis if individual women challenged the discriminatory provisions in their respective high courts.[195]

---

[189] 1968 MLJ 289

[190] AIR 1989 Cal 1 SB. Also see *Ramish Francis Toppo* v. *Violet Francis Toppo*, 1 (1989) DMC 322 (Cal).

[191] 1990 (1) KLT 130

[192] AIR 1995 Ker 252 FB. This case is also cited as *Mary Sonia Zachariah* v. *Union of India*, (II) 1995 DMC 27 FB.

[193] *Pragati Verghese* v. *Cyril George Verghese*, AIR 1997 Bom 349 FB.

[194] *Debra Seymour* v. *Pradeep Seymour*, II (2002) DMC 144 Del and *Annie Mathews* v. *Rajimon Abraham*, AIR 2002 Kar 385.

[195] The comments of the Karnataka High Court in *Annie Mathews* v. *Rajimon Abraham* (cited above) are interesting. The court chided the family court judge for refusing to follow the decisions of three high courts on

Apart from this, there were several other lacunae which needed to be addressed. A decree of dissolution of marriage passed by the district court needed confirmation by the full bench of a high court and the ground of mutual consent divorce was not available to a Christian couple. Further, the gains which the Christian women had won resulted in a strange situation which in effect proved to be reverse discrimination. The grounds of cruelty and desertion were not available to Christian husbands,[196] though Christian women in certain states had been awarded this right. The archaic provisions which entitled the husband to obtain a divorce only on the ground of wife's adultery prevailed until 2001 when through a central amendment the archaic law was changed as per the needs of the contemporary times.

Non-recognition of Divorce by Mutual Consent

In 1973, the 'fault' theory, where a couple has to prove a matrimonial fault like cruelty or adultery against the other, was abolished altogether and irretrievable breakdown of marriage' or 'no fault divorce' was introduced as the sole ground of divorce in England. Either spouse could obtain divorce merely by pleading that the marriage has broken down irretrievably. This was to avoid 'washing dirty linen in public' in matrimonial disputes. Though this concept has not yet been introduced in Indian matrimonial statutes, the option of a divorce by mutual consent is available in all the matrimonial statutes, where

the couple is not required to prove a matrimonial fault.

However, until 2001, Christian couples were denied this right which was available to couples belonging to all other communities. In order to circumvent the law, the consenting couple had to take the circuitous route of first re-registering their marriage under the provisions of the Special Marriage Act and then filing a joint petition for divorce by mutual consent under that Act. The other shorter and more commonly adopted route was to collude and fabricate a false ground of adultery. Usually the husband would accuse the wife of adultery, and in the hope of a decent settlement, the wife would consent.

When this issue came up for scrutiny before the Supreme Court in *Jorden Deigdeh* v. *S. S. Chopra*,[197] the Court commented that there was no point or purpose to be served by the continuance of a marriage which had completely and signally broken down, and recommended legislative intervention to remedy the situation. But it held that even while adopting a policy of social engineering, the judiciary cannot introduce a new remedy into the matrimonial statutes. In an earlier case, *Reynold Rajamani* v. *Union of India*,[198] the Supreme Court had examined the issue of mutual consent divorce for Christians and expressed its inability to intervene as the function of law making is the domain of the legislative and had urged the government to suitably amend the law.

The Process of Reform

From 1950 onwards, Christian women began approaching the courts and the Law Commission, demanding changes into their divorce laws. Pursuant to this, in 1960, the Law Commission

---

the ground that the same are not binding on it in Bangalore and for not granting divorce to the wife on the ground of cruelty.

[196] See the decisions in *Henry Fernandes* v. *Succorinha Fernandes*, II (2001) DMC 536 Bom, *Philip* v. *Susan Jacob*, II (2001) DMC 290 Ker, and *Rajesh Suryawanshi* v. *Ujwala Suryawanshi*, I (2002) DMC 536 Bom FB.

[197] AIR 1985 SC 935
[198] AIR 1982 SC 1261

of India held meetings with leaders of various Christian religious denominations, legal experts, and community representatives. Based on these discussions, the commission drafted a bill, titled the Christian Marriage and Matrimonial Causes Bill, to reform the archaic laws governing the Christian community and submitted it to the government in its 15th report. At this time, the Roman Catholic Church hierarchy approached the government and raised objections that as per the doctrine of the church, divorce is not permissible. The Law Department referred the matter back to the Law Commission.

The objections raised by the Roman Catholic Church regarding divorce were overruled by the Law Commission on the premise that the statutory remedy of divorce has been in existence since 1869 and the church had not raised any objection to divorce since then. What the Commission had recommended was merely to expand the grounds of divorce. It was not introducing any new remedy. Despite this, there was no further debate on this issue and the matter was shelved.

Thereafter, responding to letters received from Christian women experiencing cruelty at the hands of their husbands, the Commission, in its 90th report, again suggested that the government should immediately amend section 10 of the Indian Divorce Act and issued a warning that if the government does not act, the courts will strike down this provision as unconstitutional. The government still did not respond.

From 1983, there was a renewed campaign and negotiations by Christian women's organizations and several efforts were made to bring the church hierarchy of various Christian denominations on a common platform and draft a consensus bill. While support from the Protestant churches was forthcoming, the Roman Catholic Church raised several objections. After prolonged discussions, in 1994 a new bill was submitted to the government, which had the support of all Christian churches. Despite this, the government did not act and the struggle for reforms continued well into the new millennium. Meanwhile, the judiciary intervened and in 1995, the Kerala High Court and in 1997, the Bombay High Court, struck down the discriminatory provisions as arbitrary and violative of Articles 14 and 21 of Constitution.[199]

Finally, in August 2001, the Parliament passed a bill amending the archaic Indian Divorce Act. The word 'Indian' was deleted from the title of the Act and the Act was renamed as the 'Divorce Act'. The most significant aspect of the amendment was that it extended the gains of the high court rulings to all Christian women in India, making cruelty, adultery, and desertion independent grounds of divorce. The amendments were also beneficial to Christian men as they could also avail of the grounds of desertion and cruelty to obtain a divorce from their wives.

The amendment also introduced the remedy of mutual consent divorce. Finally, as a result of a long ordeal, a couple could obtain an honest and straightforward divorce with consent, without the necessity of fabricating false grounds or having to wash dirty linen in public.

Another significant aspect of the amendment was to remove the ceiling set upon maintenance. The stipulation under the earlier statute was that the maintenance to the wife should not exceed one-fifth of the husband's income, while women from other communities could avail of maintenance to the extent of one-third of the husband's income.

---

[199] *Ammini v. Union of India*, AIR 1995 Ker 252 and *Pragati Verghese v. Cyril George Verghese*, AIR 1997 Bom 349 which have been discussed earlier.

Yet another dichotomy which affected Christian divorces in Mumbai was in the area of jurisdiction. The Bombay High Court had retained its original jurisdiction awarded to it by Letters Patent under Clause 35—ecclesiastical jurisdiction[200] to adjudicate over Christian matrimonial matters—despite the institution of family courts in 1989. Hence, Christian couples could not avail of the procedures stipulated under the family courts Act for dispute resolution, like counselling, informal atmosphere, simplified procedures, etc. Finally, in 2001, in *Romila Shroff* v. *Jaidev Shroff,*[201] the high court relieved itself of all original matrimonial jurisdictions awarded to it under Clause 12 (civil jurisdiction) and Clause 35(ecclesiastical jurisdiction) of the Letters Patent.[202] But the high court retained the original jurisdiction awarded to it under the Parsi Marriage and Divorce Act of 1936.[203]

The Indian Divorce Act also contained an archaic stipulation of a provisional decree (*decree nisi*), which needed to be reconfirmed after six months (Sections 16 & 17). This was another Victorian-era colonial baggage, with a very conservative view regarding divorce. This provision caused a great hardship to Christian couples who had to move the court again after six months of their divorce to obtain the required decree of confirmation. The Karnataka High Court in *Joseph Varghese Cheeran* v. *Rosy Kurian Kannaikai*[204] struck down this section as

---

[200] This is discussed in Sub-section, 'Matrimonial Law – From the Ecclesiastical to the Civil Law Regime' in the Introduction to this chapter.

[201] II (2001) DMC 600 FB

[202] For further discussion on the original jurisdiction of the High Court of Bombay regarding matrimonial matters see Chapter 3 of the second volume of this book.

[203] The issue of Parsi matrimonial courts is discussed in the subsequent section on 'Parsi Law of Marriage and Succession'.

[204] I (2000) DMC 107

being infructuous after the coming into force of the Family Courts Act and held that a decree of the family court would have to proceed in accordance with the procedure prescribed under the said Act and not in accordance with the procedures under the Indian Divorce Act. The Bombay High Court in *Maria Sera Pinto* v. *Milton Dias*[205] reconfirmed this view and emphasized that Section 20 of the Family Courts Act has overriding effect on anything inconsistent therewith contained in any other Act.

The initiatives by individual Christian women and the consequent judicial interventions are important markers in the Christian law of marriage and divorce. The struggle by Christian women to reform their laws needs to be acknowledged as acts of assertion and subversion. Strengthening the theory of 'reform from within' in the realm of personal laws, as opposed to the premise of 'enactment of a uniform civil code' in order to obtain gender justice, Christian women finally succeeded both in legal battles within courts as well as in their negotiations with the church and the State, to shed the century-old shackles under which they had been burdened for well over a century.

Law of Succession

In matters of succession, the Christian subjects of British India were governed either by the provisions of Indian Succession Act of 1865 or their own customary laws. The Indian Succession Act was re-enacted in 1925. This is a progressive piece of legislation as it grants equal rights to daughters and sons in parental property. The concept of ancestral property or coparcenary is also not recognised. Hence it provides greater safeguards to women than the Hindu legal system (including the Hindu Succession Act of 1956) as well as the Muslim

---

[205] I (2002) DMC 554

and Parsi (until it was amended in 1991) legal systems. But this legislation seemed to apply mainly to Europeans and other foreigners than the Indian Christians, as a large section of the Christian community, which was governed by customary laws, was excluded from the application of this Act. [206]

As has already been mentioned, many communities continued to follow the pre-conversion laws regarding succession even after conversion. Most Christian communities followed the rule of coparcenary or joint Hindu family property and continued to practice the discriminatory laws which prohibited daughters from inheriting the property.

A leading case of the colonial period on this issue is *Abraham v. Abraham,*[207] decided by the Privy Council in 1863. The case concerned the issue of succession to the property of a Roman Catholic who had subsequently converted to the Protestant sect. The dispute was between the widow and her husband's brother. The brother pleaded that although they had converted to Christianity, they continued to follow the Hindu law of coparcenary. While holding that the property is joint, the Privy Council laid down the rule regarding conversion as follows:

The profession of Christianity releases the convert from the trammels of the Hindu law but it does not of necessity involve any change of the rights or relations of the convert in matters with which Christianity has no concern such as his rights and interests in and his powers over property.

But subsequently the Indian Succession Act of 1865 came into force and when the issue came up before the court again in 1886, the Madras High Court, in *Tellis v. Saldanha,*[208] held that after the enactment of the Indian Succession

Act, the Christian converts are governed by its provisions. The case concerned Roman Catholics of Mangalore who had converted several centuries ago. While the widow pleaded the application of the Indian Succession Act, the brother of the deceased pleaded that they are converts from a Brahmin sect and are governed by the Mitakshara law of coparcenary. But a subsequent decision of the Bombay High Court in 1907, in *Francis Ghosal v. Gabri Ghosal*[209] dissented from the view expressed in *Tellis v. Saldanha* and held that Christians are governed by the Hindu law of coparcenary.

Customs were also granted validity under Section 5 of the Punjab Laws Act, 1872. In *Premchand v. Lilavathi,*[210] while validating a custom which grants sons the right of inheritance to the exclusion of daughters, the Himachal Pradesh High Court held that Christians are governed by Section 5 of the Punjab Laws Act of 1872 and not by the Indian Succession Act which grants equal inheritance rights to daughters.

Despite the enactment of the Hindu Succession Act of 1956, which improved the situation of Hindu women and granted daughters and wives a share in the parental property (but not in the ancestral property), Christians continued to be governed by the discriminatory provisions of uncodified Hindu law which denied daughters a share in the parental property.

The law of Cochin and Travancore was particularly discriminatory against the daughters. Under the Travancore Christian Succession Act of 1910, the right of daughters was limited to one-fourth of the share of the son or Rs 5000, whichever was less. Under the Cochin Christian Succession Act, 1922, the share of daughters was one-third of the son or Rs 5000, whichever

---

[206] Section 29(2) of the Indian Succession Act, 1925.

[207] *Abraham v. Abraham,* (1863) 9 MIA 195.

[208] (1986) ILR 10 Mad 69

[209] (1907) 31 Bom 25

[210] AIR 1956 HP 17

was less. Property in excess to this would be inherited by sons and if there were no sons, then by the nearest male relative.

In 1957, the Cochin and Travancore High Court affirmed that Christians in the region are not governed by the Indian Succession Act and the discriminatory statutes enacted by the princely states apply to them.

In 1974, a single judge of the Madras High Court adopted a progressive stand and ruled that the Travancore Succession Act stood repealed after Independence and Christians in the region are not governed by this discriminatory statute, but by the Indian Succession Act.[211] But this decision was overruled in 1978 by the Full Bench of the Madras High Court in *D. Chelliah Nadar* v. *Lalitha Bai*,[212] which reaffirmed that Christians in Tamil Nadu are governed neither by the progressive provisions of the Indian Succession Act nor by the Hindu Succession Act, but by the uncodified Hindu customary law and under this law, the son was the sole heir to the father's property to the exclusion of the daughter.

The controversy was finally resolved in a ruling given by the Supreme Court in the *Mary Roy case*.[213] The Court struck down the discriminatory provisions on a technical ground that after Independence, the laws enacted by the erstwhile princely states which were not expressly saved have been repealed. While the repeal was welcome and overdue, the Court restrained from examining the provision under the constitutional mandate of equality and non-discrimination on the ground of sex under Articles 14 and 15, which could have set the precedent for examining gender discrimination under other personal laws.[214]

---

[211] *Solomon* v. *Muthiah*, (1974) 1 MLJ 53.
[212] AIR 1978 Mad 66
[213] *Mary Roy* v. *State of Kerala*, AIR 1986 SC 1011.
[214] Part B, States (Laws) Act ,1951.

Section D

PARSI LAW OF MARRIAGE AND SUCCESSION

The Parsi Community in India

The Parsis (also referred to as Parsees) are a small and well-knit community. Numerically they are so insignificant that in the Census report, under the classification of religious communities, they are listed under the head 'other communities'. As per a recent study, in 1986, the Parsi population of the world was around 2,50,800 (Cabinetmaker 1991: 2–3). As per the 2001 census, the Parsi population in India is around 76,000.

The Parsis originate from Iran (abode of Aryans). In AD 636, when the Arabs invaded Persia and Caliph Omar defeated the Parsi king Yezdezind, they sailed off in boats in search of a new land to escape persecution, carrying with them their sacred fire. After a great ordeal at sea, the boat landed twenty five miles south of Daman (Framjee 1858:10). The head of the group implored the local king, Jadao Rane, to give them refuge, with a promise that they would enrich his land. The history of India bears testimony to the fact that they kept this promise.

The King laid down five conditions:

1. The Parsis should adopt the local language
2. They should translate their holy texts into the local language
3. Their women must change their dress and wear the local saree
4. Their marriage ceremony should include the local rite of tying of the sacred knot
5. They should surrender their arms (Cabinetmaker 1991: 2–3).

They consented to all the five terms and in return the King granted them permission to build their fire temples[215] and allotted to them a

---

[215] The first fire kindled when they landed is preserved in the holiest of the holy shrines, Imamshah at Udwada near Navsari.

stretch of undeveloped country near Diu. They renamed the place as Navsari, which literally means 'New Sari', as it reminded them of a place they had left behind in Persia, which was called Sari. They settled down to agriculture (some were also weavers and craftsmen) and lived amicably with the local Hindu community. Navsari became the centre of learning of the Parsi community. Due to the rigid caste system followed by Hindus, assimilation was not possible and hence they were able to maintain their separate and distinct identity.[216] But they adopted many local customs.[217]

Within this integrated community there are two sects—Shensoys (or Shuhursaees) and Kudmis. The Kudmis are a breakaway sect formed in 1746 and consists of only around 10,000 Parsis. The difference between the two sects is not as major as the Shia and Sunni Muslims or the Catholic and Protestant Christians.

The fortunes of this community seem to have transformed when they were touched by the magic wand of colonisation. After the island of Bombay was gifted to the King of England by the Portuguese, the Parsis started trickling in and were able to obtain various commercial contracts for building the new commercial centre of the British empire.[218] The contribution of the Parsi community to building the city of Bombay after the English take-over is particularly significant. They were the first to adapt to English education, new trading patterns, and later to commerce and industry. This helped the community to acquire a new economic and political status and over a period, 70 per cent of the Parsis in India began to live in Bombay. They fitted in well with the new colonial administrative structure and also played an important role in the nationalist politics. The more prosperous among them built hospitals, gardens, schools, and housing schemes and were also significant contenders in the field of commerce, industry, science, and art.[219] It is through their close interaction with the British that the community, though numerically insignificant in the post-colonial political map, evolved as an important economic and political force during the colonial regime and were able to negotiate for themselves a separate set of personal laws.

Law of Marriage and Succession

Development of Law

The development of the Parsi legal system must be viewed in the context of the above

---

[216] The community also prescribes rigid rules which discourages Parsis from marrying outside the community.

[217] For instance, washing the toes of bridegroom with milk during marriage rituals, offering *pan-sopari* on auspicious occasions, sprinkling of rose water, etc. (Framjee 1858: 84).

[218] In 1735, when the British started building the Bombay dockyard, a Parsi from Surat, Lowjeee Wadia, was granted the contract of ship building. Rustom Patel, another Parsi, helped the British to stall the Moppala attack. Rustomjee Cursetjee wrote the first book in English in 1780 called *Bombay Calendar*. On 1 July 1822, Mobed Fardoonje Marzben started the first newspaper in Gujarati, the *Bombay Samachar*. When

the British started building the railways, the contract of laying the tracks was granted to Jamsetjee Dorabjee. In 1857, Rustomjee Byramjee, obtained a commission as a surgeon (Framjee 1858; Cabinetmaker 1991).

[219] For a numerically insignificant community, the list of Parsi dignitaries in every field is endless. Sir Jamsetjee Jeejeebhoy—the first Baronett, Sir Nes Wadia, Dinshaw Jamsetjee Petit—the philanthropists, Sir Cowasjee Jehangir—the Patron of Art, Jamsetjee Tata, Homi Mody, and Godrej—the industrialists, Behram Malabari—the social reformer, Homi Bhabha—the scientist, Sir Phirozshah Mehta, Sir Dadabhai Naoroji, Sir Dinshaw Wacha, Madam Bhicaji Cama—the nationalist leaders, Sir Dinshaw Mulla—the legal luminary and member of the Judicial Committee of the Privy Council, and so on.

mentioned role played by Parsis within the colonial scheme. As already mentioned, after settling down, the Parsis adopted the local language and customs, while maintaining a distinct and separate identity. The adaptation of the institution of local panchayats for administration of their affairs is an important indicator of this adaptation.

During the initial phase of the Company rule, the various British Charters explicitly saved the customs and usages of Hindus and Muslims in civil matters as they were deemed religious. But no such saving provision was granted to other communities—Parsis, Jews, Armenians, etc. Within the newly evolving colonial legal structure, the courts applied the principles of English law in the Presidency towns (Calcutta, Bombay, and Madras) and in the Provinces, the local customs and usages followed by the parties (or the law of the defendant, in case of disputes). In exercise of the discretion granted to the judges, English principles of justice, equity, and good conscience were also applied as a residuary rule of law (Jain 1966: 59). Under this legal scheme, English laws were applied to Parsis in all civil matters, except marriage and bigamy.[220]

In 1778, after the Parsis petitioned to William Hornby, the Bombay Parsi Panchayat was granted recognition and a lawfully constructed Panchayat came into effect from 1 January 1787 (Framjee 1858: 99). This fitted in well with the legal scheme devised subsequently by Elphinstone of granting recognition to customary usages (See Introduction to this chapters).

In 1835, a suit was filed by a son to appropriate the whole of the father's property. The suit was decreed in favour of the son by applying the English principle of primogeniture through which the eldest son inherits the whole property. Since this was not the custom followed by Parsis, the community was alarmed and pressed for a separate legislation. In their submission to the government, they pleaded that they were subjected to serious disadvantages in the absence of a fixed written code. The claim of protecting women's rights became a vehicle to establish a legal identity for the Parsis and to stake their claim for a separate law of marriage, divorce, and succession in later years.

In response to their appeal, an act was passed in June 1837[221] which relieved the Parsis of Bombay from the operation of the English law of primogeniture. Through this statute, widows were granted a share in the property and the residue was divided equally amongst the children and their descendants. But English principles continued to be applied to them in all other respects.

In the case of the mofussil Provinces, it was almost impossible to ascertain the Parsi customs with precision because the Parsis of Surat, Broach, Poona, and Ahmedabad differed from each other on many points and all of them differed from the Parsis in Bombay. So in November 1838, various associations of Parsis forwarded to the Legislative Council a petition along with the answers which they had prepared to Borrodaile's queries[222] and prayed that a

---

[220] As per a case decided on 16 December 1817 by the Court of Appeal of Surat, *Adawlut Kaoosjee Roostumjee v. Mt.Awan Baee*, matters concerning marriage and control over women's sexuality were regulated by Modees, Dustoors, and members of the *Parsee Unjoomun* and bigamous marriages were permitted under certain conditions. The case is discussed in *Mihirwanjee Nuoshirwanjee v. Awan Baee*, 2 Borradaile's Reports SDA Vol. I, 1800–24, p. 209.

[221] Succession to Parsees Immovable Property Act, 1837 (Act IX of 1837).

[222] In 1828, a questionnaire was administered to the Parsis of Surat by Borradaile who was assigned the task of recording the customs of various castes in the Gujarat region. The Surat Parsis did not respond to

regulation might be framed on the basis of those answers as embracing the rights of inheritance and succession that are acknowledged by the Parsee nation (Roy Chowdhury and Saharay 1988: 73).

The Parsis wanted to be protected from two primary principles of English law:

1. The English Statute of Distribution in case of intestacy
2. The English common law relating to husband and wife which denied married women independent control over their property during covertures.

Sometime in 1850, a Parsi lady sued her husband for a decree of restitution of conjugal rights before the Supreme Court at Bombay. Since there were no clear directions as to how a matrimonial suit of a community other than Hindus and Muslims should be decided, the Court decided to hear the case as per the jurisdiction awarded to it on the Ecclesiastical side, applying the principles of English (Christian) law. When the issue of jurisdiction was challenged, the Privy Council upheld the objection to jurisdiction. It was ruled that it was a gross error to apply the law of the Diocese of London, a Christian law, to persons professing the Zoroastrian religion and held further that the Supreme Court, in the exercise of its Ecclesiastical jurisdiction, could not entertain a suit between Parsis for restitution of conjugal rights (*Ardaseer Cursetjee* v. *Peerozeboye*[223]). The Lords of the Privy Council held that the suit could not be decided as per the Ecclesiastical proceedings which apply only to Christians and

hence the suit was not maintainable, and commented as follows:

But we should much regard if there were no court and no law whereby a remedy could be administered to the evils which must be incidental to married life amongst the Parsees. We do not pretend to know what may be the duties and obligations within a matrimonial union between Parsees, nor what remedies may exist for the violation of them. There must be some laws, or some customs having the effect of laws, which apply to the married life of Parsees. It may be that such laws and customs do not afford what we should deem, as between Christians, an adequate relief. But it must be recollected when the parties themselves could have contracted for the discharge of no other duties and obligations than such as, for time out of mind, were incident to their own caste, nor could they reasonably have expected more extensive remedies, if aggrieved, than were customarily afforded by their own usages. Such remedies, we conceive, that the Supreme Court on the civil side might administer, or at least, remedies as nearly approaching to them as circumstances would allow. In suits commenced on the civil side, the peculiar difficulties which belong to the exercise of Ecclesiastical jurisdiction in some matrimonial cases would not arise. Proceedings might be conducted on the civil side with such adaptation to the circumstances of the case as justice might require, though on the Ecclesiastical side such modification would be wholly irreconcilable with Ecclesiastical law.

The Privy Council commented further,

An examination of the case cited in the ruling in *Mihirwarjee* v. *Awan Baee*[224] that there was no doubt as to the jurisdiction of the Sudder Adawlut at Bombay to entertain a suit by a Parsi lady for a divorce from her husband. The parties resided outside the jurisdiction of the Supreme Court. The Court could take cognizance of matrimonial suits between Parsees, and award them such relief, with due regard, their own laws and customs will allow. It must be expected, that those laws and customs are wholly at variance with the principles which govern the matrimonial law of the Diocese of London, and incompatible with the Eccleesiastical law, as in such cases is administered. One instance will

---

the questionnaire. So the Bombay Parsee Panchayat published it in 1832 and obtained the response of the Bombay Parsis to these queries (Framjee 1858: 120).

[223] (1856) 6 MIA 348. This case is also discussed in the Introduction to this Chapter.

[224] 2 Borrodaile's Report of Civil Cases (SDA), 1820–4, p. 209.

suffice. It appears that, under many circumstances, the husband is permitted to take a second wife, the first being alive.[225]

Perturbed by the ruling of the Supreme Court of Bombay, the community renewed the demand for separate legislative acts to govern Parsi marriage, divorce, and succession. But the third Law Commission rejected this demand as it felt that the demand was not substantiated. This left the community highly dissatisfied.

So on 20 August 1855, a meeting of the Parsis of Bombay was convened in the central hall of the main fire temple to campaign for a separate law. The meeting was attended by 3,000 Parsis. A committee was appointed to prepare a draft Code of Laws adapted to the Parsi nation and to petition the Legislative Council of India for the enactment thereof.

On 5 December 1859, the Managing Committee of the Parsee Law Association settled and adopted a body of rules titled 'A Draft Code of Inheritance, Succession and Other Matters'. On 31 March 1860, this Draft Code was presented to the Legislative Council and was referred to a Select Committee. On 10 August 1861, the Select Committee of the Legislative Council presented their report and recommended that the Government of Bombay may appoint a commission to make preliminary inquiry into the usages recognized as laws by the Parsi community of India.

On 26 December 1861, the Government of Bombay appointed the Commission, which recorded the evidence, both written and oral, of the community representatives. As regards inheritance, succession, and property between husband and wife, the mofussil Parsis objected to the rights of females to inherit family property upon the death of a male Parsi dying intestate and to the right of married women during coverture to hold or dispose of their separate property. The mofussil Parsis, however, agreed with the Bombay Parsis that the English Law of inheritance and succession was unsuited to the requirement of the Parsi community. The Commission submitted its report on 13 October 1862 and disallowed the contention that there should be two separate inheritance laws, one for the Parsis of Bombay and another for the Parsis in mofussil towns.

As a next step, in 1864, the Parsee Law Commission was appointed and based on its report, in February 1865, two bills were introduced, the Parsee Marriage and Divorce Bill and the Succession and Inheritance (Parsees) Bill. They were referred to the Select Committee, which presented its report on 31 March 1865 (Roy Chowdhury and Saharay 1988: 74). Based on this report, the two statutes were enacted—The Parsee Intestate Succession Act, 1865 and the Parsee Marriage and Divorce Act, 1865. Thus, due to their perseverance, the Parsis finally succeeded in securing a separate law for themselves.

Salient Features of the Codified Law

The Parsee Marriage and Divorce Act has the unique distinction of being the first matrimonial law to be codified in India.[226] Through the enactment of the Act in 1865, the provisions of the English matrimonial statute, the Matrimonial Causes Act, 1857, which transformed the marriages in England from a sacrament to a dissoluble contract, were incorporated into a codified law governing an Indian community. Following the Christian model, Parsi marriages were made

---

[225] This is reproduced from the ruling of Justice Crump in *Rachel Benjamin v. Benjamin Soloman Benjamin*, (1926) Vol.28 BLR 328, where the case was discussed in detail. The particular case of Rachel Benjamin is discussed in the section on Jewish Law of marriage and divorce later in this chapter..

[226] The Indian Divorce Act, 1869 was enacted four years later.

monogamous and adultery was made into a ground of divorce (Manchanda 1991: 14).

Rather curiously, the very basis of the objection of the community and the Privy Council in *Ardeseer Cursetjee* v. *Peerozeboye* that Christian law, particularly the principle of monogamy, cannot be applied to Parsis became redundant as they adopted a law of their own which was modelled on English law. But the relevant point is that this was done through community initiatives and through this enactment, the community was able to get legal recognition to their identity.

They also secured legal recognition to their customary arbitration forum of panchayat. Under the Act, a jury system consisting of seven representatives of the community was introduced. Through this process, the community obtained a hold over matters of marriage and divorce within the Anglo-Saxon court structure. In the process of emulating English statutes, certain biases against women crept into matrimonial laws. Despite the enactments, in matters not covered by the statute, either the English common law or principles of justice, equity, and good conscience continued to be applied to Parsis.[227]

Judicial Pronouncements: 'Parsi' not a Religion but a Race

Like other communities, the characteristics of the Parsi community also were 'fixed' in the process of litigation over property disputes. In an important case involving the head of the Parsi Anjuman of Bombay, Sir Dinsha Petit, and Sir Jamsetji Jeejeebhoy, the industrialist,[228] decided in 1908, the courts ruled that there is no conversion among the Parsis.

The issue before the court was the creation of private trusts and relegating huge properties to it by the industrialist. The Parsi Anjuman objected to the creation of such private trusts. But the issue which was foregrounded during litigation was that of conversion. The Parsi Anjuman pleaded that Juddins (converts) to whom the Navjot (initiation ceremony) is performed and are given the *sudra* and *kusti*, become Parsis. In a lengthy judgment of around 100 pages, a two-member bench comprising of one Parsi (Justice Davar) and one English judge ruled in favour of Jamsetji and validated the creation of private trusts. In the process, they also invalidated conversions among Parsis. Adopting a rather curious logic, the court explained that while Zorastrianism is a religion, Parsis are a race and there cannot be conversion to a race. Just like a person cannot convert and 'become' an Englishman or a Frenchman, no one can convert and 'become' a Parsi, the court explained.

In order to prevent the Parsi trust property and fire temples from slipping away from the Parsi fold, in *Saklat* v. *Bella*,[229] it was ruled that converts to Zorastrianism and children born to a Parsi woman who has married a non-Parsi are not Parsis. Endorsing patriarchal norms, it was held that children of a Parsi father and a non-Parsi mother acquire a Parsi status. Interestingly, the issue before the court did not concern the rights of children born of Parsi women through non-Parsi husbands. The case concerned a Goan Christian girl, Bella, who was adopted and was raised as a Parsi by a Parsi benefactor settled in Rangoon. Attracted to Zorastrianism,

---

[227] See the decisions in *Manchersha* v. *Kamirunissa Begum*, 5 BHCR 109 and *Mithibai* v. *Limji N. Banaji*, ILR 5 Bom 506.

[228] *Dinsha Petit (Sir)* v. *Jamsetji Jeejeebhoy (Sir)*, (1909) ILR 33 Bom 509.

[229] 1925 ILR 53 IA 42. The court held that in a marriage between a Parsi woman and a non-Parsi man, there is a presumption that the wife will have to accept the religious faith of her husband. So it would follow that the children will be brought up according to the religion of the father.

she expressed a desire to convert and was initiated into the faith through a ceremony of initiation by a Parsi priest. But when she started attending worship at the fire temple, the community elders raised an objection and filed a suit for injunction restraining her entry into the fire temple. They pleaded that her presence in the fire temple causes distraction and prevents the Parsis from offering worship. Ironically, the land upon which the fire temple was built was a state endowment for religious worship to the Parsis. The two lower courts held that since Bella had converted to Zorastrianism, her entry cannot be prevented and she was entitled to worship in the fire temple. But the Privy Council, relying upon the Bombay High Court decision in *Dinsha Petit* v. *Jamsetji Jeejeebhoy*,[230] held that the double requirements of religion and race are essential to worship in the fire temple despite the fact that the legal deeds were drawn specifically in the context of religion. Through these two significant decisions, the avenues for conversion and adoption among the Parsis were sealed.

In 1925, when the Indian Succession Act was enacted, (which governs mainly Christian succession,) the Parsi Intestate Succession Act was verbatim incorporated in Chapter III of this Act. Interestingly, during the years 1870 to 1925, considerable progress was made in the realm of married women's property rights under English statutes and the concept of equality between men and women regarding inheritance had been accepted. Based on these developments, the Indian Succession Act did not discriminate between male and female heirs. But the Parsi inheritance laws continued to maintain the discrimination, and females continued to inherit half the share of their male

counterparts.[231] This is a rather surprising development, given the context that the demand for a separate law for Parsis originated with their resentment against the anti-women provisions of the English statutes being inadvertently applied to them.

A Wave of Reforms during the 1930s

When reforms were initiated in the family laws of Hindus and Muslims,[232] the Parsis also initiated a process of reform. In 1933, the Council of the Parsi Central Association submitted a draft bill for the opinion of the Parsi public to amend the Parsi law of succession. The main objective was to improve the position of widows and daughters under the statute and the allotment of a share to parents. The changes were incorporated into the Indian Succession Act in 1939.[233]

From 1865 to 1930, the status of women in England was radically transformed through various statutes and great strides were made in English matrimonial laws. Against this backdrop, the Parsi Marriage and Divorce Act of 1865 had become outdated. So the Parsi Central Association took up the question of reforms in 1923 and a sub-committee was appointed to suggest suitable changes. The Parsee Laws Revision Sub-committee submitted its report in 1927. The Parsee Central Association sent copies of this report to various trustees of the Parsi Panchayats, Parsi Associations, Parsi Anjumans, the delegates of the Parsi Chief Matrimonial Court, and to Parsi jurists all over India as well as to Parsi Associations in China

---

[230] Discussed earlier.

[231] This principle was borrowed from the then progressive Islamic law in 1865.

[232] The Hindu Married Woman's Property Rights Act, 1937 and the Application of Shariat Act, 1937.

[233] The Amending Act (XVII of 1939).

and Persia.[234] The report was also published in the press.

The Parsi Central Association made some modifications to the bill, after which it was circulated for public opinion. A conference was arranged under the auspices of the Parsi Panchayat. Twenty-five Parsi associations participated in this process and twenty-one associations approved the modifications.[235] Based on the various views expressed, a draft of the proposed Act was prepared and circulated which had the approval of the illustrious members of the Parsi community (who were also legal luminaries of their time), including Sir Dinshaw E. Wacha and Right Hon'ble Dinshaw F. Mulla.

A bill was introduced into the Council of State in 1935 by Sir Pheroze Sethna. It was circulated for opinion and a Joint Select Committee was appointed to consider the bill. The Select Committee reported to the Council of State in the same year and the bill was passed on 13 March 1936. The Federal Assembly considered the bill in April 1936. Sir Cowasji Jehangir who moved the bill, explained that an overwhelming majority of the Parsi community held progressive views and were anxious to modify the provisions of their archaic laws to suit modern conditions (Parashar 1992: 192–3). The reforms expanded the scope of dissolving marriage by introducing several new grounds—non-consummation of marriage, insanity, pre-marriage pregnancy, grievous hurt, and desertion.

Reforms during the 1980s

The 1980s witnessed the emergence of a new women's movement in India. The reforms were based on the recommendations of the Law Commission's 110th report. The process was initiated by the Board of Trustees of the Bombay Parsi Panchayat. It submitted the recommendations to the government. The then Law Minister, Dhiraj Goswamy introduced two bills for reforming the personal laws of the Parsis. While the amendment to marriage laws was passed in 1988, the amendment to succession laws had to be shelved and was enacted in 1991 during the Congress rule.

The Parsi Marriage and Divorce (Amendment) Bill was introduced in the Rajya Sabha on 24 November 1986. It was passed by both the houses in the following year, received President's assent on 25 March 1988, and came into force in April, 1988.[236]

The provisions of marriage and divorce were modified along the lines of the Hindu Marriage Act. Grounds of divorce were further liberalized and divorce by mutual consent was introduced.[237] The disparity between the rights of legitimate and illegitimate children was abolished. In 1991, by amending the succession laws, the discrimination between female and male descendants was abolished.

The following aspects need to be highlighted in the context of Parsi law reforms:

1. At each juncture, the process of reforms was initiated from within the community and a broad consensus was reached before the bills were introduced. So, finally when the bills were presented to the legislature, they were passed unanimously without much debate.

---

[234] Mentioned in the Statement of Objects and Reasons of the Act (Gazette of India, 1934, Part V, p. 221).

[235] The non-concurrence of the rest of the associations was explained by Sir Phiroze Sethna as 'This opposition chiefly comes from a small section who are ultra conservative in their views and do not, as a rule, approve of any changes in keeping with the changing times'.

[236] The Parsi Marriage and Divorce (Amendment) Act 1988 (Act No.5 of 1988).

[237] Sections 32 (a), (b), (c), (e), and (g) of the Act.

2. Women from the community were conspicuously absent from the discourse. Although the community is liberal and holds a progressive stand on women's issues, women's names do not figure in any phase of the reform. The process seems to have been initiated at the instance of a few liberal male members who had made a mark in public life as social reformers and legal luminaries. From their high status in society, they could interact with both the conservative community leadership at one level and with state institutions at the other.

3. Although gender justice was the stated agenda, the motive of reform seems to be dual—(i) Maintaining a separate community identity, and once this is achieved, (ii) Ensuring that the laws do not lag far behind the dominant ideology, that is, in the pre-Independence period, the British statutes and in the post-Independence period, the Hindu Marriage Act. Since Hindu Marriage Act grants the husband a right to maintenance, the same was also introduced in the Parsi laws. Under the Special Marriage Act of 1954, husbands do not have a similar right. It is significant to note that the reforms followed the provisions of Hindu law rather than the Special Marriage Act, which is a secular legislation and more beneficial to women than the Hindu Marriage Act.

4. The premise that gender equity was not the primary object is substantiated by the retention of certain outdated discriminatory notions inherited from the British statutes in 1865. The law provides for settling the property of an adulterous woman in favour of the children (Section 50). The statute also treats women as legal minors and provides for a trust to be set up in respect of the maintenance allowance with the power to restrain women's access to the maintenance (Section 41).

5. Even while modernising the statutes, the community has maintained its hold over matrimonial matters by retaining the jury system introduced in 1865. The jury system has been abolished under other Indian statutes. While all original matrimonial jurisdiction is transferred to family courts and the procedure there has been simplified, the high court has retained original jurisdiction under the Parsi Marriage and Divorce Act of 1936 (Part III of the Act). A special court is constituted twice a year by the Bombay High Court, and it functions for about a week. This causes severe hardships and delays to the litigants. Though a high court judge presides over the court, the delegates have to be members of the Parsi community (Section 24). Even in the name of uniformity or modernity, this system has not been abolished. This clause did not meet with any criticism during the legislative debate.

6. The debate in Parliament when the bills were enacted was cursory.[238] The members did not concern themselves with the implications of the bill on Parsi women. The debate was confined to two spheres:

(i) Since Parsis have willingly modified their laws, it is time to enact a uniform civil code

(ii) Praises to the Parsi community that they are an enlightened and progressive community and thereby insinuating that other communities (more specifically the Muslims) are backward and reactionary. The fact that the Parsi community had also opposed the imposition of a Uniform Civil Code and the Adoption Bill, that they had retained the jury system in matrimonial adjudication, and the relief of divorce by consent was being introduced as late as in 1988 did not even figure in the debates.

[238] For discussion on the Inheritance laws, see Lok Sabha Debates (LSD), 10th Series, VI/10 4.xii.91, pp. 662–7; 5.xii.91, pp. 442–51.

The Act also retained the sexist provisions (see point 4 on the preceding page).

In conclusion, it is obvious that it is only through its political and economic significance during the colonial rule that the Parsi community could negotiate for a separate law, where none existed. The liberal leaders of the community, during each phase of reform, have ensured that the law does not lag behind the dominant social norms, that is, of the British, during colonial rule and of the Hindus, in the post-colonial rule. Although their initial demand for a separate law was premised on protecting the rights of women from the vagaries of the British legal principles, in the process of codification and reform, the community incorporated the biases inherent in the dominant system, both of the British and of the Hindus. This aided and reaffirmed the biases inherent within the customary practices. Hence their claim for a separate law to safeguard women's rights cannot be substantiated. But the existence of a separate law has substantially aided the numerically insignificant community to retain its own separate identity within the legal arena and granted statutory recognition to community interventions in judicial processes.

Section E

JEWISH LAW OF MARRIAGE AND DIVORCE

Jewish Community in India

India has a legacy of three distinct Jewish communities—Jews from coastal Kerala, known as Cochin Jews and Paradesi Jews, Jews from the Bombay region - the Bene Israel (literal meaning—sons of Israel) and Baghdadis and the Jewish community in the North East. The Jewish migration into India took place in several phases and there is a great diversity among them in terms of their culture, language and religious practices. Their migration is linked to their history of persecution in their homeland. A process of reclaiming their Jewish identity occurred much later during colonialism.

Jews from Coastal Kerala

It is believed that Jews first entered India as traders from the Kingdom of Judah (or Judea) during the time of King Solomon and traded in teak, ivory, spices, pepper and peacocks. Some of them settled down over time in the coastal towns of Kerala. The major migration occurred in around AD 70 during the Roman take over of Judea when the second temple of Solomon was destroyed and the Jews were persecuted.

The Jews landed in Cranganore (an old fort near Cochin with the local name Kudungallur) and sought the patronage of the local Raja. It is believed that around the fourth century, a leader of the Jewish community, Joseph Raban was declared a Prince by the local raja and was given a principality through a charter engraved on two copper tablets which are known as *sasanam*. This village later came to be known as the Jewish nation (Katz 2000). They engaged in trading and farming, and also joined the armies of local rulers. It is said that the local rulers refused to fight battles on Saturdays as the trusted Jewish soldiers would not fight on the day of Sabbath (Katz and Goldberg 1993).

The Jewish community in this region was known as Cochin Jews or Malabar Yahudan. They mingled with local communities and adopted local customs and languages. They spoke Judeo Malayalam, an adaptation of the local language, but retained their separate Jewish identity. They built their synagogues, maintained dietary regulations, and observed Sabbath as a day of rest. However, they did not follow the strict Jewish code, and they did not have a rabi (priest) for their rituals.

In 1524, the local Malabari Muslims (known as Mopillahs), backed by the ruler of Calicut (presently known as Kozhikode), attacked the Jewish community in Cranganore on the pretext that they were interfering with the pepper trade. The Jews fled to Cochin and sought the protection of the Hindu Raja then ruling over Cochin. The Raja granted them a site to build their own town, which later acquired the name 'Jew Town'. The town has retained its name down the centuries to the present day.[239]

The European Jews arrived later during the early phase of colonial perod from Spain, Portugal and Holland as merchants and traders. They were known as *Paradesis* (foreigners). They maintained a distinct identity and did not mingle with the local Cochin Jews and built their own separate synagogues. A synagogue built by the Paradesi Jews in 1568 is still functioning and is declared a protected heritage. The copper tablets given to the Cochin Jews in 4th century are preserved in this synagogue.[240]

In the 17th century, when the Portuguese occupied Cochin the Jews were again persecuted. But in 1660, the Dutch defeated the Portuguese and since the Dutch Protestants were more tolerant, the Jewish community prospered. In 1795, Cochin came under the rule of the British and this resulted in further prosperity among the Jewish community, who were predominantly traders.

The Jewish travellers from Europe who visited Cochin during the early years of colonialism recorded that the Cochin Jews knew the law of Moses and the prophets but did not follow the Jewish law as prescribed in the Talmud (Karz and Goldberg 1993: 40). In the 17th century, the Dutch merchants carried some copies of the printed Torah, scrolls and prayer books which helped the local Jews to follow the Jewish code more accurately. But they also retained their local traditions and customs.

During the seventeenth and eighteenth centuries, Cochin had an influx of Jewish settlers from Middle East, North Africa, and Spain. In the 19th century, the Jewish community in Kerala lived in the towns of Cochin, Ernakulam, and Parur. After Independence, there was a sharp decline in the Jewish population in Kerala due to migration to Israel. Presently, only a dozen Jewish families are left in Cochin.

Jews from the Bombay Region

Two distinct communities of Jews lived in this region, the Bene Israel and Baghdadi Jews. The Bene Israel lived primarily in the Bombay region and spoke Marathi. They claim that their ancestors were oil pressers in Galilee who fled the country to escape from persecution in the second century BC. They trace their origins to a shipwreck off the Maharashtra coast in around BC 175. According to the legend, the shipwreck left seven Jewish couples stranded in a small village, south of Mumbai. This was the beginning of the Jewish community in the Bombay region. They adapted the local culture and spoke an adaptation of Marathi. Except for a few outward symbols, their assimilation into the local culture was complete (Roland 1989: 34-5).

In the eighteenth century, the Baghdadi Jews started arriving in Bombay. These newer settlers 'discovered' the older settlers, the Bene Israels, who at that time were observing only a few outward symbols of Judaism, which is how they were recognized. But they had no scholars of their own, so teachers from Baghdad and Cochin came to Bombay and taught them mainstream Judaism during the eighteenth and nineteenth centuries. By late eighteenth century, Bombay had the largest Jewish population in India which

[239] http://adaniel.tripod.com/cochin.htm accessed on 30 May 2010.

[240] http://philtar.ucsm.ac.uk/encyclopedia/judaism/cochin.html accessed on 2 June 2010.

comprised Bene Israels, Baghdadi, and Persian Jews. The Baghdadis, many of whom were wealthy traders and businessmen, were anglicized and were comfortable under the British rule. So they achieved the maximum prosperity. Around 5000 Baghdadi Jews lived in Bombay during the early twentieth century.

The Bene Israels also prospered during colonialism as they were termed as 'Anglo-Indians' which helped them to get better jobs and trade contracts. The Jewish population in Mumbai and surrounding districts was estimated to be around 6000 in 1830 and increased to around 20,000 in 1948. During the years preceding Independence, the Jewish community played an important role in many different fields.

Several Jewish women entered the Bombay film industry during the early days in the thirties and forties. Ruby Myers who was known as Sulochana, Miss Musleach who was known as Miss Rose, Esther Abraham who acted by the name Pramila and who was the first Miss India, Ferhet Ezekiel who was known as Nadira, the stunt queen, Rachel Cohen who was known as Ramola and Susan Solomon who adopted the name Firoza Begum are some stars who made a mark for themselves. Film directors and produces like Ezra Mir and Bunny Reuben were also Jewish. Some prominent citizens of Bombay – Nissim Ezekiel the renowned poet and David Sassoon, the renowned philanthropist belonged to the Jewish community. Ruth Prawar Jhabvala, a writer of international repute and Esther David a well known writer were also Jewish.

Because of their identification with the British, after India gained independence, the Jews began to feel insecure and subsequently, the Jewish population declined dramatically with large scale migration to Israel, England, and the United States. While the Jewish identity of Baghdadi Jews was not in dispute, there was a struggle for the Bene Israels to be accepted as authentic Jews due to their assimilation into the local language and culture. In 1964 Bene Israels were accepted as Jews by the Israeli government which helped further escalate the process of migration. After decades of migration, the Jewish population in India dwindled to a mere 5000, of which around 4000 live in Maharashtra. Today, only a few Baghdadi Jews are left in Mumbai and their number has dwindled to less than 200.

The Jewish Community in North East

The Jews from Manipur and Mizoram view themselves as descendants of the Menashe tribe, which is believed to be one of the ten lost tribes of Jerusalem. They call themselves *Beni Menashe* (children of Menasseh) and are the latest to reclaim their Jewish identity and trace the history of their persecution. They claim that their forefathers were exiled and enslaved by Assyrians from where they escaped into China. After many centuries they moved to the Chinese-Burmese border and thereafter migrated into India. They claim that there were around two million Jews in this region but in the nineteenth century, many were forcibly converted to Christianity by the Christian missionaries. Their features resemble the Chinese-Mongolian and they hardly observe any Jewish culture or traditions.

Since 1951, there is a movement to return to their original land and religion and attempts were made to learn Judaism. So they contacted the rabis in Israel and converted to Judaism after observing the strict Jewish laws. Thereafter, they staked their claim to the promised land of Israel. Since then, they have been negotiating with the Israeli authorities to recognize them as belonging to one of the lost tribes of Jerusalem.

Origins and Development of Jewish Law

Like all ancient legal systems, Jewish law also lays its claim to divine origin. According to the

Jews, the law and moral dictates were revealed by God, in the wilderness of Sinai, to Moses, who transmitted it to his people. This law is laid down in the first five books of the Old Testament (Genesis, Exodus, Leviticus, Numbers, and Deuteronomy), commonly known by the Greek word 'Pentateuch', meaning 'the five rolls'. The Jews call these five books the Torah ('The law' or, literally, 'direction' or 'guidance'). In course of time, enormous bodies of law and commentary came to be compiled known as the '*Talmud*' ('teaching' or 'instruction'), which interpreted, modified, expounded, and adapted the original scriptural law to changed times and circumstances. Modern Jewish law is an adaptation of the Mosaic (divine) and Talmudic (evolved) law.

The *Talmud* came to be compiled after the conquest of Judea by Titus in AD 70 in the reign of the Roman Emperor Vespasian. It consists of: (1) the *Mishnah*, a systematic collection of religious—legal decisions developing the laws of the Old Testament; and (2) the *Ganara*, which is a supplementary commentary based on the *Mishnah*. The *Mishnah* states a law in a few lines, while the *Ganara* is discursive, being in the nature of a commentary on the *Mishnah*, giving the diverse opinions of leading rabbis on the *Mishnah* text. It also describes the circumstances which might require the law to be modified, giving illustrations. Orthodox tradition ascribes divine origin also to the *Talmud* (the legal decisions and commentaries) stating that 'Moses left to his people not only a 'written law' in the Pentateuch but also an 'oral law' which had been handed down and expanded from teacher to pupil, from generation to generation' (*Catholic Encyclopedia*, 1913). Jewish law was interpreted and adjudicated over by the rabbis or the religious heads, and hence it is also known as 'Rabbinical law'. During the

subsequent centuries, it evolved through these interpretations.

The *Mishnah*, the *Palestinian Talmud,* and the *Babylonian Talmud* were reduced to writing in the second, fourth, and sixth centuries respectively. In the sixteenth century, the Jewish law was codified in a work titled, *Shulchan Aruch* by Rabbi Joseph Karo. The third part of this legal text which is titled, *Eben Ha-Ezer*, contains the matrimonial law.

After the Roman conquest, the Jews were dispersed. Through all their wanderings, through the long centuries of cruel persecution, to the ghettos into which they were herded or to countries which treated them with a tolerable degree of liberality, they carried with them their laws and customs. Though the Rabbi (religious head) ceased to be a civil judge and became only a spiritual guide, he continued to be the interpreter of the Jewish law. To people so widely scattered as the Jews, the *Talmud* acted as a unifying force and enabled them to cling to their identity.

Jewish Law of Marriage and Divorce

The codified Jewish law of marriage and divorce is derived from Mosaic law through analogy and deduction. It includes norms and usages which had become a part of the law, as well as new regulations enacted by religious and civil authorities to meet the exigencies of changed times and circumstances. The *Talmud* defines and regulates the forms of contracting and dissolving marriage, marital rights and duties, and innumerable issues concerning matrimonial relationship. The regulations stipulated in the *Talmud* underwent some modifications by the decisions of the *Gaonim*, who, after the Talumudic period, flourished until the eleventh century as the heads of Babylonian academics.

A standard text book on Jewish law relied upon by courts in India, is written by the renowned Jewish scholar and Professor of Talmudic Literature at the Hebrew Union Collage, Rev. M. Mieliziner, titled, *Jewish Law of Marriage and Divorce in Ancient and Modern Times*, the second edition of which was published in 1901, and *Jewish Code of Jurisprudence* by Rabbi Kadushin, published in 1921. The courts in India have opined that these two legal texts contain very valuable expositions on Hebrew law and give a clear and accurate account of the law of marriage and divorce based on the original scriptures. The following account of Jewish law of marriage and divorce is based on these legal texts, as cited with approval in various decisions of the High Courts of Bombay and Calcutta.

Though the institution of marriage is founded on Biblical injunction and has a religious basis, the modern Jewish marriage is a monogamous and dissoluble contract. The three essential requirements for a valid marriage are—free consent of the parties, mental capacity, and legal age. No marriage can take place without the consent of both parties and a marriage performed without consent is void, even if the prescribed formalities are complied with. Since consent is an absolute pre-condition to the marriage contract, idiots and lunatics who lack the capacity to give free consent cannot contract a valid marriage. The consent of the parties has to be manifested through certain legally established formalities.

The minimum legal age for contracting a valid marriage according to the Talmudic law was thirteen for boys and twelve for girls. But during the early Rabbinical and Talmudic era, in exceptional circumstances, a girl below the age of twelve years was permitted to be given in marriage by her father, or if he was dead, by her mother or brother. This was due to the necessity of having a protector in the event of her

father's death or due to poverty. Though the permissible legal age of marriage for girls was twelve, as a general rule a man was prohibited from marrying girl below thirteen years.

Legal age, mental capacity, and free consent, though essential, are not by themselves sufficient for a valid marriage. It is essential to perform formal ceremonies of betrothal and nuptial for the marriage contract to have legal validity. The groom was required to give the bride money (*Kaseph*) or any other object of equal value in the presence of two witnesses. This formality was called *Kaseph Kidushen*. During the middle ages, a plain gold ring replaced the requirement of giving money. The formality of betrothal included a pronouncement by husband in the following words: 'be thou wedded (consecrated) to me' or 'be my betrothed'. Later, additional words were added, 'according to the law of Moses and Israel'. The ritual law of the *Talmud* required that a benediction be pronounced at the betrothal invoking the Lord's praises and alludes to the law that the betrothed parties are not permitted to enter into conjugal relationship before the nuptials.

The nuptial are termed *Chuppa* (the term denoted the bridal chamber and in later years, the bridal canopy) or *Nissuin* (which means 'taking') and comprises the ritual of the groom taking the bride from her natal home to the bridal chamber. The ritual indicates that now she is under his matrimonial authority. On completion of this ritual, the marriage is deemed valid, irrespective of whether the marriage was consummated. During the early Judaic period, sufficient period lapsed between betrothal and nuptials, but after sixteenth century, betrothal and nuptial form part of the same ceremony.

As per traditional Jewish law, before the nuptials, the groom was required to make a commitment in writing, which would entitle the wife to receive a certain sum from his estate in the case of his death or a divorce. This was termed as *Kethuba*. This was a protection from the power of the husband for arbitrary divorce and was deemed as a marriage settlement. But when the husband's right of divorcing the wife against her will was restricted in the eleventh century by the generally adopted Decree of Synod of Rabbenu Gershom, the Kethuba lost its former importance but was retained as an ancient custom. Gradually, formal marriage settlements, made in a more legal form, replaced it. Later, when the wife was sufficiently protected by the civil laws of the country, the Kethuba came to be regarded as an unnecessary and useless formality and often was dispensed with.

The legal texts spell out in detail the mutual rights, duties, and obligations between the spouses. The husband's duties towards his wife are primarily to maintain her according to his status in life, that is, to furnish her with necessaries including food, clothing, and dwelling, to have conjugal cohabitation with her, to provide suitable medical care and nursing when she is sick, to protect her and to ransom her in the eventuality of her abduction and captivity (a reminder of the war torn tribal Arabia and feudal Europe), and to provide for her burial in case of her death.

Conversely, the husband was entitled to the wife's earnings, to the usufruct of her inheritance, donation, legacy, etc., except where it was given to her on the specific condition that it is for her own exclusive use. Upon her death, the husband became the sole heir to her property. The husband's right to the wife's earnings is regarded as the consideration for his duty of economically supporting his wife and protecting her. So, if the wife renounced her claim to be supported by her husband, she acquired control over her own earnings and it could be retained by her exclusively, free from the husband's claims.

Under Jewish law, the wife takes the domicile of her husband and she must follow where he goes to reside, except into a foreign country where a different language is spoken. It is her primary duty to manage the household.

Rabbinical law permitted polygamy. So though polygamy was abolished in the eleventh century by Rabbenu Gershom, in certain exceptional situations, a man could marry a second wife. But if a custom of a city prohibited a man from taking a second wife, he could not remarry. This appears to be in keeping with the Talumudic law, which stipulates that the law of the country is the binding law.

The marriage could be dissolved by death of one of the parties or by divorce. Under the strict Rabbinical Code, a ritual executed by the husband, *Get* (Bill of Divorcement or, in other words, a Deed of Divorce), was necessary to release the wife of the matrimonial bond. But subsequently, other forms of obtaining divorce acquired legal validity—a decree of divorce to the wife upon a petition filed by her, a decree of divorce enforced by a competent court in the interest of public morality (for instance in a case of wife's adultery), and divorce by mutual consent.

Until the eleventh century, a husband could divorce his wife through a Get even without her consent. Later, the husband's right of divorce was restricted. The principal passage concerning divorce in the *Torah* is to be found in *Deuteronomy* (xxiv 1–2) and reads as follows:

When a man has taken a wife, and married her, and it comes to pass that she find no favour in his eyes, because he hath found some uncleanness in her; then let him write her a bill of divorcement, and give it in her hand, and send her out of his house. And when she is departed out of his house, she may go and be another man's wife.

Under the modern Jewish law, the husband is entitled to petition the court for divorce on the following fault grounds:

1. Wife's adultery, even on strong suspicion of her having committed this crime.
2. Public violation of moral decency.
3. Change of religion or proved disregard of the ritual law in the management of the household, by which she caused him to transgress the religious precepts against his will.
4. Obstinate refusal of connubial rights during a whole year.
5. Unjustified refusal to follow him to another domicile.
6. Insulting her father-in-law in the presence of her husband or insulting the husband himself.
7. Certain incurable diseases, which render cohabitation impracticable or dangerous, such as epilepsy, etc.

In Jewish law, adultery by the wife was not only a matrimonial offence but also a criminal offence, the punishment for which was death by stoning.

The wife could also obtain divorce from her husband under the modified Jewish law on the following fault grounds:

1. Loathsome chronic diseases which the husband contracted after marriage.
2. A disgusting trade in which the husband engages after marriage, which renders cohabitation with him intolerable.
3. Repeated ill treatment like beating, throwing her out, or prohibiting her from visiting her parental home.
4. Change of religion by husband.
5. Notorious dissoluteness of morals.
6. Wasting his property and refusing to support her.
7. Having committed a crime, compelling him to flee the country.

8. Impotency or persistent refusal of matrimonial intercourse.

As per the modern Jewish law or by statutes prevailing in different countries, the wife can obtain a divorce on the following grounds:

1. Adultery
2. Cruelty (described by laws of different countries, such as intolerable severity, injurious treatment indignities making life burdensome, etc.)
3. Desertion without good cause or abandonment (the period ranges from one to five years as per the custom, usage, or statute of different countries)
4. Habitual drunkenness
5. Impotency
6. Joining a religious society which holds marriage to be unlawful
7. Imprisonment for crime
8. Neglect to provide for the wife's maintenance and support, though being able to do so.

If the wife obtains a divorce on a fault ground, she is also entitled to maintenance as well as for the marriage settlement or for Kethuba.

Judicial Interpretations of the Jewish Law

While adjudicating over matrimonial disputes between Jewish couples, the colonial courts encountered many difficulties, both in terms of substantive law as well as procedural law. The initial British charters stipulated that Hindu law is to be applied to Hindus and Mohammedan law to Mohammedans. But there were no mention of other communities living in India, basically Parsis and Jews. So, initially the colonial courts applied the principles of justice and right (or justice equity and good conscience—basically the principles of English law) to disputes among these communities. When the Supreme Court of Bombay decided a suit for restitution of conjugal rights under its Ecclesiastical jurisdiction and applied the law of the Diocese of London (a Christian law), the decision was overruled by the Privy Council, which indicated that the matrimonial disputes between non-Christians should be adjudicated under civil law and not under Ecclesiastical (Christian) law.[241] Subsequently, Clause 12 of the Letters Patent awarded the widest possible jurisdiction to newly set up high courts to entertain matrimonial suits of other communities. Cases concerning Jewish couples were decided by the high court under its original civil jurisdiction. But subsequently, statutes were enacted for all other communities—Christian, Hindu, Parsi, as well as for determining issues of divorce for Muslim women, which awarded specific jurisdiction to civil courts to entertain matrimonial suits.

But the Jews did not have any specific statute governing marriage and matrimonial reliefs. So the courts were constrained to examine Jewish law as laid out in certain legal texts and commentaries, using its power of civil jurisdiction under Clause 12 of the Letters Patent. But the power of the high court to entertain Jewish matrimonial disputes continued to be a contentious issue, which was constantly raised by defendants in matrimonial suits.

In 1924, in Sasson v. Sasson,[242] the Privy Council held that there may be a Jewish body competent to grant divorce. In this particular case, the divorce was pronounced by the Grand Rabbinat at Alexandria. But in the leading case of 1925, Rachel Benjamin v. Benjamin Soloman Benjamin,[243] Crump J. of the Bombay High Court held that the High Court has jurisdiction to adjudicate over matrimonial matters concerning Jews. The wife had filed a suit for divorce on the grounds of cruelty and bigamy. According to her, the husband had driven her out of the house and had contracted a second marriage. She pleaded that the husband should be compelled to give her a 'bill of divorcement', or in the alternative, the court should decree dissolution of the marriage and direct the defendant to pay her Rs 25,555 specified in the Kethuba executed at the time of the marriage. The husband denied cruelty and pleaded that the second marriage is valid under Jewish law. His further plea was that the high court had no jurisdiction to entertain a suit between parties professing the Jewish faith.

While affirming the power of the high court to adjudicate over matrimonial matters under Clause 12 of the Letters Patent, it was held that the law to be applied in such cases is the Jewish law, with such adaptations to the circumstances of the case as justice may require. It was further held that there are no Rabbis in Bombay who are empowered to pronounce divorce, the power lies solely with the civil courts. But Das J. of the Calcutta High Court, in a later decision, Jacob v. Jacob,[244] dissented from this opinion and expressed doubt as to whether high courts have jurisdiction to entertain a suit between a Jewish couples.

Madon J. in the case of Mozelle Robin Soloman v. Lt. Col. R. J. Soloman,[245] reviewed the entire law on the subject of marriage and divorce among Jews—the old Mosaic law with its Rabbinical interpretation and provisions and the modern legislation. It was held that a ground which would entitle a Jewish wife to obtain divorce also entitled her to reside separately from her husband and claim her right to be maintained by him. In effect, this amounts to the relief of judicial separation under modern matrimonial law.

[241] *Ardaseer Cursetjee v. Perozeboye*, (1856) MIA 348.

[242] (1924) AC 1007

[243] (1926) Vol.28 Bom.LR 328

[244] (1944) ILR 2 Cal 201

[245] (1979) 81 BLR 578

Regarding the practice of polygamy, it was held in *Rachel Benjamin* v. *Benjamin Soloman Benjamin*,[246] that the Bombay Jews are generally monogamous. They cannot lawfully contract a second marriage, except in certain exceptional cases. Hence, the wife was granted the decree of divorce on the ground of husband's cruelty and bigamy. It was further held that the court has the power to grant a *decree nisi* for dissolution of marriage and to order permanent alimony in a matrimonial suit between a Jewish couple. In this judgment, Crump J. issued a note of advice to the Jewish community regarding codification of their laws in the following words:

The Jews in Bombay come mainly from Baghdad and it was improbable that they regard the Jewish law in precisely the same light as the Jews living in England or in America. It was, therefore, plain that the custom of the community must be considered on points where there was a room for doubt.

Because of the uncertainty that prevailed within the Jewish law at the time, Crump J. suggested that it would be in the interest of the community if they consolidated the law relating to matrimonial disputes based upon legal principles which govern community practices. This could be either by the establishment of a *Beth Din* (Jewish Matrimonial Council), such as is found in Jerusalem and Baghdad, or by special legislation similar to the Parsi Marriage and Divorce Act. It was observed that the community was enlightened and progressive and should appreciate the benefit of certainty of law and procedure upon these matters which vitally affect domestic life among them.

But the codification of Jewish law did not take place during the pre-Independence period, and the legal discourse, as contained in judicial interpretations, continued to be the main source of law for the Jewish community in India. Since there has been a sharp decline in the Jewish population, the number of cases which come to court have also reduced. Recently, the high court relieved itself of the original jurisdiction awarded to it by the Letters Patent and the jurisdiction has been transferred to the family courts in Mumbai.[247] *Bension Joseph Hayeema* v. *Sharon Bension Hayeema*[248] is a case in point where the high court upheld the decision of the family court at Mumbai dismissing the husband's petition for divorce on the ground of wife's cruelty as the same was held to be not proved.

Section F

CIVIL LAW OF MARRIAGE AND DIVORCE

The Special Marriage Act, 1954 provides for a civil marriage of two Indians, without the necessity of renouncing their respective religions. The statute operates as an optional secular code of marriage and divorce. Though the Act has been in existence for a long time, it is the least publicized legislation and is shrouded by misconceptions. The most common misconception which prevails is that this law is to be used only in cases of inter-religious or inter-caste marriages, or 'love' marriages, which term refers to marriages of choice contracted against parental wishes. The fact that any one, including those belonging to the same religion, can opt to get married under this Act has not been sufficiently highlighted. The Act also offers an option to re-register marriages performed as per one's own personal laws. This provision, of subsequent registration, enables parties to avail of secular and uniform remedies despite the solemnization of the marriage through performance of religious ceremonies.

---

[246]   (1928) Vol.28 Bom.LR 328

[247]   *Romila Shroff* v. *Jaidev Shroff*, II (2001) DMC 600 FB.

[248]   I (1996) DMC 546

This aids them in overcoming the constraints posed by their own personal laws.

The present Act is a re-enactment of a statute enacted during the colonial period, the Special Marriage Act of 1872. The aim of the enactment was to provide for a civil law of marriage that would enable individuals to get married outside of their respective community mandates, as many community based laws did not provide for inter-community or inter-caste marriages. Contracting a marriage outside of one's own caste could result in loss of social standing and could also lead to a person being declared an 'outcaste'. The Special Marriage Act provided legitimacy to such marriages.

The statute was enacted in response to the demand raised by the Brahmo Samajis, as part of their campaign against Brahminical rituals and idol worship within the Bengal Presidency. They campaigned for a law enabling registration of a simple, non-ritualistic civil marriage, based on consent of the parties.

The Act (which was also referred to as the Native Marriage Act III of 1872) was a progressive piece of legislation for its time and brought far reaching changes within Hindu family relationships. It paved the way for modern and secular legislation along the lines of the English matrimonial statute, the Matrimonial Causes Act of 1857. In an era of ritualistic marriages and unrestrained Hindu polygamy, it rendered marriages contractual and monogamous and provided the option of divorce. The Act also laid down a minimum age of twelve years for marriage, which, as the controversy around the Age of Consent Act reveals,[249] was considered to be fairly high at that time. It ruled out caste or religious barriers to marriage and provided for a purely secular and non-ritualistic marriage

ceremony where the marriage vows were administered by a state authority, the Registrar of Marriages, in a civil registry.

This was blasphemous as per the Brahminical traditions where marriages were ritualistic. The Hindu orthodoxy opposed the move. Due to this, the scope of the Act was eventually narrowed down to people who would declare themselves as not Hindus, Christians, Jains, Buddhists, or Sikhs. Finally, it became applicable only to Brahmos, who had demanded the legislation. It was made mandatory for the parties contracting the marriage to declare that they have renounced their religion. People who were willing to enter into secular marriages were not willing to forsake their religion.

Since this stipulation narrowed the scope of the Act, in 1912, a demand was raised for the deletion of this provision, which was not conceded. But in 1923, this clause was deleted, which facilitated the registration of civil marriages without the accompanying encumbrance of religious renouncement. So, even prior to the enactment of the Hindu Marriage Act, two Hindus could avail of the provision of a contractual, monogamous marriage with the option of divorce, if they married under this Act. Similarly Muslims could marry under it and be bound by the provision of monogamy.

During the post-independence period, when the controversy over the enactment of the Hindu Code Bill was raging, the government felt it safer to re-enact this statue and make it more relevant to its time. Hence, the 1954 legislation was enacted. The Act contained several redeeming features. It introduced the concept of 'breakdown theory' of marriage[250] into the Indian legal regime by incorporating the provision of divorce

---

[249] See the discussion on Age of Consent earlier in the chapter.

[250] This is a later doctrine of English law than the earlier 'fault theory', where one spouse is required to prove a matrimonial fault against the other.

by mutual consent. After the marriage, for matters of property inheritance, the couple would be governed by the provisions of the Indian Succession Act, 1925 (which is more egalitarian and gender just), and not by the provisions of their respective personal laws. The Indian Succession Act contained separate sections for Parsis and non-Parsis. Although the non-Parsi section was applied primarily to Christians, the statute could be deemed a residuary law since it was also applicable to persons contracting civil marriages.

In order to contract a marriage under the Special Marriage Act, the following conditions have to be met:

1. Neither party has a spouse living at the time of marriage.

2. Neither party is incapable of giving a valid consent to the marriage due to unsoundness of mind.

3. Neither party has been suffering from mental disorder of such a kind or to such an extent as to be unfit for marriage and the procreation of children.

4. Neither party has been subject to recurrent attacks of epilepsy or insanity.

5. The bridegroom has completed the age of twenty-one years and the bride the age of eighteen years at the time of marriage.

6. The parties are not within the degrees of prohibited relationship (unless such marriage is recognized under customary law).

Prior to the marriage, a notice of intention to marry must be given to the Registrar of Marriages. The marriage is contracted at the civil registry in the presence of a marriage officer appointed by the state as well as three witnesses. The oath of marriage is administered by the marriage officer without the fanfare of any religious rituals and ceremonies. Signatures of the parties and witnesses are obtained in the

register maintained by the marriage officer. A certificate of marriage is issued to the parties, which constitutes a concrete proof of a valid marriage having been performed for all future litigation purposes. This also serves as a restraint against husbands contracting subsequent bigamous marriages. In case of re-registration of a marriage performed under personal laws, it is also necessary that the ceremony of marriage has been performed and the parties have been living as husband and wife.

After solemnizing or registering a marriage under this Act, secular provisions regarding divorce, succession and adoption will apply, the highlights of which are as follows:

1. Where any member of an undivided family who professes the Hindu, Buddhist, Sikh, or Jain religion marries a non-Hindu under this Act, he shall be severed from such family. However, if two persons who are Hindus get married under this Act, no such severance takes place.

2. Succession to the property of any person whose marriage is solemnized under this Act, and to the property of the children of such marriage, is governed by the Indian Succession Act. However, if two persons who are Hindus get married under this Act, the above provision does not apply and they are governed by the Hindu Succession Act.

3. Since a marriage under this Act is a secular and civil contract, conversion or apostasy of the spouse is not a ground for divorce under this Act.

Since the provision of divorce by mutual consent was not available under the Hindu Marriage Act, until 1976, parties wishing to avail of the provision could re-register their marriage under the Special Marriage Act and then subsequently obtain the divorce. Since the Indian Divorce Act, 1869 governing Christian marriages did not provide for a divorce by mutual consent until 2001, Christian couples desirous of a mutual consent divorce could re-register their marriage under this Act and later obtain divorce by mutual consent.

The development of this Act in subsequent years and the manner in which certain concessions were made to Hindus marrying under this Act are discussed later in Chapter 2. The problems with the Act and judicial comments regarding its outdated procedures are discussed in Chapter 1 of the second volume.

Section G

VALIDITY OF CUSTOMARY LAWS

Customary Law and Women's Rights

Scriptural law received ascendance during the colonial period and was projected as the law of the Hindus. But despite this, a large section of the Indian population was governed by community based customary laws, both during pre-colonial and colonial period. Inspite of this codification of Hindu laws, many tribes and castes continue to be governed by customary laws to the present day. Hence a discussion on personal laws would remain incomplete without negotiating and interrogating the role of custom.

The subject of customary law is vast. There are several tribes and castes which follow their are customary practices in every region in India. While tribes and castes designated as 'schedule tribes and castes' are provided constitutional protection for safeguarding their customs, rituals and laws, even those that are not similarly protected follow their own customary practices and this forms a vibrant part of personal laws. The exploration into customary laws is undertaken, keeping in view the constrains of dealing with this subject within the limited scope of this book.

Custom was recognized as an important source under smriti law. But apart from its validity under scriptural law, it was the sole source of law for many tribes and lower castes who were not governed by the smritis. During the early smriti period, roughly estimated as the period between 600 BC and AD 200, the smriti law validated various customs regarding marriage and sonship,[251] but gradually, Brahminicial practices received ascendance over other forms and were recognized as the primary pattern of marriage and sonship among the Indo-Aryans in the Gangetic Plains and the hilly terrain of North India.

One glaring distinction between this region and the southern-dravidian region can be found in marriage patterns. Among the north Indian upper castes, families sought marriage alliances with people to whom they are not already linked by ties of blood, under the *sagotra* and *sapinda* pattern of exogamy. The sagotra concept is based on the belief that all persons belonging to the same *gotra* have descended from the same male ancestor and, hence, same gotra marriage is prohibited. A related concept is sapinda exogamy, which means that persons who offer *pinda* to the same ancestor share particles of the same body and thus cannot be joined in marriage. A system of fictive kinship exists wherein people who have no actual kinship connection are regarded as part of the same kin group. Thus a whole village or a group of villages can be considered as fictive kin of each other. In addition, daughters were not married to men from villages where daughters of the family or even of

---

[251] Sonship was an important institution during the vedic and smriti period. The desire for a son was so great that smritis lay down 12 different ways of acquiring a son–the legitimate son, *aurasa*, an adopted son, *dattaka*, a daughter's son, *putrikaputra* , a son born to the wife through another man, *kshetraja*, the son of a slave *daaasiputra* and so on.

the natal village have previously been married into. This meant that in most cases, the woman was marrying into a family of total strangers, located in a distant place.

Visits from the natal family were kept at a minimum and customs in some region discouraged the natal family from visiting the girl in her marital home and partaking in a meal at her in-laws' place. In essence, this meant that the woman was isolated from her natal family and was devoid of all kinship support networks. This rendered her extremely vulnerable. She was left totally at the mercy of the members of her marital family and was expected to assimilate within this family and adopt their customs and practices. In some communities, the bride acquires not just a new family name but even a new first name to enable her to acquire a totally new identity. This was meant to wipe out her pre-marriage identity. Girls were married before they attained puberty, so, in most cases, the women had only faint memories of their natal home. The severing of ties with the natal family was total.

The Brahminical-Aryan customs followed by the upper castes of North India exercised strict control over women and their sexuality and the status of women among them was low as compared to women from the lower castes and the Dravidian regions. Brahminical norms such as pre-puberty marriage, restraint on widow remarriage and divorce, the ceremony of kanyadan (the ritual of gifting away a bedecked bride to a scholarly groom), and the theory of *kshetra* and *beeja* (soil and seed symbolizing that the woman was a mere carrier of children who actually belong to the man), are an indication of the lower status of women among the North Indian upper castes.

This system practiced by the upper castes in a particular region came to be projected as the dominant system of marriage and kinship throughout Hindu India. In reality, there were numerous local variations, customs and practices which were contrary to this practice and which placed women in a far more advantageous position. These variations have been extensively described and analyzed by anthropologists (Karve 1953; Srinivas 1962; Mandelbaum 1970). Among the myriad pro-women practices that prevailed, a few are summarized below.

The marriage pattern among the south Indian-Dravidian communities was a total contrast to the Indo-Aryan practice of sagotra and sapinda exogamy. Here, the attempt was to strengthen existing kin ties through marriage, preferably with blood relatives like cousins. *Menarikam* is a marriage, among many tribes/castes of Andhra Pradesh and other South Indian states, between a maternal uncle and his niece or between first cousins, similar to Islamic, Jewish, and Zorastrian traditions.

Among Maharashtrian communities such as Marathas, Kunbis, Malis, Mahars, etc., the marriage of a brother's daughter with a sister's son is common. Among some tribes and castes of Andhra Pradesh, Desastha Brahmans of Maharashtra, as well as among some Tulu speaking communities of coastal Karnataka such as the Bunts (also known as Shetty community which is a peasant community), Billavas (weaver community), and the Maraveers (fishing community), a man is considered to have a preferential right to marry his cousin or his sister's daughter. It is a right of first refusal, but some castes consider it improper for him to refuse. Murias and Bhils of north and central India also practice cross-cousin marriage.

A distinction is made between cross-cousins and parallel-cousins. While cross-cousin marriages are preferred, parallel-cousin marriages are prohibited and come within the incest taboo. First-cousins related through one's paternal uncle or maternal aunt are parallel cousins. Sons and daughters of a maternal uncle or a paternal aunt are cross-cousins. These are of three different categories, bilateral, patrilateral or matrilateral. The mother's brother's daughter is matrilateral cross-cousin and the father's sister's daughter is a patrilateral cross-cousin. While some communities adopt the pattern of bilateral cross cousin marriages, others may prescribe either patrilateral or matrilateral and proscribe the other. The cross-cousin and uncle-niece marriages, which are common in south India, are prohibited among the upper castes of north India (Trautmann 1981).

An important aspect of these cross-cousin or uncle-niece marriages was that the girl was familiar to the custom and culture of the family she was marrying into. In many instances, her mother-in-law would also be her aunt or her grand mother. The girl never left the familiar surroundings of her matrilineal family and would have easy access to her own natal family. In fact, there would an overlap between her natal and marital relatives. This provided a more secure setting than the alien and unfamiliar environment of a marriage outside the gotra or the village. Since marriages were contracted within the family, these communities also did not practice the custom of dowry.

The south Indian, predominantly Dravidian, regions followed various pro-women practices of property inheritance even under smriti law. One indication of this is the liberal construction of stridhana under the Bombay and Madras schools. There were also several other lesser known local customs and practices prevalent in this region. For instance, there are many references to women and their use of property in inscriptions in Tamil Nadu which can be traced back to the thirteenth and fourteenth centuries. These inscriptions indicate that the ownership

rights of women included the power of alienation through gifts and sales (Mukund 1992: WS3).

A custom of handing over a piece of land to the daughter at the time of her marriage prevailed within the Madras Presidency. The income from this land was meant for the woman's exclusive use. This was her stridhana and devolved upon the female heirs and passed from mother to daughter. Known as *manjal kani*, the land was perhaps meant to provide an independent income to the daughter, which would be sufficient to provide for her personal expenses—*manjal* (turmeric) and *kumkum* (vermilion)—while in her husband's house (Mukund 1992: WS5). A similar custom of providing a piece of land for the daughter's personal expenses also prevailed in the Maratha region of Bombay Presidency by the name *bangdi-choli* (which literally means bangles and blouse).[252] A woman's right to one-third of her husband's property upon her husband's remarriage was also recognized within certain lower castes of Madras Presidency and was termed as *patnibhagam*.[253]

Among some castes in coastal Andhra Pradesh, a custom of giving land to the daughter at the time of her marriage prevailed. This was known as *katnām* (Upadhya 1990: 38–42). In another study of *Virasaiva* women from Karnataka, it was observed that 12 per cent of the women inherited property in the form of land from their mother and this property customarily passed on only to daughters, even when boys did not inherit from their fathers (Mullati 1986). The Lingayat women of the Dharwar region, who were categorized as *sudras*

---

[252] See the decision in *Yadeorao Jogeshwar* v. *Vithal Shamaji*, AIR 1952 Nag 55, where a reference to this custom is made.

[253] This principle was upheld in *Palaniappa Chetiar* v. *Alaganchetti*, (1921) 48 IA 539.

in various judicial pronouncements, also had rights of divorce, remarriage, and property ownership. An illegitimate son was recognized as an heir, which is a marker of the status enjoyed by women in informal alliances. Buddhist literature also indicates that women could own and gift property in their own right (Talim 1972).

Marriages among the various lower castes were less sacramental and more contractual. The ritual of *saptapadi* (seven steps round the sacrificial fire, which is essentially a Brahminical ritual) or kanyadan (*kanya*–daughter, *dan*–gift)[254] did not prevail among these communities. Child marriages were not the norm. Marriages were based on the consent of adult women and the rituals and ceremonies reflected this element of consent and contract.

The most striking differences from the Brahminical notions of marriage and relationships were found amongst the tribal communities in India. Almost all tribes had a system of separate dormitories for unmarried men and women of a certain age, such as the *rangbarang*, *daa saala*, etc. These were places for cultural transmission and learning of myths, taboos, songs, and dance. Free interaction between the sexes was encouraged without restrictions. Anthropologist Verrier Elwin, who lived among the Murias of Bastar in southeastern Madhya Pradesh, described the life in a dormitory (*ghotul*), where young men and women could share friendship as well as physical intimacy for a number of years (Elwin 1964). Ultimately, their parents would arrange their marriages, usually with cross-cousins and the delights of teenage romance were replaced with the serious responsibilities of adulthood. In his survey of

some two thousand marriages, Elwin found only seventy-seven cases of ghotul partners eloping together and very few cases of divorce. In such a system, there was no premium placed on virginity or the purity of women and neither were marriages seen as sacred alliances.

A careful scrutiny of the contemporary customs of various castes reveals that different customary forms of divorce and remarriage are prevailing within these communities, even to the present day. In the Deccan (Maratha) and Gujarat regions, such practices are termed as *kadi mod* (literally, breaking of a twig, symbolizing the termination of the relationship) or *chhod chittee* (deed of divorcement drawn up by community or family elders after breaking the auspicious black bead chain, which is a symbol of marriage for the woman). This custom is also referred to as *chor chitte* or *chutta cheda*. If the process is initiated by the woman, either she or her father would have to return the bride price and also a part of the marriage expenses.[255] Normally, the mother is given the custody of her younger children, while the father retains the custody over older children and is under an obligation to bear their marriage expenses. The remarriage of widows and divorcees was also practiced among these communities and the term used for these marriages was *pat* marriages (Maharashtra) and *Natra* marriages (Gujarat). Several contemporary judgments make a reference to these practices of customary divorce

---

[254] Giving away the daughter as a gift to the bridegroom at marriage. The term *dan* was used usually for gifts made to Brahmins.

[255] The recording of customs of the Deccan and Gujarat region by Steele and Borradaile during 1820–30 provides ample proof of these practices. The fact that these customs still prevail among the lower castes was confirmed during various legal workshops in the Padra, Vagoria, and Daboi districts, organised by the Mahila Samakhya, Gujarat, which were coordinated by the author during the years 1996 and 1997. Women from various lower castes—Vankar, Baria, Vasava, Ratodia, Chamar, and Rohit—participated in the workshops.

and subsequent remarriage.[256] The prohibition of divorce and remarriages of widows and divorcees prevailed only among communities which emulated the Brahmins in order to rise up the social ladder. As a community progressed economically, it took on Brahminical practices and exercised a stricter sexual control upon its women (Srinivas 1998: 146–7).

Among various castes and tribes along the Malabar Coast, there were women headed joint family households and matrilineal inheritance patterns.[257] Of these, the *marumakkathayam* and *aliyasanthana* received judicial recognition during the British period. These systems were in existence until recently and were brought to an end through specific state intervention in the form of legislations in the post-Independence period.[258] Under these systems, specifically amongst the Nairs, women contracted loose marriage alliances which were called *sambandham* (literal meaning, relationships) which would be easily terminated with the consent of the parties.[259] The basis of the family system was the matrilineal *tharavad* which comprised a central woman character, her sisters, daughters, and sons. Though the husband in a position of authority was missing, the effective control of the *tharavad* and its property vested with the mother's brother. Even though the control remained in male hands, since property devolved along the female line, there was no premium on the sexual purity of women (Gough 1989). The Malabar Marriage Act, 1896, clearly shows the manner in which legal interventions in the colonial period prepared the ground for the later development of patrilocality and the development of the patrilineal individual family.

Similar matrilineal systems were, and still remain, prevalent amongst the Garos and Khasis of Meghalaya. In Garo society, the tribe is divided into *phratries*, which are further divided into many *sibs*. These sibs and phratries are matrilineal. Each married couple chooses one daughter to become the heiress of the household and property. (The heiress need not be the youngest daughter, though usually the youngest one is chosen.) The heiress and her husband are expected to care for the old couple as long as they live. The young couple resides in the house, and after the death of the elder couple, the chosen daughter becomes the head of the family (Majumdar 1978).

In Khasi society, descent is matrilineal; a person is a member of his or her own matrilineage from birth. Khasis follow a matrilineal system of inheritance. While among the Garos there is a choice as to which daughter can be appointed an heiress, among the Khasis there is no choice and only the youngest daughter, or the *Ka Khadduh*, who is eligible to inherit the ancestral property. If Ka Khadduh dies without any daughter surviving her, her next elder sister inherits the ancestral property, and after her, the youngest daughter of that sister. Failing all daughters and their female issues, the property goes back to the mother's sister, mother's sister's daughter, and so on.

A distinction can be made between the north Indian upper castes and lower castes through the

---

[256] See the decisions in *Rameshchandra Daga* v. *Rameshwari Daga*, I (2005) DMC 1 SC; *Pushpabai* v. *Pratap Singh*, I (2001) DMC 110 MP; *Parikshat* v. *State of UP*, I (2007) DMC 798 All; and *Parmanand* v. *Jagrani*, AIR 2007 MP 242. These cases are discussed in detail in Chapter 2 in the second volume.

[257] According to Mayne, *marummakkathayam* was practised by the Warriers, Unnis, Padvals, Chakkiars, Thiyas, Nambiars (Brahmin), and Mopillas (Muslim). The *aliyasanthana* was prevalent in south Kanara region, among the Billavas, Bunts, Maraveers, etc. (Kuppuswami 1993: 1209).

[258] The Hindu Succession Act, 1956 and the Kerala Joint Hindu Family System (Abolition) Act, 1975.

[259] Through the Malabar Marriage Act, 1896, sambandham marriages were granted legal recognition.

practice of bride price. Women from the lower castes worked and contributed to the household and hence were not totally dependent on their men. Lower castes practiced the custom of bride price (*kanya sulka*) where the father of the girl had to be compensated for the loss he suffered by the marriage of his daughter. This custom was followed by several castes in south India, the northern Himalayan regions, and various tribes right up to the pre-Independence period (Srinivas 1962). Even today, it is widespread amongst the Ho, Santhal, Jharia, Oraon, and other tribes of the central Indian belt and in some tribes of the North-Eastern belt. Marriage by purchase and marriage by service are accepted ways of finding a bride. The amount of bride price varies according to the economic conditions of tribe. In some tribes, a suitor who is not able to pay the bride price is asked to work under the father-in-law's house till his final payment.

The main aim of Brahminical law and ritual was to maintain caste purity through a very strict control over women and their sexuality. Since women of the lower castes were relatively free from these notions of purity and pollution, they were governed by a relatively lenient code of sexual morality and held a slightly higher social status. The lower castes or sudras were considered to be out of the *varnā* system and hence were not governed by the smriti code. The code was applicable only to *dwijas* or the twice born (upper castes) who had the sanction to study the sacred texts (Srinivas 1962).

From the above discussion, it becomes evident that among the lower castes and tribes in the Dravidian South, the North East and also Central India a strict sexual code did not prevail as compared to the strict sexual morality prevailing among the higher castes of North India. Correspondingly, there was a wider scope for negotiating women's rights of divorce, remarriage and property ownership among them. ·

Customary Law Versus Textual Law

Local customs were held in high esteem under the smritis and were acknowledged as an important source of law.[260] The high status awarded to custom made Hindu law plural and Hindu society amorphous. Despite the claims of divine origin, smriti law was based on local and well-established customs (Diwan and Diwan 1993: 19). According to Mulla, the importance attached to the law creating efficacy of custom in Hindu jurisprudence was so great that the exponents of law were unanimous in accepting custom as a constituent part of law (Desai 1994: 2). Bhattacharjee has extended this reasoning further and has made a highly provocative comment that smritis and commentaries were mere recordings of existing customs (Bhattacharjee 1994: 12–39).

While Manu, Yagnavalkya, and Katyayana recognized the role of custom, a later smritikar, Brihispati, exalted local, tribal, and family usages and laid down that time honoured institutions of each country, caste, and family should be preserved intact.[261] Narada went further and proclaimed that custom overrides the sacred law. In addition, there were several castes and communities who were not governed by the Brahminical smriti law, but by their own customary law. For these communities, custom was the sole source of law.

The status awarded to custom under the Hindu law was far greater and its application far wider than the Roman (and subsequently

---

[260] The importance of custom as a source of ancient Hind law has been discussed earlier in the introduction to this chapter.

[261] The famous quote of Brihaspati regarding the importance of custom: '*Deshe deshe ya acharah paramparayakramagateh; Sa shastrarthabalavanaiva langhaniyah kadhachava*' [Brihaspati. II. 18 as cited in *Mayne's Treatise on Hindu Law* (Kuppuswami 1991: 45)].

English) legal maxim *Lex Loci* (Law of the land). The relationship between positive law with its scriptural origin and the originally unwritten law, which we call 'custom', was subtle and complicated. The British and the French appreciated the distinction between these two sources of law to a certain extent but failed to provide a full juridical discussion of the relationship between the two (Derret 1999: 148).

Derrett comments that the scriptures turned a blind eye to the customs of non-Aryan peoples, which awarded a high social status and independent capacity to women as known in various parts of the peninsula. The *shastric* requirements for a valid marriage—virginity, avoidance of prohibited degrees, compliance with grounds before the supercession of an existing wife—were not practiced by large communities. While the shastra viewed the husband as the virtual owner of his wife and children, customs gave the married couple equal rights in matrimonial property. A custom, which was wide spread in south India, but not confined only to this region, allowed a wife and a widow to alienate property, even that which was inherited from a male owner, without the consent of near relatives of the husband. It also restricted the son's freedom in respect of his deceased father's property while his widow or widows survived. Remarriage of widows, anathema to the shastra, was common among these communities.

The Aryan rule that the father had an absolute right in the person and property of his son was much diluted, even in the shastra, by the growing rights, under the influence of customs. South India retained its customary concern for the 'rights' of sons and other male relatives to supervise dealings in property, and the consent of many relatives had to be obtained prior to any dealings in property contrary to the scriptures

(Derrett 1999: 205–6). Further, according to Derrett, 'the sudra's dasiputra, the favoured illegitimate son, is usually supposed to have been a pre-Aryan customary heir, retained with reluctance by the sastra'[262] (*ibid.*: 210).

During the early colonial period, there was a tendency to view Hindu society as homogeneous and hence to strictly adhere to the textual scriptures and ignore traditional customary practices. This led to the extension of shastric laws to communities that had previously been regulated by their own local customs. Several customary practices, which had previously been recognized even by Hindu laws, were de-legitimized in this period. One important area of this de-recognition concerned women. There were several instances of lower caste widows being denied their customary rights of property inheritance upon remarriage due to the erroneous interpretation by British judges of the role of custom in Hindu society.[263]

This position began to be modified during the later half of the nineteenth century. The turning point was the decision of the Privy Council in *Collector of Madura* v. *Moottoo Ramalinga*,[264] which laid down, 'clear proof of usage will outweigh the written text of law'. If the antiquity of a custom and its continuous usage by a community could be proved, it could override the stipulation in a written text. Customary rights were recognised in 1872, when the Indian Evidence Act was enacted.

---

[262] The term dasiputra literally means the son of a slave. The term was also applied to the son of a concubine. Though the right of this illegitimate son was not equal to that of the legitimate son, smriti law awarded a recognition to him regarding inheritance of property and maintenance.

[263] See the discussion on the Widow Remarriage Act, 1856 earlier in this chapter.

[264] (1868) 12 MIA 397

Section 13 of the Act dealt with the facts relevant for the proof of customary law. However, there was no attempt to codify such customary laws. The existence of customary rights was dependant upon the judicial recognition of such right as a pre-existing, valid custom. The broad parameters for validating a custom were antiquity, continuity, uniformity, and certainty. In addition, a custom had to be not unreasonable, immoral, or opposed to public policy or law.

But despite this renewed averment, according to Derrett, the British period saw the elimination of a great many customs diverging from Anglo-Hindu law because the standard of proof required were very strict. Unless the preferred customs were shown to be ancient, invariable, certain, obligatory, reasonable, and not against public policy, it had a very slight chance of being recognized. In this manner, Anglo-Hindu law, with its dharmashastra background, spread more widely during the colonial period than it had ever before (Derrett 1957: 78). The only customs which have, on a wide scale, escaped this steam roller of uniformity were those which were specially gathered for the benefit of agricultural classes in the Punjab (Oldenburg: 2002). The Malabar statute also provides an example of customary law being saved from the crushing effect of the presumption in favour of Hindu law (Derrett 1957: 78). But even there, Mitakshara was applied when the statutes was silent.

The legal maxim, 'justice, equity and good conscience', was used to determine 'reasonableness' and 'public morality'. Immorality and public policy became convenient sticks to beat women with and deny them their crucial customary rights. One such instance, where denial of rights occurred in the name of public policy, was in the case of women from the dancing communities. The *Devadasis* (temple dancing girls) and *naikins* were first classified as prostitutes and then they were denied the right of inheritance as well as the right of adoption, custody, and guardianship over their children. The custom amongst them of adopting daughters was invalidated by the Bombay High Court in *Mathura Naikin* v. *Esu*[265] on the ground that such a custom is opposed to morality and public policy. This ruling was followed by the Madras and Bombay High Courts in later years.[266] In one of these cases, *Gasito* v. *Umrao Jan*,[267] where the rights of a Muslim dancing girl were concerned, the Privy Council upheld the view that the custom of adoption of daughters by a woman of the prostitute class or her family aims at the continuance of prostitution as a family business and that it has a distinctly immoral tendency and should not be enforced in courts of justice.

The Madras High Court, in *Kalavagunta Venkata Kristnayya* v. *Kalavagunta Venkatachalam*,[268] invalidated the custom of bride price which was followed by several lower castes. But the custom of payment to the groom (*vara dakshina* or in modern terms, dowry) which was followed by the higher castes was validated.[269]

In subsequent years, the courts attempted to formulate a more rational legal framework in which customary rights could be integrated. In the absence of guidance from any substantial legislative law, it was left to the courts to develop customary laws as a new branch of civil law.

---

[265] ILR (1880) Bom 545
[266] *Venku* v. *Mahaling*, ILR (1880) Mad 393 ; *Hira* v. *Radha*, ILR (1913) Bom 116, and *Gasito* v. *Umrao Jan*, ILR (1894) Cal 1499.
[267] ILR (1894) Cal 1499
[268] ILR (1908) 32 Mad 185
[269] See the decisions in *Jagdishwar Prasad* v. *Sheo Baksh Rai*, AIR 1919 All 248 and *Dharmdhar* v. *Kanhji Sahay*, AIR 1949 Pat 250.

Box 1.5   Validity of Custom under the Hindu Marriage Act

Section 5—Conditions for Hindu Marriage: A marriage may be solemnized between any two Hindus, if the following conditions are fulfilled, namely:-

(iv) the parties are not within the degrees of prohibited relationship *unless the custom or usage* governing each of them permits of a marriage between the two;

(v) the parties are not sapindas of each other, *unless the custom or usage governing each of them* permits of a marriage between the two.

Section 7—Ceremonies for a Hindu Marriage:

(1) A Hindu marriage may be solemnized *in accordance with the customary rites* and ceremonies of either party therto.

Section 29—Savings:

(2) Nothing contained in this Act shall be deemed to *affect any right recognized by custom* or conferred by any special enactment to obtain the dissolution of a Hindu marriage, whether solemnized before or after the commencement of this Act.

In the post-Independence period, the Constitution of India provided validity to customary practices. Article 13 of the Constitution treats customary law at par with other branches of civil law. A custom or usage, if proved, would be 'law in force' under this Article. Courts can take judicial notice of these customary rights, which have the force of law, under Section 57 of the Indian Evidence Act, 1872.

'Custom' Under Codified Hindu Law and the Constitution

The Hindu Law Reforms of the fifties did not introduce any principle which had not already existed somewhere in India. Despite this, they were projected as a vehicle for ushering in Western modernity. There were, however, several liberal customary practices which were discarded by the Hindu code for the sake of uniformity. In their stated determination to put an end to the growth of custom, the reformers were in fact putting an end to the essence of Hindu law, and yet persisted in calling the codification 'Hindu'.

Despite this attempt to assimilate the Hindu scriptural law with the modern English matrimonial law, deep rooted customary practices could not be completely eradicated even when they were contradictory to both Hindu scriptural law as well as the English law. So one can observe that even within the codified Hindu Marriage Act of 1955, the spaces for validating local customs are left wide open. For instance, a Hindu could marry the person of his/her choice, over-riding the constraints of consanguinity and affinity stipulated under the Hindu Marriage Act, perform ceremonies of marriage as per the custom and also obtain a divorce under customary practices through non-state legal fora.

Contrary to popular perceptions, denying customary laws in favour of statutory law has not always been beneficial to women as the cases discussed below reveal.

In a case decided by the Himachal Pradesh High Court, *Rattan Devi* v. *Padam Singh*,[270] a

---

[270] 1981 CriLJ 1422

non-tribal man married a tribal woman according to tribal customs. While a bigamous marriage is invalid under Hindu law, according to the custom of the community to which the wife belonged, bigamy was accepted and her marriage was valid. Later, the husband abandoned the wife and the wife filed for maintenance under Section 125 of the Cr.PC. Her claim for maintenance was rejected by both the sessions court as well as the high court as the courts held that the validity of the marriage would have to be decided by the law applicable to non-tribals, that is, the Hindu Marriage Act. Since bigamy is not recognized, the court held that the marriage between a woman, who is the second wife, and a man whose first marriage was subsisting, is invalid. Even while agreeing that the principle governing the provision of Section 125 Cr.PC was to give summary relief to prevent vagrancy and destitution among abandoned wives, the courts rejected the tribal wife's claim to maintenance.

The second case, decided by the Orissa High Court, *Anupama Pradhan v. Sultan Pradhan*[271] is in contrast to the first. Here too the wife had filed for maintenance. In response, the husband pleaded that since the woman was his second wife, he was not obliged to pay her maintenance. To protect the woman's right, the court took recourse to uncodified Hindu law and held that since the couple is governed by ancient Hindu law (which permits bigamy) and not by the reformed code, the second wife is entitled to maintenance.

The case of Jordan Deigdeh[272] is another instance of a statutory provision discriminating against a tribal woman. A non-tribal Christian married a Christian woman from the Khasi tribe of Meghalaya. Under the tribal law, she could have divorced her husband alleging any fault ground. Under statutory law applicable to Christians at that time, the grounds of divorce were extremely discriminatory against women. Faced with this problem, Chinnappa Reddy J. of the Supreme Court berated the legislature and the State for not introducing changes in divorce laws applicable to Christians but declined to grant any relief to the women concerned.

According to legal scholars Lotika Sarkar and B. Sivaramayya, 'an obsession with statutory laws even on the part of activist judges is clearly visible', even when the statute is discriminatory against women and customary laws would provide a remedy which is beneficial to women (Sarkar and Sivaramayya 1994: 11).

To deal with the conflict between statutory law and customary practices, some scholars have suggested that judicial discretion should be used to inquire and uphold customary law, giving it precedence over textual or/and statutory law wherever it is found to be advantageous to women. It could be treated as a measure of protective discrimination in favour of a weaker section in society, that is, women (Agrawala and Ramanamma 1994: 248–68).

Inheritance Rights Under Tribal Customs

The Constitution has placed special importance on customary laws of tribal communities in the North, East. Article 244, read with the Sixth Schedule, provides for a unique system of district administration in the tribal areas in the States of Assam, Meghalaya, Tripura, and Mizoram. Under this system, certain areas are designated as autonomous districts. If there are a number of Scheduled Tribes in an autonomous district, then the area of each tribe is designated as an autonomous region.

[271] 1991 Cri.LJ 3216 Ori
[272] *Jordan Deigdeh v. S.S. Chopra*, AIR 1985 SC 935.

Each autonomous district and region has a district and regional council respectively. These councils have wide ranging powers, including the right to allot land, regulate money lending activities, manage forest lands, use of water resources, etc. Amongst these rights are included the right to make laws with respect to:

1. Inheritance of property
2. Marriage and divorce
3. Social customs

The regional council is superior and the district council only has those powers that are delegated to it by the former. This safeguards the laws of the tribal areas as a whole and also ensures that customary laws of each tribe are respected. There is no scope for the customs of a weaker tribe to be subsumed by the usages or customs of a stronger one.

The authority of the councils also extends to the administration of justice in the designated regions. Other than some disputes that are specifically entrusted to the courts by the Governor, all other disputes, including those related to marriage, divorce, inheritance, etc., are decided by the councils.

The general assumption is that the customary practices of tribal communities must necessarily be favourable to women, but there are several customs followed by tribes and castes, particularly in the realm of marriage and inheritance which discriminate against women. For instance, among some tribal communities, women do not have inheritance rights. Under some customary practices, if a tribal woman marries a non-tribal, she is not entitled to inherit. This rule is observed to save tribal land from usurpation by non-tribals or 'outsiders'.

A leading case where tribal law came into conflict with the constitutional provision of equality and non-discrimination is *Madhu Kishwar* v.

State of Bihar.[273] The public interest litigation challenging the validity of Sections 7 and 8 of the Chhota Nagpur Tenancy Act 1908, which confines succession of property to the male line, was filed on behalf of women members of the Ho and Oraon tribes of Bihar. Since the provision discriminates against women, it was contended that it was *ultra vires* of Article 14 of the Constitution. The court opined that as citizens of the country, female members of these tribes were entitled to the guarantees of the Constitution. But instead of deciding the case on merit, the court directed the State of Bihar to explore the possibility of permitting inheritance by women while regulating it in a way that limits the property going out of the family. The majority judgment however upheld the validity of the legislation on the ground that it was in accordance with the custom of inheritance/succession of the Scheduled Tribes. However, the dissenting judgment, K. Rama Swamy J. held that the law made a gender-based discrimination and violated Articles 15, 16 and 21 of the Constitution of India. The learned Judge observed:

Legislative and executive actions must be in confirmation of the fundamental rights guaranteed in Part III and the directive principles enshrined in Part IV and the Preamble of the Constitution which constitute the conscience of the Constitution. Covenants of the United Nations add impetus and urgency to eliminate gender-based obstacles and discrimination. Legislative action should be devised suitably to constitute economic empowerment of women in socio-economic restructure for establishing egalitarian social order. Law is an instrument of social change as well as the defender of social change. Article 2(e) of CEDAW[274]

[273] (1996) 5 SCC 125
[274] The Vienna Convention on the Elimination of All Forms of Discrimination Against Women, which was adopted by the United Nations on 18 December 1979 and which was ratified by the Government of India on 19 June 1993.

enjoins this Court to breathe life into the dry bones of the Constitution, international conventions and the Protection of Human Rights Act, to prevent gender-based discrimination and to effectuate right to life including empowerment of economic, social and cultural rights.

The above judgment brings to the fore the tension between religion based personal laws as well as customary laws and constitutional provisions of equality and non-discrimination, particularly in the context of the mandate of Article 44—enactment of a uniform civil code.

There is a tendency, even among social activists and women's groups, to be extremely critical of all customary laws, to exalt statutory enactments, and to constantly campaign for codification and legislations, even while the experience on the ground is that courts and statutes are also equally patriarchal and discriminatory against women. Regarding the demand for codification of tribal laws, Nandita Haksar, a human rights lawyer, contends that the demand is not made by people but by administrators since it is administratively convenient and empowers the state (Haksar 1996: 39). Codification of tribal laws will only enhance the power of the state over indigenous people and impose a totally alien legal system on them. Though tribal societies are patriarchal, there is a difference between patriarchal customary law and patriarchal statutory law and it is wrong to assume that customary law has existed unchanged from time immemorial, without any state intervention. The strength of customary law is that it adapts to the changing needs of a society. Many tribal communities, especially in the North-East, have modified their customary practices. For instance, within the Naga communities, village panchayats had no women representatives. A few years ago, through the initiatives of women, the panchayats passed a resolution admitting women. Codification of

tribal laws will not necessarily improve the status of women within tribal societies. On the contrary, it will pit women against the community, just as it pitted Shah Bano[275] against hers and will prove to be divisive. It will break up common property, the basis of tribal society. Democracy is strengthened by legal pluralism. The demand for unification and codification is undemocratic and anti people (Haksar 1996: 39).[276]

CONCLUSION

Through a historical analyses of personal laws governing various communities and religious denominations, this chapter has attempted to evolve an intersectional framework of women's rights in India.

The realm of personal laws or family laws is an important arena of intervention for women, as it serves to determine their status and their rights. Their engagement with family law is far more dynamic than their engagement with other branches of law (Parashar 1992). This is because while other laws deal with 'public' affairs of state and civil society such as law and order, crime and punishment, trade contracts and property transactions, personal laws deal with the 'private' or 'personal' domain of the family which forms the women's universe. Their negotiations in the public sphere are influenced and shaped by the codes set within the 'private' domain of marriage and family (Okin 1989). Their status in society gets defined through these relationships. It is not that these aspects don't affect men, they do. But for men, the public aspects of civil society have greater significance and hence, the 'personal' does not

---

[275] The reference here is to *Mohd. Ahmad Khan* v. *Shahbano Begum*, AIR 1985 SC 945. The judgment and its aftermath is discussed in 'Communalizing the demand for UCC' in Chapter 2.

[276] The contesting claims of legal universality versus legal pluralism are dealt with in Chapter 2.

constitute their entire universe. Theories of state and civil society are evolved keeping in view men's involvement in the public domain of civil life, ignoring the 'private' which constitutes the women's universe (Pateman 1988 and Roy 2005). It has been an uphill task for women to break the boundaries of the 'personal' to enter into the domain of the 'public' or the political. It is in this context, the slogan, 'personal is political' was coined within the women's movement. Hence the 'personal' aspects of the family relationships need to be examined within the paradigm of the 'political'.

The family laws evolved in the context of the socio-political and economic demands of their times and were the means through which social relationships could be regulated. While evolving the codes, the sanction of the 'divine' had to be invoked for greater validity. The social codes could be made binding only with divine sanction keeping in view the context of the community. In keeping with the norms of a patriarchal social order, despite their diverse origins, across religious boundaries, the personal laws are inscribed with patriarchal norms. Women had to struggle against these normative dictates in order to render these relationships more egalitarian.

As we trace the origin and developments of various personal laws, the similarities between them are striking. Though most personal laws claim a divine origin as 'revealed law', their development has been solely through human interventions. Law is not static and moves with the times. Legal principles are adapted to social norms and are evolved to suit the demands of a particular era. There is a dynamic interaction between the legal order and social processes (Cotterrell 2006: 29–30). While tracing the history of personal laws, an attempt has been made to contextualize them within this broader framework.

The transition from a feudal agrarian society, to an urban capitalistic economic order, patterns of trade, commerce and migrations, British influence brought in through colonialism, the dynamics of the post-colonialism independent nation-state governed by a modern constitution, the international human rights conventions–these various processes have impacted the realm of the personal laws. But at the same time, when group or community identities are threatened, personal laws become a marker of identity and their immutability is invoked.

While we examine the rights of women located within personal laws, it is revealing to note that the history of women's rights is not linear—with religious and customary laws forming one end of the scale and statutory reforms slowly and steadily progressing towards the other end—as it is popularly believed. The history is complex with various interactive forces constantly at play. Women's rights are not only constrained by a uniform set of patriarchal norms but are also shaped by several social processes and these locations contribute to framing their rights.

For instance, the rights of Hindu women need to be examined in the context of the caste system of the Hindu society. A social structure determined by caste hierarchies, necessitates relocation of women's rights within this hierarchy. Women situated within the higher strata of the caste structure were governed by a strict code of sexual control to maintain caste purity and secure property devolution through legitimate children. Women of the lower castes were out of the varna system prescribed by Manu and hence, the smriti code of sexual morality did not apply to them. As wage earners, these women contributed to the household. The patriarchal control of men in matrimonial relationships was lax and women had greater freedom of divorce and remarriage. The labour and sexuality of these women, as well as the labour of their men, was at the disposal of the higher castes and the seat of oppression was located within this social hierarchy. Most marginalised communities did not own property and hence the issue of being maintained from family property and resources was not relevant. The concept of maintenance envisages a non-working, dependent woman—a description that did not fit the working class woman.

The social norms were regulated through interventions of local caste, community, or village elders. Since most communities were patriarchal, a clear patriarchal bias permeates various customary regulations and practices. Yet it would be incorrect to presume that women had no status and no rights within these communities. Within pluralistic legal traditions it would also be incorrect to presume that patriarchies operated with equal rigour in enforcing anti-women practices among all communities. There were spaces within customary traditions for women to negotiate their rights to a certain extent.

It is generally projected that the interventions by the colonial state in the realm of family law were meant primarily for the liberation of Indian woman from the barbaric customs of sati, female infanticide, and marital rape of infant brides. There is also a misconception that the right to ownership of property came from the West and was ushered in through colonial interventions as a modernizing mission. But this premise overlooks the fact that Roman law as well as English common law contained several anti-women biases. These biases crept into India through Anglo-Saxon jurisprudence and subverted the traditional legal systems which provided women with a certain measure of economic security. Traditional systems were remoulded into linear, formal, and stringent structures, which exercised greater patriarchal control over women and their right to property.

Changes brought about in land tenure in regions such as Punjab and Kerala also contributed to a consolidation of male power and denial of traditional and customary rights to women.

Colonial interventions facilitated the construction of distinct and mutually hostile religious communities of Hindus and Muslims, to be governed by their respective personal laws along the model of the canon law. The basis of the legal system was the ancient scriptures translated with a Western mind set. These scriptures were never meant to be used as rigid legal principles of an adversarial legal system. The translated texts drastically changed the nature and character of customary and scriptural Hindu law and Hindu woman's right to property suffered a severe set back. In the process of streamlining a pluralistic society, several customary rights of women were crushed as they could not meet the legal requirements set by the British courts to prove a custom. Ironically, the character of the communities was fixed and the mutually exclusive communities of Hindus and Muslims were constructed through litigation over property disputes.

The restructuring of the easily accessible non-state, judicial fora, dispensing quick redressal through community based interventions, into an alien model of English courts, rendered justice adversarial, expensive, and dilatory. Within a system of hierarchy of courts, the decisions of the Privy Council became binding principles of law and the process of evolving laws at the local level to suit the needs of local communities was arrested. Concepts of justice, equity, and good conscience became direct channels of introducing English laws, principles, and puritanical notions of morality into India. The new legal order created a new set of problems for women while accessing justice within alien structures.

As compared to other realms of revealed laws (Hindu, Christian, Parsi and Jewish), in its conception, Islamic jurisprudence was far more progressive. Much before the notion of 'contract' began to dominate public discourse in Europe through theories of social contract, Islamic law viewed marriages as dissoluble contracts. Within this framework, it was possible to introduce ingredients of consent, conditions and dissolution. In addition, the stipulation of a predetermined amount as mehr to provide future security to the wife was an essential ingredient of the marriage contract. Stipulation of high mehr amounts was meant to act as a deterrent on the husband's power of arbitrary divorce.

The legal premise of contractual marriages, dispute resolution through mediation, and the breakdown theory of marriage, all of which were part of the Muslim law of marriage, are considered to be progressive principles of matrimonial law in contemporary times. But since this law differed a great deal from the sacramental marriages of native Hindus as well as European Christians, it came to be projected as archaic, obscurantist and anti-women and Muslim marriages came to be viewed as loose sexual unions devoid of rights which could be easily dissolved, as compared to the sacramental nature of Christian and Hindu marriages. This notion served to tip the balance in favour of men, and Muslim women were stripped of the safeguards which the Quranic law had provided them. Ironically, during the same period, English women were campaigning for transformation of their marriages from the notion of an indissoluble sacrament to a dissoluble contact.

There were several religious communities which did not fit the legal binary of Hindu and Muslim—Parsis, indigenous Christians, the Jewish people etc. Since there was no separate law to govern them, English legal principles were applied to them, which led to a great deal of discontent within these communities. The Parsis successfully campaigned for a separate law of marriage, divorce, and property rights. The situation of Jews was difficult and they continued to be governed by the general principles of English civil law. Indigenous Christians were governed by the principles of English law, local customs, and religious dictates of canon law. Within these contradictory pulls, Christians had to struggle for well over a century, to rid themselves of the archaic principles of Victorian morality which they were saddled with for well over a century.

While the nationalist struggle helped to foreground women's rights within the family, there was also a political undercurrent that was palpable. The aim of the two legislations enacted in 1937, the Hindu Married Women's Right to Property Act and the Application of Shariat Act was to restore property rights subverted through the legal precedents set by the Privy Council. But there was also an underlying motive of structuring communities around their religious identities.

Independence brought an end to the colonial era. The new constitution with its mandate of equality and social justice, brought in visions of gender justice. But the other major political event of this time, the partition of the composite British India into two nations brought in its wake unprecedented violence and served to create an insecure minority for whom the personal laws became an important marker of their identity. In this context while it became imperative to reform the family laws of the majority Hindu community through state intervention, bringing reforms within laws governing minority communities became an extremely tenuous task which had to be dealt with cautiously.

Restructuring of feudal family laws to suit the needs of women within a modern democracy was the challenge before the newly independent state while reforming Hindu family laws. But the much trumpeted Hindu law reforms of the post-Independence period were concerned more with homogenizing the culturally diverse Hindu communities through a uniform set of state regulated enactments than widening the sphere of women's rights. Hence crucial women's rights located within diverse customary laws were compromised. The enactments turned out to be a curious mixture of English law and shastric law, with the worst biases of both written into them.

The highly contested right of inheritance was subverted by surreptitiously granting Hindu men the right to will away property. The protective restraint against bequests under Islamic law to safeguard women's rights did not find a place in the codified Hindu law since it was remoulded on the English model of exclusive and absolute rights to the individual. To facilitate the transformation of the economic system from feudalism to capitalism, it was crucial that property be alienable in the hands of individual men. Inalienable and immovable property could now be converted into liquid and negotiable capital. Within this new economic order, women's rights of maintenance and inheritance became transient and illusory.

Traditionally, the Hindu woman had a distinct economic right called stridhana. The definition of stridhana, its changing character during various phases of a woman's life, the woman's power of disposal over it, etc., had been the subject of elaborate discussions under smriti law. The commentators of the post-smriti period were engaged in widening its scope and strengthening its base and yet, while restructuring the traditional sacramental form of marriage into a dissoluble contract and bestowing upon the Hindu woman a new status of a divorcee, the character of her stridhana and control over it during this new phase of life, did not find a

mention in the Hindu Marriage Act. This is perhaps due to the fact that most nationalist leaders were advocates trained in English law, which they held as a model for reform within family laws. They had imbibed the colonial contempt for non-state, pluralistic legal systems. So the Hindu Marriage Act turned out to be a poor imitation of the English Matrimonial Causes Act. Based on the legal premise of formal equality, the codified Hindu law of marriage and divorce was stripped of all its protective measures. Even the traditional right of maintenance was now extended to husbands, a concept unheard of under either scriptural or customary Hindu law.

The end of the colonial era affected other minority communities in various ways. The insecurity among the Jewish community resulted in a mass exodus and Jewish personal laws lost their significance. The Parsi community lost the political patronage which they enjoyed during the British period and had to remould itself in the context of the Hindu majority and their personal laws followed closely the reforms within Hindu laws. However, they continued to view their personal laws as important markers of their identity even while bringing in changes within them. In this context the Parsi matrimonial court with a jury system in which the community elders could participate became an important feature of their personal laws which needed to be retained.

Paradoxically, the 'native' or 'indigenous' Christians became the depositories of the then progressive law, the Indian Divorce Act, enacted by the British within a Protestant framework. But in the post-Independence period, the Roman Catholic dogma of indissolubility of marriage resisted all changes within it. Hence at the advent of the 21st century, Christian women in India were still struggling for their basic right of divorce on grounds such as cruelty and desertion, a right which was awarded to women of every other religious community.

The Muslim law provides an example of the disjunct between the traditional Shariat and its patriarchal subversions where mehr is reduced to a token amount and is replaced by dowry a concept alien to the Arab world within which the Islamic law and religion had its roots. The meagre amounts stipulated as mehr have failed to act as a deterrent against instant divorce. The rulings of the British period which validated the mere utterance of the word 'talaq' as a legal and binding divorce further eroded the rights of Muslim women. More recently, after the enactment of the Muslim Women (Protection of Rights upon Divorce) Act 1986, the popular misconception that a divorced Muslim woman has no right of maintenance further impinged the rights of Muslim women and divested them of all their economic security. In this context, the courts had to step in to safeguard their rights and provide a measure of security. However, the plethora of positive rulings by various high courts and the Supreme Court have filed to receive the publicity they deserve and the misconception continue. Even the mandate of halala gets invoked as a legal ploy to subvert women's rights as is demonstrated by cases discussed in this section. The Muslim law does not lend itself easily to the technical treatment applied to it by modern lawyers (Schacht 1964). While deciding a claim of rights and entitlements, the courts are constantly faced with the challenging task of reinterpreting the protective provisions of classical law and mould them in the interest of justice.

A similar manipulation can also be found within the codified Hindu law. The principle of monogamy, which was modelled on Western and Christian doctrine, was not suited to the cultural conditions of a diverse and pluralistic Hindu society. So at one level, the law was ineffective in curbing polygamy but conversely, it strengthened the patriarchal base by depriving women in informal relationships of their customary rights as concubines and mistresses.[277] This move was supposed to bring in the Christian model of sexual morality, despite the fact that the English law itself has moved on from its own outdated Victorian morality and provides for easy divorces, facilitating multiple sequential marriages. Simultaneously, legal recognition has been awarded to cohabittees and illegitimate children. It has taken much longer to accept these principles within the Indian family laws modelled on archaic English traditions and values.

Despite the legislative and judicial interventions, the institution of marriage continues to be firmly rooted within customs and traditions of a community. Hence the Special Marriage Act, 1954, a progressive piece of legislation which was meant to be a secular and optional code, has failed to make a dent. The codes governing marriage continue to be governed by social norms and community mores. Arranged marriages, with rules of hypergamy[278] and exogamy[279] are strictly observed. The lower status of bride givers is indicated by the custom of dowry with bride takers dominating the marriage markets. Legislative interventions of bringing a curb to this practice have been ineffective due to its social acceptance. At another level the strict community control is evident in the threats issued to young couples contracting marriages of choice, defying the marriage codes of the community. In cases where a girl from a

---

[277] This issue is discussed in detail in Chapter 2 of the second volume.

[278] An anthropological term which indicates the pattern of boys marrying girls from a lower or equal social strata.

[279] Marrying outside of one's clan or village.

higher caste marries a boy from the lower caste or a Hindu girl marries a Muslim boy, the couple is subjected to extreme violence which may result in murder, maiming, public humiliation or social/caste ostracization.

Paradoxically while among the southern-Dravidian states cross cousin marriages are a norm, several North Indian communities observe the sagotra (gotra--denotes a clan or sub-caste and sagotra implies marriage within the same clan) rule, where marrying within a village or even a cluster of villages is a taboo. The ruling of the district and sessions judge, Karnal, Haryana by Judge Vani Gopal Sharma, delivered on 30 March 2010, awarding death penalty to five members of the girls family and life imprisonment to the head of the Khap Panchayat, by naming it as a 'rarest of rare crime', has evoked much public response.[280] While urban civil society groups have been demanding a ban on such panchayats, the Khap Panchayats have approached the government for recognition of their customary rule of prohibition of sagotra marriages within the codified Hindu Marriage Act.[281]

The question that needs to be foregrounded is, from where do these Khap Panchayats derive their authority to enforce community sanctions. The members of these panchayats are upper caste men who wield considerable economic and political power. The Khap Panchayats have authority over not just one village but a cluster of villages within a prescribed geographical area. They address issues concerning the community—*aikya* (unity), *izzat* (honour), *biradari* (community) and *bhaichara* (brother-

hood). People prefer to approach them for resolution of their disputes rather than the formal courts which are distant, alien, and expensive and bogged down with backlogs and delays (Yadav 2009). As against this, the 'justice' in the Khap Panchayat is cheap, instant and accessible. The criminal transgression take place with active collusion of the local administration and under political patronage.

Even more important—most often, the girls family is implicated in the crime. It is a murder of a daughter and/or her lover/husband carried out by her own family in collusion of either the state authorities or the local Khap Panchayats. Sensationalizing these crimes by prefixing them with a title of 'honour killings' by 'Khap Panchayats' only serves to shroud the reality of the brutal power which the natal family wields upon their daughters when they transgress the patriarchal boundaries which are drawn for them. This can happen in both urban and rural areas. Hence the demand for banning the panchayats will not address the root cause of the problem, sexual control of the girl by her natal family.

The brief discussion on Khap Panchayats serves to further complicate an already complex question, of women's rights within diverse family laws, which are entwined within tensions between state, community and family. Women's rights hinge upon the power dynamics between them and the spaces which this dynamics opens up for their own negotiations. So moving on from the historical, the following chapters, in this and the next volume, will attempt to situate women's rights into the following locations.

- The intersections of the personal and political arena of rights within the constitutional framework of citizenship, its inclusions and

---

[280] Gajinder Singh, 'Death for Honour Killling' Calcutta: *The Telegraph* 31 March 2010.

[281] Vrinda Sharma, 'Khap Panchayat Leaders Condemn Ruling' Chennai: *The Hindu* 14 April 2010.

exclusions and the manner in which the issue of Uniform Civil Code gets framed within the context of majority minority politics.

- The social institution of the family, its progression from 'status' to 'contract' and from 'indissolubility' to 'dissolubility' and examine its impact upon women in the context of formal equality and gender neutrality.
- The economic and familial rights accruing from the marriage contract–maintenance,

matrimonial property and custody of children and the notions of sexual morality that hover over these claims.

- The procedural realm of family courts within which the claims arising out of family disputes are currently situated within the formal court systems.

These diverse locations will help us to re-locate the historical realm of family laws within their contemporary moorings.

2

Constitutional Law and Citizenship Claims

The Indian Constitution is a fundamental document of the Bill of Rights and reflects the aspirations of its framers. While providing an overview of the constitutional scheme of protections and checks and balances, the first section of this chapter examines the notions of equality, special protection, freedom and liberty. Some landmark rulings which have breathed life into the constitutional proclamations and have advanced women's rights, are outlined in this section.

The divide between the public and the private spheres, which seeks to confine women to their domestic existence, affects their role and position in society and within their families. Inequalities between the sexes at the workplace and at home reinforce and exacerbate each other. Hence the struggle to break these binaries through claims of citizenship serves to redefine gender roles both in the public as well as the private spheres. Women's struggle to enter the public domain of politics by acquiring basic literacy and professional skills, and by forming associations are also traced in this section.

The political debate around the enactment of the Uniform Civil Code (UCC), in the context of Article 44 of the Constitution, is discussed in detail in the second section. Within a communally vitiated atmosphere, the manner in which a pro-women demand of equal rights within family laws was converted into an anti-minority agenda is examined. The role of the media and the adverse impact of communally-tinted judicial pronouncements are also analysed. In this context, individual struggles of Muslim women who defied community norms and popular misconceptions projected by the media, to stake their claims of citizenship are important milestones and hence are highlighted.

In the third section, some legislative drafts which attempted to frame a Uniform Civil Code are discussed in the context of their feasibility and conceptual clarity. The argument here is that smaller and specific reforms would make a more significant contribution to protecting women's rights than an all-encompassing Uniform Civil Code. The 'magic wand' rhetoric around the Uniform Civil Code must give way to pragmatism and legal realism.

The concluding section examines constitutional assurances in the context of gendered notions of citizenship within a broader political context. The projection of women as the nation's 'honour', pose a challenge to the constitutional assurances of equality. The construction of an 'ideal' woman worthy of citizenship leaves out large sections of poor, marginalised, and 'sexually-tainted' women, for whom, the constitutional claims remain empty assurances and unfulfilled promises. An attempt is made to examine their claims within the context of citizenship.

Section A

LOCATING WOMEN'S CLAIMS WITHIN THE CONSTITUTIONAL DOMAIN

Contextualising the Indian Constitution

Indian Constitution: A Covenant of Social and Economic Justice

Words are magic things often enough, but even the magic of words sometimes cannot convey the magic of the human spirit and of a Nation's passion. (The Resolution) seeks very feebly to tell the world of what we have thought or dreamt of so long, and what we now hope to achieve in the near future.

Pandit Jawaharlal Nehru
December 13, 1946[1]

A constitution is the fundamental legal document of a democratic country, and lays down the principles for its governance. All laws have to conform to it and any provision of law or regulation which is inconsistent with it is void. The Indian Constitution, which came into force on 26 January 1950, provides a framework for governance and assigns roles to different institutions such as the executive, legislature, and

[1] Constituent Assembly Debates: Lok Sabha Secretariat, New Delhi: 1999, Vol. I, pp.57-65, as cited in *Naz Foundation* v. *Government of NCTA* 2010 Cri.LJ 94 Del.

judiciary. It is also a covenant of social and economic justice.

India's founding fathers and mothers incorporated in the constitution the nation's ideals—national unity and integrity and a democratic and equitable society—and the institutions which would aid the process of achieving them. The new social order was to be achieved through a socio-economic revolution, pursued with a democratic spirit, using constitutional institutions. The framers of the constitution perceived unity, social revolution, and democracy as the three interdependent goals which had to be sought together and could not be pursued or achieved disjointedly, which Granville Austin refers to as the three strands of a seamless web (Austin 2001: ix-x).

Three important documents of the pre-Independence period provided the framework for the Constitution, the Nehru Report of 1928, the Karachi Resolution on Fundamental Rights of 1931 and the Sapru Report of 1945.

The Nehru Report was produced by a sub-committee headed by Motilal Nehru, father of Jawaharlal Nehru. The impetus for producing this document came from a challenge posed to the Indian leaders by the Secretary of State for Indian Affairs, Lord Birkenhead in the House of Lords in 1927, that they should draft a Constitution which would be acceptable to all communities. The underlying premise of this challenge was that the Indian leaders would not be able to produce such a document. However, after several consultative sessions, a document produced by the sub-committee constituted for this purpose, was approved by the All Party Conference held at Lucknow in August, 1928 (Austin 2001: 55). It was a Declaration of Rights and it proclaimed that the main aims of the Constitution would be to secure for Indians fundamental rights and provide certain safeguards to minorities. The Independence perceived at this time was of a dominion, which would function under the authority of the British, and not total independence.

The Congress Convention held at Karachi in March 1931, adopted the resolution on Fundamental Rights and economic and social changes. This was both a declaration of rights and a humanitarian, socialist manifesto. The Karachi Resolution, as it came to be known, held that social revolution would have a vital share in shaping India's Constitution. The provisions contained in this document did in fact become the spiritual and, in some cases, the direct antecedents of the Directive Principles (Austin 2001: x). Credit for drafting the Karachi Resolution has been bestowed upon Pandit Jawaharlal Nehru, the first prime minister of Independent India.

The Sapru Report, published in 1945 concerned itself mainly with the problems of minority fears which were overshadowing the political scene, vitiated by communal tensions and conflicts. By now, it was becoming clear that India would achieve Independence in the near future and the minorities had to be reassured about their security in a Hindu majority state. The Sapru Report declared that Fundamental Rights within the new Constitution would have to include certain safeguards for minorities. The report stated:

That what the constitution demands and expects is perfect equality between one section of the community and another in the matter of political and civic rights, equality of liberty and security in the enjoyment of the freedom of religious worship and the pursuit of the ordinary applications of life (Sapru 1945: 260).

The period in which the Constitution was drafted coincided roughly with the post Second World War sentiments regarding gross human rights violations using excessive and arbitrary state power by certain states. Hence concerns reflected in the Universal Declaration of Human Rights of 1948 regarding protection of life and liberty, are also reflected in the Indian Constitution.

The Constitution was drafted by the Constituent Assembly which was formed under the British Cabinet Mission through a process of indirect elections and held its first session in December, 1946. Initially it had 207 members including 15 women and was headed by Dr. Rajendra Prasad who later became the first President of Independent India. It was approved by the Constituent Assembly on 26 November, 1949 and came into effect on 26 January, 1950 which is celebrated as the Republic Day. Thereafter, until the first elections were held in 1952, as per the guidelines laid out in the Constitution, the Constituent Assembly functioned as India's first Parliament.

Parts III and IV of the Constitution, the Fundamental Rights and the Directive Principles of State Policy are perceived to be the core values of the nation. The Fundamental Rights are justiceable rights which protect individuals from arbitrary, prejudicial State actions. Equality, non-discrimination, freedom, liberty, and protection to minorities are its primary pillars. In addition, three Articles have been designed to protect the individual against actions of other private citizens. Article 17 abolishes untouchability, Article 15 (2) lays down that no citizen shall suffer any disability in the use of shops, restaurants, wells, roads, and other public places on account of his religion, race, caste, sex, or place of birth, and Article 23 prohibits forced labour. Although this is a violation practiced many-a-time by the State, it relates more commonly to violations by landowners or zamindars. Thus the State, in addition to obeying the Constitution's negative injunctions regarding interference with citizen liberties, must fulfill its positive obligation to protect citizen's rights from encroachment by other influential members of the society. This concept of Fundamental Rights was introduced to foster a social revolution by creating a society which is egalitarian in which all its citizens would be equally free from coercions or restrictions by the State or by the society. Liberty would no longer be the privilege of the few.

The Directive Principles contain an even clearer statement of the social revolution. They aim at making the citizens of India free in the positive sense, free from the passivity engendered by centuries of coercion by society, and free from the abject physical conditions that had prevented them from achieving the full human potential. To do this, the State is to apply the precepts contained in the Directive Principles when making laws. These Principles are not justifiable; courts cannot enforce them, but they are, nevertheless, to be 'fundamental in the governance of the country'.[2] The essence of the Directive Principles lies in Article 38 which echoes the Preamble:

The State shall strive to promote the welfare of the people by securing and protecting as effectively as it may a social order in which justice, social economic and political shall inform all the institutions of the national life.

To foster this goal, other provisions of the Directive Principles exhort the State to ensure that citizens have adequate means of livelihood, that operation of the economic system and ownership and control of the material resources of the country serve the common good, that the health of workers, including children, is not abused, and that special consideration is given to pregnant women. Workers, both agricultural and industrial, are to have a standard of living that allows them to enjoy leisure and social and cultural opportunities. Among the primary duties of the State is the welfare of the people.

By establishing these positive obligations of the State, members of the Constituent Assembly

made it the responsibility of future governments of India to find a middle way between individual liberty and public good, between preserving the property and privilege of a few and bestowing benefits on the many.

While Fundamental Rights (civil and political rights) are justiceable, the Directive Principles (social, cultural, and economic rights) are non-justiceable and are more in the nature of aspirations than rights. This became a site for contestation within the Constituent Assembly. B.N. Rao, A. K. Ayyar, B.R. Ambedkar, K.M. Munshi, and K.T. Shah who shared a liberal socialist outlook were in favour of making the Directive Principles justiceable (Austin 2001: 77). They felt that within the prevailing social and economic structures, a large segment of the Indian population was poor and illiterate. This segment, according to them, might not be in a position to access the Fundamental Rights if the larger issues of land reforms, re-distribution of wealth, and eradication of illiteracy were not addressed first. Hence, for them issues of social, cultural, and economic rights were far more crucial to ensure a constitutional democracy and to usher in a new egalitarian social order. B.N. Rao, Constitutional Advisor to President, Dr. Rajendra Prasad, while suggesting an amendment to render Directive Principles enforceable in a court of law, stated as follows:

It is to make it clear that in a conflict between rights conferred by Chapter III - Fundamental Rights which are for the protection of rights of individuals and the principles of policy set forth in Chapter IV which are intended for the welfare of the State as a whole, the general welfare should prevail. Otherwise it would be meaningless to say that the principles are fundamental and it is the duty of the State to give effect to them in making laws. (Tope 1992: 336)

Dr Ambedkar, who himself belonged to a backward caste, argued that while the Constitution adopted formal equality of all

---

[2]   Article 37, Constitution of India.

citizens, the social and economic life in India was deeply caught in variegated expressions of equality and that unless democracy became a way of life, political democracy might not endure for long, or at least endure in a robust manner. But the suggestion to make Part IV justiceable was rejected. However, over the years, the judiciary has stepped in and incorporated some of the Directive Principles of State Policy into the domain of Fundamental Rights by expanding the notion of the Right to Life and Liberty (Article 21 of the Constitution). In *People's Union of Democratic Rights* v. *Union of India*,[3] the Supreme Court read the right to minimum wages into Article 21. In *Olga Tellis* v. *Bombay Municipal Corporation*,[4] it was held that the right to life includes the right to livelihood. Landmark judgments such as these have been instrumental in furthering the mandate of social justice as enshrined in the Constitution.

Constitutionalism and the Power of Judicial Review

Where the law is unsettled, a duty may be cast upon the courts to declare it retrospectively in exercise of power frankly legislative in function.

Benjamin Cardozo,
Supreme Court, USA 1932-38[5]

The Indian Constitution envisaged a system of governance which was largely inspired by the British. However, unlike the British notion of parliamentary supremacy, the Indian Constitution incorporated American federalist principles of separation of power and a powerful Supreme Court, which was to be the guardian of the Constitution.

The separation of powers between the judiciary, executive and the legislature under the Indian Constitution is not strict and there is a substantive overlap in the functions of the different organs. The need of the day was to guarantee that while executing either original or quasi functions, none of the state organs largely overstep so as to violate the basic essential functions that were required to be performed by them as an organ. The judiciary was entrusted with the power to oversee these essential checks and balances which would ensure smoother operation between and within these organs. This was essential for the protection of Fundamental Rights, which constitutes a check on the powers of both the legislature and the executive with a view to ensure liberty of the individual as guaranteed by the Constitution. In this context, out of the three organs of the State, the judiciary plays the most decisive role in the development of constitutionalism. A Constitution that guarantees Fundamental Rights to individuals affords a larger scope to its judiciary to develop constitutionalism.

The Indian judiciary has been vigilant in its role as the protector of the Constitution. Through the years, an expansion of its role has occurred on many fronts, the primary being the interpretation of the Right to Life under Article 21, meaning of the term 'due process of law', the balance between Fundamental Rights and Directive Principles, and the expansion of writ jurisdiction. The judiciary has innovatively used the wide powers awarded to it by the Constitution to uphold its basic structure and its core values.

Judicial review signifies the power of the highest judiciary to declare a parliamentary law *ultra vires* the Constitution. This power was born in the United States of America through the path breaking judgment of Marshall C.J. in 1803, in *Marbury* v. *Madison*,[6] through a detailed

---

[3] (1982) 3 SCC 235
[4] (1985) 3 SCC 545
[5] Cardozo, Benjamin N. (1921) *The Nature of the Judicial Process*, New Haven: Yale University Press pp. 128-9.

[6] (1803) 1 Cranch 137.

examination of the term 'due process of law' in the 5th Amendment to the American Constitution. The term 'due process' needs to be examined within two different contexts— i) 'substantive due process', in which a court examines the law both in terms of the written word and spirit behind the words; and ii) 'procedural due process', in which a court examines whether a law is duly enacted under legal provisions.

In India, the first draft of the Constitution used the words 'due process of law', but later this was replaced with the wordings, 'procedure established by law', in Article 21. Thus, the power of judicial review of the Indian judiciary, as envisaged by the Constitution, was truncated and constrained. But through various strands of interpretation, the judiciary expanded the scope of the provision, and thus expanded their powers of judicial review.

A series of judgments have brought to the fore, the contest between the Parliament and the Supreme Court for supremacy. These cases address the tensions between the Fundamental Rights and the Directive Principles. In *Sankari Prasad*[7] and *Sajjan Singh*[8] the Supreme Court conceded to the Parliament the power to amend the Constitution and upheld the land reforms introduced by the Parliament which impinged upon the fundamental rights of individuals to hold property. But in *Golak Nath*,[9] the Supreme Court held that Fundamental Rights cannot be tempered with through a constitutional amendment. In retaliation, the Parliament brought in the 24th Amendment to the Constitution to restore to itself the power of Constitutional Amendment. The Supreme Court struck down two important reforms introduced by the government regarding nationalization of Banks[10] and abolition of Privy Purses to the erstwhile royal families of Princely states.[11]

Thereafter, in *Kesavananda Bharati*,[12] the Supreme Court introduced the concept of a 'basic structure of the Constitution' which cannot be amended by Parliament and held that the power of judicial review is part of this basic structure. To undo the harm caused by this ruling, the Parliament enacted the 42nd and 44th Amendments to the Constitution. The 42nd Amendment (1976) was passed during the emergency (June 1975–March 1977) and brought in sweeping changes and gave the ruling government wide powers to declare emergency and suspend Fundamental Rights. But the 44th Amendment (1978) passed in the post - emergency period has held that the right to life under Article 21 cannot be suspended even during an emergency. The right to hold property has been deleted from the provisions under Article 19 and it is no longer a Fundamental Right.

The harmonious balance between Fundamental Rights and Directive Principles is an essential feature of the 'basic structure' of the Constitution and one should not be given absolute primacy over the other. The Directive Principles of State Policy enable the legislature and the executive to improve the quality of life of socially disadvantaged groups in various ways. While spreading the gains of economic advances to the less privileged, the rights of individuals from the elite sections cannot be adversely affected. The vision of the founding fathers was clearly that the directive

---

[7] *Sankari Prasad v. Union of India*, AIR 1951 SC 458.

[8] *Sajjan Singh v. State of Rajasthan*, AIR 1965 SC 845.

[9] *Golak Nath v. State of Punjab*, AIR 1967 SC 1643.

[10] *R. C. Cooper v. Union of India*, AIR 1970 SC 564 : (1970) 1 SCC 248.

[11] *HHM Madhav Rao Scindia v. Union of India*, AIR 1971 SC 530.

[12] *Kesavananda Bharati v. State of Kerala*, AIR 1973 SC 1461.

Principles of State Policy should remain subservient to the Fundamental Rights and in keeping with this, in the *Minerva Mills* case,[13] the judiciary invalidated a constitutional amendment which gave Directive Principles primacy over Articles 14 and 19. However, while upholding the principle of harmonious construction, the Court also conceded that social welfare laws were beyond challenge and could be read into Fundamental Rights such as Articles 14, 19, or 31 of the Constitution.

Over the years, the judiciary has sought to creatively introduce the spirit of the Directive Principles into Fundamental Rights through a liberal and expansionist view of the constituents of the 'right to life' under Article 21. Through a long line of precedents,[14] the Court has included liberty, dignity, health, peaceful life, clean drinking water, clean environment, absence of noise pollution, and many other aspects as essential for the right to life.

The constraints on the power of the Supreme Court through the term 'procedure established by law' have been circumvented by the application of an integrated idea of reasonableness and interconnectedness of the Fundamental Rights. In the initial case which dealt with this issue, *A. K. Gopalan* v. *State of Madras*,[15] the Court took a restricted view of its own powers. It interpreted Article 21 literally, to hold that the expression 'procedure established by law' meant 'any procedure which was laid down in the statute by the competent legislature to deprive a person of his life or personal liberty' and that it was not permissible to read any concept such as

natural justice, due process of law, or reasonableness into this article. The Court also ruled that Fundamental Rights were independent of each other and that Article 19 did not apply where Article 21 applied. Article 19 applied to a free man and not to a person in preventive detention. Thus the procedure could not be challenged even if it were unreasonable or inconsistent with the principles of natural justice.

This view prevailed for twenty-five years, but the judicial attitude changed in 1978, perhaps because the emergency revealed how fragile the base of democratic rights in India was in reality. In *Maneka Gandhi* v. *Union of India*,[16] the very first case which came before the Supreme Court after the emergency, the Court settled some of the prevailing problems about Article 21. By a majority, the Court decided that Articles 21 and 19 were not mutually exclusive, that they had to be read together, and so the procedure affecting any of these rights had to be reasonable. The Court also held that the procedure established by law in Article 21 was in itself right, just, and fair and not arbitrary, fanciful, or oppressive. Any procedure which was not right, just, and fair was no procedure at all. A procedure that failed to meet the standard of Article 21 would not appear satisfactory to the Court. The Court further held that the concept of reasonableness must be projected in the procedure contemplated by Article 21 and that this was because of the link between Articles 21, 19, and 14. Through this ruling, the Indian judiciary moved to the position held by the American Supreme Court, as established and laid down in *Marbury* v. *Maddison* (discussed above).

The judiciary has also developed innovative principles of interpretation based on concepts such as *locus standi*, reasonableness, *ultra vires*, *male fide*, natural justice, government largesse,

---

[13] *Minerva Mills Ltd.* v. *Union of India*, AIR 1980 SC 1789.

[14] For example see *C. Masilamani Mudaliar* v. *The Idol of Sri Swaminathaswami Swaminathaswami Thirukoli*, (1996) 8 SCC525 and *In re: Noise Pollution*, (2005) 5 SCC 733.

[15] AIR 1950 SC 27

[16] AIR 1978 SC 597

and public interest litigation. The theory of unamendability of the basic structure of the Constitution, as laid down in the landmark. *Kesavananda Bharati* case (discussed above), has helped considerably in further developing the principles of constitutionalism.

The consciousness on the part of the activist judges of the Supreme Court of India to protect the liberty of the people led to the devising of a new remedy in the form of public interest litigation. The Court accepted an expanded interpretation of the concept of *locus standi* to protect the interests of the weak and unprivileged who are not in a position to access the courts. The expanded notion recognized the right of citizens to approach the courts on behalf of these disadvantaged groups in order to ensure that their Fundamental Rights are not violated by state authorities. According to Tope, constitutionalism has advanced more in India than in the United States of America, especially in the area of protection to life and personal liberty and securing social justice (Tope 1992: LXXII).

Expansion of the principle of natural justice by the Supreme Court of India is another dimension of constitutionalism. The Court laid down that the principles evolved and followed by quasi-judicial bodies and even the executive must be in line with the principles of natural justice when their decision is likely to adversely affect the rights of any individual. The concept of *audi alteram partem,* i.e., the right to fair hearing, has thus been evolved by the judiciary on the basis of its constitutional mandate.

In a plethora of judgments it has been held that judicial review cannot be barred totally. Any decision which denies an individual the right to either do or to abstain from doing something, has to be decided upon fairly. The power of judicial review need not necessarily be executed by the judiciary and can, alternatively, be exercised through another duly constituted body with

unbiased members. But the crucial governing principle that must prevail is to be *'fair'*.

Women's Entry into the Public Domain

The Indian Constitution awards equal rights to women and prohibits the State from discriminating against them. This principle, along with the notion of adult franchise, has proven to be one of the basic pillars upon which the notion of gender justice has been pegged in the post-Independence period. While we applaud the gender equality enshrined in the Indian Constitution, it is imperative to acknowledge the century long struggle in which women strived for their right to basic literacy, formal education, and political participation, which in turn laid the foundation for the demand for right of legal equality.

While grappling with the notion of inequality at the grassroots and the constitutional challenges this situation poses, a mere appreciation of constitutional principles will not provide a complete picture unless we place these milestones within the context of an earlier movement and the struggle of women therein.

The Constitution Drafting Committee reckoned the inclusion of traditionally marginalized sections to be of prime importance in order to ensure that their concerns were reflected in the Constitution. The Committee had women representatives, though not in large numbers. Towards the conclusion of the debates, demands for more female elected members were raised. However, this became a contentious issue with several male members opposing the demand.[17] This is a small indication that women's entry into the realm of political formations has not been easy.

Several social reformers, particularly women reformers, and nationalist leaders focused on

[17]   Constitution Assembly Debates – comments of Shri B. Das dated 24 January 1950.

issues such as women's education, discriminatory personal laws, and access to health. Later, some women leaders formed associations to bring women's concerns into the realm of social reforms. Gandhiji's call for political participation in the Swadeshi and Non-Cooperation movements gave an additional boost to women. Only from this historical plank could women agitate for their fundamental rights of equality, non-discrimination, protective provisions, adult franchise, and right over their bodies. This section briefly sketches this important political evolution which culminated in gender equality being included as a fundamental right and went further to ensure one-third reservation for women in local bodies through the 73rd and 74th amendments to the Constitution, which gave a boost to the process of women's political participation.

History of Women's Education in India

After some time, the desire to learn how to read properly grew very strong in me. I was angry with myself for wanting to read books. Girls did not read. How could I? … What was I to do?

"Books were not printed in those days. The handwriting was difficult to decipher. Oh, the trouble I had to take to read. In spite of all that, I did not learn to write. One needs a lot of things if one is to write: paper, pen, ink, ink pot and so on. You have to set everything before you. And I was a woman, the daughter-in-law of the family. I was not supposed to read or write. It was generally accepted as a grave offense. And if they saw me with all the writing paraphernalia, what would they say? … So I gave up the idea of writing and concentrated on reading."

Rassundari Devi

Amar Jiban (My Life) 1876)[18]

This excerpt from the autobiography of Rassundari Devi succinctly captures the struggle women had to go through to achieve basic

literacy. Rassundari Devi taught herself to read by stealing a few minutes from her housework and the task of looking after her twelve children. She had taught herself to read and write in secret by scratching the letters of the alphabet onto the corner of a blackened kitchen wall. Rassundari overcame all opposition and obstacles, learnt to read and write and wrote about her own experiences. There were many others like her who endured great hardships to acquire basic literacy. Many of these early literate women wrote their autobiographies depicting their struggles. The autobiographies and other writings by women of this period, provide us with not just glimpses of their own struggles but also a world view of their times from their perspectives.[19]

During the nineteenth century, the Christian missionaries and Indian social reformers, who were committed to the cause of women's education, started several schools for girls. The first to attend the schools of Christian missionaries were Christian converts, orphans, and girls from lower castes and poor families. 'Respectable' Hindu girls were not sent to these schools for fear of conversion (Basu 2005: 185). The work of the Missionaries was not supported by the English East India Company due to the fear that it would amount to dereliction of the principles of religious neutrality to which the Company was pledged. The credit for changing this official attitude of indifference goes to John Drinkwater

[18] Tharu and Lalita (1991) pp. 199 and 202.

[19] Ramabai Ranade, *Amachya Ayushyatil Kahi Athawani* (Memoirs of Our Life Together); Muktabai, *Mang Maharachya Dukhavisayi* (About the Griefs of the Mangs and Mahars); Pandita Ramabai Saraswati, *The High Caste Hindu Woman*; Tarabai Shinde, *Stri Purush Tulana* (A Comparison of Men and Women); Binodini Dasi, *Amar Katha* (My Story); Bahinabai Chaudhari, *Ata Maza Male Jeeva* (Now I Remain for Myself); Janaki Bai, *I remember the days of love's first flowering*. (Translated from Urdu) etc. See Tharu and Lalita (1991).

Bethune, the Law Member in the Governor-General's Council and President of the Council of Education. Convinced of the need for female education, Bethune opened a school for girls in Calcutta in 1849.

Jyotiba Phule started a school for girls in Pune in 1851 despite stiff opposition from orthodox Hindus. He remained undaunted and went on to start two more schools for girls in Pune. In his memorandum submitted to the Indian Education Commission in 1882, Phule pleaded that the Education Commission be kind enough to sanction measures for the spread of female primary education on a more liberal scale (Phooley 1884: 140-54).

Around this time, Maharshi Karve also decided to educate the young girls along with widows and started a school in a small structure known as 'Karve Kutir' with five girls, in a village near Pune. But his associates opposed this move as they felt that unmarried girls should not study along with widows. So he started Mahila Vidyalaya for higher education in 1907. But his greatest achievement was the institution of the famous Karve Women's University in 1916, which later came to be known as the Shrimati Nathibai Damodar Thakersey (SNDT) Women's University (Desai 1977: 121). The Deccan Education Society started by Agarkar in 1884, which initially admitted only boys, later started schools for girls as well. Out of the eleven institutions run by the society, nearly seven had facilities for women (Desai 1977: 118).

In the Western region, the Parsis were the first among Indians to educate their daughters. From the 1840s onwards, Parsi girls were educated at home. By 1886, literacy among Parsi girls was very high—nearly 70 per cent of girls of school going age were in schools (Basu 2005: 188).

Among Muslim reformists, Sir Badruddin Tyabji, in 1882, encouraged schools for Muslim girls and regretted that there was not a single Muslim girls' school in Bombay that taught English. At Aligarh, Sir Syed Ahmad Khan in 1898, rejected the idea of any education being imparted to girls outside their homes. Serious efforts for education of Muslim girls began in U.P. with Karamat Hussain's girls school at Lucknow, which was established in 1900, and Shaikh Abdullah's girls school at Aligarh, which was established in 1906. The Muhammedan Education Conference, at its annual meeting in 1912, passed a resolution which proclaimed that the spread of education among Muhammedan girls was a matter of paramount importance and necessary for the progress of the community (Basu 2005: 190).

The movement towards educating women had its own ups and downs. The conservatives and revivalists, opposed the attempts by reformers and missionaries to educate women. Some among them viewed it as a way of appeasing the English and as an endorsement of their political agenda. The Hindu revivalist movement, which was committed to the ideal of Hindu ethos and values as enshrined in the ancient scriptures, viewed it as an encroachment into their religious beliefs. There was also the fear that it would be difficult to control an educated woman because she would challenge her traditional role. For the reformers themselves, the status of women was only an issue of concern due to the relation it had with the general welfare of society, the upbringing of children, and as a part of the nation-building agenda. As Saraladevi Choudhurani wryly observed:

They are the so called social reformers. They advertise themselves as the champions of the weaker sex; equal opportunities for women, female education and female emancipation are some of their pet objects of oratory at the annual show. They even make honest efforts at object lessons in the above subjects by persuading educated ladies to come up on the platform and speak for themselves. But woe to the women if they venture to act for themselves. (Choudhurani 1911 : 345)

The 1891 Census recorded male literacy at 11 per cent and female literacy at 0.5 per cent; thus there was only 1 literate woman to every 23 literate men. The wide disparity between male and female literacy rates continued even after Independence. Hence, the report of the First Backward Classes Commission, 1955 popularly known as the Kaka Kalelkar Commission, recommended that women as a class be treated as backward. One of the factors taken into consideration for classification by the Commission was the percentage of literacy or the general advancement made by them.[20] Though some progress was made in the later half of the twentieth century, the disparity persists.

In 1992, in *Mohini Jain* v. *State of Karnataka*,[21] the Supreme Court held that the right to education has the status of a Fundamental Right and thus belongs in the enforceable Part III of the Constitution rather than in the unenforceable Part IV. In 1993, the Apex Court expanded this concept further in *Unnikrishnan J.P.* v. *State of A.P.*[22] and held that the right to education flows directly from the right to life and is related to the dignity of the individual. Following these decisions, and in the context of the dismal state of affairs regarding education in the country, the 86th Amendment to the Constitution added Article 21A, making it a duty of the State to provide free and compulsory education to all children from the age of six to fourteen years. This amendment made right to education a part of the basic right to life under Article 21, which

was a great leap ahead. It also amended Article 45, directing the State to provide early childhood care and education for all children till they complete the age of six years.

Article 21A: *The State shall provide free and compulsory education to all children of the age six to fourteen years in such as a way as the State may, by law, determine.*

Article 45: *The State shall endeavour to provide early childhood care and education for all children until they complete the age of 6 years.*

As a sequel to this, the Right to Free and Compulsory Education, 2009 was passed which came into effect on 1 April 2010. After this enactment, every child in India between the ages of four to fourteen is supposed to be in school. Though the Act is not based on a gendered premise, in effect, since literacy rates are lower among girls than boys, it is intended to benefit a large number of girls from rural, marginalized and poverty stricken areas.

From Basic Literacy to Professional Education

After breaking the barrier against basic literacy, the next major hurdle that needed to be crossed was in the realm of professional education. Kadambini Basu and Sarala Ray, two pupils of the Banga Mahila Vidyalaya cleared the entrance examination to the Calcutta University in 1878. Thereafter the University Senate resolved that female candidates shall be admitted for university examinations subject to certain rules. In 1886, Anandibai Joshi, graduated from the Women's Medical College in Philadelphia as their first Indian student and the first Hindu woman to study medicine abroad. The first woman to qualify in medicine from Bombay University was Miss Annie Walker in 1889. The Madras Medical College admitted four girls in 1875 for a certificate course and in 1881-2, the

---

[20] See *Annual Report 2003–4* of the National Commission for Backward Classes. The report of the Kaka Kalelkar Commission was not accepted by the Central Government.

[21] (1992) 3 SCC 666

[22] (1993) 1 SCC 645

first woman was admitted for the medical course (Basu 2005: 192).

In 1883, Bombay University allowed girls to appear for the matriculation examination and pronounced that henceforth the pronoun 'he' and its derivatives used in the University Act would also apply to women. In 1888, Cornelia Sorabji passed the Bachelor of Arts examination, standing first in the university. But the issue of admitting women into the bar remained unresolved for a further thirty years. In 1916 and 1921, applications by Regina Guha in Calcutta[23] and Sudanshu Bala Hazra[24] in Patna respectively, for enrollment as pleaders under the Legal Practitioners Act, 1879 were rejected because they were not 'persons' under the law.

However, around the same time, the Allahabad High Court, through its ruling dated 24 August 1921, accepted a similar application by Cornelia Sorabji, making her the first lady advocate in the country. She was the first Indian woman to qualify for the Bar examination and was the only woman barrister for many years (Basu 2005: 192). These events ultimately led to the enactment of the Legal Practitioners (Women) Act, 1923 which provided that women will not be disqualified from becoming legal practitioners only on the ground of their sex.[25]

[23] *In re: Regina Guha*, ILR (1916) 44 Cal. 290.

[24] *In re: Sudanshu Bala Hazra*, AIR 1922 Pat 269.

[25] Section 3 of the Act reads: Women not to be disqualified by reason only of sex.—Notwithstanding anything contained in any enactment in force in the territories to which this Act extends or in the letters patent of any high court or in any rule or order made under or in pursuance of any such enactment or letters patent, no woman shall, by reason only of her sex, be disqualified from being admitted or enrolled as a legal practitioner or from practising as such; and any such rule or order which is repugnant to the provisions of this Act shall, to the extent of such repugnancy, be void.

Women's Associations and Political Participation

By the end of the 19th century, major battles in the realm of women's education had been won and the prejudices against women's education had been reduced. Education of women had become an issue of public concern. The new slogan for social reformers was: 'educating a girl means educating a family'. The stage was now set for women to enter the political domain. The first step in this direction was the formation of women's associations.

Pandita Ramabai formed the Arya Mahila Samaj in 1882 in Western India. In the same year, in Calcutta, Swarna Kumari Debi, sister of poet Rabindranath Tagore, founded Sakhi Samiti. Her daughter, Saraladevi Chaudhurani, started the first all India women's association, Bharat Stree Mandal, in 1910 (Basu 2005: 194). After the First World War, in 1917, the Women's Indian Association (WIA), was started in Madras by Annie Besant, Margaret Cousins, and Dorothy Jinarajdasa for agitating for the right to vote for women within the new Constitution which was to be introduced by the Montague-Chelmsford Reforms. The announcement on 20 August 1917 by Edwin Montague, Secretary of State for India, regarding the development of self-governing institutions in India and his subsequent visit in November 1917 to ascertain Indian opinion on specific reform proposals, provided the first avenue for women to enter the political domain and initiate a struggle to secure franchise for women.

It is interesting how the colonial administration viewed the women's delegation which met Motague. When Margaret Cousins and Saraladevi Chaudhurani requested an audience for delegates from their respective organizations to discuss education resulting in social reform, they were informed that only deputations with political agendas would be received.

In this context, the issue of political rights for women gained precedence in women's activism. Later, Margaret Cousins has recorded how the first demand for women's franchise was born soon thereafter:

I then circulated a couple of extra sentences about political rights or rather opportunities in the draft of the memorandum. I know that women interested in the deputation believed in being citizens of their country and they wrote agreeing to the condition, so the vote was born. (Cousins, 1941: 33)

On 15 December 1917, a 14-member women's delegation led by Sarojini Naidu met Montague and Chelmsford to present their demands for political rights. Montague's entry for the day in his diary has the following recording: 'The women's deputation assured [him] that the Congress would willingly pass a unanimous request for women's suffrage' (Roy 2005 : 131). He thought of the deputation as nothing more than 'interesting' and the Montague-Chelmsford Reforms did not make any mention of it. His comments were personal in nature – 'one very nice looking woman from Bombay, Dr. Joshi', Sarojini Naidu, 'the poetess, a very attractive and clever women, but [he believed] a revolutionary at heart', and Mrs. Cousins, 'a well-known suffragette from Bombay' and 'one of Mrs. Beasant's crowd' (Moraes 1958: 91). A WIA publication records that many years later Sarojini Naidu was to recall that the idea of meeting important people such as the Viceroy of India seemed a 'bold and daring' adventure to the deputation. The delegates subconsciously spent a lot of time 'worrying over their appearances', wishing somehow to reinforce their arguments 'by a colourful and picturesque appearance' (Reddy 1956 : 8).

In order to get the support of male political leaders, it was important that the demand was framed in a manner which would not threaten them. The women leaders had to project that voting rights for women were congruent with the language of equality in the political domain and yet in harmony with tradition (Roy 2005: 131). In August 1918, Sarojini Naidu exhorted a large special session of the Indian National Congress attended by 5000 delegates, assuring her audience that extending franchise to women was rational, scientifically and politically sound, compatible with tradition, and consistent with human rights (Forbes 1998: 94). Saraladevi Chaudhurani presented the resolution supporting vote for women in the thirty-third session of the Indian National Congress in December 1918 at Delhi. In 1919, a British Parliamentary Committee recommended that female franchise should be considered a 'domestic' subject, leaving it to the provincial legislatures to decide the matter (Roy 2005: 132). So from 1920s, the focus of the women's struggle for the right to vote shifted to the provincial level.

Women's participation in the Swadeshi movement where they learnt to picket shops, march in processions and court arrests, served to redefine traditional roles and helped them gain entry into active politics, a clear shift from educational and social welfare oriented activities. This was an important development which marked the end of women's seclusion. This was followed closely by the formation of the All India Women's Conference (AIWC). The creation of these organisations brought women out of their homes and gave them a consolidated voice, forcing the nation to give due importance to women's issues and their demands.

A.I.W.C.: Educational Reforms to Political Participation

In 1926, when a call was given for an all India women's conference to discuss women's issues, little did the organisers envisage that the conference would give birth to a national level women's organisation by this very name or that its name would be engrained in the political history of the nation and would become synonymous with campaigns for women's rights. This also proved to be a turning point for women's groups, marking a shift from the reformist agenda of women's education to a claim for political participation and legal equality. The organisation, which was formally registered in 1930, boasted of many political stalwarts such as Sarojinidevi Naidu, Kamaladevi Chattopadhyay, Muthulakshmi Reddy, Begum Shah Nawaz, Vijay Laxmi Pandit, Renuka Ray, Rajkumari Amrit Kaur, Hansaben Mehta, Begum Hamid Ali, Lakshmi Menon, and Rameshwari Nehru.

The first meeting of the AIWC was held in Poona in January 1927 and was attended by a large number of social reformers, professional educationists, the wealthy, and the titled. The immediate context within which the AIWC was formed suggests that its basic intent was to organise women to demand reforms in the system of education. The debates within the AIWC reveal that education itself was initially perceived as a kind of panacea for solving problems of women, family, and society. It started with a conservative agenda—to produce better wives and mothers—but there was also the need to produce better teachers, doctors, professors, and lawyers. The presidential address of Maharani Chimanbai Gaekwad of Baroda reads:

... Here, with the rising tide of revival of Indian culture, here, at the beginning of what may rightly be regarded as the Indian renaissance, we are assembled to discuss ... those things which are essential for the education and the general well being of the future mothers of the race.... Let us recognize that womanhood should be able to produce not just healthy bodies, but healthy souls....(Chaudhuri 2004: 118)

The second AIWC, held in 1928 and presided over by Begum Sultan Jahan of Bhopal, focused on educational reforms. The third, held in 1929, was presided over by Rani Saheb of Mandi. As one can note, the women of royal families of

Princely States were invited to preside over these gatherings of professional women to bring glamour to the association. Some members like Kamaladevi Chattopadhyaya and Sarojini Naidu were dissatisfied with the agenda of social reform and expressed the desire to move into the political domain. They argued that 'the burning question of the day is political—such as freedom of the country' (Chaudhuri 2004: 122). But many members felt that the conference should remain apolitical and persist with its social reform agenda and that there should not be any discussion on 'controversial topics'. But gradually the voices in support of politics grew louder. Margaret Cousin's Presidential address at the eleventh session was decisively in favour of political participation. She raised some probing questions: Can the Indian man or woman be free if India remained a slave? How can we remain dumb about national freedom, the very basis of all great reforms? Has not the political status of the whole country as much to do with the welfare of women and children as the political status of women within an admittedly unsatisfactory new constitution? (Chaudhuri 2004: 123)

Rajkumari Amrit Kaur, in her Presidential address at the 12th AIWC session, asserted:

Life is an indomitable whole and we cannot separate social and educational reform from political and economic reform any more than we can separate women from men. Our conference is pledged not to take part in 'party politics' and I am quite certain that we have never broken this pledge. But if we are to eschew politics altogether we might as well give up all our work in connection with vital matters that pertain to the welfare of our sex....(Chaudhuri 2004: 123)

Vijayalakshmi Pandit expressed her distress regarding the rigid aloofness of the AIWC from the political life of the country and commented that as long as India is not a free country; no progress in the real sense is possible. There was a gradual change of opinion. For instance, though initially Lady Abdul Qadir considered the exclusion of politics to be critical for the unity of the conference, she later argued that the franchise of women was a political issue. Yet the conference could not leave the issue unconsidered as it had an important bearing on education and reform (Chaudhuri 2004: 123). Gradually the AIWC became an integral part of the nationalist movement. In her Presidential speech at the seventeenth session of the AIWC, Kamaladevi Chattopadhyaya declared, 'To a subject people, politics is its very life breath. To deny that urge, is to deny life.'

In 1931, the Karachi Session of the Indian National Congress in the Resolution on Fundamental Rights committed itself to women's equality in the following words:

Resolution on Fundamental Rights:

1. All citizens are equal before the law, irrespective of religion, caste, creed or sex.

2. No disability attaches to any citizen, by reason of his or her religion, caste, creed or sex, in regard to public employment, office of power or honour, and in the exercise of any trade or calling.

3. The franchise shall be on the basis of universal adult suffrage.

4. Women shall have the right to vote, to represent and the right to hold public offices.[26]

This declaration was largely the outcome of the mass participation of women in the national movement as well as the activities of several women's organisations, notably the AIWC, the WIA, and the NFIW (National Federation of Indian Women), who had pioneered the first women's movement in India (Kasturi 2004: 136).

Later, when the Joint Parliamentary Committee Report, published in 1933, rejected the principal of universal adult franchise, members of the AIWC opposed the same and argued

[26] Report of the Sub-Committee, 'Woman's Role in Planned Economy', 1947:37–8.

that property and literacy qualifications were contrary to democratic principles. They argued that the requirement of owning property would be meaningless for the vast majority of poor people of India. The literacy qualification would discriminate against the large illiterate population. Both these qualifications would drastically affect women and deny them the franchise.

Several AIWC members have recorded the difficulties they faced in bringing leaders of the Indian National Congress to accept the demands made by them for strengthening women's rights. Lamenting the plight of women, Captain Lakshmi Menon stated at the 1933 AIWC meet: 'The members of the Legislative Assembly who are men will not help us in bringing any drastic changes which will benefit women' (Basu and Rai 1992: 46). At the urging of Renuka Ray, the AIWC declared 24 November 1934 as 'legal disabilities day'.

The AIWC members played an important role, both in the Legislative Assembly and the Constituent Assembly, in foregrounding women's concerns within broader political debates. In the Legislative Assembly, Renuka Ray, who was appointed as the AIWC representative, raised the demand for Hindu law reforms. She also tried, albeit unsuccessfully, to have a clause incorporated in the draft constitution to prohibit discriminatory marriage and inheritance laws. Rajkumari Amrit Kaur and Hansa Mehta were prominent members of the sub-committee on Fundamental Rights of the Constituent Assembly. When the sub-committee accepted K.M. Munshi's draft on the freedom of conscience and the right to freely profess and practice religion, Rajkumari Amrit Kaur expressed her apprehension that the clause was defective to the extent that it might conflict with a legislation invalidating anti-social customs which have the sanction of religion.

She also sent a letter, on behalf of Hansa Mehta and herself, to the sub-committee, voicing their concern over this clause. Their apprehension was that it might create hurdles in introducing any future legislation to wipe out social evils practiced in the name of religion such as child marriage, dedication of girls to temples, prevention of inter-caste marriages, unequal laws of inheritance, polygamy, and seclusion of women. It might even render invalid prevailing legislation like the Child Marriage Restraint Act, 1929 and the Widow Remarriage Act, 1856.

While claiming legal and political equality, there was a concern not to equate the movement with the Western women's rights movement. Sarojini Naidu, while seconding the resolution on women's franchise, assured the Congress that Indian women would not transgress the existing gender roles. The dominant discourse on women was marked by a desire to distinguish the more 'strident' nature of women's demands in the West from the 'legitimate, yet proper' character of the Indian movement. The AIWC laid emphasis on the non-antagonistic relationship between Indian men and women based on mutual acceptance of gender roles, the positive contribution of women in lending a higher tone to public life, and the imperative for women to take up women's and children's issues to help in the progress of Indian society (Chaudhuri 2004: 126).

A slight departure from this position can be found in an important document of this period titled, 'Women's Role in Planned Economy' which was brought out by a 16-member all women sub-committee constituted under the National Planning Committee (NPC), of which Jawaharlal Nehru was Chairman. This was a major attempt to draw up a blueprint for the planned economic development of women in the post-Independence period. The Report addressed some crucial issues concerning women such as women's equal right to develop themselves and to improve their unsatisfactory economic status. It highlighted the unremitting labour of women of all classes, women's economic dependence, and their lack of resources. The sub-committee was of the opinion that one of the objectives of a planned economy should be to relieve women of their great and unequal burden and to provide conditions wherein they might develop their fullest potential through equality, education, and opportunity in all spheres. Emphasis was laid on action at the local level where the need is the greatest.

Among the various issues debated were–the nature of household labour and the need to recognize its value, the rights of the unmarried women, the irrelevance of legitimacy for determining the rights of children so far as the state is concerned, and 'identical moral standards' (Choudhuri 1996 : 216). The document, radical not only for its own time but even for ours, disappeared in the years after Independence. It was discussed by the National Planning Committee and some resolutions were passed reiterating the principle of women's equality, but this major landmark in the evolution of women's status remained largely unnoticed in the debates in the post-Independence period (Kasturi 2004: 137-8).

From the struggle for basic literacy, the onward march to higher education, and then on to the formation of women's associations and political participation in nationalistic struggle, the stage was set for the demand for constitutional equality and special protection to women. Women members of the Constitutional Assembly were entrusted with the responsibility of transforming the gains achieved through individual struggles during the preceding century into constitutional claims to safeguard the rights of future generations of women. It is to these women and women's organizations that we must pay tribute as we examine women's constitutional claims. Making women's equality, non-discrimination, and positive discrimination a part of the basic structure of the Constitution, they have ensured that we do not lapse back into the dark abyss of yester-years.

During the post-Independence period, organizations such as the AIWC lost their political edge and stagnated into organizations of upper middle class women with a desire to do social work (Desai 1977: 163).

Women's Claims and Constitutional Provisions

In the post-Independence period, the Constitution became the benchmark for determining the scope of women's rights. The provisions of adult franchise, non-discrimination on the basis of sex, and positive discrimination (or affirmative action) in favour of women and children placed Indian women far ahead of many of their Western counterparts.[27] The promise of equality is not just a formal equality but an egalitarian equality. Over the years the Supreme Court has read various socio-economic rights to include them in the realm of Fundamental Rights, particularly Article 21, the right to life.[28] Following is a brief outline of the important provisions within the Constitution which have contributed to enhancing women's rights.

The Preamble

The Preamble to the Constitution proclaims the ideals and aspirations of the people of India. One of the primary ideals it enunciates is 'equality of status and of opportunity'. This clause has

provided the basis for several legislations, in the realm of family laws and labour laws.

Part III: Fundamental Rights

The Fundamental Rights are contained in Articles 12 to 35 of the Constitution and can be accessed by all citizens irrespective of sex. However, certain Fundamental Rights contain specific and positive provisions to protect the rights of women. Of the various rights conferred in this part, the provisions of equality, non-discrimination and special protection have special significance for women.

i. Right to Equality: Articles 14–16

The phrase 'equality before law' (Article 14) has been further elaborated under Article 15 (1) of the Constitution which lays down that the State 'shall not discriminate against any citizen' on grounds of sex. In addition to equality, this clause contains an express prohibition of discrimination on the ground of sex.

ii. Special/Favourable Treatment: Article 15 (3)

Acknowledging the historical disadvantage suffered by women, Article 15 (3) is a departure from the established principle of equality and enables the state to make special provisions to protect women. This is a correctional measure of positive discrimination in favour of women (and other disadvantaged groups like children, scheduled castes and scheduled tribes). In addition,

---

[27] In contrast, Canadian women were granted the right of equality in 1982, Swiss women were granted the right to vote in 1972, and the United States has not yet endorsed the Equal Remuneration Act.
[28] Article 21 of the Constitution guarantees protection of life and personal liberty.

Box 2.1 Right to Equality

Article 14: Equality before law and equal protection of laws
Article 15(1): Non discrimination on grounds of sex
Article 15(3): Special provision for women and children
Article 16(2): Non discrimination in respect of employment

the gender-role stereotypes and subordinate and inferior social and economic status also necessitates that the state caste upon women its protective mantle.

This provision enables the state to secure women's rights through special provisions overriding the norm of equality and non-discrimination under Articles 14 and 15. The provision of maintenance under section 125 of Cr.PC, special provisions under criminal law regarding arrest and detention of women, and special protection to pregnant women and lactating mothers under labour laws come within the purview of Article15(3) of the Constitution. Similarly, setting up of special educational institutions for women and reserving places for women in public conveyances and places of entertainment would not violate the constitutional mandate of equality and non-discrimination.

Numerous laws have been enacted relating to prohibition of female infanticide, prevention of dowry and dowry related violence, prevention of indecent exposure of women in advertisements and films, prevention of child marriages, prevention of rape and sexual violence, medical termination of pregnancy, prohibition of prostitution and trafficking in women, protection in employment, etc. The decisions of the courts have served as a stimulus for the Indian legislators to enact new laws or to bring about changes in existing ones with a view to affording better protection to women. Reservations for women in panchayats and other self-governing bodies such as municipalities and corporations are protected through this constitutional safeguard. Similarly, legislation that gives tax concessions for women entrepreneurs and reservations for women in educational institutions and government services also come under this provision.

While this protection is necessary as an intermediary measure to attain equality, the protectionist approach is laden with an inherent danger of viewing women as minors, imbeciles, or dependents incapable of making decisions for themselves and is reflective of a paternalistic attitude towards women.

iii. Equality of Opportunity and Special Protection in Matters Relating to Employment: Article 16

Clause (1) of Article 16 provides equality of opportunity in matters relating to employment or appointment to any office under the state. This right to equality is also in terms of recruitment, promotion, wages, termination of employment, periodical increments, leave, gratuity, pension, age of retirement, etc. Article 16 (2) lays down specific grounds on which citizens are not to be discriminated against each other in offices under the State. Discrimination on the basis of sex has been specifically prohibited under the Constitution so as to bring women at par with men in the realm of public employment. Sex shall not be the sole ground of ineligibility for any post. Article 16(3) provides an additional safeguard and confers power on the Parliament to make special provisions to protect women in terms of employment.

iv. Right to Life and Liberty: Article 21

The right to life is the most basic of all fundamental rights and has been widely interpreted to imply several Articles included in Part IV of the Constitution, including the right to health and education. This right has been used to protect women's rights related to their ability to procreate, to be or not to be a parent, to give birth, to terminate unwanted pregnancies, to use or not to use contraceptives, and to be or not to be sterilized. It has established that the right of the mother to preserve her own health outweighs the right of the unborn child. It also includes the right to privacy, to be free from unwarranted government intrusion in matters which are very personal and fundamentally affecting a person. The right to life further includes the right to live in dignity, to be free from violence, and the right to dissolve an oppressive marriage.[29]

v. Right against Trafficking or Forced Labour: Article 23

Article 23 of the Constitution specifically prohibits traffic in human beings. In this context, traffic in human beings includes the Devadasi system,[30] a custom by which women and girls are dedicated as Devadasis to Hindu deities in temples, in reality being forced into prostitution. Trafficking in human beings has been prevalent in India for a long time in the form of prostitution, bonded labour, and even simply selling and purchasing human beings for a price. On the strength of Article 23(1) of the Constitution, the legislature has passed the Suppression of Immoral Traffic Act, 1956 (later renamed as the Immoral Traffic (Prevention) Act) which aims at abolishing the practice of forced prostitution and other forms of trafficking. This is an act made in pursuance of the International Convention for the Suppression of the Traffic in Persons and of the Exploitation of the Prostitution of Others, signed at New York on 9th May, 1950 for the prevention of immoral traffic. The Bonded Labour (Prohibition) Act, 1976 has helped curb the practice of bonded labour.[31]

The employment of children below the age of 14 years is strictly prohibited as per the constitutional mandate. Therefore, females below the age of 14 cannot by law be employed in any factory or mine, or in an organization engaged in any hazardous activity. The provision is in the interest of the health and well being of adolescent boys and girls. It is also consistent with Article 39, a Directive Principle of State Policy, which asserts that it is the duty of the State to protect the health and strength of workers, men or women. The Constitution casts a duty on the State to ensure that children of a tender age are not abused and that citizens are not forced by economic necessity to enter vocations unsuited to their age or ability.

Part IV: Directive Principles of State Policy

Articles 36 to 51 contain the Directive Principles of State Policy, which forms Part IV of the Constitution. Several of these provisions are meant to improve the status of women.

i. Article 39 (a) directs the State to provide adequate means of livelihood for men and women.

ii. Article 39 (d) mandates the State to secure equal pay for equal work for men and women.

iii. Article 39 (e) aims to protect the health and strength of workers, men and women.

iv. Article 42 directs the State to make provisions for securing just and humane conditions of work and for maternity relief.

v. Article 43 gives workers the right to a living wage and decent standard of living.

vi. Article 51-A explicitly protects the dignity of women.

To give effect to the various constitutional provisions which protect women, several laws have been enacted, some of which are listed below:

i. Devadasi Protection Act, 1957

ii. Female Infanticide Prevention Act, 1961

---

[29]   See *Neera Mathur* v. *Life Insurance Corporation of India*, AIR 1992 SC 392 and *Mary Sonia Zachariah* v. *Union of India* II (1995) DMC 27 FB which are discussed in detail in the section, *'Judicial Interpretations of Constitutional Provisions'*.

[30]   *Vishal Jeet* v. *Union of India*, AIR 1990 SC 1412.

[31]   This was enacted after the United Nations General Assembly adopted the International Covenant on Civil and Political Rights in 1966 which came into effect in 1976.

iii. Dowry Prohibition Act, 1961

iv. Maternity Benefits Act, 1961

v. Medical Termination of Pregnancy Act, 1971

vi. Equal Remuneration Act, 1976

vii. The Bonded Labour (Prohibition) Act, 1976

viii. Child Marriage Restraint Act, 1978

ix. Suppression of Immoral Traffic in Women & Girls Act, 1956, (SITA) (Later renamed as Immoral Traffic Prevention Act, 1986 (ITPA))

x. Indecent Representation of Women (Prevention) Act, 1986

xi.Pre-Natal Diagnostic Techniques (Regulation) Act, 1994 (PNDT Act) (Later renamed as Pre-Conception and Pre-Natal Diagnostic (Regulation) Act, 2002 (PCPNDT Act) (This act aims to prevent selective abortions of female foetus)

xii. Protection of Women From Domestic Violence Act, 2005

In addition several statutes contain special provisions for the protection of women such as:

i. Indian Penal Code, 1860

ii. Indian Evidence Act, 1872

iii. Code of Criminal Procedure, 1973

iv. Minimum Wages Act, 1948

v. Factories Act 1948

vi. Plantation Labour Act 1951

vii. Mines Act, 1952

Judicial Interpretations of Constitutional Provisions

The constitutional power of judicial review has been crucial in securing women's rights. An activist judiciary has tried to breathe life into the bare skeleton provided by the Constitution and has contributed to expanding the realm of women's rights by striking down laws, rules, and regulations which violate them and by upholding the constitutional validity of protective provisions. Constitutional provisions would have remained at the level of mere proclamations without the intervention of the judiciary. In landmark rulings, the Supreme Court and various high courts have been called upon to examine contested claims of women to legal equality and their positive rulings have served to bring in a culture of women's rights in the public domain. The transition of Indian women from the private to the public domain and their struggle to redefine traditional gender-based, stereotypical roles and acquire a new identity for themselves, alongside the resistance to this change from the patriarchal social order, has resulted in several challenges to the constitutional claims. Following is a summary of some of the landmark rulings in this realm.

Discrimination in Employment and Service Conditions

Issues concerning discrimination in the public domain of employment were the first to be challenged and had to be tested against the constitutional mandate of equality during 1970s and early 1980s. They reflected the transition that Indian women were making, from the private to the public domain. Issues such as marital status of women workers, their right to have children, sex stereotypes reflected in the age of retirement of women workers, and wage discrimination, etc. have been some of the important areas of struggle. The courts attempted to bridge the gap between the dichotomy of women's lives as home makers and wage earners.

The expansion of the scope of Fundamental Rights could occur only because some women, who felt violated by discriminatory laws, dared to approach the courts to challenge the validity of these offensive provisions. They were amply rewarded when these provisions were struck down. However, despite the positive rulings, discriminatory aspects persist and continue to haunt a large number of women workers.

Despite the constitutional mandate, the provision of equality and non-discrimination in employment remained an empty promise for nearly three decades after Independence. In 1966, in *Bombay Labour Union* v. *International Franchise*,[32] a rule requiring an unmarried woman to give up her employment on marriage was successfully challenged. However, continuing with the assumption of women being the primary caregivers of children, the court deduced that widows were just as likely to have such responsibilities and held that it could not be said that married women posed a greater problem of absenteeism, in the following words:

There is nothing to show that married women will necessarily be more likely to be absent than unmarried women or widows. If it is the presence of children which may be said to account for greater absenteeism among married women that would be so more or less in case of widows with children also.

The landmark ruling on this issue was pronounced in late 1970s in *C.B. Muthamma* v. *Union of India*[33] when the Supreme Court was called upon to address the issue of employment related discrimination. Rule 18 (4) of the Indian Foreign Services (Recruitment, Seniority and Promotion) Rules, 1961 stipulated that 'No married woman shall be entitled as of right to be appointed to the service'. Further, as per Rule 8 (2), women were required to obtain written permission from the government before marriage. The rule further stipulated that '... At any time after marriage, a woman member of the service may be required to resign from service, if the government is satisfied that her family and domestic commitments are likely to come in the way of due and efficient discharging of

duties.' Ms. Muthamma, a senior member of the Indian Foreign Services challenged these discriminatory provisions as *ultra vires* Articles 14, 15, and 16 of the Constitution. The Supreme Court upheld her contentions and declared that both these provisions were discriminatory against women and thus violative of Articles 14, 15, and 16 of the Constitution and struck them down. While upholding the principle of equality, the court placed women employees at par with male employees. In his historical ruling, Justice Krishna Iyer commented as follows:

Discrimination against woman, in traumatic transparency, is found in this rule...In these days of nuclear families, inter-continental marriages and unconventional behaviour, one fails to understand the naked bias against the gender of the species.

A few years later, yet another landmark case on the issue of discrimination in rules of employment was presented before a three-judge bench of the Supreme Court—*Air India* v. *Nergesh Meerza*[34] (also known as the Air Hostess Case). The Supreme Court struck down Air India Regulations relating to retirement and the pregnancy bar on the services of air hostesses as unconstitutional on the ground that the conditions laid down therein were entirely unreasonable and arbitrary. But the Court rejected the challenge to the lower retirement age for female members of the crew on the ground that this cannot be held to be discrimination based only on sex, upholding the stand of the employer that the different ages of retirement and salary structure for male and female employees in Air India are based on their different conditions of service and not on sex alone.[35] The impugned Service Regulation 46 provided that an air hostess would retire from the service of the

---

[32]   AIR 1966 SC 942
[33]   AIR 1979 SC 1868

[34]   AIR 1981 SC 1829
[35]   Nearly twenty years later, the Supreme Court reaffirmed this stand in *Air India Cabin Crew Association* v. *Yeshawinee Merchant*, AIR 2004 SC 187.

Corporation upon attaining the age of 35 years or on marriage, if it took place within four years of service, or on first pregnancy, whichever occurred earlier.

Under Regulation 47, the Managing Director was vested with absolute discretion to extend the age of retirement until the employee attains 45 years. The argument advanced on behalf of Air India, a Public Sector Undertaking, was that the air hostesses 'have to deal with passengers of various temperaments, and a *young and attractive* air hostess is able to cope with difficult or awkward situations more competently and more easily than an older person with less personal prepossessions' (emphasis added). It was also argued that air hostesses do not stay very long in the service of Air India and that young and attractive women are more inclined to look upon service in Air India as a 'temporary occupation than as a career'. Both the regulations, i.e., Regulations 46 and 47 were struck down as violative of Article 14 which prohibits unreasonableness and arbitrariness. Justice Fazal Ali, while declaring the provision of termination of service on the first pregnancy as violative of Article14, observed that 'It seems to us that the termination of the service of an air hostess under such circumstances is not only a callous and cruel act but an open insult to Indian womanhood.' The judgment, while recognizing the biological imperatives of a woman, went far in asserting a woman's right to private choices and to professional opportunities. 'Why should a woman be penalized for bearing a child and be made to give up her job?', the court queried. 'Therefore, if some disqualifications are attached to the condition of being a woman, it amounts to discrimination which is in violation of Article14.'

In 1986, in *Maya Devi* v. *State of Maharashtra*,[36] the requirement that married women obtain their husbands' consent before applying for public employment was successfully challenged as a violation of Articles 14, 15, and 16. The Court emphasized the importance of economic independence of women, in overcoming traditional disadvantages.

With these judgments, some headway was made towards gender equality in conditions of employment. The traditional roles of women within the domestic sphere could not be viewed as impediments to professional advancement. But despite the Supreme Court ruling, discrimination continued both in private as well as public sector. Despite the mandate of equality and statutory provisions of the Equal Remuneration Act, several loopholes could be invented to deprive women of their legitimate dues. These judgments, therefore, marked not the end but just the beginning of a long journey for women's right to equality in service conditions and employment rules. Women workers soon found out that despite the claim to legal equality, discrimination could be camouflaged under various labels. Also, while the Fundamental Rights were guaranteed against the State, discrimination within the private sector continued unabated. Further, women's rights could be defeated through contractual agreements between the employers and employees or their unions.

The next landmark judgment, *Mackinnon Mackenzie & Co Ltd.* v. *Audrey D'Costa*,[37] addressed some of these concerns. This was a case where the lady stenographers were paid less by a private sector firm than the male staff. Though the nature of the duties was the same, female stenographers were discriminated against by labeling the male staff as private secretaries. The employer had held negotiations with its employees and a settlement was arrived at, which agreed that lady stenographers would be given a lower pay scale than their male counterparts.

---

[36]   1986 1 SCR 743

[37]   (1987) 2 SCC 469

When this settlement was challenged by a lady stenographer, the petitioners argued that there was no gender discrimination and that the nature of work performed itself was very different by the male and the female stenographers. The Supreme Court overruled this argument and held discrimination with regard to unequal payment on the grounds of sex of the employee to be illegal and directed equal pay for equal work or work of a similar nature. Further it held that the provisions of the Equal Remuneration Act, 1976 would override any settlement that the employer may have with the employees. Through this judgment, the principal of equality was extended to the private sector as well.

In *Uttarakhand Mahila Kalyan Parishad* v. *State of Uttar Pradesh*,[38] the State Government discriminated against women in two respects: firstly with disparity in the pay scales whereby male teachers and employees in the Education Department were getting a higher salary than female teachers and employees, both doing administrative business and the same job; and secondly, male teachers had several promotional avenues available to them, which were denied to female teachers. It was also held that there was no particular reason for providing promotional avenues for male teachers while denying the same to female teachers. The court held that under the constitutional arrangement, there is neither occasion for a differential treatment between men and women employees in the Educational Department when they are doing the same job, nor is there any justification for a preferential treatment in the matter of affording promotional avenues for the male teachers. The Supreme Court issued a writ of Mandamus, directing the State Government to stop these discriminatory practices and directed that the pay scales for male and female teachers should comply with the constitutional provision of equality and discrimination.

In *Neera Mathur* v. *Life Insurance Corporation of India*,[39] the Supreme Court addressed the issue of the right to privacy and dignity of working women. In this case, the services of a probationer were terminated on the ground that she had falsely stated in her application the last date of her menstruation and had conveyed an impression that she was not pregnant at the time of filling it. The Supreme Court struck down the termination and directed the Corporation to delete the questions included in the application form, which were not only extremely personal but also offensive. The Supreme Court held that such questions are awkward and infringe the right of privacy under Article 21 of the Constitution.

More recently, in *Anuj Garg* v. *Hotel Association of India*,[40] the Supreme Court upheld the Delhi High Court ruling which had struck down section 30 of the Punjab Excise Act, 1914 which prohibited employment of 'any man under the age of 25 years' or 'any woman' in any part of such premises in which liquor or intoxicating drug is consumed by the public. The court held that the provision is ultra vires of Articles 14, 15, and 19 (1) (g).[41] This ruling opened up the scope for women to seek employment in bars serving liquor.

By the 1990s, there was a gradual shift in the nature of the judicial interventions, from delivering basic rights to assuring conducive working environment for women. The ratification of the convention on the Elimination of all Forms of Discrimination Against Women (CEDAW) in 1993 placed an additional onus upon the Supreme Court to eliminate all forms of discrimination against women. The Supreme

---

[38]   AIR 1992 SC 1695

[39]   AIR 1992 SC 392
[40]   AIR 2008 SC 663 : (2008) 3 SCC 1
[41]   Freedom to practice any profession or to carry on any occupation, trade or business.

Court relied upon the provisions of the Maternity Benefit Act, 1961 read with Article 11 (2) (a) and (b) of the CEDAW[42] to hold that muster roll employees were also entitled to maternity leave. The issue before the court was whether maternity leave is available only to regular employees of the Corporation or whether casual workers (known as 'muster roll employees') are also entitled to the benefit of this provision. Despite its existence on the statute books for several years, the beneficial provisions of the welfare legislation, the Maternity Benefit Act, were denied to women who were casual or contract workers. Muster roll employees of the Municipal Corporation of Delhi challenged this provision in *Municipal Corporation of Delhi* v. *Female Workers (Muster Roll)*[43] and the same was struck down by the Supreme Court in 2000.

Discrimination against the daughter is an issue which lies within the domain of personal laws, but the same also cropped up as an issue concerning the workplace in *Savita Samwedi* v. *Union of India*.[44] The Railway Board issued a circular that disentitled a married daughter living with her father, both being employees of the Railways, from claiming regularization of the government accommodation on the retirement of the father, if he had a son. The petitioner challenged this provision as discriminatory and violative of Articles 14 and 15 of the

Constitution. The Supreme Court struck down the Railway Board's circular holding that it was a clear case of gender bias. The Court clarified that if the father desired that upon his retirement the allotment of a government accommodation made to him be regularized in favour of his daughter who was also an employee of the Railways and who was not claiming House Rent Allowance, there was no reason why his request could not be acceded to. The Court commented that it is not mandatory for a father to live only with a son and that he is not prohibited from living with a married daughter.

It has been a long and sustained struggle from C.B. Muthamma and Nergesh Meerza cases, where women workers had to fight for their right to enter into marriage, to Neera Mathur, Savita Samwedi and the Muster Roll cases, through which women raised concerns of privacy, dignity, and discrimination. The hard won victories of a few women have helped to usher in a culture of women's rights within workplaces, both in the public as well as the private sector.

Positive Discrimination in Favour of Women
The validity of several protective legislation in favour of women was challenged on the ground that they violate the constitutional mandate of equality, as they 'discriminate in favour of women'. While upholding the validity of these provisions, the courts have relied on Article 15 (3) of the constitution to defend these positive enactments which aimed to set right the centuries of discrimination suffered by women.

In *Om Narain Agarwal* v. *Nagarpalika, Shahjahanpur*,[45] the provision under the U.P. Municipalties Act which provides for the nomination of two women on the municipal board was challenged in the Supreme Court. It was

---

[42] Article 11(2) (a) and (b) read: 'In order to prevent discrimination against women on the grounds of marriage or maternity and to ensure their effective right to work, States/parties shall take appropriate measures: (a) to prohibit, subject to the imposition of sanctions, dismissal on the grounds of pregnancy or of maternity leave and discrimination in dismissals on the basis of marital status; (b) to introduce maternity leave with pay or with comparable social benefits without loss of former employment, seniority or social allowances.'

[43] (2000) 3 SCC 224
[44] (1996) 2 SCC 380

[45] AIR 1993 SC 1440

held that the nominations are protected by Article 15 (3). In *T. Sudhakar Reddy* v. *Govt. of A.P.*,[46] the Supreme Court upheld the constitutional validity of the proviso to section 31 (1) (a) of the Andhra Pradesh Cooperative Societies Act, 1964 and the Rules 22 (c) and 22-A (3) (a) framed thereunder, relying upon the mandate of Article 15 (3) of the Constitution. The proviso along with the said rules provided for the nomination of two women members by the Registrar to the managing committee of the Cooperative Societies with a right to vote and to take part in the meetings of the committee. The Court upheld the validity of these provisions on the ground that Article 15 (3) of the Constitution permitted the making of special provisions for women. In *Govt. of Andhra Pradesh* v. *P.B. Vijayakumar*,[47] the Supreme Court relied upon Article 15 (3) of the Constitution and held that the decision taken by the State government of giving preference to women, other things being equal, to the extent of 30 per cent posts in recruitment to the subordinate service was protected. This protection was differentiated from reservation and was described as an instance of 'limited affirmative State action' and was perhaps the first occasion that Article 15 (3) of the Constitution was invoked affirmatively by the Supreme Court in matters of employment.

Paternalistic Approach to the Offence of Adultery

While in the above instances the mandate for enacting special legislation in favour of women has proved to be beneficial, a protectionist approach can not always be construed as favouring women. This becomes evident when we examine various cases, wherein the penal

provisions regarding adultery under section 497[48] of the IPC and section 198 (2)[49] of the Cr.P.C. In these cases, the Apex Court used a paternalist argument to defend these legal provisions which only serve to undermine women's role as equal partners in marriage. The arguments used for upholding the constitutional validity of these provisions, which are not just discriminatory against men but are sexist and anti-women in their intent and reflect archaic victorian values, are rather absurd. The Supreme Court invoked the constitutional mandate of positive discrimination under Article 15 (3) while defending these sexist provisions. The challenges to these provisions have come from the perspective punishment for the woman involved, right of the adulterer's wife to prosecute her husband etc., as the following cases illustrate.

In *Yousuf Abdul Aziz* v. *State of Bombay*,[50] the validity of section 497 of the IPC, which punishes only the men in the offence of adultery and exempts women from punishment, was challenged as violative of Articles 14 and 15 (1) of the Constitution. The petitioner contended that even though women may be equally guilty,

---

[48] Section 497 (IPC) Adultery: '*Whoever has sexual intercourse with a person who is and whom he knows or has reason to believe to be the wife of another man, without the consent or connivance of that man, such sexual intercourse not amounting to the offence of rape, is guilty of the offence of adultery, and shall be punished with imprisonment of either description for a term which may extend to five years, or with fine, or with both. In such case the wife shall be punished as an abettor.*

[49] Section 198(2) (Cr.PC): Prosecution for offences against marriage: '*For the purposes of sub-section (1), no person other than the husband of the woman shall be deemed to be aggrieved by any offence punishable under section 497 or section 498 of the said code: Provided that in the absence of the husband, some person who had care of the woman on his behalf at the time when such offence was committed may, with the leave of the court, make a complaint on his behalf.*

[46] 1993 (4) SCC 439
[47] AIR 1995 SC 1695
[50] AIR 1954 SC 321

only the man was punished, which violates the right to equality on the ground of sex. A Constitutional Bench of the Supreme Court upheld the validity of the provision on the ground that the classification was not based on the ground of sex alone. The Court relied upon the mandate of Article 15 (3) to uphold this provision. The position was made explicit when it was ruled:

It was argued that clause (3) should be confined to provisions which are beneficial to women and cannot be used to give them a licence to commit and abet crimes. We are unable to read any such restriction into the clause; nor are we able to agree that a provision which prohibits punishment is tantamount to a licence to commit the offence of which punishment has been prohibited.

In *Sowmitri Vishnu* v. *Union of India*,[51] the validity of section 497, IPC was challenged once again before a three-judge bench of the Supreme Court on the ground that it recognizes only the husband of the adulteress as an aggrieved party but does not confer similar rights upon the wife of the adulterer. It was contended that the provision is a flagrant instance of 'gender discrimination' and 'male chauvinism'. Once again the Supreme Court declined to strike down the provision and held that it does not violate Article 14 or 15 of the Constitution and validatēd it on the ground that it is a protection awarded to women under Article 15 (3) of the Constitution. Subsequently, in yet another case, *Revathi* v. *Union of India*,[52] the Supreme Court held that section 198 (2) of the Criminal Procedure Code (Cr.PC) which gives the husband of an adulteress the right to prosecute the adulterer but does not award similar rights to the wife of the adulterer, is not discriminatory. Thus the Court was consistent in its apparent mandate to 'protect' women.

These judgments by the Supreme Court are contrary to the recommendation made by the Law Commission, in its 1971 Report and recommended an amendment of the law to render it gender-neutral by extending its provisions to both men and women. The Malimath Committee Report recommended further changes and suggested:

The object of this section (S.497, IPC) is to preserve the sanctity of marriage. Society abhors marital infidelity. Therefore, there is no reason for not meting out similar treatment to the wife who has sexual intercourse with a man (other than her husband).[53]

The provisions of IPC and Cr.PC are reflective of the value system then prevailing in England where marriages were deemed to be monogamous and indissoluble. Within this concept, women were treated as the property of the husband. Any man who violated these norms of proprietorial ownership was equated with a man who commits theft and was punished. This notion is based on the Ten Commandments of the Biblical era, where the Sixth and the Ninth commandment restrained men from indulging in sexual relationship with the wife of one's neighbour or even coveting her by prescribing, '*Though shall not covet your neighbour's wife*'. It is interesting to note that the provision does not recognize the role of the married woman in the sexual act as she was viewed only as a passive object or a mere chattel. On the other hand, sex with an unmarried woman was beyond the purview of this provision. Since women were mere chattels, the sanction against sex with a married woman could be applied only to the man who indulged in such an act, the wife of the adulterous man had no remedy against her own husband.

---

[51] AIR 1985 SC 1618
[52] AIR 1988 SC 835

[53] Malimath Committee Report, Committee on Reforms of Criminal Justice System, Government of India, Ministry of Home Affairs at p. 190.

In the modern day where women have ceased to be regarded as the property of their husbands and are competent of leading an independent existence, matrimonial law in England has moved far from this archaic notion of sacramental and indissoluble marriages. A marriage can be dissolved at the behest of either of the parties by proving a matrimonial fault or through mutual consent. Therefore there is no reason to uphold this archaic provision in our Penal Code when it has been abandoned even by the English law a long time ago.

While the Supreme Court decisions are problematic, the recommendations to usher in the notion of equality as suggested by the Malimath Committee are equally problematic. Granting married women the right to file a criminal complaint against her husband and the woman who had committed adultery with the husband or granting the husband the right to file a criminal complaint against his wife who has been adulterous with another man will not serve any purpose as it would be contrary to the prevailing principles of matrimonial jurisprudence. Marriages are no longer treated as sacramental and indissoluble unions which need to be protected by providing for punishment as a deterrent to sex with a married woman.[54] An act of adultery either by the wife or the husband can be addressed by filing a petition for divorce on this ground rather than resorting to penal provisions based on archaic principles. Archaic and sexist patriarchal notions cannot be validated or remedied by introducing an element of equality within them.

Right to Life Includes Right to Privacy and Dignity

As has been discussed above, the Supreme Court, in *Neera Mathur* v. *Life Insurance Corporation of India*, applied the constitutional provisions of Article 21 (right to life and liberty) to protect women's right to privacy and dignity at workplace. In subsequent years the Court extended this principle to issues of public life and the domain of personal laws. At times the courts have had to step-in to protect women when the very measures introduced for their betterment were used to discriminate against them. In *Neera Gupta* v. *University of Delhi*[55] the Court was called upon to examine the issue of leave which a woman is entitled to under the provision of the Maternity Benefits Act. A female student who had availed of such leave was barred from appearing for the university exam on the ground of insufficient attendance. The Delhi High Court struck this down holding that if students were entitled to avail of various kinds of leave, why could a lady student not avail of maternity leave? The court commented that there was no explanation as to why a long leave is permitted to all other students for various reasons while only female graduate students are discriminated against for availing the maternity leave by denying them permission to appear for university exams. The court expressed the view that there appears to be no rational or logical explanation for this discriminatory treatment.

The application of Article 21 to the realm of personal law has been an important and innovative step taken by the higher judiciary. While striking down the discriminatory provisions under the Indian Divorce Act, the Kerala High Court, in *Ammini E.J.* v. *Union of India*,[56] introduced the notion of right to life with dignity within the ambit of Article 21.[57]

---

[54] See Section 1 of Chapter 1 of the second volume of this book *Marriage and Its Dissolution* for detailed discussion on this issue.

[55] AIR 1997 Del 175

[56] This judgment is discussed in detail in Chapter 1 Personal Laws and Women's Rights.

[57] See later the sub-section, constitutional validity of personal laws for a more detailed discussion of this judgment.

An important ruling in the context of the right to privacy and dignity is the Delhi High Court ruling in *Naz Foundation* v. *Government of NCT*.[58] In this historical ruling, the high court held that section 377 of IPC, insofar as it criminalises consensual sexual acts of adults in private, is violative of Articles 14, 15, and 21 of the Constitution. This judgment protects the rights of lesbians, gays, bisexuals and transgender persons (LGBT) who have a different sexual orientation and legalizes homosexuality. The court explained its reasoning in the following words:

If there is one constitutional tenet that can be said to be underlying theme of the Indian Constitution, it is that of 'inclusiveness'. This Court believes that Indian Constitution reflects this value deeply ingrained in Indian society, nurtured over several generations. The inclusiveness that Indian society traditionally displayed, literally in every aspect of life, is manifest in recognizing a role in society for everyone. Those perceived by the majority as 'deviants' or 'different' are not on that score excluded or ostracised. Where society can display inclusiveness and understanding, such persons can be assured of a life of dignity and nondiscrimination. ... It cannot be forgotten that discrimination is antithesis of equality and that it is the recognition of equality which will foster the dignity of every individual.

Provisions to Secure Social and Economic Advancement of Women

There are several other measures, both legislative and judicial, which have served to enhance women's rights. One significant move in this direction has been the introduction of reservations for women in order to increase their political participation. This has been a great boon to Indian women, particularly to women from backward castes and scheduled tribes.

The Vienna Convention on the Elimination of All Forms of Discrimination Against Women (CEDAW)—which was ratified by the United Nations Organization on 18 December 1979 and by the Government of India on 8 August 1993. This has strengthened the arms of the judiciary in ensuring gender justice. The Supreme Court, in *C. Masilamani Mudaliar*,[59] invoked the CEDAW provisions while highlighting the right of women in India to eliminate gender-based discrimination, particularly in respect of property, so as to attain economic empowerment.[60]

The Vishaka Guidelines have been another instance where the Apex Court has gone beyond its constitutional mandate to defend women's rights at their workplace. While usurping the powers of the legislature, the Supreme Court relied upon the provisions of the CEDAW. Hence provisions of the CEDAW have now become part of the domestic law which can be invoked to protect women against discrimination in various other areas as well. This section deals with these developments.

Reservations for Women in Local Bodies: 73rd–74th Amendment

The 73rd and 74th amendments to the Indian Constitution, affected in 1992, provide for reservation of seats for women in elections to *panchayats* and municipalities respectively. This was perhaps the first attempt by the Parliament to provide reservations for women in elected representative bodies. According to Article 243D of the Constitution of India, not less than one-third of the total number of seats to be filled by direct election in every panchayat shall be reserved for woman. Such seats may be allotted by rotation to different constituencies in a

---

[58] 2010 Cri.LJ 94 Del

[59] *C. Masilamani Mudaliar* v. *The Idol of Sri Swaminathaswami Thirukoli*, (1996) 8 SCC 252.

[60] See later the sub-section, constitutional validity of personal laws for a more detailed discussion of this judgment.

panchayat. Not less than one-third of the total number of posts of chairpersons in the panchayat, at each level, shall be reserved for women. Article 243T of the Constitution of India, which was added by the Constitution (74th Amendment) Act, 1992, makes similar provisions for reservation of seats for women in the direct elections to every municipality.

The two child norm for members of elected bodies which has been introduced in several states since 1992, has had an adverse impact upon scheduled castes and tribes (Rao 2003). Such moves only serve to widen inequalities of communities which have low health indicators, inadequate health care facilities and high mortality rates. The elections of many members who were unaware of this provision have been set aside. In one particular instance, when a male Sarpanch was disqualified, all his children were compelled to leave the school because the states population policy recommends that government facility for education be withheld to persons having more than two children. The children had to bear the brunt of their parents action and were denied their Fundamental Right to free and compulsory education (Hariharan 2003).

The impact upon women has been even more adverse since the men have resorted to various manipulations to retain their seats like discarding their wives, forcing them to undergo abortions, abandoning their children, or giving away the children in adoption. For women, such options do not exist. Women lack decision making power regarding their bodies and reproductive choices, but are compelled to face consequences (Buch 2006). At times the younger women have been forced to quite their seats in favour of their mother-in-law or any other male member of the family. The Supreme Court has upheld the constitutional validity of this provision on the ground that it is in public interest

and consistent with the national population policy and that it promotes health of the masses and socio-economic welfare of the people.[61] There appears to be a disjunct between the understanding of the Supreme Court and the ground realities of the 'masses'.

In September 1996, the Parliament introduced the Constitution (81st Amendment) Bill seeking to reserve one-third of the seats in the Lok Sabha and state legislative assemblies for women. This move is an extension of the 73rd and 74th constitutional amendments and represents a light towards correcting gender imbalance in state and central legislatures and will ensure greater political participation and representations in elected bodies for women. However, there is also a concern that the gains will be reaped only by women of upper strata at the cost of men from the lower strata. Due to opposition from political parties from Bihar and Uttar Pradesh, it was stalled. A demand was also raised for 'reservations within reservations' for women from lower castes, backward tribes and minority communities. But this demand was not conceded. After much skepticism, the Bill which is now titled as, The Constitution (108 Amendment) Bill, 2010, was finally passed in the Rajya Sabha on 9 March 2010 and is awaiting its passage in the lower house.[62]

Reservation of seats for women in local bodies and educational institutions, as well as those which aim to promote self-employment among women, are held to be valid. Some illustrative cases on this issue as discussed below.

In *Government of A.P. v. P.B. Vijay Kumar*,[63] the Supreme Court held reservations for women in State services, to the extent of 30 per

---

[61] *Javed* v. *State of Haryana* AIR 2003 SC 3057.
[62] "Rajya Sabha Passes Women's Reservation Bill" *Times of India*, March 10 2010 (news report).
[63] AIR 1995 SC 1648

cent, by the Andhra Pradesh government candidates as valid. The Division Bench of the Supreme Court emphatically declared that the power conferred upon the State by Article 15 (3) is wide enough to cover the entire range of State activity, including employment under the State. Special provisions for women in respect of employment or posts under the State were held to be an integral part of Article 15 (3). The Court held that since Articles 15 (1) and 15(3) go together, the protection of Article 15 (3) would be applicable to employment under the State, falling under Article 16 (1) and (2) of the Constitution.

In *Union of India v. K.P. Prabhakaran*,[64] the Supreme Court upheld the decision of the Railway Administration to reserve the posts of Enquiry-cum-Reservation Clerks in Reservation offices in the metropolitan cities of Madras, Bombay, Calcutta, and Delhi exclusively for women and the further decision that the Reservation Offices in the said metropolitan cities should constitute a seniority unit separate from the rest of the cadre of Enquiry-cum-Reservation clerks. The Court while coming to the above conclusion relied upon its decision in *Government. of A.P. v. P.B. Vijay Kumar.*[65]

In *Gayatri Devi Pansari v. State of Orissa*,[66] the Supreme Court upheld a Government order which gave preference to women in opening up to 30 per cent of the medical stores in hospitals on the ground that it is a beneficial provision and its purpose was to provide self-employment opportunities to women.

In 2007, in *Women's Education Society v. State of Maharashtra*,[67] the Nagpur Bench of the Bombay High Court reaffirmed the trend and held that 'eligibility condition of being women imposed by the Petitioners for employees being recruited in the college concerned cannot be held to be violative of Article 14 or Article 16 of the Constitution'. The concerned college was exclusively for women. Its decision to invite only women applicants for teaching and non-teaching positions was challenged by the Nagpur University, according to which such a move was violative of the Constitution and the Maharashtra Universities Act, 1994. However, the court held that the latter act recognised exclusive women colleges and permitted not only admission but also appointment to be restricted only to women. The high court also stated that the petitioner college was established to encourage women's education, and the appointment of female teaching staff was neither erroneous nor arbitrary and hence was not violative of the Constitution.

Sexual Harassment of Women at Workplace: The Vishaka Guidelines

In *Vishaka v. State of Rajasthan*,[68] a Division Bench of the Supreme Court, speaking through J.S. Verma, C.J., laid down a number of guidelines remedying the legislative vacuum on the subject of sexual harassment of women at their workplace. Taking into consideration the definition of women's rights contained in section 2 (d) of the Protection of Human Rights Act, 1993, the court defined 'sexual harassment' in the following words: Any unwelcome, sexually determined behaviour, whether directly or by implication, like physical contact and advances, a demand or request for sexual favours sexually-coloured remarks, showing pornography, and any other unwelcome physical, verbal, or non-verbal conduct of sexual nature.

---

[64] 1997 (11) SCC 638
[65] AIR 1995 SC 1695
[66] (2000) 4 SCC 221
[67] 2007 (109) BLR 1562

[68] (1997) 6 SCC 241

Box 2.2 Vishaka Guidelines

- It is the duty of the employer or other responsible persons in workplaces or other institutions, to prevent or deter the commission of acts of sexual harassment and to provide procedures for the resolution, settlement, or prosecution of acts of sexual harassment by taking all steps required.
- All employers or persons in charge of workplaces, whether in the public or private sector, should take appropriate steps to prevent sexual harassment.
- Appropriate work conditions should be provided in respect of work, leisure, health, and hygiene to further ensure that there is no hostile environment towards women at workplaces and no woman employee should have reasonable grounds to believe that she is disadvantaged in connection with her employment.
- Where such conduct amounts to a specific offence under the Indian Penal Code or under any other law, the employer shall initiate appropriate action in accordance with law by making a complaint with the appropriate authority.
- It should be ensured that victims or witnesses are not victimized or discriminated against while dealing with complaints of sexual harassment.
- Victims of sexual harassment should have the option to seek transfer of the perpetrator or their own transfer.
- Where such conduct amounts to misconduct in employment as defined by the relevant service rules, appropriate disciplinary action should be initiated by the employer in accordance with those rules.
- Whether or not such conduct constitutes an offence under law or a breach of the service rules, an appropriate complaint mechanism should be created in the employer's organization for redress of the complaint made by the victim. Such a complaint mechanism should ensure time bound treatment of complaints.
- The complaint mechanism should be adequate to provide, where necessary, a Complaints Committee, a special counsellor, or any other support service, including the maintenance of confidentiality.
- The Complaints Committee should be headed by a woman and not less than half of its members should be women. Further, to prevent the possibility of any undue pressure or influence from senior levels, such Complaints Committee should involve a third party, either NGO or other body who is familiar with the issue of sexual harassment.
- The Complaints Committee must make an annual report of the complaints received and action taken by them to the government department concerned.
- The employers and person-in-charge will also report on compliance with the aforesaid guidelines, including on the reports of the Complaints Committee, to the government department concerned.
- Employees should be allowed to raise issues of sexual harassment at workers' meetings and in other appropriate fora and it should be affirmatively discussed in employer-employee meetings.
- Awareness of the rights of female employees in this regard should be created, particularly by prominently notifying the guidelines, and appropriate legislation when enacted on the subject, in a suitable manner.
- Where sexual harassment occurs as a result of an act or omission by any third party or outsider, the employer and person-in-charge will take all steps necessary and reasonable to assist the affected person in terms of support and preventive action.

The Supreme Court referred to the CEDAW and the violation of gender equality as enshrined in Articles 14 and 15 and the right to life and personal liberty of women under Article 21 of the Constitution. As a result of this judgment, any woman employee who is subjected to sexual harassment of any kind at the workplace can take recourse to initiating criminal proceedings and/or disciplinary action and can also seek compensation from the guilty employer and other persons responsible for the harassment. The court further directed that the guidelines laid down in this case should be followed until the legislature enacts a statute in this regard.

Constitutional Validity of Personal Laws

This section analyses the interface between provisions of equality and non-discrimination contained in a modern constitution at one end and the religious or customary, gender-discriminatory personal laws at the other. Therefore many of the cases cited here have also been discussed under the various religion-based personal laws or the customary laws in the preceding chapter. This section also briefly discusses the interface between diverse personal laws and the call for a UCC as stipulated under Article 44 of the Constitution which are discussed in greater detail in the subsequent section.

Issues such as monogamy, restitution of conjugal rights, discriminatory grounds of divorce and property inheritance, rights of maintenance upon divorce and discriminatory personal laws have come for judicial scrutiny from time to time. Most challenges, barring a few, have been in the context of statutes enacted by the legislature. The courts were testing the validity of these specific provisions in the context of the mandate of the constitution for equality, non-discrimination, freedom and liberty. It is interesting to note that the decisions are at times contradictory. There is also an apprehension

that through these rulings the judiciary may encroach upon the legislative powers, leading to controversial judicial law-making. The rulings were shaped by the need of the hour, political exigency, and social concerns of an individual judge. Therefore what has evolved is a cautious and case by case approach rather than a broad framework of rights.

One of the first constitutional challenges to the existence of personal laws in the post-Constitution period was in *State of Bombay* v. *Narasu Appa Mali*.[69] The petition was in defense of the prerogative of the Hindu male for polygamy. The petitioner pleaded that the norm of monogamy imposed upon him by the Bombay Prohibition of Bigamous Marriages Act, 1946, violated the provision of equality under Article 14 and non-discrimination under Article 15 of the newly enacted Constitution on the ground that Muslim men could contract polygamous marriages. While upholding the validity of this social legislation enacted for the protection of women, the Bombay High Court ruled that personal laws are not 'laws in force' under Article 12 of the Constitution as they are based on religious precepts and customary practices and that the principles enshrined in Part III of the Constitution cannot be applied to the personal laws. In the subsequent ruling, *Srinivasa Aiyar*,[70] it was contended that the right to practice polygamy is based on Hindu religious precepts and a prohibition on polygamy violates this right to practice religion. The Madras High Court held that even assuming that the term 'laws in force' includes personal laws, the Act does not offend Article 15 which stipulates non-discrimination on the basis of sex.

---

[69] AIR 1952 Bom 84

[70] *Srinivasa Aiyar v. Saraswati Ammal*, AIR 1952 Mad 193.

Nearly half a century later, the position was clarified by the Supreme Court in *C. Masilamani Mudaliar v. Idol of Sri Swaminathaswami Thirukoil*,[71] the Supreme Court held as follows:

The personal laws conferring inferior status on women is anathema to equality. Personal laws are derived not from the Constitution but from the religious scriptures. The laws thus derived must be consistent with the Constitution lest they became void under Article 13 if they violated fundamental rights.

With these wordings, though not directly, yet implicitly, the apex court overruled the earlier two judgments which had held that personal laws are not laws in force. The implication of the observations of the Supreme Court, which dealt with the right of a Hindu woman to execute a will in respect of the property acquired or possessed by her, under Section.14 of the Hindu Succession Act, 1956, is that the right of women to eliminate all kinds of gender based discrimination, particularly in respect of property, is an implicit right, it forms part of Articles 14, 15 and 21 of the Constitution of India, which the judgment referred to as 'the trinity of justice – equality, liberty and dignity of person'. Hence it can be surmised that after this ruling 'personal laws' can be construed as 'laws in force' under Article 13 and can be struck down if they violate fundamental rights.

In *Dwarakabai v. Prof. Mainam Mathews*,[72] where the stipulation that the husband could get divorce on the ground of adultery but the wife had also to prove cruelty or desertion, was challenged. The Madras High Court, adopting an extremely anti-women posture, ruled that the discrimination is based on a sensible and reasonable classification, after taking into consideration the ability of men and women and the results of their acts and hence it is not arbi-

trary. Subsequently, in 1995 in *Ammini E. J. v. Union of India*,[73] the constitutional validity of section 10 of the Indian Divorce Act was challenged on the ground that it violates Articles 14, 15, and 21 of the Constitution. Accepting this argument, the Kerala High Court struck down the offensive provisions and introduced the notion of right to life with dignity within the ambit of Article 21 in the following words:

The legal effect of the provisions of Section. 10 is to compel the wife who is deserted or cruelly treated to continue a life as the wife of a man she hates. Such a life will be a sub-human life without dignity and personal liberty. It will be humiliating and oppressive without the freedom to remarry and enjoy life in the normal course. Such a life can legitimately be treated only as a life imposed by a tyrannical or authoritarian law on a helpless deserted or cruelly treated Christian wife quite against her will and will be a life without dignity and liberty ensured by the Constitution. Hence the provisions which require the Christian wives to prove adultery along with desertion and cruelty are violative of Article 21 of the Constitution of India.[74]

In *Mary Roy v. State of Kerala*,[75] provisions of two pre-Independence statutes—the Travancore Christian Succession Act, 1910 and Cochin Christian Succession Act, 1922—which discriminated against daughters, were challenged on the ground of discrimination against women and violation of Articles 14 and 15 of the Constitution. Under the Travancore Christian Succession Act, 1910, the share of the daughter was limited to one-fourth of the share of the son or Rs 5000, whichever was less. Under the Cochin Christian Succession Act, 1922, the share of daughter was one-third of the son or Rs 5000, whichever was less. Although the Supreme Court struck down the discriminatory provisions, this

---

[71] (1996) 8 SCC 525
[72] AIR 1953 Mad 792

[73] AIR 1995 Ker 252 FB. Also reported as *Mary Sonia Zachariah v. Union of India*, II (1995) DMC 27 FB.
[74] AIR 1995 Ker 252 (FB)
[75] AIR 1986 SC 1011

was done based on a technical ground that after Independence the laws enacted by the erstwhile princely states which were not expressly saved have been repealed.[76]

In *Madhu Kishwar* v. *State of Bihar*,[77] the constitutionality of certain provisions of the Chhota Nagpur Tenancy Act, 1908 which disentitled tribal women from inheritance rights were examined. The court, while upholding the discriminatory provisions, read them down to preserve their constitutionality. It ruled that destitute women could assert a right of occupation against the male inheritors. The court was unwilling to declare that the custom of inheritance, which disinherited the daughter, offend Articles 14, 15, and 21 on the basis that customs differ from tribe to tribe and region to region.[78]

The constitutional validity of the Muslim Women (Protection of Rights on Divorce) Act, 1986 was challenged in *Daniel Latifi* v. *Union of India*.[79] The Supreme Court upheld the validity of the Act but provided a more egalitarian and gender-just interpretation of the Act. The court explained that the new Act has substituted the earlier right of recurrent maintenance under section 125 of the Cr.P.C. with a new right to claim a lump sum amount as a divorce settlement. If the husband fails to make such a settlement, a divorced Muslim woman has the right to approach the court for enforcement of the right under section 3 of the Act.

In 1983, in *T. Sareetha* v. *T. Venkatasubbiah*,[80] the Andhra Pradesh High Court struck down section 9 of the Hindu Marriage Act, 1955, which deals with restitution of conjugal rights as unconstitutional. The court held that this provision violates the right to privacy and human dignity guaranteed by Article 21 of the Constitution and causes the grossest form of violation of an individual's right to privacy. It denies the woman her free choice whether, when, and how her body is to become the vehicle for the procreation of another human being. In 1984, the Delhi High Court, in *Harvinder Kaur* v. *Harminder Singh*,[81] upheld this provision, invoking the old argument that constitutional principles cannot be applied to personal laws. The court ruled:

Introduction of constitutional law in the home is most inappropriate; it is like pushing a bull into a china shop. It will prove to be a ruthless destroyer of the marriage institution and all that it stands for. In the privacy of the home and married life, neither Article 21 nor Article 14 have any place.

Later in the same year, the Supreme Court affirmed this decision in *Saroj Rani* v. *Sudarshan Chhadha*.[82] It attempted to reconcile the contradictory views by upholding the Delhi High Court judgment that section 9 is constitutional and by overruling the Andhra Pradesh judgment.

The stipulation under the Hindu Minority and Guardianship Act, 1955 that the father is the natural guardian of the child was challenged in *Githa Hariharan* v. *Reserve Bank of India*.[83] Rather than giving a finding of unconstitutionality, the Apex Court used the interpretative tool of 'reading down' the law to include the mother as also the 'natural' guardian of a child. The interpretation that the mother is the 'natural guardian' in the case of an absentee father had already been upheld by the Supreme Court in 1970 in *Jijabai Gajre* v. *Pathan Khan*[84] and

---

[76]   Part B, States (Laws) Act, 1951

[77]   (1996) 5 SCC 125

[78]   However, K. Ramaswamy J., in a dissenting judgment, held that the provision is unconstitutional.

[79]   (2001) 7 SCC 740: 2001 Cri.LJ 4660 SC FB

[80]   AIR 1983 AP 356

[81]   AIR 1984 Del 66

[82]   AIR 1984 SC 1562

[83]   (1999) 2 SCC 228 : AIR 1999 SC 1149

[84]   AIR 1970 SC

hence the *Githa Hariharan case* did not break any new ground.

The courts have adopted a cautious approach and have responded more on a 'case to case' basis rather than advocating a universalized position regarding its authority to enter the domain of the 'sacred and the personal'. While there have been some gains by striking down discriminatory provisions, a clear and unambiguous set of principles regarding the relationship between Articles 14 and 15 (equality and non-discrimination) and Article 25 (right to practice and propagate religion) is yet to emerge. The courts have also resisted the pressure for judicial law-making and if an alternate plea could be upheld, as in the *Mary Roy case* discussed above, they have refrained from testing the validity of a discriminatory provision on the basis of equality and non-discrimination.

This approach is exemplified in a ruling in the public interest petition filed by an Ahmedabad-based women's organization, the Ahmedabad Women Action Group (AWAG).[85] This petition urged the courts to enter the arena of judicial law-making. The petition had challenged various discriminatory aspects of Muslim law, including polygamy and triple talaq. While dismissing this petition (and other similar petitions challenging the discriminatory aspects of Hindu and Christian law), without examining the merits of the contentions, the Apex court ruled that it is not within the jurisdiction of the courts to make laws for social change. The Court observed that the petitions raised issues of state policy and it is the function of the legislature to lay down these policies of social change. The courts have responded more favourably when there is a *lis* and when women who are aggrieved by the discriminatory provision have approached

the courts rather than in public interest litigation demanding judicial intervention to usher in an era of gender justice.

Though the domain of personal laws remains contested and controversial, one can gradually see a new trend where the courts are willing to test the constitutionality of these provisions against notions of justice, equity, equality, non-discrimination, right to life and personal liberty. In this context, while the ruling in *Narasu Appa Mali*, which held that personal laws are not subject to judicial review, forms one end of the spectrum and the more recent rulings, such as *Ammini* and *Danial Latifi*, make up the other end.

Section B

UNIFORM CIVIL CODE: CONTESTING CLAIMS AND COMMUNAL HUES
Minority Claims within a Nationalist Agenda

The State shall endeavour to source for the citizens a uniform civil code throughout the territory of India.

– Article 44, Constitution of India

The discussion on the constitutional validity of diverse 'personal laws' brings us to the debate around the enactment of a Uniform Civil Code. The debate encompasses the tension between two constitutional guarantees—equality and non-discrimination (Articles 14 and 15) and religious freedom and cultural plurality (Articles 25 to 28). While the mandate for enacting a UCC (Article 44 of the Constitution) is a Directive Principle of State Policy, right to equality and protection of minority culture are justiciable Fundamental Rights. It is within this scheme of seemingly conflicting constitutional claims that one needs to frame the discourse on the enactment of a common or uniform family law.

---

[85] *Ahmedabad Women Action Group (AWAG) v. Union of India*, JT 1997 (3) SC 171.

The Indian Constitution contains an inconsistency regarding family law. While Article 44 directs the State to enact a uniform civil code, the power to legislate in the realm of family law is situated in the Concurrent List (Entry 5, List III of the Seventh Schedule), which means that the power is granted to both central and state legislatures. Since the Constitution provides for a federal structure with clearly defined legislative powers, depriving the states of this power through the enactment of one set of rigid and uniform family laws would lead to the dominance of the centre over the states. While this would affect the overall centre-state relationship, it would particularly cause a serious dent in relationships with the North-Eastern states which are further protected through specific Constitutional guarantees of protection of customary laws and practices of certain tribes.

The genesis of the demand for uniform family law is situated within the women's movement of the pre-Independence era. The AIWC was an active protagonist of this demand and raised the issue in the context of women's rights within the larger political debates within the Indian National Congress. One of the first issues addressed by the AIWC was the unequal treatment of men and women within personal law. Although initially the demand for reform was articulated in terms of 'women's upliftment', later the scope was widened to 'equal rights'. The demand was for a comprehensive code regulating marriage, divorce, and inheritance, based on principles of equality. As a first step in this direction, the AIWC undertook a comparative study of family laws of different communities with a view to recommend reforms within them.

In 1940, the National Planning Committee, while focusing on the economic dimension of women's rights, resolved that women should be equal to men in a planned society. To achieve this goal they recommended the enactment of a Uniform Civil Code (Lateef 1994: 48). During the initial phase, the UCC was to be an optional code which could gradually replace the various personal laws.[86]

The political astuteness of the AIWC members was visible in the subsequent parliamentary debates on the Hindu Code Bill in the 1950s. Representatives of Hindu fundamentalist parties termed the proposed code as anti-Hindu and anti-Indian and raised the demand for a uniform code as a delaying tactic. But the AIWC members rejected the proposition for a Uniform Civil Code and pressed for Hindu law reforms. This was a significant political move since supporting the demand for a uniform code at that juncture would have meant an alliance with the most reactionary and anti-women lobby and would have been a further set back to the rights of Hindu women.

Later, during the Constituent Assembly debates, the focus shifted from gender equality to national integration. The demand for a UCC was seen as a corrective measure for divisive colonial policies. Integration of communities in the modern state was sought to be achieved through uniformity of personal laws. While pressing for setting a timeframe for the enactment of a UCC, M. R. Masani, Hansa Mehta, and Amrit Kaur bemoaned the continuance of personal laws which, they argued, was keeping India back from advancing to nationhood.[87] Proceedings of the Constituent Assembly show a marked absence of discussion about the

---

[86] This position seems to have continued till the Draft Bill which was presented at the Convention held by the Bar Council in 1986.

[87] The note of dissent attached to the Draft Report of 14 April 1947 of the sub-committee on Fundamental Rights and the note of dissent attached to the Draft Report of 17 to 20 April 1947 (Rao 1968:162 and 177).

significance of a UCC for women. The issue of women's rights seems to have been subsumed by the political concerns of building a modern state. However, there was a presumption that the modernity ushered in by a modern state would transform the patriarchal social order and ensure gender justice.

The Constitutional Assembly debates around the enactment of a UCC were framed within the dynamism between group identity and individual rights—multiculturalism and legal pluralism at one end and legal universalism and citizenship claims on the other. At this historical juncture of India's freedom, the overarching concern of the founding fathers was the formation of the new nation-state and its smooth governance. Within this paradigm, the provision of a UCC was debated primarily in the context of the authority of the State to regulate civil life and family relationships of its citizens and the right of minorities to their cultural identity.

Within the political turmoil surrounding the partition of the country and the bloodbath that followed, an insecure and defensive Muslim minority had to be reassured of their right to religious and cultural freedom in the new democracy. What emerges was a duality of concerns for the newly evolving Indian State. While it was deemed necessary that the various sects, castes, and tribes—from the erstwhile Princely States, territories under the control of various tribes, and the British Raj—be integrated as one community by enacting a uniform set of family laws by introducing a concept of 'legal Hinduism'. The flip side of this objective of smooth governance was assuring minorities (not just Muslims, but also Christians, Parsees, Jews, and tribal communities) of the intactness of their separate religious and cultural identity, symbolised by the continuance of their personal laws.

In the years immediately following Independence, the issue of a UCC, for ensuring gender equality or to further the cause of national inte-

gration, did not figure in any important national debate. But a passing reference to this demand was made by conservative sections while opposing Hindu law reforms.[88] While enacting a code for Hindus, the attempt was not to abandon ancient scriptural law or established community customs altogether but rather to assimilate them within a code along with certain principles of English law and, while doing so, establish the law making authority of the newly independent nation, which was, until then, vested with the heads of various religious sects (Parashar 1992).

In 1974, the Report of the Committee on the Status of Women shifted the focus and situated gender justice at the core of the demand for a UCC but did not quite distance itself from the premise of a modern and secular nation.[89]

During the subsequent decades, the issue was further complicated by judicial comments. While examining gender bias within Muslim personal law, the courts have explicitly commented that oneness of the nation, as well as loyalty to it, would be at stake if different minority groups follow different family laws.[90] It is a matter of debate whether a UCC will ensure national

---

[88] The opponents of Hindu law reform used the occasion to remind the government of the constitutional directive to enact a UCC for all communities. Some members of Parliament argued that if a constitution could be enacted on the principles of equality and equity for the entire country, then personal laws could be made for the whole country on those principles too. This was a tactic adopted by the conservatives to forestall Hindu law reforms. See comments of various members in Parliamentary Debates 5.2.1951– Vidyavachaspati pp. 2387, 2389-90; Sarwate pp. 2374-75; Deshmukh p. 2399.

[89] The Report stated that the absence of a UCC in the last quarter of the twentieth century, twenty seven years after Independence, is an incongruity that cannot be justified with all the emphasis that is placed on secularism, science, and modernism. p. 142 of the report.

[90] See for instance, the comments in *Sarla Mudgal v. Union of India*, (1995) 3 SCC 635.s.

integration and communal harmony.[91] But the comments have enabled communal forces to appropriate the demand and turn it into a political question. Protagonists of the communal propaganda have projected that the non-implementation of Article 44 of the Constitution has resulted in a growth in the Muslim population and that this constitutes a danger to the majority community. The image of a polygamous Muslim has been constructed to support this propaganda.[92] It is in this context that monogamy, imposed by a compulsory code, is projected as the need of the hour. The gains to gender concerns by the imposition of monogamy seem to only be incidental. Some Muslim scholars like Badshah (1995) have countered this with statistical data and have focused on sociological factors such as poor socio-economic conditions and low level of education among the Muslims, which, according to them, are the root causes of a slight increase in the Muslim population. Thus they have pointed out that a UCC will not resolve this problem (Badshah 1995). But the concept of monogamy, which is basically a tenet of Christianity, also draws the unquestioning support of liberals moulded in Western ethos. Here bigamy is considered reflective of pre-modern barbarism and monogamy symbolises civilization, enlightenment, modernity, and progress.[93]

This appropriation has posed insurmountable obstacles in the path of family law reforms from the perspective of gender justice. To counter the communal propaganda, some scholars, in recent times, have differentiated between a uniform civil code and a common civil code and have held that the demand for a uniform code is premised upon modernity and gender justice whereas the common code would only ensure commonality of oppression (Dhagamwar 1989). But this differentiation between the words 'common' and 'uniform' appears to be rather stretched and does not serve any purpose within the larger political context.

Erosion of Secular Values

Prior to the controversy in 1986 regarding the erosion of 'secular values' within the Indian polity in the context of the Muslim Women's Act (discussed later), there were several instances when there was a departure from the constitutional mandate of Article 15 that the State '*shall not discriminate on the basis of religion or sex*'. The enactment of a family code for Hindus in 1955-56 was the first major departure after the enactment of the Constitution. In subsequent decades, there were other instances, like the amendment to the Special Marriage Act in favour of Hindus. But ironically these instances did not stir a political debate on departure from the stated objective of Article 15. A presumption prevailed that personal laws are out of the purview of the Constitution, a view reflected initially in the *Narasu Appal Mali case*[94] and later, in the 1908s, in the *Harvinder Kaur case*.[95] The debate around a common adoption law in the 1970s did raise some questions regarding opposition

---

[91] See Kamila Tayabji quoted in Mahmood 1976, Aggarwal 1975 and Bhattacharjee 1996.

[92] '*Since Muslims are allowed to marry four wives, the Muslim population is growing at a faster rate*', is the communal propaganda.

[93] While not holding a brief for male bigamy, one is only questioning whether sexuality can be controlled through state regulations when the economic restraints for such measures, which were rooted in European feudalism (bastardization of children and denying them the right of property inheritance), have broken down. The modern tendency is towards laxity in marriage contracts, conferring rights to spouses in informal relationships as stipulated in the Domestic Violence

Act, 2005, and dissolving differences between legitimate and illegitimate children.

[94] *State of Bombay v. Narasu Appa Mali*, AIR 1952 Bom 84.

[95] *Harvinder Kaur v. Harminder Singh*, AIR 1984 Del 66.

to a uniform law by minority communities; but at that time this was just a murmur. This section will examine these departures from the stated objective of uniformity.

Hindu Law Reforms

Within the first decade of the adoption of the new and revolutionary Constitution, the State enacted special laws for its 'Hindu' citizens. By validating diverse customary practices and rituals as 'Hindu', by grouping various castes and sects under the banner of a 'legal Hinduism', and by naming the attempts of modernising family laws as 'Hindu' reforms, the State departed from its declared goal of secularizing the family law. These enactments took Hindus out of the application of some statutes which had, hitherto, been uniformly applicable to all citizens. For instance, the scope of the Caste Disabilities Removal Act, 1850, which prohibited loss of rights upon conversion, was constrained as apostasy now constituted a matrimonial offence.[96] The non-Hindu spouse was not entitled to maintenance from the Hindu spouse, whether living together or separately.[97]

The converted parent lost the right to be the natural guardian of a minor child.[98] Children born after a parent, originally Hindu, had converted were disqualified from inheriting the property of a Hindu relative.[99] The scope of another secular legislation, the Guardians and Wards Act, 1890, was restricted by the Hindu Adoption and Maintenance Act, 1956. Hindus were taken out of the purview of this secular and uniform legislation and were placed under the new statute, which validated adoptions through the Brahminical Hindu ritual of giving and taking in adoption,[100] while customs and practices of lower castes, which were more fluid and secular, were disallowed (Kishwar 1994: 2145). Section.18 (a) of the Hindu Marriage Act, took Hindus out of the general provisions of the Child Marriage Restraint Act, 1929 and were now liable for lesser punishment for the same offence. In addition, while child marriages performed under other matrimonial statutes (for instance the Parsi Marriage and Divorce Act, 1936 and the Special Marriage Act, 1954), were held to be void, such marriages were deemed valid under the Hindu Marriage Act (Bhattacharjee 1996: 11-14). Further, certain tax benefits were also conferred upon Hindu coparcenaries within taxation laws.[101]

These enactments violated the constitutional mandate under Article 14 and Article 15 as Hindu religion was the sole criteria for the classification (Bhattacharjee 1996: 10-27).

---

[96]   Section 13 (1) (ii) of the Hindu Marriage Act, 1955.

[97]   As per Hindu law, conversion results in the legal death of a Hindu. Hence the Hindu husband is not under obligation to maintain his converted wife. In *Sundarambal* v. *Subbaiah Pillai*, AIR 1961 Mad 323, the courts went even further and held that an order for maintenance obtained prior to the conversion cannot even be enforced after it.

[98]   A change of religion by the mother will disentitle her to the custody of her child under Hindu law; since the father is the natural guardian, it is presumed that the child will follow his religion.

[99]   Although the bar on conversion or change of caste was removed by the Caste Disabilities Act, 1850 and a convert cannot be denied rights in ancestral property, under the modern statute, the children of a converted parent cannot inherit property of a Hindu relative unless at the time when the conversion opens, the child is a Hindu. (Section 26, Hindu Succession Act)

[100]   See Section 11 (vi) of the Hindu Adoption and Maintenance Act, 1956.

[101]   Under section 10.2 of the Income Tax Act, an exemption is granted to income from the Hindu Undivided Family (HUF). Under Section 20 and 20A of the Wealth Tax Act, certain tax concessions are granted to members of the HUF at the time of Partition.

During the decades that followed, the State moved further away from its declared objective of a uniform and secular family law. In several instances, the vested patriarchal and community interests of influential sections superseded the rights of women and children.

Special Marriage Act, 1954

The enactment of the Special Marriage Act in 1954 has been the only significant move in the post-Independence period to secularise family laws.[102] In 1952, while introducing the bill, Law Minister C.C. Biswas described it as *'an attempt to lay down a uniform territorial law for the whole of India.'*[103]

The Act provided for a civil marriage of two Indians without the necessity of renouncing their respective religions. Since a marriage under this Act is a secular and civil contract, conversion or apostasy is not a ground for divorce. Marriage is contracted at the civil registry in the presence of a marriage officer appointed by the State, without the necessity of performing any religious rituals and ceremonies. A certificate is issued to the parties, which constitutes clear proof of a valid marriage for all future litigation purposes. Once the parties opt for a secular form of marriage, in matters of succession they are governed by the Indian Succession Act, 1925, which is more egalitarian and gender-just, and not by their respective personal laws.[104] This was a concrete step towards gradual unification of family laws.

[102] This was a re-enactment of the 1872 Act discussed in Chapter 3 of the second volume.

[103] LSD (1954), Vol. V, Part II col. 7797.

[104] Section 21 of the Special Marriage Act, 1954. The provision was meant to further secularize inheritance laws. The Indian Succession Act grants better rights of inheritance to daughters than the Hindu Succession Act of 1956 which continued to recognize male coparcenary.

Conservative Hindu, Muslim, and Christian opinion was strongly opposed to the Act. Although the concept of contractual marriage was closest to the Islamic concept of marriage, during Parliamentary debates, a demand was raised by a section of Muslims that the Muslim community should be exempted from the purview of the Act as persons marrying under it would not be governed by the Shariat. But this demand was not conceded. Prime Minister Jawaharlal Nehru pointed out that the constitutional provision which guarantees freedom to practise religion also includes the freedom not to practise a religion. He emphasized that since it is a facilitating legislation, no one was compulsorily bound by it and the State would not come in the way of any one opting for its provisions (Parashar 1992).

The Act had the potential of being developed further into a comprehensive code of marriage and divorce which could incorporate adequate safeguards for women, without invoking the controversy regarding freedom of religion. The premise that the Act is merely a facilitating measure which would apply only to consenting couples had already been accepted, both politically and legally. Unfortunately, the Act has not been well publicised and there seems to exist a manipulation to subvert its provisions.[105]

However, despite its secular credentials, the Act largely mirrored dominant Hindu, upper caste practices, which prohibit marriages between first cousins and close family relatives. Such prohibitions are not found in the customary practices of several lower castes as well as among Muslims, Parsis, and Jews. Among several South Indian communities, marriages

[105] See the difficulties in registering a marriage under the Special Marriages Act in sub-section, *Registration of Marriages* in Chapter 1 of the second volume.

between uncles and nieces and first cousins are a norm.[106] Similarly, marriages among first cousins are a norm among many Muslims and other minority communities.

In 1963, in order to rectify this lacuna and to widen the scope of the Act, an amendment was introduced, which subordinated the Act to customary practices.[107] During the Parliamentary debate, the amendment was criticized as a retrograde measure by several members of the Parliament.[108] Prior to this Act, personal laws were made subordinate to the stipulations under the Special Marriage Act. The amendment reversed this norm, subordinating the Act to provisions of personal laws. The stated reason for the amendment was to recognize the practices of South Indian communities which permit marriages between uncles and nieces and among first cousins.[109] The objective was to synchronize the Act with the provisions of the Hindu Marriage Act which validated customary practices. Its relevance to minority communities and practices prevailing among them was not a concern which the law makers addressed at the time.[110] The amendments placed the Act further away from its objective of a secular code.

In 1976, major amendments were introduced in the Hindu Marriage Act by incorporating additional grounds of divorce and by introducing divorce by mutual consent. Now, superficially it appeared that the Hindu Marriage Act and the Special Marriage Act were synonymous and has similar provisions. However, anomalies in the Hindu Marriage Act regarding proof of valid ceremonies were not addressed by these reforms and Hindu marriage continued to be an illusory legal incident.

At the other level, amendments introduced in the Special Marriage Act in 1976[111] conferred concessions on Hindus marrying under the Act, which undermined the secular provisions of the statute. If a Hindu couple married under this Act, they were taken out of the purview of the Indian Succession Act and were permitted to be governed by the Hindu Succession Act. This move was made to ensure that coparcenaries (and male privileges that accompany it) were not abdicated while contracting a marriage under the secular civil law. But the interests of the Hindu male who contracted a civil marriage were protected only as long as he married a woman within the broad Hindu fold.[112] It gave a further lease to coparcenaries, which, in any case, are anti-women. But the move was deemed progressive because it protected the interests of a Hindu male contracting a civil marriage. Even if one concedes to this reasoning, why a similar benefit was not conferred on a Hindu male contracting an inter-religious civil marriage remains unexplained. In effect, the amendment was a deterrent to a Hindu male wishing to marry a woman from a minority

[106] This issue is discussed in detail in the Section on *Validity of Customary Laws* in Chapter 1. Also see Uberoi 2008:54-85.

[107] The Special Marriage (Amendment) Act of 1963 added the following proviso to section 4 (d): *Provided that where a custom governing at least one of the parties permits of a marriage between them, such marriage may be solemnized notwithztanding that they are within the prohibited degrees of relationship.*

[108] See the comments of U.M. Trivedi, L.M. Singhvi etc., LSD (1962) Vol.XX /12 col.3234 and 3250.

[109] Speech by Deputy Minister Bibhudhendra Mishra, LSD (1962) Vol.XX/12 col.3228.

[110] First cousin marriages are an acceptable custom among the Muslim, Parsi, and Jewish communities but no concession based on customary practices was granted to these communities.

[111] The Law Commission of India, Fifty Ninth Report (1974) p. 98.

[112] This would include inter-caste and inter-regional marriages and marriages with women from Buddhist, Jain, and Sikh religions as well as Brahmos, Prarthana Samajis, Arya Samajis, and even atheists.

religious community. Such an event would result in the dissolution of the coparcenary and would deprive the male of his interests in it. Interestingly, no such deterrent has been placed to the marriage of a Hindu male to a woman belonging to a lower Hindu caste. While this is to be appreciated, the reasoning that the broad Hindu fold is only a legal fiction and that the notion of a Sudra or a neo-Buddhist woman entering the household would be as, if not more, abhorrent to an orthodox Hindu household, ridden with concepts of caste purity, as the idea of a Muslim or a Christian woman entering the household, seems to have escaped the law makers. The provision was clearly unconstitutional as the basis of discrimination was religious belief. Further, atheist Hindus who married under the secular Act were not given a choice to be governed by a uniform and secular law of succession and were automatically placed under a law governing 'Hindus'.

This clear violation of the mandate for uniformity and secularization of family laws did not attract a public debate. The benefits conferred on Hindu males contracting a civil marriage were deemed as a progressive step for the Hindu community. Hence the deterrent it would pose to marriages of Hindu males with minority women and to the secular principles of the nation did not figure in the public discourse. The criticism against this amendment remained within the confines of legal academia and did not result in a media furore (Sivaramayya 1978).

The Adoption Bill

The Adoption Bill, which was introduced in the Rajya Sabha in 1972[113] and was referred to a Joint Parliamentary Committee, was yet another attempt at uniformity.[114] This Bill was meant to be enacted in the interest of minor, abandoned children and to provide a home for them by enacting a uniform law across community dictates. The Bill provided that any citizen of India would be entitled to adopt and any child would be entitled to be taken in adoption. Since it would encroach upon the domain of personal laws, the Joint Select Committee held public hearings with representatives of various communities who would be affected by this enactment. At these hearings, the representatives of Muslims and Scheduled Tribes expressed their desire to be excluded from its application.[115]

Although opposition to the Bill was based on various factors, the economic motive was the most dominant. Adoption would affect the inheritance rights of other stipulated shares of legal heirs under the Muslim law and also make inroads within the common property of tribal communities. These were the two major concerns expressed by the dissenting communities.

The tribal communities opposed adoption of children from outside the tribe as this could lead to the inheritance of the tribal property by adopted, non-tribal children. They also opposed the provision of registering the adoptions as it would pose technical difficulties. The change of name after adoption was also considered to be contrary to tribal custom. They claimed that the Bill would violate the constitutional protection awarded to tribal customs.

Muslim religious leadership argued that the Bill would be against the tenets of Islam. Adoption could create prohibited degrees of relationships in matrimonial alliances (with the adopted parents), which would violate Islamic principles. But most importantly, the adopted child would become an heir to the property of the adopting parents and the shares of the natural

---

[113] Gazette of India, Part II, 1972, pp. 601-10.
[114] LSD, 26 August 1972.

[115] Joint Select Committee, Evidence on Adoption Bill, Vol. II, 1972, p. 111.

heirs would be altered. This would amount to an interference with the scheme of succession under the Shariat.

Although the conservative segment of the Muslim religious leadership opposed the Bill, it received the support of several prominent Muslim scholars and jurists.[116] Some scholars suggested modifications to the Bill which would make it more acceptable to the Muslim community. Justice Hameedullah Beg suggested that instead of excluding Muslims, the Bill should contain a provision to declare that adoption is not contrary to their religious beliefs and added that the Constitution gives every individual his or her religious freedom.

The committee agreed to exclude the Scheduled Tribes but not the Muslim community. The three Muslim members of the committee, in their note of dissent, pressed for the exclusion of the Muslim community from its application.[117] The Joint Select Committee submitted its report to the Parliament in August 1976. But in order to avoid any politically costly controversy over this issue, the Bill was not presented till the Parliament was dissolved in March 1977 and consequently, the Bill lapsed. The Janata government which was voted to power after the election introduced a new bill but withdrew it following opposition from a section of Muslims (Baig 1980).

In 1980, when the Congress party regained power, the government re-introduced a modified version of the Bill and paid heed to the Muslim demand for exclusion. This time the Bill was referred to the Minorities Commission. At this juncture, the Parsi community demanded

exemption from its application[118] as they did not want their charitable trust funds and their fire temples to be thrown open to non-Parsi children. They, however, had no objection to inter-religious adoption if the rights of the non-Parsi child were restricted to inheritance of private property and would not extend to community resources. In the face of opposition from so many fronts, the Bill was eventually abandoned.

While the Bill was ultimately unsuccessful, the debate that surrounded it indicated a shift in the government's stance. In 1954, while enacting the Special Marriage Act, the government had not accepted the claim that it would encourage Muslims to leave the fold of Islam. But two decades later, while debating the Adoption Bill, the government accepted the religio-political leaders as spokespersons for the entire community.

Communally Tinted Judicial Pronouncements

The 1970s and 1980s witnessed an erosion of secular principles within the Indian judiciary, which further complicated the issue of enacting the UCC. A steady decline of secular values can be traced through the debates on the enactment of the Special Marriage Act in the 1950s, the fate of the Adoption Bill in the 1970s, and the controversy around the Muslim Women's Bill in the 1980s. The policy on secularism had changed from the Nehruvian concept of maintaining equidistance from all religions to the instrumental use of religion for political gains during Rajiv Gandhi's rule in the 1980s. The State became increasingly entangled with the communal factions. If one concession was granted to one communal group, it was compelled to grant another concession to another

---

[116] Justices Chagla, Hidayatullah, and Beg and jurists Asaf Ali Fyzee and Daniel Latifi to name a few. For more details see Parashar 1992: 171.

[117] Joint Select Committee, Evidence on Adoption Bill, 1972 Minutes of Dissent at IX –XI.

[118] Fourth Annual Report, the Minorities Commission (1983).

group to set the balance right. The Muslim Women's Act was a direct outcome of this political jugglery.

The Nehruvian model of a modern, democratic, and secular nation-state was dented by periodic communal strife and the Hindu and Muslim communities continued to be constructed within polarized oppositions. It is against this backdrop of rising communal tension that Muslim law, which was until then perceived as more modern and advanced in terms of women's rights, began to be viewed as obscurantist and anti-women.[119]

The Shah Bano Controversy

It is in the above context that the Shah Bano[120] ruling by the Supreme Court created political controversy. Rather unfortunately, certain stray comments contained in this judgment against Islam and the Prophet, as well as its call for a uniform civil code, gave it a communal hue and contributed in politicising the demand for the enactment of a UCC.

The issue before the Court was a simple one—the right of a divorced Muslim woman to claim maintenance from her husband under a secular legal provision, section 125 of the Cr. P.C., which entitled the magistrate's court to order a sum not exceeding Rs 500 as maintenance in order to prevent destitution of women. But by the time it reached the Supreme Court, the issue became entangled in the binaries of community identity and legal provisions of a secular state. The Muslim Personal Law Board,

which joined as an intervener in the appeal filed by the husband, argued that it was un-Islamic for a divorced wife to claim maintenance from her husband after the *iddat* period and that Muslim law secures her right through the institution of mehr. While rejecting the argument and upholding Muslim women's right to post-divorce maintenance, the controversial judgment, delivered by Y. V. Chandrachud, C.J. speaking for a full bench comprising five judges, commented on Islam, the Quran, and Muslim personal law and called for a UCC.

Interestingly, two significant decisions of the Supreme Court, delivered by Justice Krishna Iyer in 1979 and 1980, had already placed divorced Muslim women's right to maintenance on a secure footing without arousing a political controversy.[121] These decisions had examined the rights of a Muslim woman from a humanitarian perspective of the right to survival and basic dignity.

The unwarranted comments of the court evoked a communal backlash. Relenting to the pressure exerted by Muslim orthodoxy, the government introduced the Muslim Women (Protection of Rights on Divorce) Bill, which sought to exclude divorced Muslim women from the purview of section 125 Cr.PC. This move by the Congress government, led by Rajiv Gandhi, met with severe opposition from women's organizations and progressive sections. It came to be considered as a glaring defeat of principles of gender justice and secularism within the Indian polity.

As the controversy around this Bill raged on, the media projected two insular and mutually exclusive positions—those who opposed the Bill and supported the demand for a UCC were

---

[119] The earlier view that Muslim law is more favourable to women was based on the fact Muslim women were entitled to property inheritance and were granted the right of a judicial dissolution of marriage nearly two decades prior to Hindu women acquiring similar rights.

[120] *Mohd. Ahmad Khan v. Shah Bano Begum*, AIR 1985 SC 945.

[121] *Bai Tahira v. Ali Hussain Fideali Chotthea*, AIR 1979 SC 362 and *Fuzlunbi v. K.Khadil Vali*, AIR 1980 SC 1730.

painted as modern, secular, rational, and nationalist while those opposing the code were projected as fundamentalist, orthodox, male chauvinist, communal, obscurantist and antinational. As the controversy escalated, Muslims were defined as the 'other', both of the nation and of Hindus. Muslims, in turn, could be mobilised to view this as yet another threat to their tenuous security. A large number of Muslims, including women, came out to the streets to denounce the judgment and to demand the enactment of Muslim Women's Act. The rigid approach of the Muslim leadership provided further fuel to Hindu right-wing forces in their anti-Muslim propaganda. Within this polarised position, there was no space for moderates to forge a position which would reconcile the two extreme ends of the debate.

Ironically, the fury which was whipped up seemed to be divorced from the core of the controversy, that the maintenance settlement, a paltry sum of Rs 179 per month, was far too inadequate to save a 73-year old ex-wife of a successful Kanpur-based lawyer from vagrancy and penury. The raging controversy and the communal turn of events finally led Shah Bano herself to make a public declaration renouncing her claim, strengthening the popular misconception that Islam subverts the economic rights of women. If this entitlement was against her religion, she declared, she would rather be a devout Muslim than claim her right to maintenance. A sad comment, indeed, which warranted reflection from campaigners on both sides of the divide. The statute, passed under a party whip, further strengthened the 'Muslim appeasement' theory in judicial discourse and in popular media.

The demand for a UCC was framed within a modernist discourse and was endorsed not only by the Hindu right-wing but also by secular civil society groups and women's rights organiza-tions. It was marked by three distinct undertones—gender equality, national integration, and concepts of modernity embedded within notions of middle class morality. Secular and women's rights groups projected the UCC as a magic wand which would ameliorate the woes and sufferings of Indian women in general and Muslim women in particular. This formulation placed gender as a neutral terrain, distanced from contemporary political processes. Minority women were projected as lacking a voice and agency to enforce their basic human rights, both within their communities and through litigation. For the liberal, modern, English-educated middle classes, the demand was laden with a moral undertone of abolishing polygamy and other 'barbaric' customs of the minorities and extending to them the 'egalitarian code' of the 'enlightened majority'. This position relies upon the western model of liberal democracy and scorns simultaneous sexual relationships in the nature of polygamous marriages, in the name of modernity, while endorsing sequential plurality of sexual relationships (through frequent divorces). Within a communally vitiated political climate, the demand also voices concerns of 'national integration' and 'communal harmony'.

Analysing the political developments around this period, Zoya Hasan argues that the compromise of surrendering women's rights has to be viewed from the perspective of a communalised polity (Hasan 1994: 67-8). It was an outcome of a rightward shift in politics and economy in the 1980s, resulting in a close interaction between politics and religion, marked by a decline in the commitment to secularism, equal opportunities for all, and social welfare benefits for the under privileged and disadvantaged.

The Congress faced defeat in several state assembly elections in 1985-86 as the Muslim vote, angered by the Shah Bano verdict, tipped the balance in favour of opposition parties.

The Congress responded to the crisis by a shift in strategy, highlighted by the appropriation of pro-Hindutva themes which were gaining popularity in North India. This won the support of some Hindu factions but further alienated Muslims, the traditional supporters of Congress, who were dissatisfied with the party's failure to alleviate their long-standing grievances. Their disenchantment was further aggravated by the Ram Janmabhumi movement, started by the Vishwa Hindu Parishad in 1984, for the 'liberation' of the Ram temple in Ayodhya. Against this background of declining political support, the Congress government, in February 1986, decided to open the locks of the disputed Babri Masjid and enact the Muslim Women's Bill. Together, these two decisions were part of a 'grand' Congress strategy of using religious issues and sentiments to regain its hold over Hindu and Muslim votes.

The Muslim Women's Act[122] was thus an effort to pacify Muslim sentiments which were ruffled over the reopening of the disputed site. The Congress government exaggerated the strength of the conservative opposition, manipulated by a politically ambitious Muslim leadership. The Congress viewed the All India Muslim Personal Law Board (AIMPLB) as the sole arbiter of Muslim interest. Opposition from liberal and progressive groups was ignored, allowing the Ullema to appropriate the task of defining the overarching concerns and interests of Muslims.[123]

Invalidating Triple Talaq

The judgment of the Lucknow bench of the Allahabad High Court invalidating triple talaq,

delivered by Hari Nath Tilhari J. on 15 April 1994,[124] served to further communalise the demand for a UCC. On the face of it the judgment could be interpreted as pro-women. It proclaimed that since the practice of triple talaq denigrates women, it is 'violative of the constitution'. The judgment was hailed as bold and progressive because it had apparently served the cause of Muslim women.[125] But one had to read between the lines to grasp its anti-Muslim bias.

The response of Muslim religious leadership was predictable.[126] The comments by the *amicus curie* during the proceedings—that knowledge of Arabic is essential for commenting on the provisions of the Quran and the Hadis (which constitute the Shariat)—further fuelled the communal myth that Muslims do not owe allegiance to the sovereign Indian State and that they are not governed by the State-enacted legal system (Ahmad 1994: 104).

The judgment caused concern among progressive scholars who, while criticising the inertia of the AIMPLB in declaring the practice invalid, apprehended that it might hamper the process of reform from within the community.[127] Legal scholars also questioned whether a retrospective judgment of a single judge in a land ceiling dispute was the proper forum to

[122] The Muslim women (Protection of Rights upon Divorce) Act, 1986. The Act is discussed in greater detail later in this chapter.

[123] See Chapter 2 of Volume 2 of this book for the subsequent reinterpretation of this Act.

[124] *Rahmat Ullah* v. *State of U.P.*, WP No.45 of 1993 and *Khatoon Nisa* v. *State of U.P.*, WP No.57 of 1993 (unreported).

[125] 'Triple Talaq Again', *Times of India* 19 April 1994, 'The practice is contrary to the spirit of Islam', *Indian Express* 22 April 1994, 'Muslim women welcome court verdict on talaq', *The Statesman* 22 April 1994, Anjana Basu, 'Behind the Four Walls The Veil', *The Statesman* 30 April 1994.

[126] 'Muslims resent talaq verdict', *Times of India* 18.4.94; 'Divorced From Reality', *The Pioneer* 25.4.94.

[127] See comments Tahir Mohammed quoted in 'Beyond the law The Strange case of Justice Tilhari', *Frontline* 20.5.94 p. 35.

examine the validity of triple talaq (ibid. and Latifi 1994). Several Muslim scholars and leaders, who had supported the Supreme Court judgment in the Shah Bano case[128] and had opposed the Muslim Women's Bill in 1986, were critical of the judgment and expressed their resentment of the sensationalization of the issue by the media.[129]

Media reporting of the case led to the misconception that the high court had upheld a Muslim woman's petition challenging triple talaq, protecting her rights and consequently, the rights of all Muslim women. The implications of the judgment on the woman concerned received least media attention (Agnes 1994: 1169).

Briefly, the facts of the case were as follows: When a notice was issued to one Rahmatullah in 1974 under the U.P. Land Ceiling Act,[130] he pleaded that he had divorced his wife Khatoon Nisa in 1969 and that land belonging to her was erroneously added to his assets. The case, initiated in 1974, went through several stages and was examined by several state authorities. Finally the issue before the high court, in two separate writ petitions filed by Khatoon Nisa and Rahmatullah, was whether the plea of divorce was genuine or was it resorted to only to defraud the State. Originally, Khatoon Nisa was not a party to the case. But in 1980, she deposed before the concerned authority that she had been divorced eleven years ago. Under the Land Ceiling Act, a woman who is married relinquishes her right to hold separate property. However, the Act recognises the right of a divorced or judicially separated woman to separate property, in which case property of the spouses is not clubbed together.[131] Hence the second issue before the court was whether a woman who is divorced as per the rules of her personal law is entitled to similar benefits as a woman who is separated or divorced through a court decree.[132]

The woman concerned did not dispute the fact of the divorce nor challenge the Constitutional validity of oral and unilateral divorce (triple talaq). The opposing party was not her husband but the state authorities. At the initial stage of the case, she had not even entered the litigation arena. It is pertinent to note that not just the advocates representing the parties and the *amicus curie* assisting the court, even

---

[128] AIR 1985 SC 945.

[129] Arif Mohammed Khan, the Congress Minister who had resigned in protest against the Muslim Women's Bill criticized the judgment in an interview with Neena Vyas (Vyas 1994). In another article, several scholars expressed their resentment about the media coverage. Historian Harbans Mukhiya drew a parallel between the way the West covers India and the response of the media to Muslim issues. Mushirul Hasan opined that the media and Muslim tend to stereotype each other. (Ashraf 1994).

[130] The U.P. Imposition of Ceiling on Land Holding (Amendment) Act 1972. (U.P. Act No.13 of 1972).

[131] Sections 3 (7) and 3 (17) provided for wives who were legally separated and divorced through a court decree to hold separate property.

[132] Triple talaq under the Shariat has statutory recognition under section 2 of the Application of Shariat Act, 1937. Further, talaq either in one sitting or in three consecutive months is the only remedy available for a Muslim man to divorce his wife. A Muslim man cannot approach a court for a divorce, either by consent or on fault ground. The Dissolution of Muslim Marriages Act of 1939 is applicable only to women. The matrimonial relief of judicial separation is of western origin and is not recognized under Muslim law. The fact that an orally divorced wife's right to hold separate property does not figure in the provisions of the Act, while a legally separated wife's rights are recognised, is an indicator of the State's blinkers towards the specificity of minority practices, while enacting legislations. In *Sita Devi* v. *Additional Commissioner, Agra*, AIR 1996 All 75, the court upheld the plea that the property of a judicially separated Hindu wife cannot be clubbed with that of her husband. If this is the legal position there was no basis for holding that an orally divorced wife is not entitled to hold separate property.

the Advocate General appearing for the State had pointed out to the judge that the validity of triple talaq was not an issue before the court. But overriding these objections, Justice Tilhari hastily pronounced the judgment after he received his transfer orders. When the Advocate General questioned the constitutionality of such a move, rather curiously, the Avadh Bar Association passed a resolution to suspend him.[133]

The sum effect of the judgment for the concerned woman was that her marriage, which had been dissolved twenty five years earlier, was held to be valid and subsisting against her own wishes and depositions. Consequently, the land belonging to her was held to be surplus for the purpose of acquisition by the State under the Land Ceiling Act.

The judgment examined a serious issue such as invalidating triple talaq in a flippant manner and relied upon a couplet written by an Urdu poet:

Talaq de rahe ho bare gharur ke saath; Mere shabaab bhi lautaa do mere mehr ke saath
(You divorce me with such pride; Give me back my youth along with my mehr)

A romantic poem cannot be treated as an authority and relied upon in a judicial decision. While dealing with an issue of such magnitude, quoting a romantic couplet does not seem appropriate. The stanza had no relevance to a case where the wife herself affirmed her divorce (Ahmad 1994: 108).

The rambling judgment of over 150 pages lamented the position of Muslim women under their personal law and relied on legal arguments, prose, and poetry to prove the point. But the preoccupation with gender justice seems to be limited to the issue of Muslim women and triple talaq and does not extend to issues of gender discrimination under the Land Ceiling Act. The provision of clubbing a married woman's property with that of her husband is blatantly anti-women and smacks of European medievalism. It is based on the premise that the husband and the wife are one unit (and that unit is the husband) and that the unit is of a permanent nature. Under this concept, a woman loses her right over her individual assets upon marriage and the husband acquires power to not only manage it but even to alienate it. Incidentally, Muslim law does not recognize the concept of merging of a wife's assets with that of her husband.[134]

This blatantly discriminatory aspect of the Land Ceiling Act had been declared as constitutionally valid in an earlier judgment.[135] The Act also provides for two additional hectares of land for each adult son, but no such benefits are provided for adult daughters who formed part of the domestic unit. The Act presumes either that women are not capable of owning and administering property or that property is of no concern to adult females. Therefore, neither as unmarried daughters nor as married wives do they have an additional entitlement and their status is confined to that of dependants. The Tilhari judgment which claims to address the

[133] 'Avadh Bar to Suspend Advocate General' 'Times of India' 19 April 1994. The interest of the Bar Association of Avadh is another curious aspect of the case. Perhaps it is relevant to note that the advocates of the Avadh Bar led a demonstration to Ayodhya demanding public worship of Ram idols installed at the newly constructed temple after the demolition of Babri Masjid in December 1992.

[134] The press note issued by the AIMPLB on 1 May 1994 from Lucknow stressed that Muslim law is more progressive than the Land Ceiling Act in this respect. But ironically, the AIMPLB had not opposed this provision of clubbing together the properties of the spouses with that of her husband's, raising the plea of religious dictates, prior to this judgment.

[135] Ambika Prasad Mishra v. State of U.P., 1980 (3) SCC 719.

issues of gender equality, does not concern itself with this issue.

One curious aspect of the judgment is that while the court went out of its way to declare the discriminatory aspect of Muslim personal law as unconstitutional, even though the issue was not under challenge, in several instances when the discriminatory aspects of personal laws were an issue directly before them, the courts have upheld their constitutional validity.[136]

Even presuming that there was an intention to attain monetary advantage by defrauding the state through the misappropriation of the provision of oral and arbitrary talaq, such misappropriations and manipulations are not unique to this case. The right to form Hindu coparcenaries, which grants tax benefits, are routinely used for monetary gains. Several Hindu couples have also obtained collusive decrees for saving their land from the provisions of the Land Ceiling Act (Mali 1994 and Kannabiran 1994). Here the collusive factor had not led to an invalidation of the decree of divorce.

In another instance when the issue of collusive decrees was examined by the high court of Bombay, the court specifically ruled that so long as the necessary conditions have been met, it is not up to the court to examine the motive for a divorce by consent. The question had arisen because the family court had refused to grant a divorce by consent on the ground that the petition was based on an ulterior motive of defrauding creditors.[137]

The press reports drew a comparison between the Shah Bano controversy and the triple talaq judgment.[138] But the comparison was based on a warped understanding of the issue. The only common denominator between the two judgments was the judicial interpretation of the Shariat; but the comparison ends there. While Shah Bano herself had approached the court and had gained personally from the judgment, the judgment by Justice Tilhari had in fact deprived the woman concerned of her right to property.

Viewed within this broader context, there is reason to infer that the motive for the judgment lay elsewhere. Gautam Navalakha (1994) has pointed out the communal tendencies underlying the judgment as well as other instances where a communal motive can be attributed. Immediately after the demolition of the Babri Masjid, when the issue of public worship of the idols of Ram in the newly erected temple was before the court, the judge permitted public worship on the site on the ground that Lord Ram is a 'Constitutional identity'. He based his logic on the fact that a picture of Ram appears on the copy of the constitution given to him by his father. In another judgment, while granting the custody of a minor child born of a Christian mother and a Hindu father, the judge held that the father would be a better guardian as he is a Hindu.[139]

In his press interviews following the judgment on triple talaq, Justice Tilhari reaffirmed that he is a firm Hindu and that he believes that

---

[136] See *Dwarakabai* v. *Prof. Mainam Mathews*, AIR 1953 Mad 792; *Harvinder Kaur* v. *Harminder Singh*, AIR 1984 Delhi 66; and *Krishna Singh* v. *Mathura Ahir*, AIR 1980 SC 707.

[137] *Leela Mahadeo Joshi* v. *Mahadeo Sitaram Joshi*, AIR 1991 Bom 105.

[138] The report which appeared in the *Times of India* 25 April 1994, was titled, 'Another Shah Bano in the Making'. Several articles while commenting on the judgment carried a picture of Shah Bano. See for instance, 'Fear Behind the Purdah' Blitz 21 May 1994, 'One Nation, One Law', Sunday 17 May 1994.

[139] Judgment of Justice Tilhari in the case of *Indumati Koorichh* v. *Yogendra Pal Koorichh*, W.P. No. 325 of 1993 dated 29 July 1993. See Bindra 1994: 11. Also see 'Beyond the law—The strange case of Justice Tilhari', *Frontline* 20 May 1994, at p. 35.

everyone born in Hindustan is a Hindu as this is his motherland. The rhetoric of 'motherland' and 'cultural Hinduism for all Indians' bears close resemblance to the propaganda by the communal Hindu factions in their anti-Muslim agenda (Basu 1993:11).

The Supreme Court Ruling in the Case of Hindu Bigamy

Another significant development in the debate on Muslim personal law and the UCC was the decision of the Supreme Court in the case of *Sarla Mudgal* v. *Union of India*[140] concerning polygamy of Hindu men after conversion to Islam. While the issue before the Court was that of bigamy of Hindu men and the validity of their marriage contracted prior to conversion, it primarily addressed the issue of the UCC in the context of the nation, national integration, and minority identity.

In the much publicised judgment delivered by Kuldip Singh J. (with a concurring judgment by R.M. Sahai J.), the court commented:

Since Hindus along with Sikhs, Buddhists and Jains have forsaken their sentiments in the cause of the national unity and integration, some other communities would not, though the Constitution enjoins the establishment of a common civil code for the whole of India.... Those who preferred to remain in India after the partition, fully knew that the Indian leaders did not believe in two-nation or three-nation theory and that in the Indian Republic there was to be only one nation, the Indian Nation and no community could claim to remain a separate entity on the basis of religion. In this view of the matter, no community can oppose the introduction of common civil code for all citizens in the territory of India.[141]

The obvious reference to partition and to the choice to remain in India clearly indicates that the judgment targets the Muslim minority

community. The discourse of choosing 'to remain in India after Partition' has long been a warning to Indian Muslims from the Hindu right-wing. The judgment's language pits those who oppose the Code (Muslims) against the rest of 'the Indian Nation', which is assumed to be in favour of a common civil code. The comments seem to suggest that Hindu family laws are entirely secularized and gender just, while the Muslim community is boorish, uncivilized, and an enemy to national integration.

Ratna Kapur and Brenda Cossman have argued that the language of the judgment, in deflecting attention away from the continuing religious and discriminatory aspects of Hindu personal law and in attacking the Muslim community, is disturbingly similar to the political rhetoric of the Hindu right-wing. As per this view, all religious communities must be treated the same and it is the dominant Hindu community which is to be the norm against which equality is judged (Kapur & Cossman 1995: 260).

But the 'norm' of monogamy among Hindus, which was the issue under scrutiny before the Apex Court, escaped all public debate. It is an issue which needs further scrutiny. Monogamy was introduced among the Hindus through the Hindu Marriage Act in 1955. Prior to this, Hindu men were absolved of the criminal consequences of bigamy under section 494 of the IPC. After 1955, a Hindu wife could divorce her husband on the ground of bigamy and also prosecute him under the penal law. The right to dissolve the marriage on the ground of bigamy is available to a Muslim wife under the Dissolution of Muslim Marriages Act.[142] The

[140] (1995) 3 SCC 635
[141] *Ibid.* at para 34 and 35

[142] Section 2 (viii) (f) of the Dissolution of Muslim Marriages Act, 1939. Under this section, if the husband does not treat both wives equitably, the woman has a right of dissolution of marriage. A similar right also exists if the husband associates with women of ill repute.

only additional relief that a Hindu wife can avail is criminal prosecution for bigamy. But since only the first wife can initiate prosecution, a popular notion prevails that a Hindu husband can remarry with the consent of his wife; practically, this notion is not far from the truth. Statistics of bigamous marriages among Hindus and Muslims are comparable.[143] By declaring that the earlier marriage was valid, the only legal remedy, apart from a petition for divorce on the ground of bigamy, that the litigating women were entitled is a prosecution for bigamy.

It is in this context that the judicial attitude towards bigamy by Hindu men has to be posited as the central issue. The judgment seemed to indicate that the judiciary has dealt severely with all breaches of monogamy among Hindus and the only loophole through which a husband can escape is conversion. But an examination of the decisions of the Supreme Court and various high courts reveals that bigamy of the Hindu male persists despite statutory restraints and that judicial attitude has been extremely lax towards the issue.[144] Instead of examining the norm of Hindu bigamy, the judgment turned the spotlight on polygamy of Muslim men and the plight of Muslim women. The solution

offered to curb polygamy was the immediate enforcement of a UCC. There was a presumption that a uniform code would render Hindu marriages more stable by curbing the bigamous tendencies of Hindu men (Agens 1995). A reading of the judgment seemed to indicate that the only way that monogamy was breached among Hindus was by conversion to Islam. To quote from the judgment, '...there is an open inducement to a Hindu husband, who wants to enter into a second marriage to become a Muslim...'

Dichotomy between Cultural Plurality and Legal Uniformity

The judgment pronounced by V.N. Khare C.J. in the *John Vallamattom case*[145] was yet another instance of unwarranted comments by the court acquiring a communal hue. The case concerned a Christian priest's personal freedom to make a bequest of religious-charitable nature. While examining the constitutional validity of section 118 of the Indian Succession Act,[146] the Supreme Court ruled:

A charitable disposition of property for the benefit of the public in the advancement of religion, knowledge, commerce, health, safety, or any other object beneficial to the mankind has specifically been acknowledged not only in different religious texts but also in different statutes. Charitable purposes are philanthropic and since a person's freedom to dispose of property for such purposes has nothing to do with religious influence, the impugned provision treating bequests for both religious and charitable purposes is discriminatory and

---

[143] As per the Census report 1961, incidences of polygamous marriages for the decade 1951-60 are as follows: Tribal 17.98 per cent, Hindus 5.06 per cent, and Muslim 4.31 per cent. According to another study, the incidence of polygamy among tribals was 15.25 per cent, among Buddhists was 7.97 per cent, Jains was 6.72 per cent, Hindus was 5.8 per cent, and Muslims was 5.7 per cent (Towards Equality pp. 66–7 and p. 104). Since Buddhists and Jains are also governed by Hindu law, the statistics for Hindus collectively would be 6.83 per cent as compared to 5.7 per cent for Muslims.

[144] *Bhaurao Shanker Lokhande* v. *State of Maharashtra*, AIR 1965 SC 1564; *Kanwal Ram* v. *The H.P. Administration*, AIR 1966 SC 614, and *Priya Bala Ghosh* v. *Suresh Chandra Ghosh*, AIR 1971 SC 1153.

[145] *John Vallamattom* v. *Union of India*, AIR 2003 SC 2902.

[146] Section 118 deals with bequests for religious or charitable purposes. It states that no man having a nephew or niece or any nearer relative shall have power to bequeath any property to religious or charitable uses, except by a will executed not less than twelve months before his death and deposited within six months from its execution in some place provided by law for the safe custody of the wills of living persons. However nothing in this section applies to a Parsi.

violative of Article 14 of the Constitution. Once it is held that the underlying purpose for enacting the said provision was merely to thwart influence exercised by people professing religion resulting in death-bed disposition, having regard to the fact that such a contingency has adequately been taken care in other provisions under the Act, the purpose and object of the Act must be held to be non-existent.

Based on this reasoning, the Court struck down the provision as being unreasonable, arbitrary, and discriminatory and therefore violative of Article 14 of the Constitution. While striking down the provision, the Court also relied on the Declaration on the Right to Development, adopted by the World Conference on Human Rights, to which India is a signatory and on Article 18 of the United Nations Covenant on Civil and Political Rights, 1966 which provides as follows:

Everyone shall have the right to freedom of thought, conscience and religion. This right shall include freedom to have or adopt a religion or belief of his choice, and freedom, either individually or in community with others and in public or private, to manifest his religion or belief or belief in worship, observance, practice and teaching. Freedom to manifest ones own religion or beliefs may be subject only to such limitations as are prescribed by law and are necessary to protect public safety, order, health, or morals or the fundamental rights and freedom of others.

The question before the Court was not of gender justice or national integration, but that of personal freedom of a Christian priest. Contrary to popular belief, through this petition, the petitioner-priest sought to protect his right of religious freedom and the right to follow the dictates of one's religion. While defending cultural plurality of belief, worship, and practice by invoking the United Nations Covenant on Civil and Political Rights, the Court ruled in favour of religious minorities by upholding their right of religious-charitable bequests. The Court held that violation of this right amounted

to discrimination under Article 14 of the Constitution.

But a stray and uncalled for comment regarding the UCC helped the media to convert a judgment in defence of personal freedoms and cultural plurality into one in defence of the UCC and hence, anti-minority. It is indeed a matter of concern that some stray and uncalled for comments have come to the aid of Hindu communal organizations in their call for a UCC for national integration. It is also interesting to note that no matter what the core issue litigated before the Apex Court, comments regarding the enactment of a UCC are always made in reference to 'national integration' and are either a veiled or direct insinuation against Muslim law, thus creating a fiction that Hindus are governed by a secular, egalitarian, and gender-just family code and that it was high time that this code was extended to Muslims in order to usher in modernity and gender equality among them. In is interesting to contrast the comments in this ruling with the comments of the Delhi High Court in the context of the Hindu law: "Introduction of constitutional law in the home is most inappropriate. In the privacy of the home and married life, neither Article 21 nor Article 14 have any place."[147]

Framing the Muslim Woman

Sensational and Communalised Media Reportage

It is true that the sporadic, at times unwarranted, comments regarding national integration, the two nation theory, or the denial of women's rights under Islam in judgments urging the State to enact a UCC served to ignite a communal controversy. But the blame for repeatedly fanning the controversy and for keeping

---

[147] See the *Harvinder Kaur case* discussed above.

the issue alive in the public mind lies with the media.

The Shah Bano judgment provided the first impetus for formulating the issue within the binaries of Islam versus women. The media morphed the polarized opinions into mutually exclusive segments—the progressive-modernist in support of a UCC and the fundamentalist-obscurantist in opposition. Since then, every stray comment of the Supreme Court has evoked a frenzied media response. The issue is constantly framed within these binaries even when the lines between these two were blurred. In the two decades since the Shah Bano ruling, ground realities have changed substantially. The demolition of the Babri Masjid in 1992 and the communal riots that followed, the rise of the Hindu right-wing, and the gruesome sexual violence upon Muslim women unleashed during the Gujarat riots in 2002 have been factors that have necessitated a re-examination of the earlier call for a UCC, ostensibly to secure the rights of minority women. The Muslim intelligentsia, which spoke out in favour of a UCC during the Shah Bano controversy, has been constrained to change its position in the context of a threatened Muslim identity and as a response to the framing of the demand for a UCC as an anti-Muslim agenda. Many secular, human rights and women's rights groups no longer support this demand. Despite this, the polarization in the media continues and the same old controversy gets whipped up again and again and is savoured with relish by the urban, 'liberal' middle class.

News reports are accompanied by images of purdah-clad Muslim women and comments from an orthodox clergy. At times, the core issues litigated before the Supreme Court are blurred (as in the *John Vellamathom case*) and the call for a UCC is projected as a pronouncement against the Muslim minority. Within this preordained formulation, there is no space for the moderate opinions within Muslim leadership as they do not make a 'good story'.

The media is guilty not only of sins of commission but also of omission. While giving undue publicity to stray comments which do not reflect the core issues litigated before the Supreme Court, it has deliberately failed to give due importance to the extremely positive interpretations by the judiciary which upheld the rights of divorced Muslim women to lump sum settlements in cases under the Muslim Women's Act.

Within this communally vitiated atmosphere, the advances made by divorced Muslim women were made invisible and glossed over.[148] During the Shah Bano controversy, the denial of the right to a meagre maintenance dole was lamented by all and sundry, not withstanding the fact that the maintenance awarded to the wife of an advocate with a flourishing practice was just Rs 25 in the first instance and Rs 179 in appeal. So long as the debate could be used as a stick to beat the community with, these 'minor' details didn't seem to matter. What did matter was the fact that a communal campaign could be mounted upon a patriarchal paradigm and thereby legitimised.

Innovative Judicial Interpretation of the Muslim Women's Act

It is in this context that the Muslim Women's Act needs to be revisited. The hurriedly drafted and hastily enacted statute was full of contradictions and was ridden with controversies. But despite its limitations, the Act was of immense historical significance as it was the first attempt of Independent India to codify Muslim personal law. But since it was enacted amidst protests

---

[148] In this context also see the discussion on *Validity of triple talaq under* Islamic Law of Marriage and Succession in Chapter 1

from women's rights groups and social organizations, it was viewed with suspicion and foreboding. The first response of the protesting groups was to challenge its constitutionality, rather than to examine its viability.

While the writ petitions filed by many such groups challenging the validity of this provision were pending in the Supreme Court, the Act gradually unfolded itself in the lower courts. Appeals from the decisions of various high courts gradually started accumulating before the Supreme Court, along with original writ petitions. What was intriguing was that while the writ petitions were filed by groups agitating for women's rights, the appeals were from husbands aggrieved by verdicts of various high courts.

If the Act was in fact depriving women of their pre-existing rights and was enabling husbands to wriggle out of their economic liability towards their ex-wives, why were the husbands finding themselves 'aggrieved' by the orders passed under a blatantly anti-women statute? Lurking beneath this query was a faint suspicion that perhaps the manner in which the Act was unfolding itself in the lower courts was indicative of a different reality, defying the premonitions. This fascinating phenomenon provided the first indication that perhaps the ill-famed Act could be invoked to secure the rights of divorced Muslim women.

A seemingly innocuous clause, which had missed the attention of protesters and defenders alike, had been invoked by a section of the lower judiciary to pronounce judgments which provided a greater scope for protection against destitution. Section 3(1)(a) of the Act stipulated that a divorced Muslim woman is entitled to 'a reasonable and fair provision and maintenance to be made and paid to her within the iddat period by her former husband.' This clause, along with the preamble which proclaimed 'An

Act to protect the rights of Muslim women who have been divorced by, or have obtained divorce from their husbands', had been invoked by the judiciary in defense of Muslim women's rights.

Though initially just a trickle, the judgments were a pointer towards a possibility. They affirmed that the new Act was to protect, rather than deprive, the rights of divorced Muslim women. They further stressed that any ambiguity within section 3(1)(a) must be interpreted in such a manner as to reconcile with the proclamation contained in the title of the Act. Banishing divorced women to a life of destitution would not amount to protecting their rights as stipulated by the statute, they declared. Drawing on the Islamic concept of *mataaoon bil ma'aroofe* (as reflected in the wordings, 'fair and reasonable provision'), the high courts opened a new portal for the protection of divorced Muslim women. Endorsing the spirit of Islam and the shariat and reflecting the sensitivity of the Prophet, the courts read notions of justice and equity into the statute. Doing precisely what the Act in its title proclaimed, i.e., protection of rights of divorced Muslim women, the judiciary turned what had initially appeared to be a misnomer and a mockery into a factual reality and ushered in a silent revolution in the realm of Muslim women's rights.

This broadened the scope of women's right to maintenance and provided a better safeguard to them than the one provided under section 125 of Cr.PC. A reading of the judgments indicates that the Act had rid itself of the agenda of alleviating vagrancy and destitution among divorced women and had extended itself to the claims of women from a higher social stratum. Suddenly, the lump sum provisions for future security, which the courts were awarding within the framework of Islamic principles, seemed to be a better safeguard against destitution than the meager, monthly recurring sums which women were entitled to under section 125 of the Cr.PC.

The first significant judgment on this issue was pronounced by M. B. Shah J., then presiding over the Gujarat High Court, on 18 February 1988.[149] But the dice had already been cast in favour of women by a woman judicial magistrate in Lucknow on 6 January 1988. The woman concerned, Fathima Sardar, was awarded Rs 85,000 as maintenance during iddat period, mehr entitlement and a lump sum settlement for the future (Agnes 1999). Following the judgment of the Gujarat High Court, the Kerala High Court upheld this view in two significant rulings.[150] In another unreported judgment, the Kerala High Court upheld the woman's right to Rs 3,00,000 as fair and reasonable and also awarded Rs 7,500 as maintenance during iddat.[151] In the years that followed, Full Benches of Punjab and Haryana and Bombay High Courts, the Division Benches of the Bombay, Kerala, Madras, and Calcutta high courts, and single judges of several other high courts upheld this view. The courts ruled that even when a wife has some source of income, the right under section 3 of the MWA is not extinguished.

Finally, after a decade and a half of its enactment, in September 2001, a five-judge Bench of the Supreme Court in *Daniel Latifi* v. *Union of India*,[152] pronounced that the controversial Act is valid and constitutional and upheld the positive interpretations of various high courts regarding fair and reasonable settlement for a life time. The Apex Court clarified that at the time of divorce, the Muslim husband is required to contemplate the future needs of the wife and make preparatory arrangements in advance in order to meet those needs. Reasonable and fair provision would include provision for residence, food, clothes, and other articles.

Within a communally vitiated atmosphere, even this landmark ruling did not attract much media attention and lay hidden from public view. The under reporting of this ruling caused a great disservice to Muslim women as scholars and activists continued to mouth the 'appeasement' theory and endorse the outdated and erroneous view that a divorced Muslim woman does not have a right to post-divorce maintenance. Hence the positive tidings could not filter down and reach the poor, marginalized, and illiterate Muslim women who needed it most in order to secure their rights against arbitrary pronouncements of divorce by their husbands and to create a culture of rights within their own community.

Muslim Women and Dominant Ideologies

In the final battle in the Supreme Court, both sides—the women's rights groups who had challenged the constitutionality of the Act as well as the Muslim religious leadership who had pressed for their claim that the Muslim women's entitlement ought to be limited to three months of Iddat period—lost. It was the divorced Muslim woman, who had waged a relentless battle to defend her rights, who emerged victorious.

The judgment was the outcome of numerous applications filed by Muslim women for their right of post-divorce maintenance in lower courts in smaller cities and moffusil towns across the country. It was crucial that the media took note of this silent revolution waged by individual Muslim women and acknowledge their agency in bringing about changes within their personal laws. The struggles of individual

---

[149] *Arab Ahemadhia Abdulla* v. *Arab Bail Mohmuna Saiyadbhai*, AIR 1988 Guj 141.

[150] *Ali* v. *Sufaira* (1988(2) KLT 94) and *Aliyar* v. *Pathu* (1988 (2) KLT 172).

[151] *P. K. Saru* v. *P. A. Salim* (unreported).

[152] *Daniel Latifi* v. *Union of India*, 2001 (7) SCC 740.

divorced Muslim women who defied their culture and tradition and the dictates of patriarchy need to be acknowledged as acts of assertion. Focusing on these struggles and identifying their locations of resistance is crucial for our understanding of the dynamism of Muslim family law in India and is of great political and emancipatory value.

A legal provision has to be assessed not merely by its wording or the political context in which it was enacted, but by its application to real life situations. The wording of a statute comes to life when it is contested in court rooms and is interpreted through judicial pronouncements. While examining the provisions of the MWA, there have been several instances of innovative judicial interpretations where courts have gone beyond the wording of the statute and have located the rights within a contemporary social reality, thereby expanding the horizon of women's rights.

But the struggle has not been easy for divorced Muslim women who have had to fight every inch of the way for their rights, right from trial courts in small district towns to the Supreme Court. Their crucial right of survival hinged upon interpretations and explanations of simple words like 'within'/'for', 'and/or', 'maintenance'/'provision'. The ambiguities which surfaced due to callous drafting posed hurdles in the struggle to claim their rights. The Act provided ample scope for husbands to exploit the situation, which led to protracted litigation, to the benefit of the husbands and the nightmare of women. But women withstood the ordeal with courage, determination, patience, and perseverance and overcame the seemingly insurmountable hurdles. Through this laborious process, the civil right of divorce settlement has been taken out of the earlier legal premises such as 'inability to maintain', 'prevention of vagrancy', 'a dole to hold together body and soul'. After a decade and a half, the end results of this persistent struggle are clearly discernible.

One needs to examine the invisibilising of the Muslim woman's struggle within the cultural construct of hegemonic claims. Communal fervour could be sustained only by denying the fact that the Act provided for an alternate remedy which was far superior to the one that had been denied to Muslim women under section 125 of the Cr.P.C., by negating the fact that since 1988, the Act was being positively interpreted by various High Courts by awarding substantial amounts as 'settlements', and by glossing over an important development in the realm of family law—that of determination of economic entitlements upon divorce, rather than the prevailing right of recurring maintenance.

The Shah Bano controversy and the Supreme Court ruling validating the Muslim Women's Act are reflective of an emerging legal discourse on legal pluralism versus legal universalism. Many legal scholars today endorse the view that liberalism's subordination of difference to an abstract individualism has become increasingly problematic. Even in mainstream legal thought, issues concerning the marginalized have contributed to the evolution of a new 'jurisprudence of difference'. I rely upon a quote from a renowned scholar and a proponent of legal pluralism to sum up my concern regarding the liberal approach to the Shah Bano controversy:

(L)aw's social environment can no longer be thought of as made up merely of individuals addressed equally by law. Law addresses--not necessarily explicitly or directly--groups of many kinds. Law means different things to different people and has different consequences for them in the light of plurality of religious beliefs and practices, ethnic identifications and historical patterns of collective experience. (Cotterrell 2005: x)

In the West, issues of legal pluralism have emerged in the context of ethnic groups and their rights for recognition of their diverse cultural histories and social realities within the English (and Continental) legal domain. The growth of distinct populations that, during their settlement history, brought different ways of life from foreign places of origin is hardly a new phenomenon in British history. But its recent scale is striking. According to Cotterrell, the vital challenge today is to create a sound legal framework for Britain as a society not only of stimulating diversity, but also of solidarity and individualism, involving a constant reaching out to others across cultural divides (Cotterrell 2005).

In England, various cultural-legal issues have emerged, such as recognition of polygamous marriages and cultural differences, interaction of the South Asian legal traditions and the official legal system, the role of experts in immigration cases and more generally, in fostering understanding of cultural and legal pluralism. Other scholars such as Prakash Shah have persuasively advocated a legal pluralist perspective in law teaching and legal scholarship and an outlook that links law to ideas of the community, including transnational and 'trans-local' networks of a community having boundaries not coterminous with those of the nation-state (Shah 2005).

Perhaps a similar legal framework needs to be evolved in India, in the context of a nation-state and its relationship to minority communities, their cultures, and practices while keeping in view issues of justice, equality, and human rights. The issue of women's rights and legal reforms need to be framed within this, more inclusive, framework of rights rather than the existing binaries of women versus minority communities.

While examining the plurality of law, one must transcend the shackles of doctrinal legal thinking. Even though law is not, and never has been, a unitary phenomenon, an assumption to the contrary has played a central role in most legal discourses and theories. Law is a complex

of practices, discourses, and institutions. Like any other institution of society, it is interconnected with other institutions. Over this plurality of legal forms 'state law', persistently, but never with complete success, seeks to impose a unity. This approach to law can be identified by the label of 'legal pluralism' (Mensky 2003).

The developments of the law of maintenance to Muslim women in the post-Shah Bano phase are reflective of a larger social and political reality which we need to accept as we begin to explore the issue rationally and dispassionately.

Section C

ATTEMPTS AT FORMULATING THE UCC

While advocating a cautious approach towards legal universalism and advancing an argument in defence of legal pluralism in the Indian context, one needs to also scrutinize the efforts to draft a secular civil code. After the Supreme Court ruling in the Shah Bano case, there have been several attempts to draft a model civil code. Rather curiously, these drafts, which were discussed at various workshops, do not substantiate the premise that a UCC will better protect women's rights. While they hold a brief for monogamy, which is directed against the Muslim law, they endorse a conservative notion regarding women's sexuality and link maintenance for women with sexual purity. Some suggestions like compulsory registration of marriages enhance State power over civilian life and at the same time jeopardise women's rights as the court would have the power to invalidate legal marriages merely because they are not registered. They also reproduce the prevailing, at times conservative, matrimonial remedies. Overall, there is nothing novel or path breaking in these drafts which would make it a revolutionary code from the perspective of women's rights. A few suggestions which may be beneficial to women have, over the years, been brought into effect, either by amendments to existing statutes (for example removing the ceiling of Rs 500 for awarding maintenance under section 125 of the Cr.P.C. in 2001) or by a specific enactment (such as the Protection of Women from Domestic Violence Act, 2005 which is applicable to all women across the religious divide). Campaigns which led to the enactment of these beneficial provisions have been smooth, without churning up a communal controversy in the political domain. Hence these campaigns and enactments substantiate the view that these focussed piecemeal legislations are more advantageous for protecting women's rights than an all encompassing UCC ridden with political controversy.

The Civil Code of Goa

In the debate on the UCC, the Goan Code is often projected as the model of uniformity for the rest of India (Vargo *et al.* 1995: 21). This projection is based on an erroneous understanding of the Goan Code, which in fact grants recognition to various customary practices, including Hindu polygamy.[153] The situation in Goa is unique as compared to the rest of the country. Here, Hindus are granted the customary right of polygamy, while Muslims are governed by the principle of monogamy. Neither nikah nor talaq is recognized and Muslim marriages and divorces are regulated by the code. The fact that this situation has not led to any political controversy can be attributed to the non-politicization of issues concerning Muslims, who in any case are numerically insignificant.[154]

The Code also needs to be viewed within the context of colonial rule. The Portuguese brought Roman Catholicism into Goa. Religion and politics mingled under the Papal authority. They introduced the Continental system of family law which prevailed in Portugal and was based on the French Civil Code. But like the French Civil Code, there was no total separation of Church and State. The Code, enacted for a predominantly Roman Catholic population, grants certain concessions to them. While marriages of other communities have to be performed in the Office of the Registrar, a marriage solemnized in church, as per the church law (Canon law), is valid. Hence the sacramental aspect of only a Catholic marriage is granted statutory recognition.[155] An annulment granted by an ecclesiastical tribunal is also granted automatic recognition.[156] Therefore, Catholics in Goa do not have to go through a dual process of obtaining a civil divorce and a canonical annulment like Catholics in the rest of India. After liberation in 1961, Goa and Daman and Diu were incorporated into the Indian nation as Union Territories, but the Hindu Code Bill or other personal laws were not made applicable to these territories and the laws which were then in force were allowed to be retained.[157]

---

[153] Article 3 of the Usages and Custom of Gentile Hindus of Goa. [Year?] Identical statutes were enacted also for Daman and Diu.

[154] It is less than 4 per cent. The Portuguese did not resort to the divide and rule policy of the British which led to the constitution of Hindus and Muslims as distinct and mutually hostile communities. The Portuguese

policy was one of assimilation and codification to facilitate smooth administration and hence various castes within their colonies were listed and their customs and usages were codified. But Muslims in Goa have lived on the periphery of social and political activity and there does not seem to be any categorization of their customs and usages under Portuguese rule.

[155] Article 1069 of the Code. Also see Chadha 1993.

[156] Hence the Catholic community in Goa does not have to go through the rigours of a civil divorce, as is situation in the rest of India under the IDA.

[157] Section 5 of the Goa and Daman and Diu (Administration) Act, 1962.

While the Goan Code provides useful guidelines regarding the concept of joint matrimonial property (based on the Continental legal system), its claim of being a workable model of uniformity cannot be substantiated. The positive and the negative aspects of the Code can not be isolated from the context of the Continental legal system or the Portuguese colonial policies within which it is located. The legal system, which worked well for a small and homogenized territory under the rule of assimilation can not be applied to a vast and pluralistic nation which was governed for about 200 years by the British policy of divide and rule.[158]

Model Drafts and Legal Doctrines

Some attempts to formulate a UCC were made in the post-Shah Bano period, primarily as a response to the Supreme Court directive. The primary attempt of these drafts was to bring in certain uniformity in the diverse family law and to enhance state authority over civil marriages concerning minority communities. Though there was also a claim of gender equality, some of the suggestions in the proposed drafts contradict this claim. Further, they adopted a formal notion of equality which, at times, proves to be adverse to women's rights. The approach towards equality has to be substantive, not just a formal notion of equality.[159]

This section examines these drafts, categorized as drafts by legal scholars, recommendations by women's groups, and official drafts or private Bills by Members of Parliament.

Drafts by Legal Scholars

The draft presented by the Bar Council of India in 1986 (hereafter referred to as the Bar Council draft or BCI draft) addressed the whole gamut of personal laws—marriage, divorce, maintenance, custody and guardianship of children, adoption, legitimacy, inheritance, succession, implementation machinery, and procedures.

While the initial draft proposed an optional code,[160] the final recommendations favoured a compulsory code with other options built into it.[161] There was a consensus that sufficient time should lapse after the enactment of the code before it is brought into force. It was also felt that it might be more feasible to introduce reforms within small and specific aspects of personal laws by generating sufficient pressure within communities.

The draft prescribes compulsory registration of marriages and stipulates that a marriage certificate is essential for claiming maintenance,[162] which would cause a severe blow to women's rights. While the draft retains conventional matrimonial reliefs, provisions regarding permanent alimony and maintenance during litigation are absent. Instead, section 125 of the Cr.P.C. has been incorporated to provide for maintenance of wives and children during the subsistence of marriage and after its dissolution.

The draft protects children's interests by recognizing them as an independent party during matrimonial litigation and stipulates that unless adequate arrangements are made for protecting

---

[158] In this context, also see the note of caution in the Foreword by Chief Justice Sabyasachi Mukherji to Usgaocar's very useful translation of the Goan Family Code. (Usgaocar 1988).

[159] The substantive model of equality is governed by Article 15(3) of the Constitution while formal equality is based on Articles 14 and 15(1) of the Constitution.

[160] The initial draft proposed that Muslims and Scheduled Tribes be exempted from its application. An individual Muslim could opt to be governed by it. Tribal communities could be governed by it only by a notification in the Government gazette. Section 1 (a) and (b) of the proposed draft. For more, see Mishra 1991: 65.

[161] Ibid.: iv

[162] Section 26 of the draft. See ibid.: 65

children's interests, the matrimonial court should not pass a decree. The property of both parents should be settled in favour of the children so that the welfare of the children is not jeopardised due to paucity of funds.[163] These are positive provisions which would safeguard children's rights.

The draft also introduces the concept of joint ownership of matrimonial property,[164] i.e., all property acquired after marriage is deemed to be the joint property of the spouses. Upon breakdown of marriage, the spouses would be entitled to a half share each. Upon death, the surviving spouse will inherit half the property while the other half devolves by testamentary or intestate succession. Property acquired by the spouses prior to marriage is deemed to be their separate property. This includes customary gifts received by a woman i.e., stridhana, mehr, etc. This suggestion for introducing the concept of joint ownership of matrimonial property is significant. But adopting a formal approach to equality by placing women's traditional rights within the realm of matrimonial property may not serve women's interests.

The draft code presented by the ILS Law College, Pune in 1986 (hereafter referred to as the ILS draft) provides for the repeal of all existing matrimonial statutes and to this extent prescribes a compulsory code. But elsewhere, the authors have examined possibilities of an optional code or reform within personal laws, in keeping with the federal structure of the Indian state.[165] 'There is great danger in enforcing a compulsory code in a sudden fashion as it might result in the alienation of the minorities which is not wise from the point of view of national integration', the authors caution.[166] Viewed in this context, the provision for repeal of all existing laws seems to be a contradiction.

In addition to the prevailing matrimonial reliefs, the draft incorporates provisions of maintenance under section 125 of the Cr.P.C., conviction for bigamy under sections 494, 495, and 496 of the IPC (which deal with the matrimonial offence of bigamy) and punishment for non-payment of maintenance.[167]

The draft provides for compulsory registration of marriages and invalidates non-registered marriages. Notwithstanding this stipulation, it seeks to marginally protect the rights of women and children in void marriages by conferring on them the right to maintenance.[168] Adopting the formal equality model (reflected in the Hindu Marriage Act), it provides for maintenance to husbands,[169] a concept which is not prevalent in other such as the Indian Divorce Act, Muslim personal law and the Special Marriage Act and section 125 of the Cr.P.C.

Regarding rights to matrimonial property, a vague and confusing provision of the Hindu Marriage Act, which confers on courts the jurisdiction over property presented jointly to the parties at the time of marriage, is incorporated.[170] Here, there is no mention of any other property acquired by the spouses during the subsistence of marriage, customary gifts, monetary security made to the bride at the time of marriage, or property of either spouses acquired prior to the marriage.

---

163   Ibid.: 121
164   Ibid.: 238
165   Dr S.P. Sathe has emphazised that federalism is not only a geographical phenomenon but also cultural and ethnic, that the need to be different is not anti-national and that nationalism does not require regimentation (Sathe 1995: 2165).

166   Ibid
167   Sections 17 & 33 of the Bill
168   Section 18 of the Act read with Section 3(a) and Section 9 of the proposed bill
169   Section 17 of the Bill
170   Section 27, Hindu Marriage Act, 1955

A Critique of the Proposed Drafts

Neither of the above detailed drafts comprised a radical departure from the reliefs which were already available under existing matrimonial statutes. Hence their claim to modernity can not be sustained. The drafts have retained conventional matrimonial remedies which were adopted from English family law principles, including the archaic remedy of restitution of conjugal rights, although the same has now been abolished under English matrimonial statutes.[171]

Surprisingly, the ILS draft, a purely civil statute, has also retained conversion as a matrimonial offence and to this extent has undermined the provisions under the Special Marriage Act. The rationale behind holding conversion as a matrimonial offence forms a part of religious law which was applicable to persons professing the same religion. Since the draft provides for the solemnization of marriages between two persons, irrespective of their religions, it is difficult to comprehend how change of religion can be a matrimonial offence. In addition, grounds such as leprosy, conversion, bestiality, sodomy, and unnatural sex are hardly used in the normal course as grounds of divorce and would have more academic than practical use.

The drafts do not provide for maintenance as an ancillary matrimonial relief in matrimonial proceedings, resorting instead to section 125 of the Cr.P.C. and recommending abolition of the ceiling of Rs 500 prescribed therein. This is neither new nor radical as the Law Commission of India, in its 132nd report, had recommended this and the same has been subsequently enacted, through an amendment, in 2001.[172]

[171] Section 20, Matrimonial Proceedings and Property Act, 1970.

[172] The report brought out under the Chairmanship of M.P. Thakkar was submitted to the government in April 1989. Subsequently, in 2001, the ceiling was removed.

The BCI draft was ambiguous on whether the forum for adjudication must shift from the prevailing magistrate's court to district courts and whether proceedings will continue to be summary. Under prevailing matrimonial statutes, the courts can order lump sum maintenance and settlements. The proposed drafts do not seem to include this very useful provision. The procedures for enforcing an order of a criminal court are more stringent than those of the civil court and hence the provisions of Section 125 Cr.P.C. will provide a better scope for enforcing maintenance orders. But the drafts have not addressed these deeper concerns.

The ILS draft retained the clause linking maintenance to sexual purity. Sub-section (4) of section 125 of the Cr.P.C. stipulates that if a woman is *living in adultery*, she is not entitled to maintenance and sub-section (5) stipulates that if subsequent to the order, the woman *lives in adultery*, the husband can move the court to vary the order (emphasis added). The ILS draft modifies this position and makes it more stringent and provides as under:

If the court is satisfied that the party in whose favour an order has been made under this section has had sexual intercourse with any person other than the spouse, it may, at the instance of the other party, vary, modify or rescind any such order in such manner as it may deem just.

Under the prevailing sections, the courts have ruled that the words 'living in adultery' used in section 125(4) and (5) of the Cr.P.C. indicate that isolated instances of adultery are not sufficient to deny the wife maintenance. The husband had to prove that the woman is living with another man and that the other man is now maintaining the wife. Even when a husband succeeds in obtaining divorce on the ground of the wife's adultery, she cannot be denied maintenance.[173] By substituting the words 'sexual intercourse' with 'living in adultery', the draft narrows the scope of claiming maintenance. This suggestion would make the situation far worse for women.

The draft renders maintenance as a premium on chastity not only during the subsistence of marriage but even after the marital bond is dissolved through a decree of divorce. Since this provision is often used by husbands to embarrass women in court proceedings, the Law Commission, in its 132nd report, had recommended its Seletion.[174] To this extent, the stipulation in the ILS draft was regressive and anti-women.

The stipulation in the Bar Council draft that maintenance would be granted only on the production of a marriage certificate would also adversely affect the rights of women and children and falls below the existing stipulation under matrimonial statutes and section 125 of the Cr.PC. In addition, proceedings under section 125 of the Cr.PC are of a summary nature and a woman is not required to prove the marriage. Women approaching the courts for maintenance are protected by a presumption in favour valid marriage laid down under section 50 of the Indian Evidence Act.

In both the drafts, the claim to 'modernity' rests on the stipulation of monogamy and compulsory registration of marriages. The provision of registration exists under the Parsi, Christian, and Special Marriage Acts and also, to a limited extent, under Muslim law (where marriages are performed through written contracts, nikahnamas, and are registered with the office of the Qazi.). Section 8 of the Hindu Marriage Act provides for registration of Hindu marriages. But keeping in view the plurality of the Hindu society, its loose social and religious organisations, and non-State regulatory structures, the Act has specifically laid down that non-registration cannot invalidate an existing marriage. Stipulations of compulsory registration seek to modify the existing legal position under the Hindu law, to the detriment of women's rights. The provision seems to stem from a concern to curb bigamy by providing for valid proof of marriage and to this extent is defended as beneficial to women. But in reality, the suggestion is extremely short sighted. The fact that far more number of women are likely to approach courts for maintenance than for criminal prosecution in cases of bigamy and that maintenance is far more crucial to women than the penalty for bigamy seems to have escaped the notice of the drafters.[175]

Some of the recommendations are also confusing and contradictory. For instance, the Bar Council draft provides for registration of two types of marriages, civil and traditional.[176] The recommended procedure for registering a civil marriage is a verbatim repetition of the provision under the present Special Marriage Act. The procedure for registering a traditional marriage is complex. After a marriage is solemnized in a traditional manner, a declaration signed

---

[173] See the decisions *in Mahalingam Pillai* v. *Amsavalli*, (1956) 2 MLJ 289; *Gulab Jagduse Kakwani* v. *Kamla Gulab Kakwani*, AIR 1985 Bom 88; *T. Raja Rao* v. *T. Neelamma*, 1990 Cri.LJ 2430 AP; *Baishnab Charan Jena* v. *Ritarani Jena*, 1993 Cri LJ 238; *Sandha* v. *Narayan* II (1999) DMC 411 Ker; and *Laxman Naik* v. *Lalita Naik* II (2003) DMC 275 Ori.

[174] Point 7 of the 132nd Law Commission Report suggested Sub-section (4) and (5) of section 125, Cr. PC which deprives a wife from claiming maintenance on the ground that she is living in adultery, should be deleted as it is invoked primarily to humiliate women during the trial.

[175] See *Registration of Marriages* in chapter Marriage and Its Dissolution (volume 2 of this book) for a critique of the recent Supreme Court rulings on this issue.

[176] Chapter III sections 15 to 24.

by the parties and three witnesses must be sent to the registrar. This serves as a mere notice. After the expiry of one month and after the Registrar satisfies himself that the requirements of a valid marriage have been complied with, the parties will have to present themselves before the Registrar along with three witnesses for completing the formalities of registration. The marriage becomes valid and binding only after a certificate of marriage is issued by the Registrar. Hence a section which elaborately lays down various traditional forms of marriage under different religions and some customs (section 21) seems redundant and illusory and a mere token gesture towards legal plurality. This will lead to unnecessary ambiguities and legal complexities. Traditional marriage is a social event with customary rituals and ceremonies which include the ritual of consummation. It is rather absurd to presume that a mandatory refrain from consummation under a statute, will prevent a couple from consummating the marriage until a certificate is obtained from the registrar after a month. The implications of consummating a marriage performed traditionally, before a certificate is obtained from the registrar, are not addressed.

In this context, the ILS draft is more direct and provides greater clarity. While civil registration is mandatory, the parties are free to perform religious ceremonies of their choice. This provision is projected as incorporating legal plurality. The marriage becomes legal and binding only upon a civil registration. Since in any case, social events are celebrated with traditional rituals and ceremonies and the sanction of the State is not necessary for these celebrations, providing for them within a statute would still amount to a gesture of mere tokenism and may lead to ambiguities which are best avoided.

The drafts lose sight of the fact that civil registration of marriages is an alien concept under Hindu law. For this stipulation to meet with a measure of success, it is essential that the procedures are simple, inexpensive, and decentralised. The drafts do not provide for this. The statutory notice of one month stipulated under the Special Marriage Act is mechanically retained. The fact that this has proved to be the greatest deterrent against registering marriages under the Special Marriage Act has not been considered. In Mumbai and other cities of Maharashtra and Gujarat, forced, fraudulent, and invalid marriages could be registered for a premium, in a matter of minutes, by manipulating the provisions of an outdated statute, Bombay Marriage Registration Act, 1953, which, in effect, provided for the registration of a mere document and not of the marriage (Agnes 1996: 25). Unscrupulous lawyers successfully mislead naive, unassuming, young couples, who wish to marry despite parental opposition, into registering invalid marriages in this manner. The stringent stipulations under SMA have led to the mushrooming of several *vivaha karyalaya*s where registration of marriages has become a lucrative business. The fact that the procedures for registering a marriage under the Special Marriage Act are stringent and cumbersome and information about correct procedures is scarce, has contributed to this dismal state of affairs. There is an urgent need to simplify and decentralize the procedures of registration and to reduce the existing notice period of one month. The drafts do not concern themselves with these social realities.

The ILS draft starts off with rigid stipulation regarding registration of marriages, but the rigidity is relaxed in a subsequent section which grants women in void marriages the right of maintenance. If a woman can prove a customary marriage and subsequent cohabitation, despite the fact that the marriage is bigamous, she will be entitled to maintenance. While this is a positive suggestion which will be beneficial to women who are tricked into bigamous marriages, it leads to an internal inconsistency in the draft and reduces registration to a mere facilitating measure. This, in any case, is the present legal position. Hence, while the Bill may rake a controversy over abolition of bigamy and compulsory registration of marriage, on closer scrutiny, the Bill would not drastically change the existing situation.

While granting women in void marriages a right to maintenance is beneficial, the provision of granting husbands a similar right of maintenance under the concept of formal equality would open up new avenues of harassment in matrimonial litigation and will saddle women with unwarranted encumbrances.

The failure to provide the right of residence in the matrimonial home, as a right flowing from the contract of marriage, and civil injunctions restraining the husband from dispossessing the wife from the matrimonial home seems to be another major drawback of both the drafts. The right to reside in the matrimonial home and the right to a share of matrimonial assets need to be clearly stipulated as matrimonial rights flowing from the contract of marriage. Further, since there is a lot of ambiguity regarding the matrimonial home in judicial discourse, there is an urgent need to statutorily define 'matrimonial home'. The drafts have failed to respond to this pressing need.

Therefore, overall, despite their stated objective, the primary concern of the drafts seems to be with uniformity and regulation of sexuality rather than a genuine concern for protecting the rights of women and children.

Recommendations by Women's Organizations

Recommendations by Vimochana and Lawyers Collective (1988)

These recommendations were evolved at a workshop organized by Vimochana, a counselling and support group based in Bangalore, along with the Lawyers Collective, in May 1988 at Bangalore.[177] Protection of economic rights of women within marriage is a major concern of this draft. The draft proposes joint ownership of property acquired after marriage and grants women the right to reside in the matrimonial home. The husband is restrained from selling the matrimonial home or relinquishing the tenancy of the house without the consent of the wife.

Departing from the outdated 'fault' theory of divorce, where one spouse has to prove a matrimonial fault (adultery, cruelty, desertion, insanity, etc.) against the other, the 'breakdown' theory is based on incompatibility between the spouses and is borrowed from the principles of contemporary English matrimonial statutes.[178] With this, the archaic provision of restitution of conjugal rights is automatically abolished. To grant additional protection to women, it is proposed that a divorce demanded by the husband on the ground of irretrievable breakdown of marriage should be granted only after he makes adequate economic provision for the wife. The draft stipulates that if the wife is in possession of the matrimonial home, her right of residence should not be extinguished upon divorce.

Since enforcement of maintenance orders is a major hurdle faced by women, the draft suggests that the husband should be required to make a

---

[177] 'Recommendations of the Lawyers Collective Bangalore Law School', *The Lawyers* III/7 (1988) p. 20.

[178] The remedy is based on a similar provision under the English law under section 2 of the 1973. (See Jackson 1983: 2499-501)

voluntary disclosure of his assets and income immediately after a petition for divorce is filed by either of the spouses. Thereafter, he must deposit three months' maintenance for the wife and children. The amount must be calculated by dividing the income in equal shares between the husband, the wife, and the minor children. The draft also stipulates that matrimonial courts should have the power to award lump sum maintenance, property settlements, and salary attachments. Criminal and civil remedies to prevent violence against women, including ouster injunctions, have also been proposed to provide protection to women within marriage.

The draft seeks to abolish the concept of the father as the natural guardian of a child. The draft specifically protects the mother's rights to custody by stipulating that custody should be given to the parent who has taken the responsibility of looking after the child in the past. The draft also suggests that the lack of earning capacity of the mother or the fact that she has no dwelling should not disentitle her to the custody of the children and further, factors like alcoholism and violence towards the mother or children should be considered while determining the best interest of the child in custody petitions.

The recommendations provide for compulsory registration of marriages but grant rights to women in informal relationships. Further, it is clarified that for the purpose of conviction for bigamy, cohabitation should be deemed as marriage. It recommends abolition of the offence of adultery under section 497, IPC. The contradiction between providing for compulsory registration of marriages at one end and granting recognition to informal marriages and providing for the rights of cohabitees has not been examined. This seems to be a major drawback of the draft. If the rights of cohabitees are on par with the rights of spouses, there would be no compulsion to register a marriage, particularly

in a society where marriages are viewed more as social functions than as legal contracts. Similarly, the contradiction between recommending abolition of the punishment for adultery and at the same time advocating for broadening the scope of the offence of bigamy from formal marriages to informal relationships has not been addressed. If marriages and informal cohabitations are both deemed as offences, then the entire premise upon which conviction for bigamy is based collapses. The existing law makes a clear distinction between solemn marriages and illegitimate and informal alliances where the ceremony of solemnization and permanency of the relationship is of greatest relevance. Widening this scope would render adultery an offence rather than bigamy. But since it is also recommended that adultery ought not to be deemed as an offence, there is an ambiguity about whether the focus of the reform is on curbing sexual immorality by a penal provision or protecting women's economic rights by widening the scope of maintenance to include women in informal alliances.

The recommendations introduce the remedy of irretrievable breakdown of marriage. This was proposed by the Law Commission in its 71st report.[179] But the issue was abandoned due to opposition from various women's organizations. This opposition was based on the fact that the remedy may not suit Indian cultural ethos and women will be worse affected by it. It will provide an avenue for husbands, after years of marriage, to opt out on flimsy grounds and leave the wife and children in a lurch. While the opposition is valid, it does not take into account subsequent developments. The remedy has already made a back door entry into matrimonial statutes. Firstly, the ground of mental

---

[179] The report was brought out in 1980 and was circulated to various women's organizations in 1981.

cruelty is used by the parties almost on the same footing as irretrievable breakdown of marriage.[180] Further, by the 1976 amendment, several new grounds of divorce have been introduced in the Hindu Marriage Act and the Special Marriage Act which amount to the ground of irretrievable breakdown of marriage.[181] So, the opposition does not have a sound legal basis. As far as the husbands are concerned, the remedy is linked to economic settlements in favour of the wives. But if the suits for maintenance are an indication, husbands will find myriad ways to wriggle out of their economic responsibilities. This is a concern which needs special attention while recommending irretrievable breakdown of marriage.

Recommendations by the All India Democratic Women's Association (AIDWA) (1995)

The AIDWA is affiliated to CPI (M) and has been active in the post-Independence campaigns for women's rights. Its campaign against

the enactment of the Muslim Women's Bill is particularly significant.[182] While initially the group endorsed the demand for a UCC, subsequently, it opposed this demand and suggested alternate recommendations.

While concern for strengthening women's rights is the governing principle, the focus of the recommendations is on the strategies of reform. At its national convention held at Delhi on 9-10 December 1995, titled 'Equal Rights, Equal Laws', the AIDWA proposed a step-by-step approach to bring in reform (Karat 1995: 25; Singh 1996: 55). The convention rejected the idea of a comprehensive code, whether compulsory or optional, and instead advocated legislation on specific issues and reforms within existing personal laws as dual strategies of achieving the goal of gender justice.

According to the organization, an umbrella legislation would require complete overhauling of all existing laws. This may pose obstacles in the path of immediate reform. Before implementing a comprehensive code, the foundation of equality between men and women would have to be laid. It believes that secular legislation in specific areas of crucial concern will be an important step in this direction. The three specific areas of legislative reform proposed by the convention are: (i) right to matrimonial property, (ii) protection against domestic violence, and (iii) marriage registration facilities.

A legislation on joint matrimonial property would grant recognition to women's contribution to the household by way of unpaid labour and reduce the incidents of destitution which are common among women of all communities. A Domestic Violence Act would provide for

---

[180] A scrutiny of the reported cases indicates that husbands file petitions on the ground of mental cruelty making frivolous allegations like refusal to cook food, asking the husband to clear the dining table in the presence of friends, not following specific instructions about taking care of his mother, quarrelsome nature of the wife, arrogance due to higher educational qualifications, pressurising the husband to set up a separate house, etc.

[181] Section 13 (1A) of the Hindu Marriage Act and Section 27 (ii) of the Special Marriage Act stipulate that if cohabitation is not resumed after one year of obtaining a decree of restitution of conjugal rights or judicial separation, either parties can approach the court for a divorce. In actual effect if the wife has obtained a decree of restitution of conjugal rights and the husband has thereafter refused to comply with the decree, he can obtain decree of divorce one year later. This provision was introduced in the Parsi Marriage and Divorce Act in 1988 by adding section 32(A). See A.5. *Irretrievable Breakdown of Marriage* of Chapter 1 of the second volume *Matrimonial Conflicts and Women's Rights* where this issue is discussed further.

[182] Memorandum dated 17 April 1986, presented to the President of India by Susheela Gopalan, General Secretary, AIDWA and *Susheela Gopalan v. Union of India*, WP No. 1055 of 1986, dated 24 July 1986.

both civil and criminal remedies.[183] The demand for a law on registration of marriages clarified that there should be no interference with the nature of rituals and ceremonies of marriages. A decentralized machinery should be provided for registering marriages at villages and local panchayats could be granted the power of registration. Such registration would be of great help to women and would provide them with documentary proof of a valid marriage in the event of a dispute. The convention resolved that campaigns within communities are important strategies for reform in personal laws.

Despite the contradictions, these drafts are based on ground realities of women in distress situations and hence are aimed at seeking practical solutions, despite some minor inconsistencies. When translated into specific acts, they would provide some relief to the economic problems faced by women.

In the decade 1991-2000, several women's groups and human rights organizations were also engaged with the process of drafting uniform laws which would weed out discrimination against women, not just within personal laws but also within civil, criminal, and labour laws. A new term, 'gender just laws', was coined during this period to shed the baggage of communal undertones of the demand for a uniform civil code. While these drafts helped focus on the contemporary concerns of various groups to a certain extent, they did not get transformed into official drafts and remained at the level of campaign issues and over time, faded out.

Official Drafts and Parliamentary Trends
The four drafts discussed above reflect the concern of social organizations and legal academia.

But unless these concerns are reflected in official discourse, the process of law reform will not get off the ground. Hence, it is relevant to examine the position reflected in official drafts as well.

Bill Formulated by the National Commission for Women (1994)
It is rather disconcerting to observe that while the recommendations by women's organizations are cautious and practical, a Bill formulated by the National Commission for Women (NCW), titled The Marriage Bill, 1994[184] makes sweeping and unrealistic recommendations, throwing all caution to the wind. The primary concern of the Bill seems to be abolition of polygamy by ensuring compulsory registration of marriages. But instead of a facilitating measure (of providing proof in case of a dispute), registration becomes an end in itself.[185] The Bill stipulates that a declaration of marriage must be sent to the Registrar of Marriages within three days of its performance. A fine of Rs 100 per day is levied for default for a period of one month and thereafter the marriage is deemed void.[186] The Bill stipulates such stringent measures for non-registration of a marriage, even while ignoring that a large section of the population is deprived of basic amenities such as clean drinking water, primary education, and health facilities. The Bill does not spell out the measures through which the government will

---

[183] Subsequently, the Domestic Violence Act was enacted in 2005 which provides for civil and criminal remedies.

[184] The draft was approved by the Expert Committee on Laws in its meeting held on 18 and 19 August 1994. The Bill is unpublished. For various provisions of the Bill see Tiwari 1995: 28.

[185] The Statement of Object and Reason declares, 'A Bill to consolidate and amend the law relating to marriages in India and to provide for their compulsory registration'.

[186] Proviso to Section 17 of the Bill.

make it possible for people to register their marriages within three days of its performance.

The Bill abolishes the concept of restitution of conjugal rights. While this could be interpreted as a positive measure, it leaves no legal avenue for a deserted woman to apply to the courts for remedies of maintenance, custody of children, right of residence in the matrimonial home, etc., unless she is willing to dissolve the marriage, either by divorce or annulment. These crucial rights are incorporated only as ancillary reliefs in petitions for divorce and annulments. The Bill does not confer a statutory right of residence in the matrimonial house during the subsistence of marriage.

While stipulating stringent measures for registration of marriages, divorce is made easy by introducing the ground of incompatibility or irretrievable breakdown of marriage.[187] The statutory period of separation for a divorce by mutual consent is reduced from one year to three months.[188] The rationality behind rendering the bond of marriage so transient at one level and prescribing such stringent measures for its registration on the other, are difficult to comprehend.

Only one section of the Bill deals with economic rights of maintenance and residence, both during the subsistence of marriage and after its dissolution.[189] Here, adopting the model of formal equality, the Bill grants husbands and wives similar rights of maintenance and residence in the matrimonial home as ancillary measures.[190]

Private Member's Bill (1994)

This Bill was introduced by a Congress member, Veena Verma, in the Rajya Sabha in May 1994

and is titled, The Married Women's (Protection of Rights) Bill, 1994.[191] It is in the nature of specific enactments like the Dowry Prohibition Act, the Medical Termination of Pregnancy Act, and punishment for cruelty to wives (section 498A, IPC). Although these enactments altered personal laws, they were not situated within the political controversy of a UCC versus personal laws.

This Bill is significant for a number of reasons: (i) it provides for a new remedy which is non-existent in any matrimonial statute, (ii) it subscribes to the step-by-step approach, (iii) it is premised on the model of substantive equality, and (iv) the debate in Parliament regarding the Bill provides insights into legislative responses to protecting women's economic rights.

While the drafts discussed earlier grant women rights over property acquired after marriage (and husbands reciprocatory rights over the wive's property), this Bill grants rights to women over all the property of the husband and does not confer similar rights to husbands. The Bill seeks to grant the wife the right to live in the house of her husband, whether owned by him or by members of his joint family, the right to food, clothing, and other facilities, the right to an equal share in the property of her husband, and the right to be consulted in matters of family business and other financial transactions regarding the husband's property.[192] It is interesting to note that the Protection of women from Domestic Violence Act, 2005 incorporated at least the limited right of residence in the matrimonial home.

The Bill was debated in the Rajya Sabha during three different sessions: 12 August 1994,

---

[187] Section 7 (2) of the Bill.
[188] Section 11 (i) of the Bill.
[189] Section 10 of the Bill.
[190] Section 14 of the Bill.

[191] Bill No. XXV of 1994 introduced by Veena Verma in the Rajya Sabha on 13 May 1994.
[192] Section 3 of the Bill.

9 December 1994, and 31 March 1995.[193] Among the twenty-three members who commented on the Bill, barring a few stray adverse comments, unanimously supported the Bill. Though the issue would encroach into the terrain marked as 'personal laws' there was no opposition to the Bill by any member of minority community. On the contrary, the Christian member from Goa welcomed it and mentioned that such a provision is already existing in Goa.[194] It is also interesting to note that the reluctance to enact the Bill was not based only on diverse laws of succession but also on taxation laws.

When reforms cause a dent in the economics of patriarchy, perhaps it is easier to stall them communalising the issue. Due to the overwhelming support, the Minister was constrained to assure the house that it will be re-introduced as a Government Bill. But the government did not keep to this assurance and after elections, when the new United Front government assumed power, no further action was taken in this regard.

While the concern for enacting a UCC faded out of the political arena, women's rights could be framed within public discourse around specific issues such as prevention of domestic violence, right of residence in the matrimonial home and maintenance rights. A major achievement for women's groups was the enactment of the Protection of Women from Domestic Violence Act, 2005, which was the result of a sustained national-level campaign.

Salient Points Emerging from the Model Drafts
i. Even though abolishing polygamy through compulsory registration of marriages

seems to form the core of the controversy over a UCC, no draft has yet been able to resolve this issue. This is due to the two opposing concerns around the issue: (i) prescribing stringent measures, both civil and criminal, as deterrents to (male) bigamy, and (ii) providing for the rights of women in informal relationships. A tilt towards the former will increase state control over people's lives and will drastically affect the rights of women and children. A tilt towards the latter will render inconsequential the provisions in favour of monogamy and compulsory registration of marriages. The drafts have not paid due attention to this internal contradiction of the demand. The consensus seems to be governed by the sense of middle class morality and the Christian conception of marriage adopted by liberals in India rather than a genuine concern for women's rights as the recommendations seem to indicate.

ii. Gradually, a consensus seems to be emerging that the process of family law reform has to be cautious. It cannot happen through a bull in the china shop approach. Enforcing a compulsory UCC from above may not be the best solution. A step-by-step approach seems to be more feasible than a comprehensive code. The fact that the debate around the UCC had to be abandoned and an alternative strategy of a step-by-step approach succeeded, proves this point. The removal of the ceiling of Rs 500 for maintenance under section 125, Cr.P.C. as well as the enactment of the Domestic Violence Act has been beneficial to women across the religious divide.

iii. If the goal is to improve the rights of women and children, the recommendations have to be based on substantive equality. The use of the term 'spouse' while determining the rights and obligations of the parties to a marriage will result in further deterioration of women's

---

[193] RSD 12 August 1994 pp 796-861; RSD 9.12.94 pp.892-967 and RSD 31-03-95 pp 865-939
[194] See comments of Shri John F. Fernandes (Congress) 12 August 1994 at p. 840.

rights. A greater clarity regarding the theoretical framework upon which the remedies are based needs to be evolved, particularly where the legal academia is concerned.

iv. A shift away from the conception of marriage as a sexual contract to control or regulate sexuality to viewing it as an economic contract where weaker partners need additionally statutory protection (as in labour legislations), is visible in the drafts by women's organizations. There is an increasing realization regarding the link between divorce or desertion and the destitution of women in the development discourse. Women's right to shelter in their matrimonial home and the right to a share in the matrimonial property upon divorce are emerging as concrete strategies of tackling this issue.

v. The drafts discussed above underscore two presumptions about women: first, that women are non-working spouses whose only contribution is unpaid domestic labour and second, that women are equal partners within marriage, hence men and women have equal rights, duties, and responsibilities. Women who are the sole providers of their families are invisible in this debate. The recommendations do not protect these women who shoulder a double burden as wage earners and home makers. The implications of introducing the concept of joint family property, equal right to matrimonial home and maintenance, etc., using a gender neutral term 'spouse', would be detrimental to the rights of these women, most of whom belong to marginalized sections of society. The concerns of this large category of women are not reflected in any of the drafts.

CONCLUSION

While concluding this chapter, an attempt is made to interrogate the claims of equality and citizenship of the post-colonial, democratic, Indian state. Equality in turn is linked to freedom and further, economic and political freedom help reinforce one another.

There is strong evidence to suggest that social opportunities such as education and healthcare, which may require public action, complement individual opportunities of economic and political participation. If we identify freedom as the main object of development, the purpose of policy should be to analyse and establish linkages that make the viewpoint of freedom coherent and cogent as the guiding perspective in the process of development (Sen 1999). This chapter attempted to examine the Constitution of India, from the perspective of female citizens. Women's constitutional claims of equality, liberty, and freedom, beyond their formal and textual meanings, are important in this exploration. The power of judicial review within the constitutional scheme and the role of the judiciary in testing constitutional aspirations against the real life situations of women are important components of constitutionalism. It is in this context that some land mark rulings which served to break traditional barriers and secure the rights of women, beyond the assurances of formal equality, and protected women's rights to life, liberty, and dignity are discussed.

Equally important, but fraught with problems, are explorations into the gendered nature of citizenship and the negotiations between state, community, and family which are carried out by individual women. The 'gendering' of citizenship is a universal concern, primarily due to the creation of the public-private divide, where the male belongs to the public sphere and the female to the private. The characteristics of citizenship are located within the public domain and have been attributed to males by philosophers such as Rousseau and Hobbes who envisaged the male as facilitating the transition from a disorderly to an ordered society. In contrast, the woman has been associated within the realm of family and community (Roy 2005: 28). The creation of the binaries of public-private has been simultaneous with the creation of binaries of active and passive citizenship, with active citizenship signifying positive contribution to the political arena. Passive citizenship signifies reaping the political benefits of an organized society without contributing to it. Here again, the former has been attributed to men while the latter has been attributed to women (Chari 2009: 48).

The notion of a 'passive citizenship' of women had led to the notion of a 'dependent' citizenship of married women, under several common law countries. 'Citizenship' relates to a person's public identity and defines the relationship between an individual and the state. The assumption that a married woman's primary location is the private sphere within the home and under the protection of her husband has prevailed under most legal regimes. Hence, her need for a separate public identity and legal relationship with State was not taken into account. This led to several women who had married foreigners being stateless person upon the death of their husbands. Upon marriage the women lost their citizenship and acquired the citizenship of their husband as dependent citizens. Upon the death of the husband they became stateless persons, despite the fact that they themselves had never left their country of birth. The Convention on the Elimination of All Forms of Discrimination Against Women (CEDAW) adopted by the United Nations General Assembly in 1978 in Article 9 specifically addressed this concern.[195]

Citizenship, nationality and domicile are interconnected and overlapping concepts which determine legal rights. Domicile refers to a person's place of permanent residence. Acquisition and transfer of citizenship and nationality are determined by legal prescriptions of individual nation states. Women in England ceased to be dependent citizens only in 1974, after coming into force of the enactment, Domicile and Matrimonial Proceedings Act, 1973. In India the situation was changed in 1992, through an amendment to the Citizenship Act of 1955 and women were empowered to pass on their citizenship to their children. This, despite Article 5 (b) of the Constitution of India bestowing equal rights of citizenship by dissent upon both male and female citizens in 1950 when the Constitution came into force. It is in this context, women's struggle to bridge the gap between the public and the private realm of their lives becomes significant.

In India, women's attempt to enter the political life of the nation is reflected in campaigns to secure franchise and ventures into the political processes in the pre-Independence period. This move was met by a degree of hostility by male political leaders. But the hostility against women's entry into the public domain does not originate at this point. Confrontations with the dictates of family, community, and state took place a century earlier when a few women attempted to acquire basic education. Women's desire for literacy and the hardships they endured to attain it are recorded through poignant autobiographies of contemporary women.

---

[195] Article 9 (1): States Parties shall grant women equal rights with men to acquire, change or retain their nationality. They shall ensure in particular that neither marriage to an alien nor change of nationality by the husband during marriage shall automatically change the nationality of the wife, render her stateless or force upon her the nationality of the husband. Article 9 (2): States Parties shall grant women equal rights with men with respect to nationality of their children.

In the nineteenth century, through the actions of missionaries and social reformers, women's education became more acceptable, though opposition persisted from conservative segments of the political leadership. Even the East India Company, despite its commitment to ushering in modernity through English education, did not particularly encourage women's education as they considered it an issue within the ambit of religious beliefs and community dictates. Professional education amongst women was rare, with only a few notable figures like Cornelia Sorabjee, Kadambini Basu, and Sarala Ray emerging victorious.

The late nineteenth and early twentieth century witnessed the formation of women's associations such as Arya Mahila Samaj, Bharat Stree Mandal, Women's Indian Association, and All India Women's Conference. Though concerned primarily with a reformist agenda of social transformation and women's education, they were soon drawn into the political fervour of the national movement. There was a realization that citizenship claims are fundamental, without which it would not be possible to achieve the goal of social transformation. However, the demands raised by various women's organizations were not translated into legal reality until the enactment of the Constitution, which guaranteed equality, liberty, and freedom and adult franchise. In addition, special protection was awarded to women and children, by incorporating Article 15 (3) into the Constitution. This move facilitated the enactment of legislation meant especially to strengthen and protect women, beyond the confines of formal equality.

Later, the judiciary intervened and protected individual women against various forms of discrimination in employment and provided to them workplace specific protection. Through these processes, women gained some ground and consolidated their claim to legal equality.

From cases such as *C.B. Muthamma*[196] and *Nergesh Meerza*,[197] where women workers had to fight for their right to enter into marriage, to cases such as *Neera Mathur*[198] and *Savita Samwedi*,[199] where women raised concerns regarding privacy, dignity, and discrimination, it has been a long and sustained struggle. Gains achieved by a few women who staked their claims and sought the intervention of courts in defense of their rights, helped in the advancement of rights of a multitude of women workers in the organized sector. There have also been efforts to apply the principles enshrined in UN Conventions such as the CEDAW as governing principles of domestic statutes through judicial intervention. To increase political participation of women, the government also introduced reservations for women in local self government bodies such as the panchayats and municipalities.

Despite these gains, discrimination and unfavourable working conditions persist, particularly in the unorganized sector where bulk of the women workforce is located. Here women continue to labour in extremely exploitative conditions, devoid of the constitutional guarantees and protective legislations. Safe transportation to the workplace, maternity benefits, facility of crèches, health care and education of children, and even minimum wages continue to be distant dreams for a large segment of the female workforce who are still awaiting the social revolution promised by the Constitution. Ironically, the protective measures introduced within the organized sector,

[196] *C.B. Muthamma v. Union of India*, AIR 1979 SC 1868.
[197] *Air India v. Nergesh Meerza*, AIR 1981 SC 1829.
[198] *Neera Mathur v. Life Insurance Corporation of India* AIR 1992 SC 392.
[199] *Savita Samwedi v. Union of India* (1996) 2 SCC 380.

such as the Maternity Benefits Act, the Factories Act, the Mines Act, the Plantation Labour Act, the Equal Remuneration Act, etc., instead of improving the condition of women, have instead resulted in pushing them out of the organized labour force.

Judicial interventions and constitutional guarantees, in themselves, do not add up to freedom. If we identify freedom as the main object of development, we confront a stumbling block. Today, developmental indicators are the measures for assessing the nation's accountability to its female citizenry in broader fora such as the United Nations conferences and conventions. India's dismal failure in these respects and the deterioration of the situation is all too apparent in the poor indices of women's status. This is reflected in sex ratio, literacy rates, employment and wages, infant and maternal mortality, life expectancy, and widespread violence against women, both in private and public domains.

Sunder Rajan argues that 'women' as a category have been identified by the State primarily through the index of their 'status' which in turn has been manipulated by the State to serve its various political agenda. For the colonial state, for instance, it indicated the degree of a colonized people's civilizational backwardness or progress. British colonial government's selective measures to improve the condition of Indian women were, therefore, sought to legitimize its rule. At the same time, these interventions, carefully planned in relation to different sections of indigenous patriarchy, left large parts untouched, referring to it as the 'private domain'. The question of women also became central to nationalism at the inception of independent nationhood. Recent feminist researches on partition reveal how fraught the problem of abducted Hindu and Muslim women became to the self-representation of the new Indian and Pakistani nations (Sunder Rajan 2003: 2).

At the dawn of nationhood, while ushering in the new Constitution with its guarantees of the Fundamental Rights of life, liberty, and freedom, the state also had to deal with the aftermath of violence unleashed during partition. The violent wrenching of a colonised country into two post-colonial nation-states and re-drawing of political boundaries resulted in the displacement of a huge population. While entire communities suffered in this process, women were subjected to extreme sexual violence, unleashed upon them as bearers of their community's identity. Apart from killing and maiming, women were also raped and abducted. As per estimates, around 75,000 to 100,000 women were raped or abducted on both sides of the border. Later, these women had to be retrieved and marked as 'citizens' of the new nation-state (Das 1995; Menon and Bhasin 1998; Butalia 2000).

The entire debate on the recovery of abducted women and children at the time was a debate among men in the Indian Constituent Assembly and Parliament. It was a debate about what was happening to 'their' honour, 'their' women, and 'their' children, in which sentiments such as the following were expressed: 'So what if the mother was a Muslim and has gone to Pakistan, the father was a Hindu, and so this child is 'our' child' (Pandey 1996: 19). When the process of 'retrieving' the abducted women and 'restoring' them into their home country, was being carried out from 1948 to 1956,[200] there was a long-drawn debate, especially among women social workers, on the advisability of 'recovering' abducted women and their children who had already settled down with some sense of security in their adoptive country. These

[200] The Abducted Persons Recovery and Restoration Act was enacted in 1949 and remained in force till 1957, after which it was not renewed.

women were not ready to trade-off this security and be uprooted yet again to face an unknown future. They did not know what terrors would await them while being thrown into new communities or camps, sometimes without their children who would be retained by the adoptive state as 'its' citizens.

Even when natal families could be located, these families did not accept the women 'tainted' by men from the 'enemy' country. In order for the women to be accepted, those who were pregnant were forced to undergo abortions. Hindu mothers were forcibly separated from children begotten from Muslim husbands, as these 'Muslim' children would have no future within the new Indian state and it was 'best' that they be left behind while the women were to be 'recovered' and marked with the seal of citizenship. While these were the concerns of women social workers at the ground level, for the male custodians of the nation's pride, it was a question of 'their' honour. The abducted women symbolised the shame of the nation as mother, and hence the honour of the nation had to be restored (Butalia 2000: 191).

It is within this formulation of 'our women' and 'nation's honour' that the gendered citizenship of a post-colonial nation-state was constructed. The relationship between 'state' and 'women' is complex and multi-layered. At one level, women staked their claim for equality with men, for 'sameness' of treatment in the public domain, for equal rights, equal opportunities, and equal protection. But at the same time, their claims were negotiated through other mediums such as tradition, culture, religion, community, and family and were framed by notions of 'honour' and 'stigma'. This leads to the construction not just of a uni-dimensional gendered citizen in opposition to men, but a multi-dimensional one, and compels women to negotiate their citizenship with the State

through a kaleidoscope of identities resulting in layered, fragmented, hierarchical, and at times, overlapping claims.

Within this hierarchy, the Hindu woman becomes the ideal and most deserving object of citizenship. She is constructed as the 'norm'. As a passive citizen, she is synonymous with the nation, deserving protection and reverence. While the male occupies the public space of political activity, she occupies the private space of domestic tranquillity and carries upon her body, the honour of a nation, community, and family.

Where does this construct of the 'ideal' gendered citizen, framed through her religious or community identity and her domestic role, leave the multitude of women who are outside of this construct? Even during the national movement, there were multiple identities of women which were subsumed by the larger than life image of the Hindu woman, the mother figure of *Bharat Mata*. The struggle against foreign rule and for national freedom seemed to have been fought by men, in her honour and for her protection.

Partha Chatterjee argues that the entire concept of tradition and women was reconstituted and reaffirmed within the inner domain of national culture during the national movement (Chatterjee 1994: 117). This 'new' woman was different from the British women and from the lower caste street woman. She was unlike the former as she didn't seek education to attain competitive equality with men and hence retained feminine virtues. She was the reverse of the 'common' woman who was coarse, vulgar, loud, quarrelsome, devoid of superior moral sense, sexually promiscuous, and was subjected to brutal physical oppression by males (ibid.:127). She was an ideal companion to the Indian male, not marred by materialism, and could uphold the sanctity of the nation. The new patriarchy conferred on women this responsibility and bound them to subordination in order to legitimize the idiom of the nation. Recovery of the nation became contingent to protecting the honour of the ideal Hindu woman (ibid.: 130).

But this new conception of the Indian woman was far removed from the ground reality and, at times, blatantly incorrect. In fact, the new construction only reflected the class concerns of the elite and conveniently ignored various categories of women who were wage-earners and were struggling against their working conditions in a colonial capitalist economy. Realities of their lives exposed the constraints and contradictions in the claim of an 'ideal' Hindu woman and notions of her emancipation within the nationalist movement. Even when the nationalists claimed that the women's question had been resolved, women themselves interpreted their struggles as not merely against colonial domination. They saw themselves as struggling on multiple fronts, against social evils of their time and they sought not just national liberation but social transformation to end their political, legal, and economic subordination (Roy 2005: 76).

Women who struggled for their basic rights of survival, like the women in the Telengana movement who entered the public domain of political struggle to fight the oppression of a feudal order, economic oppression of money lenders, and sexual exploitation by both, did not become the symbol of the nation. They defy the notion of a 'passive' citizenship. They were equal partners in the public domain. Their armed struggle along with their menfolk remained unsung and unacknowledged even by the movement, despite its pledge to equality. Male leaders related to these women through the hierarchy of gender. The mechanisms of power which had held them back physically and overtly in the past had been transformed gradu-

ally into modes of social control (Kannabiran and Lalitha 1989: 180-203).

The gendering of citizenship renders women as unequal citizens, not just in opposition to men within the binaries of the public and private domains, but also within the hierarchical order of class, caste, and community. This becomes evident when we trace the post-Independence political events in the context of the lower caste, Dalit woman (Chakravarty 2003; Pawar and Moon 2008). An example of this social hierarchy of gendered citizenship is that while the constitution empowered women through reservations to local panchayats by enacting the 73rd and 74th Amendments to the Constitution, newspapers continued to carry reports of Dalit women *sarpanches* (panchayat heads) being paraded naked and humiliated for holding these positions.[201] Rape of Dalit women continues to be a common occurrence with around 1172 dalit women having been raped during the year 2005, as reflected in the statistics compiled by the National Crime Record Bureau. The landmark cases of rape around which the women's movement built its anti-rape campaigns, Mathura, Rameeza Bee and Banwari Devi, were poor, tribal or Dalit women (Agnes 1995; Kannabiran 2008). Rape, murder, and maiming of Dalit women by upper caste men, as a retaliation for aspirations of the community for economic and social progress, still continues in the villages and towns of Independent India. While most of these violations go unchecked, the gruesome killing of a Dalit woman along with her seventeen-year-old daughter and two sons, in Khairlanji village in Buldhana district of Maharashtra in September 2006, made national headlines when six people

[201] See the news report, 'After MP, Jharkhand women paraded naked', *Times of India*, Bhopal 23 June 2006.

were convicted with death penalty and two with a sentence of life imprisonment.[202] But this judgment was criticized because the accused were charged with murder under section 302 of the IPC, but were acquitted of charges under Prevention of Atrocities Act. Dalit and human rights activists felt that this glossed over the atrocities committed upon citizens solely due to their caste positions. Also awarding death penalty to perpetrators may not be an ideal solution to the problem.[203]

Another stark incidence is the protest by women in Imphal, Manipur against the rape and murder of 32-year-old Thangjam Manorama Devi, the alleged member of Manipur's banned People's Liberation Army (PLA) by the Armed Forces, the Assam Rifles. Manorama's bullet-ridden body was found near her home in Imphal marked with signs of torture and rape. Five days later, as a mark of extraordinary outrage, and in order to get the attention of the country to the plight of Manipuri women, on 15 July 2004, around 30 women, between the ages of 45 and 73, walked naked through the streets of Imphal to the Assam Rifles bastion at Kangla. 'Indian army, rape us too,' they screamed, 'we are all Manorama's mothers'. They were ordinary women. None had met Manorama, but her torture and the government's silence horrified them. How can a civilized nation keep quiet about something like this, they queried. The women narrated that to hide her rape, the Assam Rifles had stuffed cloth in her vagina and shot bullets through her body. When they were done, her body looked like a blood stained battlefield.[204]

Across the ethnic divide, women from various tribes, Meiteis, Nagas and Kukis marched in solidarity. It was not just the death they were protesting against, but the law that made it possible, the Armed Forces Special Powers Act (AFSPA) imposed in Manipur in 1980. It was not a feminist protest of assertion, but an act of desperation, a valiant effort to get their voices heard across the Indian mainland, and question the authority and the brutality of the Indian state. They marched with no other weapons except their naked bodies through which they strived to affirm their citizenship claims within the Indian nation.

No less poignant are the stories from Kashmir where women have been caught in the cross fire between the Indian armed forces and the local militant insurgencies. Since the insurgency began in late eighties, a large number of women have been subjected to sexual violence. Their number surpasses that of women in other conflict areas such as Sierra Leone, Chechnya and Srilanka. Despite the odds, women have played an important role, not just as victims but as survivors of violence, mothers of missing sons, widows of killed men, peace keepers of their communities and bearers of their cultural identity. An informal report brought by a women's group, Women's Initiative (1994: 2) captures their anguish in the following words:

What of the sister who hears that her 13-year-old brother has been 'picked up' for interrogation, knowing as she does that she may never see him again...? How does the mother who has lost three sons find the strength to carry on? What does it mean to be the wife or a sister of a militant? How does she bear the pain of death and separation? How does the woman looking at her innocent son rendered impotent by torture at the hands of the forces keep her faith in humanity alive...? These women are perhaps the bravest of all, for they continue to live and struggle for what they believe to be right. They form the backbone of the (insurgency) movement. They are the ground which sustains life in the midst of death, humanity in the face of guns.

---

[202] 'A Strong Message', Editorial, *Times of India* Mumbai: 26 September 2008.

[203] 'Understanding the Khairlanji Verdict' in *The Hindu*, Chennai: 5 October 2008. Subsequently the high court reduced the death penalty to life imprisonment.

[204] Mihir, Srivastava, 'The Siege Within--Goes On', *Tehelka*, 2 September 2006.

The disputed stakes of national boundaries rupture their daily lives but over the years, living at the edge, they have learnt to live their lives, despite the ruptures and horrors that awaits them at every bend of the road.

The claims for citizenship staked by two other categories of marginalized women, through their composite identity of gender and community, need to be highlighted here—first, the Muslim woman and the second, the 'immoral' bar dancer.

When we examine the claims of Muslim women we are confronted with another set of problems. With the Supreme Court ruling in the controversial *Shah Bano* case, the post-colonial identity of Muslim women emerged in the public domain as a 'victim' of her personal laws. This was followed by the enactment of the Muslim Women's Act in response to the demands from the community (read 'predominantly male'). The constitutional direction to enact a UCC was raised in the context of the *Shah Bano* ruling and its aftermath and got entangled in the wider political debate on minority rights and pluralistic tradition on the one side and national integration and national unity at the other. Resonance of an earlier discourse over *sati,* where women became the site on which a contest between culture, tradition, and modernity was waged, could be discerned in this debate. Muslim women were placed at the centre of this controversy. The debate depicts the tension between two constitutional guarantees—that of equality and non-discrimination and of religious freedom and cultural plurality. While the mandate for enacting a UCC is a Directive Principle of State Policy, equality and multi-culturalism are justiciable Fundamental Rights. It is within this scheme of seemingly conflicting constitutional claims that the periodic pronouncements by the Supreme

Court urging the State to enact a UCC have been examined in this chapter.

The citizenship claims of women and their right to life with dignity, a constitutional mandate under Article 21, became the plank of the majority-minority political contestation and it further fuelled antagonism between both Hindu and Muslim fundamentalists. What began as an argument in defence of women's rights got dissipated in a vortex of patriarchal and communal formulations. The conflict of identities that emerged created a minefield of problems for feminist politics. Principles of secularism and multi-culturalism were subverted within a communally vitiated political climate. The campaign by Hindu right-wing organizations received a boost through the judgments pronounced by the Supreme Court of a secular and pluralistic state.

The media fuelled the controversy by highlighting stray incidents of violation of rights as the 'norm' of the community, while gains made by individual women within the domain of rights and litigation remained outside the public gaze because they were not 'news worthy'. This resulted in a biased and communal view of the Muslim community, Muslim law, and Muslim women. The worst sufferers of this media campaign were Muslim women themselves as the skewed projection of their rights was accepted as a norm not just by Hindu right-wing organizations but also by progressive and socially committed groups, the intelligentsia, the lower judiciary, and worst of all, representatives of Muslim women.

The motif of the vigorously self-multiplying Muslim had been effectively used to whip up Hindu sentiments in support of the Uniform Civil Code, in the post Shah Bano phase, by the right-wing Hindu nationalist political parties. Hence, during the communal riots that rocked the nation since the Shah Bano ruling, even while homes of poor Muslim women were looted, gutted and razed to the ground and teenage sons of Muslim women were killed at point blank ranges in police firings, the mainstream media continued to lament over *Muslim appeasement* and denial of maintenance to '*poor Muslim women / the Shah Banos*'. It is difficult to logically explain the recurring motif of 'Muslim appeasement' which continues even after the Supreme Court decision in *Danial Latifi*[205] case, when the controversy was finally laid to rest by upholding the constitutional validity of the Act and simultaneously securing the rights of Muslim women.

The symbolism becomes even more stark, when we confront the gruesome sexual violations of women during the Gujarat riots in 2002. As narratives of young women, running helter-skelter, slipping, falling and becoming preys to the marauding mobs, their violated and mutilated bodies being thrown into open fires are reported in the media, the question keeps haunting: where and how does one pin the culpability? (Agnes 2002)

The genocide in Gujarat, as well as the earlier communal riots, have taught a painful lesson to Muslim women, that when threatened with a life and death situation, in the face of bloodthirsty and sexually debased mobs, mosques, dargahs and madrasas are transformed into an oasis of security and solace. The bonding between people under siege, is cemented through the adhesive of shared grief and suffering. In the struggle for day to day survival, gender concerns and patriarchal oppressions seem remote. It is here that community and patriarchal identities get forged.

During the communal violence, the women's bodies become a site of almost inexhaustible violence, with infinitely plural and innovative forms of torture, their sexual and reproductive organs are attacked with a special savagery, their children born and unborn, also become the targets of violence and are killed before their eyes (Sarkar 2002). There are myriad ways in which the seemingly innocuous laws of rape, murder, and fundamental rights such as right to life tend to get subverted within the complex terrain of social hierarchies. The violators and the prosecutors merge together and form one consolidated identity mocking the constitutional provisions of separation of powers. It is due to these constitutional violations that the only rape case which came up for legal scrutiny, that of Blikis Bano, was shifted out of Gujarat through a direction of the Supreme Court and had to be prosecuted in Maharashtra, overriding the mandate of criminal trial as laid out in the Code of Criminal Procedure, to secure a conviction.[206]

Despite this, the rhetoric in the context of the Uniform Civil Code, continues. And gets invoked, even in defence of the Gujarat carnage in the post Daniel Latifi phase: '*They had it coming ... they have been 'appeased' beyond tolerance. Why should they demand a separate law in a secular country? Why should they be allowed to marry four times? Why are Hindus alone bound by an obligation of maintenance?*' Within the

---

[205] 2001 (7) SCC 740 : II (2001) DMC 714 (SC)

[206] Bilkis Bano was raped when she was 3 months pregnant. 12 members of her family including her three-year-old daughter in this incident. Her mother and sisters were also raped before they were burnt to death. A sessions court in Gujarat had acquitted the accused. But in a subsequent retrial held in Mumbai 11 rioters were given life imprisonment. See 'Gujarat rioters get life for rape, murder' in *Reuters Insider* Mumbai 21 Jaunary 2008, available at http://in.reuters.com/article/idINIndia-31509620080121 accessed on 16 June 2010.

cultural ethos of the mainstream, an injustice to a Muslim wife gets magically transformed into a Hindu injury, which can be invoked to justify communal carnage (Agnes 2002).

When the moral basis for the rights itself shifts, where can one start the process of renegotiating and reframing the covenants of equality and equal protection? This is a challenging question facing civil society and secular organizations in the contemporary times.

The second category of women who have staked their claim to citizenship in recent times, is the 'immoral woman', the bar dancer of Bombay. The dilemma which surfaced in this context highlights yet another aspect of 'gendered citizenship' demanding a more nuanced theoretical framework of citizenship. The entry of these girls into the bars, which started around 1985, helped boost the liquor trade in the city and was actively encouraged by the state government to increase its revenue by issuing the required licences to bar owners. In 2005, due to the pressure exerted by some conservative women's organizations, the state government declared a ban on dancing in bars. At this time, there were an estimated 2500 such bars which provided livelihood to an estimated 75,000 girls in and around Mumbai as well as in other cities of Maharashtra. A significant number of these women hailed from traditional dancing communities of Rajasthan, Madhya Pradesh, and Uttar Pradesh. Traditionally, these women were heads of their households, the sole breadwinners of their families; most were illiterate. After losing the traditional patronage, the communities were reduced to penury. Developmental policies of the government had bypassed this segment. The dance bars provided them an opportunity to adapt their traditional skills to suit the demands of the new economy. There were also women from other communities who had opted to dance in bars for various personal reasons. They came from Maharashtra and other states. They were young, vibrant women who were able to use their supple bodies to earn their livelihood.

The issue of the bar dancer hit the headlines when a large number of them came out in protest against the police raids. Though the raids were conducted against the bar owners for violating conditions of license, it was the girls who were arrested, detained, and humiliated in the police stations. The heightened media publicity around this protest brought the girls into the limelight which in turn raised the demand for the ban by some women's organizations.[207]

The demand for the ban was grounded on two premises which were contradictory to each other. Firstly, that the bar dancers are evil and immoral, they corrupt the youth and wreck middle class homes, they hanker after easy money and amass a fortune each night by goading innocent and gullible young men into sex and sleaze. Secondly, that bars are, in fact, brothels and bar owners are traffickers who sexually exploit the girls for commercial gains. This premise refused to grant an agency to the women dancers. Rather unfortunately, both these populist premises appealed to the parochial, middle class Maharashtrian sense of morality. What was even worse was that the demand for a ban was framed within the language of 'women's liberation'. The economic disempowerment of this vulnerable class of women came to be projected as a plank which would liberate them from sexual bondage.

The issue received wide media publicity. The sensationalized media projection caused bar dancers further harm. The debate on sexual morality and debasement of metropolitan Mumbai seemed to be revolving around their existence. The blame for every evil in the city was placed at their doorstep, including crime,

---

[207] For a more detailed discussion see Agnes 2007: 158–75.

corruption, and terrorism. Women's groups advocating the ban distributed leaflets which said: 'Sweety or Savithri—who will you choose?' 'Savithri' denoted a traditional Hindu woman, an ideal for Indian womanhood, while 'Sweety' denoted a non-Hindu, debased woman of easy virtue. Ironically, there were no simultaneous demands to close down brothels or to ban the sale of liquor. The demand was confined only to a ban on dancing in the bars. Finally, after much controversy and heated public debate, the government enacted a legislation to bring in the ban, which was passed by the state legislature unanimously. No political party or individual legislator was willing to publicly defend the lowly bar dancers, though leaders of some political parties were owners of some well known dance bars and legislators and party workers were regular patrons of these bars.

After the ban, which, ironically came into effect on 15 August 2005, as the nation celebrated its Independence, the girls lost their means of livelihood. Some returned to their villages disgraced, some opted for prostitution in the city, many had to pull out their teenaged girls from English medium schools (through which they were hoping to change their destiny) and press them into sex work. The number of women visiting clinics for sexually transmitted diseases spiralled, as did incidents of domestic violence among them. Some, pushed to the brink, committed suicide. A few sought employment in bars as waitresses, or 'welcome' girls, earning only a fraction of what they earned as dancers.

A few months later, the ban was struck down by the Bombay High Court on the ground that it violated the fundamental freedom guaranteed under Article 19(1) (g) of the Constitution.[208] 'Are our fundamental rights so fickle that a

citizen has to dance to the State's tune', the Court remarked. Further the court held:

It is true that there is material on record to show that many of those who perform dance in these bars are young girls, a large section being less than 21 years of age and with only a primary education. Can that by itself be a ground to hold that they constitute a threat to public order? Can a girl who may be semi-literate or even illiterate who may be beautiful, knows to dance or tries to dance, prohibited from earning a better livelihood or should such a girl, because of poverty and want of literacy, be condemned to a life of only doing menial jobs?

The State does not find it offensive to the morals or dignity of women and/or their presence in the place of public entertainment being derogatory, as long as they do not dance. The State's case for prohibiting dance in dance bars is, that it is dancing which arouses the physical lust amongst the customers present. There is no arousing of lust when women serve the customers liquor or beer in the eating house, but that happens only when the women start dancing …. The right to dance has been recognized by the Apex Court as part of the fundamental right of speech and expression. If that be so, it will be open to a citizen to commercially benefit from the exercise of the fundamental right. This could be by a bar owner having dance performance or by bar dancers themselves using their creative talent to carry on an occupation or profession. In other words, using their skills to make a living…

Despite this judgment, the girls could not go back to work as the state government obtained a stay in the Supreme Court. The police continued to hound the former bar dancers who were working as waitresses and detained them in custody if they did not have the money to bribe or provide surety for their release. The poorest among these were the Bengali-speaking Muslim girls who were arrested not under the obscenity law or for violating the ban, but under the Passport Act on the ground of being illegal migrants from Bangladesh. These women, living of the margins, across poverty stricken villages of West Bengal and Bangladesh had, out of sheer desperation, reached Bombay in search of livelihood options. The political boundaries drawn on a map which drastically altered their very

---

[208] *Indian Hotel and Restaurants Association (AHAR) v. State of Maharashtra*, 2006 (3) Bom.CR 705.

existence did not mean much to them. They did not have the required documents to prove their citizenship of either state across the border. They were Bengali speaking poor Muslims who had come to Mumbai in search of a livelihood. Most of them claimed Indian nationality but could not prove it as per the strict standards that were stipulated and hence were branded as 'illegal migrants'. A few malnourished women, the poorest of the poor, conceded that they had crossed the border, but did not, they and their infants would have died of starvation. The state dubbed all of them as trafficked migrants and deported them. These women had no rights, unless they could prove their citizenship. For poor migrant women living in the city, proving their nationality and citizenship as per the legal requirements is an impossible task (Agnes 2005). As per the Supreme Court ruling in the illegal migrants case, *Sarbananda Sonowal v. Union of India*,[209] they were not entitled to Fundamental Rights and hence their rights, even to a fair trial, could not be defended.

This brings us to the question of migration and citizenship claims of women. The cross-border movement of the transnational migrant female subject is inadequately addressed in law and policy. This inadequacy owes in part to two conflations—the tendency to address women's cross border movements primarily within the framework of trafficking and the conflation of trafficking with prostitution. In order to make migration policies, international and national, conducive to women's rights, there is a need to consider the nuances of the relationship between trafficking and migration and to de-link trafficking from prostitution.[210]

It is not my case here that prostitutes or sex workers should not be allowed to migrate. We need to acknowledge that sex work is a livelihood option for a large number of women, within a gender specific labour market which has rendered women's sexuality and sex appeal saleable commodities. There is a need to protect the citizenship rights of women engaged in sex work and provide a measure of dignity and protection to them. Some collectives of sex workers, such as Sangram in Nippani (Karnataka) and Durbar Mahila Sammanayee Samiti (DMSS) in Kolkata, have been fighting for de-criminalizing sex work and for health insurance and old age benefits.

However, when we address issues of prostitution, trafficking, and migration in gender specific terms, the debate gets conflated and these terms are used synonymously. In this context, feminist scholars have argued that migration is not trafficking; even irregular migration is not trafficking. Yet, there is an overwhelming tendency to address all cross-border move-

[209] AIR 2005 SC 2920: (2005) 5 SCC 665. In this case, the Supreme Court struck down the provisions of the Illegal Migrants (Determination by Tribunals) Act, 1983, applicable to the State of Assam, which had shifted the onus of proving citizenship to the prosecution. The judgment held that the prosecution cannot prove residence and date of birth, facts exclusivity within the knowledge of migrants. The judgment also held that migration of foreign nationals into the country is to be treated as aggression, as such migration results in internal disturbance. Further it was held that fundamental rights cannot be applied to illegal migrants, including the provision under Article 21 (right to life) and they can be deported without giving them an opportunity of fair hearing. Deportation does not amount to violation of right to life and liberty as the proceedings do not amount to a criminal trial. The foreign illegal migrant is not deprived of his life or personal liberty by identification and deportation.

[210] See the report of the International Seminar held on 9-10 January 2004 at New Delhi, *Cross Border Movements and Human Rights* by the Centre for Feminist Legal Research.

ments of women primarily through the prism of trafficking. Singular attention on trafficking turns the attention away from the larger context of migration and distorts the broader picture of women's movement. In tandem with the propagation of female 'victim-hood,' the trafficking agenda has come to be increasingly influenced by a conservative sexual morality that has gripped some nation-states.

Mobility of women is often viewed as an indication of immorality. It needs to be recognized that migrants and trafficked persons, including those in prostitution, exercise agency and demonstrate decision-making abilities. But since women have been cast in the mould of 'honour' and 'passive citizenship', it is easier to view migrant women as lacking agency. Women are also seen as the hallmark of the cultural and social fabric of society and challenges to 'traditional' gender constructions are seen as posing a dual threat, to women and to the security of the society. This leads to a protectionist approach towards women. Within this protectionist agenda, no distinction is drawn between consensual and coerced movement, resulting in the treatment of all movement of women as coerced and reinforcing presumptions of Third World or poor women as victims, infantile, and incapable of decision-making. The combination of sexual conservatism and the construction women as the symbol of national and cultural authenticity results in stigmatization and ostracism of migrant women who are portrayed as aberrant (Kapur 2002). There is a need to install the trans-national female migrant firmly at the centre of the anti-trafficking and migration agenda by developing a more layered and complicated analyses and more effective intervention strategies.

Developments of the late twentieth and early twenty-first century have forced us to rethink the issue of citizenship within the new paradigm of trans-national migrations, globalization, and multicultural national populations. Roy argues that within the global context, citizenship becomes not just a set of relationships that are historically created which also go beyond notions of circumscribed territoriality, so that national and trans-national citizenships constitute two interrelated and coexisting modalities of citizenship (Roy 2005: 256). She, in turn, relies upon Yuval-Davis and Werbner (1999) who argue that the notion of citizenship as multilayered and dialogical, serves not only to recognize multiple political subjectivities and simultaneous membership in several political communities, but also helps to identify the sites of 'exclusions'.

The insertion of the viable, exclusionary, citizenship concentrates on the way the different positionings of women affect their citizenship within state policies and how these positionings contribute to the construction of boundaries—between national collectivities and between the private and the public. The inclusion of a broad canvas of intersecting-dialogical layers of membership allows us to examine how these intersections and their different or discrepant positionings give rise to 'ambivalences' or 'ambivalent citizens' on the 'borders' of citizenship, viz., refugees and asylum seekers and stateless persons. The state 'protection' against other people ironically renders illegals and labour migrants devoid of their basic human rights and protection of due process law.

Within the complex labyrinth of gendered citizenship, whether the state retrieves its women and adorns them with the seal of citizenship, or inhumanely deports them as illegal migrants in 'push-back' operations by maintaining migration as a threat to national sovereignty, the issue is fraught with problems. The dilemmas which are raised here, will hopefully contribute to a more nuanced discourse over citizenship claims of women.

Cases

Debra Seymour v. *Pradeep Seymour*, II (2002) DMC 144 Del.

Deo Prashad v. *Lujoo Roy*, (1873) 20 WR 102.

Dharmdhar v. *Kanhji Sahay*, AIR 1949 Pat 250.

Dholidas v. *Fulchand*, (1898) ILR 22 Bom 658.

Dilshad Begum Ahmedkhan Pathan v. *Ahmedkhan Hanifkhan Pathan*, II (2007) DMC 738 BOM.

Dilshad Haji Risal v. *State of U.P*, I (2006) DMC 461 All.

Dinsha Petit (Sir) v. *Jamsetji Jeejeebhoy (Sir)*, (1909) ILR 33 Bom 509.

Dowlut Kooer v. *Burma Deo Sahoy*, (1874) 22 WR 54.

Dwarakabai v. *Prof. Mainam Mathews*, AIR 1953 Mad 792.

Dwarakabai v. *Prof. Mainam Mathews*, AIR 1953 Mad 792.

Emperor v. *Mt. Ruri*, AIR 1919 Lah 389.

Farida Bano v. *Kamruddin*, II (2006) DMC 698 MP.

Francis Ghosal v. *Gabri Ghosal*, (1907) ILR 31 Bom 25.

Fuzlunbi v. *K.Khadil Vali*, AIR 1980 SC 1730.

Gama Nisha v. *Chottu Mian*, II (2008) DMC 472 Jha.

Gasito v. *Umrao Jan*, ILR (1894) Cal 1499.

Gaya Prasad v. *Bhagwat*, AIR 1966 MP 212.

Gayatri Devi Pansari v. *State of Orissa*, (2000) 4 SCC 221.

Githa Hariharan v. *Reserve Bank of India*, (1999) 2 SCC 228;, AIR 1999 SC 1149.

Golak Nath v. *State of Punjab*, AIR 1967 SC 1643.

Gonda Kooer v. *Kooer Gody Singh*, (1874) 14 BLR 159.

Govt. of AP v. *P.B. Vijayakumar*, AIR 1995 SC 1648.

Gulab Jagduse Kakwani v. *Kamla Gulab Kakwani*, AIR 1985 Bom 88.

Gungbae v. *Sonabae*, (1853) POC 110.

Hamira Bibi v. *Zubaida Bibi*, AIR 1916 PC 46.

Harvinder Kaur v. *Harminder Singh*, AIR 1984 Del 66.

Hasnumiya Dadamiya v. *Halimunnisa Hafizullah*, AIR 1942 Bom 128.

Henry Fernandes v. *Succorinha Fernandes*, II (2001) DMC 536 Bom.

HHM Madhav Rao Scindia v. *Union of India*, AIR 1971 SC 530.

Hira v. *Radha*, ILR (1913) Bom 116.

Hirbae v. *Sonbae*, (1853) POC 110.

In re. Noise Pollution, (2005) 5 SCC 733.,

In re. Regina Guha, ILR (1916) 44 Cal. 290.

In re. Sudanshu Bala Hazra, AIR 1922 Pat 269.

Indian Hotel and Restaurants Association (AHAR) v. *State of Maharashtra*, 2006 (3) Bom.CR 705.

Indumati Koorichh v. *Yogendra Pal Koorichh*, WP No. 325 of 1993 dated 29.7.1993.

Jacob v. *Jacob*, (1944) ILR 2 Cal 201.

Jagdishwar Prasad v. *Sheo Baksh Rai*, AIR 1919 All 248.

Javed v. *State of Haryana*, AIR 2003 SC 3057.

Jijabai Vithalrao Gajre v. *Pathankhan*, AIR 1971 SC 315.

John Vallamattom v. *Union of India*, AIR 2003 SC 2902.

Jorden Deigdeh v. *S.S. Chopra*, AIR 1985 SC 935.

Joseph Varghese Cheeran v. *Rosy Kurian Kannaikai*, I (2000) DMC 107.

Kailash Wati v. *Ayodhia Parkash*, ILR (1977) 1 P&H 642 FB.

Kalavagunta Venkata Kristnayya v. *Kalavagunta Venkatachalam*, (1908) 32 Mad 185.,

Kanwal Ram v. *The H.P. Administration*, AIR 1966 SC 614.

Kaoosjee Roostumjee v. *Mt. Awan Baee*, Borradaile's Reports SDA Vol. I 1800–1824.

Kaur Sing v. *Jaggar Singh*, AIR 1961 Punj 489.

Kesavananda Bharati v. *State of Kerala*, AIR 1973 SC 1461.

Khwaja Mohammed v. *Husseini Begum*, (1910) 37 IA 152.

Krishna Singh v. *Mathura Ahir*, AIR 1980 SC 707.

Lalit Mohan v. *Tripta Devi*, AIR 1990 J&K 7.

Laxman Naik v. *Lalita Naik*, II (2003) DMC 275 Ori.

Leela Mahadeo Joshi v. *Mahadeo Sitaram Joshi*, AIR 1991 Bom 105.

Ma Yait v. *Maung Chit Maung*, (1921) 48 IA 553: (1921) ILR 49 Cal 310.

Mackinnon Mackenzie & Co Ltd. v. *Audrey D'Costa*, (1987) 2 SCC 469.

Madhu Kishwar v. *State of Bihar*, (1996) 5 SCC 125.

Mahalingam Pillai v. *Amsavalli*, (1956) 2 MLJ 289 DB.

Maina Bibi v. *Vakil Ahmad*, AIR 1925 PC 63: (1924) 52 IA 145 PC.

Manchersha v. *Kamirunissa Begum*, 5 BHCR 109.

Maneka Gandh v. *Union of India*, AIR 1978 SC 597.

Mansur v. *Azizul'*, AIR 1928 Oudh 303.

Marbury v. *Madison*, (1803) 1 Cranch 137.

Maria Sera Pinto v. *Milton Dias*, I (2002) DMC 554.

Mary Roy v. *State of Kerala*, AIR 1986 SC 1011.

Mary Sonia Zachariah v. *Union of India*, 1990 (1) KLT 130.

Mary Sonia Zachariah v. *Union of India*, (II) 1995 DMC 27 FB.

Masroor Ahmed v. *State (NCT of Delhi)*, MANU/DE/9441/2007.

Mathura Naikin v. *Esu*, ILR (1880) Bom 545.

Maya Devi v. *State of Maharashtra*, 1986 1 SCR 743.

Mehafoz Alam Dastagirsab Killedar v. *Shagufta*, I (2004) DMC 76 Kar.

Mihirwanjee Nuoshirwanjee v. *Awan Baee*, 2 Borradaile's Reports SDA Vol. I 1800–24 p. 209.

Minerva Mills Ltd. v. *Union of India*, AIR 1980 SC 1789.

Mithibai v. *Limji N. Banaji*, ILR 5 Bom 506.

Mohd. Ahmad Khan v. *Shahbano Begum*, AIR 1985 SC 945.

Mohini Jain v. *State of Karnataka*, (1992) 3 SCC 666.

Molly Joseph v. *George Sebastian*, (1996), AIR SCW 4267.

Moonshee Buzloor Ruheem v. *Shumsoonissa Begum*, (1867) 2 MIA 551.

Mozelle Robin Soloman v. *Lt. Col. R. J. Soloman*, (1979) 81 Bom. LR 578.

Mt. Bebee Bachun v. *Sheikh Hossein*, (1871) 14 MIA 377.

Muhammad Muin-ud-din v. *Jamal Fatima*, AIR 1921 All 152.

Municipal Corporation of Delhi v. *Female Workers (Muster Roll)*, 2000 (3) SCC 224.

Mussammat Thakoor Deyhee v. *Rai Baluk Ram*, (1886) 11 MIA 139.

Mustari Begum v. *Mirza Mustaque Baig*, II (2005) DMC 94 Ori.

N.R. Radhakrishna v. *Dhanalakshmi*, AIR 1975 Mad 331.

Najmunbee v. *Sk Sikander Sk Rehman*, I (2004) DMC 211 Bom.

Nawab Begum v. *Hussain Ali Khan*, AIR 1937 Lah 589.

Naz Foundation v. *Government of NCT*, 2010 Cri.LJ 94 Del.

Neera Gupta v. *University of Delhi*, AIR 1997 Del 175.

Neera Mathur v. *Life Insurance Corporation of India*, AIR 1992 SC 392.

Noor Bibi v. *Pir Bux*, AIR 1950 Sindh 8.

Nurannessa Khanum v. *Khaje Muhammad Sakru*, AIR 1920 Cal 463.

Olga Tellis v. *Bombay Municipal Corporation*, (1985) 3 SCC 545.

Om Narain Agarwal v. *Nagarpalika, Shahjahanpur*, AIR 1993 SC 1440.

Omprakash v. *Radhacharan*, 2009 (7) SCALES 1.

P. K. Saru v. *P. A. Salim*, (unreported).

Palaniappa Chetiar v. *Alaganchetti* (1921) 48 IA 539.

Parikshat v. *State of UP*, I (2007) DMC 798 All.

Parmanand v. *Jagrani*, AIR 2007 MP 242.

People's Union of Democratic Rights v. *Union of India*, (1982) 3 SCC 235.

Philip v. *Susan Jacob*, II (2001) DMC 290 Ker.

Poonoo Bibi v. *Puex Puksh*, (1875) 15 BLR App.5.

Pragati Verghese v. *Cyril George Verghese*, AIR 1997 Bom 349 FB.

Pratap Singh v. *Union of India*, AIR 1985 SC 1695.

Pratibha Rani v. *Suraj Kumar*, AIR 1985 SC 658 : 1985 Cri.LJ 817.

Praveenben v. *Sureshbhai*, AIR 1975 Guj. 69.

Premchand v. *Lilavathi Shanti*, AIR 1956 HP 17.

Pritam Kaur v. *State of PEPSU*, AIR 1963 Punj 9.

Priya Bala Ghosh v. *Suresh Chandra Ghosh*, AIR 1971 SC 1153.

Pushpabai v. *Pratap Singh*, I (2001) DMC 110 MP.

R. C. Cooper v. *Union of India*, AIR 1970 SC 564 : (1970) 1 SCC 248.

Rabasa Khanum v. *Khodadad Bomanji Irani*, AIR 1947 Bom 272.

Rachel Benjamin v. *Benjamin Soloman Benjamin*, (1926) 28 BLR 328.

Rahimatbae v. *Hadji Jussa & Ors*, (1853) POC 110.

Rahmat Ullah v. *State of U.P.* WP No.45 of 1993 and *Khatoon Nisa* v. *State of U.P.* WP No.57 of 1993 (unreported).

Raj Bahadur v. *Bishen Dayal*, (1882) ILR 4 All 343.

Rajesh Suryawanshi v. *Ujwala Suryawanshi*, I (2002) DMC 536 Bom FB.

Ram Kumari (In the matter of), (1895) 18 Cal 264.

Ram Prakash v. *Savitri Devi*, AIR 1958 Punj 87.

Rameshchandra Daga v. *Rameshwari Daga*, I (2005) DMC 1 SC.

Ramish Francis Toppo v. *Violet Francis Toppo*, 1 (1989) DMC 322 Cal.

Rattan Devi v. *Padam Singh*, 1981 Cri.L.J. 1422.

Rattan Lal v. *Vardesh Chander*, AIR 1976 SC 588.

Revathi v. *Union of India*, AIR 1988 SC 835.

Reynold Rajamani v. *Union of India*, AIR 1982 SC 1261.

Riaz Fatima v. *Mohd. Sharif*, I (2007) DMC 26 Del.

Romila Shroff v. *Jaidev Shroff*, II (2001) DMC 600 FB.

Rukia Khatun v. *Abdul Khalique Laskar*, (1981) 1 GLR 375.

Sabah Khan v. *Adnan Sami Khan*, 2010 (112) Bom. LR 1409.

Sajjan Singh v. *State of Rajasthan*, AIR 1965 SC 845.

Saklat v. *Bella*, (1925) ILR 53 IA 42.

Saleem Basha v. *Mumtaz Begum*, 1998 Cri.LJ 4782 Mad.

Sandha v. *Narayan*, II (1999) DMC 411 Ker.

Sankari Prasad v. *Union of India*, AIR 1951 SC 458.

Sarbananda Sonowal v. *Union of India*, AIR 2005 SC 2920 : (2005) 5 SCC 665.

Sarla Mudgal v. *Union of India*, (1995) 3 SCC 635.

Saroj Rani v. *Sudarshan Kumar Chaddha*, AIR 1984 SC 1562.

Sasson v. *Sasson*, (1924) AC 1007.

Savita Samwedi v. *Union of India*, (1996) 2 SCC 380.

Shahzad v. *Anisa Bee*, II (2006) DMC 229 MP.

Shamim Ara v. *State of UP*, 2002 (7) SCC 518.

Shastri Yagnapurushadasji v. *Muldas Vaishya*, AIR 1966 SC 1119.

Sheo Shankar v. *Debi Sahai*, (1903) 30 IA 202.

Sita Devi v. *Additional Commissioner, Agra*, AIR 1996 All 75.

Skinner v. *Skinner*, (1898) ILR 25 Cal 537 PC.

Solomon Devasahayam v. *Chandirah Mary*, 1968 MLJ 289.

Solomon v. *Muthiah*, (1974) 1 MLJ 53.

Sonubai Yeshwant Jadhan v. *Bala Govinda Yadav*, AIR 1983 Bom 156.

Sowmitri Vishnu v. *Union of India*, AIR 1985 SC 1618.

Sri Jiauddin v. *Anwara Begum*, (1981) 1 GLR 358.

Srinath Gangopadhya v. *Sarbamangala Debi*, (1868) 10 WR 488.

Srinivasa Aiyar v. *Saraswati Ammal*, AIR 1952 Mad 193.

State of Bombay v. *Narasu Appa Mali*, AIR 1952 Bom 84.

Subaratha Mudali v. *Balakrishna Swami Naidu*, (1917) 33 MLJ 207.

Sucha Singh Biswas v. *The State of Punjab*, AIR 1974 P&H 162.

Sultana Begam v. *Sarajuddin*, AIR 1936 Lah 183.

Sundarambal v. *Subbaiah Pillai*, AIR 1961 Mad 323.

Surinder Kaur v. *Gardeep Singh*, AIR 1973 P&H 134.

Susheela Gopalan v. *Union of India*, WP No.1055 of 1986 dated 24 July 1986.

Swapna Ghosh v. *Sadananda Ghosh*, AIR 1989 Cal 1 SB.

Swaraj Garg v. *R.M. Garg*, AIR 1978 Del 296.

T. M. Bashiam v. *M. Victor*, AIR 1970 Mad 12 SB.

T. Raja Rao v. *T. Neelamma*, 1990 Cri.LJ 2430 AP.

T. Sareetha v. *T. Venkatasubbiah*, AIR 1983 AP 356.

T. Sudhakar Reddy v. *Govt. of AP*, 1993 (4) SCC 439.

Tellis v. *Saldanha*, (1986) ILR 10 Mad 69.

Tirath Kaur v. *Kirpal Singh*, AIR 1964 Punj 28.

Union of India v. *K.P. Prabhakaran*, AIR 1995 SC 1695: 1997 (11) SCC 638.

Unnikrishnan J.P. v. *State of AP*, (1993) 1 SCC 645.

Uttarakhand Mahila Kalyan Parishad v. *State of UP*, AIR 1992 SC 1695.

Venku v. *Mahaling*, ILR (1880) Mad 393.

Vishaka v. *State of Rajasthan*, AIR 1997 SC 3011: (1997) 6 SCC 241.

Vishal Jeet v. *Union of India*, AIR 1990 SC 1412.

Visvanathan v. *Saminathan*, (1890) ILR 13 Mad 83.

Waghela Rajsanji v. *Shekh Masluddin*, (1887) 14 IA 89.

Women's Education Society v. *State of Maharasthra*, 2007(109) BLR.1562.

Yadeorao Jogeshwar v. *Vithal Shamaji*, AIR 1952 Nag 55.

Yousuf Abdul Aziz v. *State of Bombay*, AIR 1954 SC 321.

Yudhishter v. *Ashok Kumar*, AIR 1987 SC 558.

Zeenat Fatema Rashid v. *Mohd. Iqbal*, II (1993) DMC 49 Gau.

Zulekha Begum v. *Abdul Rehman*, II (2000) DMC 99 Kar.

Bibliography

Books

Agarwal, Bina, *A Field of One's Own: Gender and Land Rights in South Asia,* Cambridge: Cambridge University Press (1994).

Agnes, Flavia, S. Chandra, and M. Basu, *Women and Law in India,* New Delhi: Oxford (2004).

Agnes, Flavia, *Law and Gender Inequality,* New Delhi: Oxford University Press (1999).

Agnes, Flavia, *State, Gender and the Rhetoric of Law Reform,* Bombay: SNDT Women's University (1995).

Ahmad, F., *Triple Talaq: An Analytical Study,* New Delhi: Regency Publications (1994).

Ameer Ali, Syed, *Mohammedan Law* Vol. I, Calcutta: TLLS 1912 (4th ed.) and Vol. II Calcutta: TLLS 1929 (5th ed.).

Austin, G., *The Indian Constitution: Cornerstone of a Nation,* New Delhi: Oxford University Press (2001).

Balchin, C., (ed.) *A Handbook on Family Law in Pakistan,* Lahore: Shirkat Gah (1994) (2nd ed.).

Basu, Srimati, *She Comes To Take Her Rights,* New Delhi: Kali for Women (2001).

Basu, A and B. Rai, *A History of the AIWC 1927 – 1990,* Delhi: Manohar (1992).

Basu, M., *Hindu Women and Marriage Law,* New Delhi: Oxford University Press (2001).

Basu, T., et al., *Khaki Shorts and Saffron Flags,* New Delhi: Orient Longman (1993).

Baxi, U., *Towards a Sociology of Indian law.* New Delhi: Satvahan (1986).

Bhattacharjee, A.M., *Hindu Law and the Constitution,* (2nd ed.), Calcutta: Eastern Law House (1994).

Bhattacharjee, A.M., *Matrimonial Laws and the Constitution,* Calcutta: Eastern Law House (1996).

Buch, Nirmala, *The Law of Two Child Norm in Panchayats,* New Delhi: Concept Publishing (2006).

Buhler, Georg, *The Laws of Manu,* (reprint), Delhi: Motilal Banarsidass (1975).

Butalila, Urvashi, *The Other Side of Silence: Stories from the Partition of India,* New Delhi: Sage Publications (2000).

Cabinetmaker, P.H., *Parsis and Marriage,* Pune: International Institute of Population Studies (Mimeograph) (1991).

Cardozo, Benjamin N., *The Nature of the Judicial Process,* New Haven: Yale University Press (1921).

Catholic Encyclopedia, Pentateuch, New York: Robert Appleton (1913).

Chakravarti Uma, *Gendering Caste: Through a Feminist Lens,* Stree: Calcutta (2003).

Chandra, S., *Enslaved Daughters,* New Delhi: Oxford University Press (1998).

Chatterjee, Partha, *The Nation and its Fragments: Colonial and Postcolonial Histories,* New Delhi: Oxford University Press (1994).

Chaudhuri, M., (ed.), *Feminism in India,* (Issues in Contemporary Indian Feminism Series, Vol.2),

New Delhi: Kali for Women & Women Unlimited (2004),.

Cohn, Bernard S., *Colonialism and its Form of Knowledge: The British in India*, New Delhi: Oxford University Press (1997).

Cotterrell, Roger, *Law, Culture and Society: Legal Ideas in the Mirror of Social Theory*, Aldershot: Ashgate (2006).

Cotterrell, Roger, *The Politics of Jurisprudence: A critical Introduction to Legal Philosophy*, Philadelphia: University of Pennsylvania Press (1989).

Cousins, Margarete, *Indian Womanhood Today*, Allahabad: Kitabisthan (1941).

Das, Veena, *Critical Events: An Anthropological Perspective on Contemporry India*, New Delhi: Oxford University Press (1995).

De Beauvoir, Simone. *The Second Sex*, translated by H. M. Parshley, Harmondsworth: Penguin [1949] (1972).

Derrett, D.J. M., *The Death of Marriage Law: Epitaph for the Rishis*, New Delhi: Vikas (1978).

Derrett, D.J.M., *Hindu Law Past and Present*, Calcutta: Mukherjee & Co. (1957).

Derrett, D.J.M., *Religion, Law and the State in India*, New Delhi: Oxford University Press (1999).

Desai, Neera, *Women in Modern India*, 2nd ed.. Bombay: Vora & Co. (1977).

Desai, S.T. (ed.), *Mulla's Principles of Hindu Law*, Bombay: N.M. Tripathi (1994) (16th ed.) and New Delhi: Butterworths (1998) (17th ed.) .

Dhagamwar, V., *Towards the Uniform Civil Code*, Bombay: N.M. Tripathi (1989).

Diwan Paras and Peeyushi Diwan, *Law of Adoption, Minority, Guardianship and Custody*, Allahabad: Wadwa & Co. (1993).

Diwan, Paras and Peeyushi Diwan, *Law of Marriage and Divorce*, Delhi: Universal Law Publishing Co. (1988) (2nd ed.) and (1997) (3rd ed.).

Diwan, P., *Hindu Law*, Allahabad: Wadhwa & Company (1995).

Diwan, P., *Muslim Law in Modern India*, Allahabad: Allahabad Law Agency, (6th ed.), (1993).

Dube, L., *Matriliny and Islam Religion and Society in the Laccadives*, Delhi: National Publishing House (1969).

Elwin, V., *The Tribal World of Verrier Elwin*, New Delhi: Oxford University Press (1964).

Fineman, M. A., *Illusion of Equality: The Rhetoric and Reality of Divorce Reform*, Chicago: The University of Chicago Press (1991).

Fineman, M. A., *The Neutered Mother, The Sexual Family and Other Twentieth Century Tragedies*, New York: Routledge (1995).

Forbes, Geraldine, *Women in Modern India*, Cambridge: Cambridge University Press (1999).

Framjee, D., *The Parsees, Their History, Manners, Custom and Religion*, London: Smith Elder & Co. (1858).

Fyzee, A.A.A., *Outlines of Muslim Law*, (4th ed.), New Delhi: Oxford University Press (1974).

Galanter, Marc, *Law and Society in Modern India* (paperback), New Delhi: Oxford University Press (1989).

Gill, K., *Hindu Women's Right to Property in India*, Delhi: Deep & Deep Publications (1986).

Gooptu, S., *Cornelia Sorabji: India's Pioneer Woman Lawyer*, New Delhi: Oxford Univesity Press (2006).

Gough, K. E., *Rural Changes in Southeast India: 1950s to 1960s*, Oxford: Oxford University Press (1989).

Gough, K. E., *Rural Society in Southeast India*, Cambridge: Cambridge University Press (1981).

Grafe, H., *History of Christianity in India: Tamilnadu in the Nineteenth and Twentieth Centuries*, Vol. IV (Part 2), Bangalore: The Church History Association of India (1982).

Guha, R., *India after Gandhi: The History of the World's Largest Democracy*, London: Macmillan, (2007).

Hasan, Z., *Forging Identities: Gender, Communities and the State*, New Delhi: Kali for Women (1994).

Hidayatullah, M. and A. Hidayatullah, *Mulla's Principles of Mahomedan Law* (19th ed.), Bombay: N.M. Tripathi (1990).

Hunt A. and G. Wickham., *Foucault and Law: Towards a Sociology of Law as Governance*, London : Pluto Press (1998).

Jackson, J. (ed), *Raydens's Law and Practice in Divorce and Family Matters*, London: Butterworths (1983).

Jain, M.P., *Outlines of Indian Legal History*, 2nd ed., Bombay: N.M. Tripathi (1966).

Kapur, R. and B. Cossman, *Subversive Sites*, New Delhi: Sage Publications (1995).

Karve, I., *Kinship Organisation in India: A Study of Various Social Institutions in India*, Poona: Deccan College Monograph Series Vol.11 (1953).

Katz, Nathan and Ellen Goldberg, *The Last Jews of Cochin: Jewish Identity in Hindu India*, Columbia, SC: University of South Carolina Press (1993).

Katz, Nathan, *Who Are the Jews in India*, Berkeley: University of California Press (2000).

Kumar, R., *The History of Doing: An Illustrated Account of Movements for Women's Rights and Feminism in India 1800 – 1990*, New Delhi: Kali for Women (1993).

Kuppuswami, A., *Mayne's Treatise on Hindu Law and Usage*, (13th ed.), New Delhi: Bharat Law House (1993).

MacKinnon, C., *Towards a Feminist Theory of State*, Cambridge Mass: Harvard University Press (1989).

Mahmood, T., *Family Law Reform in the Muslim World*, Bombay: N.M. Tripathi (1972).

Mahmood, T., *An Indian Civil Code and Islamic Law*, Bombay: N.M. Tripathi (1976).

Maine, Henry Sumner, (1861), *Ancient Law*, (reprint), London: Everyman Edition (1972).

Maine, Henry Sumner (1875), *Early History of Institutions*, (reprinted, 7th ed.), New York: Kennikat Press (1966).

Majumdar, D. N., *Culture Change in Two Garo Villages*, Calcutta: Anthropology Survey of India, Govt. of India (1978).

Manchanda, S., *Parsi Law in India*, (5th ed.), Allahabad: The Law Book Co. (1991).

Mandelbaum, D.G., *Society in India*, Berkeley: University of California Press (1970).

Marshall, T.H., *Citizenship and Social Class and Other Essays*, Cambridge: Cambridge University Press (1950).

Mayaram, Shail (1997), *Resisting Regimes: Myth, Memory and the Shaping of a Muslim Identity*, New Delhi: Oxford University Press (1997).

Menon, Nivedita, *Recovering Subversion*, Delhi: Permanent Black (2004).

Menon, Ritu, and Kamla Bhasin, *Borders and Boundaries: Women in India's Partition*, New Delhi: Kali for Women (1998).

Mensky, W., *Hindu Law: Beyond Tradition and Modernity*, New Delhi: Oxford University Press (2003).

Minault, G., *Secluded Scholars: Women's Education and Muslim Social Reform in Colonial India*, New Delhi: Oxford University Press, (1998).

Mohanty, Chandra T., *Feminism Without Borders: Decolonising Theory, Practising Solidarity*, New Delhi: Zubaan (2003).

Mukhopodyay, Maitrayee, *Legally Dispossessed: Gender, Identity and the Process of Law*, Calcutta: Stree (1998).

Mullati, L., *The Bhakti Movement and the Status of Women: A Case Study of Virasaivism*, New Delhi: Abhinav Publications (1986).

Okin, Susan Moller, *Justice Gender and The Family*, New York: Basic Books (1989).

Oldenburg, Veena Talwar, *Dowry Murder: The Imperial Origins of a Cultural Crime*, New Delhi: Oxford University Press (2002).

Parashar, A., *Women and Family Law Reform in India*, New Delhi: Sage Publications (1992).

Pateman, Carole, *The Sexual Contract*, Stanford: Stanford University Press (1988).

Pawar, Urmila and Meenakshi Moon, *We Also Made History: Women in Ambedkarite Movement* (Translated and with an introduction by Wandana Sonalkar), New Delhi: Zubaan (2008).

Raghavachariar, N.R., *Hindu Law: Principles and Precedents*, (7th ed.) Vol I & II., Madras: The Madras Law Journal Office (1980)

Rao, Shiva, B., *The Framing of India's Constitution, A Study, and Select Documents*, Vols. I–IV. New Delhi: Indian Institute of Public Administration (1968)

Rawls, John, *A Theory of Justice*, Cambridge, MA: Harvard University Press (1971).

Reddy, Muthulaksmi, *Margaret Cousins and Her Work in India*, Madras: WIA (1956).

Roland, Joan G., *Jews in British India: Identity in a Colonial Era*, Hanover: Unverisity Press of New England (1989).

Roy Chowdhury, S.K., and H.D. Saharay (eds), *Paruck's The Indian Succession Act*, (7th ed.), Bombay: N.M. Tripathi (1988).

Roy, Anupama, *Gendered Citizenship: Historical and Conceptual Explorations*, New Delhi: Orient Longman (2005).

Sachs, A. and J. H. Wilson, *Sexism and the Law: A Study of Male Beliefs and Judicial Bias*, Law in Society Series, Oxford: Martine Robertson (1978).

Sarat, Austin and Thomas Kearns (ed.), *Justice and Injustice in Law and Legal Theory* Ann Arbor: University of Michigan Press (1998).

Sarkar, Lotika and B. Sivaramayya, *Women and Law Contemporary Problems*, New Delhi : Vikas Publishing House (1994).

Schacht, Joseph, *An Introduction to Islamic Law*, Delhi: Oxford University Press (1964).

Sen, Amartya K., *Development as Freedom*, Oxford: Oxford University Press (1999).

Sen, Amartya K., *The Idea of Justice*, London: Allen Lane (2009).

Sen, M., *Death by Fire*, New Delhi: Penguin Books India (2001).

Shah, P., *Legal Pluralism in Conflict*, London: Glass House Press (2005).

Shastri, G.C. Sarkar, *A Treatise on Hindu Law*, 7th ed., Calcutta: B. Banerjee & Co. (1933).

Shiva Rao, B., *The Framing of India's Constitution*, Vol. II, New Delhi: The Indian Institute of Public Administration (1968).

Shodhan, A., *A Question of Community*: *Religious Groups and Colonial Law*, Calcutta: Stree Publications (2001).

Srinivas, M.N., *Caste in Modern India and Other Essays*, Bombay: Media Promoters & Publishers (1962) (Rpt 1986).

Srinivas, M.N., *Some Reflections on Dowry*, New Delhi: Oxford University Press (1984).

Srinivas, M.N., *Village, Caste, Gender and Method*, New Delhi: Oxford University Press (1998).

Steele, A., *Hindu Caste, Their Law, Religion and Customs*, Bombay: Courier Press (1827).

Sunder Rajan, Rajeshwari, *The Scandal of the State*: *Women, Law and Citizenship in Post Colonial India*, Ranikhet: Permanent Black (2003).

Talim, M., *Women in Early Buddhist Literature*, Bombay: Popular Prakashan (1972).

Tayabji, Kamila cited in Mahmood, T., *An Indian Civil Code and Islamic Law*, Bombay: N.M. Tripathi (1976) p. 29.

Thapar, R., *A History of India*, Vol. I, Delhi: Penguin (1992).

Tharu, Susie and K. Lalita (ed.), *Women Writing in India: 600 BC. to the Present*, Vol. I, New Delhi: Oxford University Press (1991).

Thekkedath, J., *History of Christianity in India 1542 – 1700*, Vol. II, Bangalore: The Church History Association of India (1982).

Tope, T. K., *Constitutional Law of India*, (2nd ed.), Eastern Book Company, New Delhi: (1992).

Trautmann, T.R., *Dravidian Kinship*, Cambridge: Cambridge University Press (1981).

Usgaocar, M.S., *Family Laws of Goa, Daman and Diu*, Vol. II, Panaji: Vela Associates (1988).

Usgaocar, M.S., *Family Laws of Goa, Daman and Diu*, Vol. I, Vaso Da Gama: Devi Shreeevani Education Society (1980).

Young, Iris Marion, *Justice and the Politics of Difference*, Princeton: Princeton University Press (1990).

Yuval-Davis, Nira and Pnina Werbner, *Women, Citizenship and Difference*, London: Zed Books (1999).

Articles in Books and Journals

Aggarwal, R., 'Uniform Civil Code: A Formula not a Solution' in Mahmood T. (ed.), *Family Law and Social Change*, Bombay: N.M. Tripathi (1975) pp. 110–44.

Agnes, Flavia, 'Triple Talaq Judgment Do Women Really Benefit', *Economic and Political Weekly*, vol. XXIX, no. 20 (1994) p. 1169.

Agnes, Flavia, 'Economic Rights of Muslim Women', *Economic and Political Weekly*, vol. XXXI, no. 41–42 (1996) p. 2832.

Agnes, Flavia, 'Hindu Men, Monogamy and the Uniform Civil Code', *Economic and Political Weekly*, vol. XXX, no.50 (1995) p. 3238.

Agnes, Flavia, 'Women, Marriage, and the Subordination of Rights' in P. Chatterjee and P. Jeganathan (ed) *Community, Gender and Violence*, Subaltern Studies, Volume XI Delhi : Permanent Black (2000) p. 106–37.

Agnes, Flavia, 'State Control and Sexual Morality: The Case of the Bar Dancers of Mumbai' in John, Mathew and Sitharamam Kakarala (ed.), *Enculturing Law: New Agenda for Legal Pedagogy*, New Delhi: Tulika Books (2007) pp. 158–75.

Agnes, Flavia, 'Transgressing Boundaries Of Gender & Identity', *Economic and Political Weekly*, vol. XXXVII, no. 36, (2002) p. 3695.

Agnes, Flavia (forthcoming) 'From *Shahbano* to *Kausar Bano*: Contextualizing the 'Muslim Woman' within a Communalised Polity' in Ania Loomba and Ritty Lukose (ed.) *Feminisms in South Asia: Contemporary Interventions* Durham: Dukes University Press.

Agrawala, Raj Kumari and A. Ramanamma, 'Women and the Family Law' in Sarkar,

Lotika and B. Sivaramayya, *Women and Law: Contemporary Problems*, New Delhi: Vikas Publishing House (1994) p. 248–68.

Bartlett, Katharine T., 'Feminist Legal Methods', *Harvard Law Review*, vol. 103 (1990).

Basu, A., 'A Century and Half's Journey: Women's Education in India, 1850s to 2000' in Bharati Ray (ed.), *Women of India: Colonial and Post-Colonial Periods*, Vol. IX, Part 3, New Delhi: Sage Publications (2005) p.183–207.

'Beyond the law: The strange case of Justice Tilhari', *Frontline* 20 May 1994. p. 35.

Bindra, A., 'Child Custody for Hindus Only', *The Lawyers*, vol. IX, no. 2 (1994) p. 11.

Chari, Anurekha, 'Gendered Citizenship and Women's Movements', *Economic and Political Weekly*, vol. XLIV, no.17 (2009) pp.47–57.

Chaudhuri, M., 'The Indian Women's Movement' in M. Chaudhuri, (ed.), *Feminism in India*, New Delhi: Kali for Women & Women Unlimited (Issues in Contemporary Indian Feminism Series, Vol.2, (2004) pp. 117–33.

Choudhuri, M., 'Citizens, Workers and Emblems of Culture: An Analysis of the First Plan Document on Women' in Patricia Uberoi (ed.), *Social Reform, Sexuality and the State*, New Delhi: Sage Publicatons, (1996) pp. 211–38.

Choudhry, Prem, 'Customs in a Pesant Economy: Women in Colonial Haryana' in Kumkum Sangari and Sudesh Vaid (eds), *Recasting Women*, New Delhi: Kali for Women (1989) p. 302–36.

Choudhurani, Saraladevi, 'A Women's Movement', Calcutta: Modern Review, October, (1911) p. 345.

Cotterrell, Roger, 'Foreword' in Prakash Shah, *Legal Pluralism in Conflict*, London: Glass House Press (2005).

Crenshaw, Kimberlé, 'Mappping the Margins: Intersectionality, Identity Politics and Violence Against Women of Color', *Stanford Law Review*, vol.43, no.6 (1991) pp. 1241–99.

Crenshaw, Kimberlé, 'Demarginalizing the Intersection of Race and Sex: A Black Feminist Critique of Antidiscrimination Doctrine, Feminist Theory and Antiracist Politics', *University of Chicago Legal Forum* (1989).

Devi, Rasasundari, *Amar Jiban* in Nareshchandra Jana et al. (eds), *Atmakatha* Vol.I, Calcutta: Ananya Prakashan, (1981) (First Published in 1876).

Dube, L., 'Conflict and Compromise Devolution and Disposal of Property in Matrilineal Muslim Society', *Economic and Political Weekly*, vol. XXIX, no. 21 (1994) p. 1273.

Dube, L., 'Conflict and Compromise Devolution and Disposal of Property in Matrilineal Muslim Society', *Economic and Political Weekly*, vol. XXIX, no. 21 (1994) pp. 1273–84.

Fraser, Nancy and Linda Nicholson, 'Social Criticism without Philosophy: An Encounter between Feminism and Postmodernism', in Cohen Avner and Maracelo Descal (ed.) *La Salle, Ill*: Open Court (1988) as cited by Minow Maratha, *Making All the Difference: Inclusion, Exclusion, and American Law*, New York: Cornell University (1990).

Fyzee, A.A.A., 'The Muslim Wife's Right of Dissolving Her Marriage', 38 Bom.LR (1936) p. 113.

Haksar, N., 'The Political Issues', *Seminar*, No. 441 (1996) p. 39.

Kannabiran, K.G., 'Outlawing Oral Divorce', *Economic and Political Weekly*, vol. XXIX, no. 25 (1994) p. 1509.

Kannabiran, Kalpana, 'Sexual Assault and the Law', in Kannabiran Kalpana and Ranbir Singh (eds), *Challenging the Rule(s) of Law: Colonialism, Criminology ad Human Rights in India*, New Delhi: Sage Publications (2008).

Kannabiran, V and K. Lalitha 'That Magic Time: Women in the Telangana People's Struggle' in K. Sangari and S. Vaid (ed.), *Recasting Women: Essays in Colonial History*, New Delhi : Kali for Women (1989) pp.180–203.

Kapur, R, 'The Tragedy of Victimization Rhetoric: Resurrecting the 'Native' Subject in International/Post Colonial Feminist Legal Politics', *Harvard Human Rights Journal*, Spring (2002).

Kapur, Ratna, 'Tragedy of victimization rhetoric of the 'Native' subject in International/Post-Colonial Feminist Legal Politics' 15 *Harvard Human Rights Journal*, 1 (2002).

Karat, B., 'Step by Step Approach: Equal Rights, Equal Laws', *Women's Equality*, vol. V, no. 1 (1993) p. 5.

Karat, B., 'Uniformity vs Equality: The concept of uniform civil code', *Frontline*, 17 November 1995, p. 25.

Kasturi, L., 'Report of the Sub-Committee, *Women's Role in Planned Economy*, National Planning Committee Series (1947)' in M. Chaudhuri (ed.), *Feminism in India*, New Delhi: Kali for Women & Women Unlimited (2004) (Issues in Contemporary Indian Feminism Series) (Vol.2) pp. 136–55.

Khanna, S., 'Padmasini's Quest for Justice', *The Lawyers*, VII/2 (1992) p.25.

Kishwar, M., 'Codified Hindu Law: Myth and Reality', *Economic and Political Weekly*, vol. XXIX, no. 33 (1994) p. 2145.

Lateef, S., 'Defining Women through Legislation' in Z. Hasan, (ed), *Forging Identities: Gender, Communities and the State*, New Delhi: Kali for Women (1994).

Mani, L., 'Contentious Traditions: The Debate on Sati in Colonial India' in K. Sangari and S. Vaid (ed.), *Recasting Women: Essays in Colonial History*, New Delhi : Kali for Women (1989) pp. 88–126.

Maududi, Syed Abdul A'la, *Huquq-uz-Zaujain*, (9th ed.), Lahore 1964, translated from Urdu by Tahir Mahmood, *The Muslim Law of India*, (3rd ed.), New Delhi: LexisNexis Butterworths: New Delhi.

Mishra, V.C. (ed.), 'Special Issue on Uniform Civil Code', *Indian Bar Review*, vol. XVIII, no. 3–4 (1991).

Moraes, Frank, 'In Political Life' in Tara Ali Baig (ed), *Women in India*, Delhi: Manager Press (1958).

Mukund, K., 'Turmeric Land: Women's Property Rights in Tamil Society since Medieval Times', *Economic and Political Weekly*, vol. XXVII, no.17 (1992) p.WS-2.

Navlakha, G., 'Triple Talaq: Posturing at Women's Expense' *Economic and Political Weekly*, vol. XXIX, no. 21 (1994) p.1264.

Pandey, Gyan, 'Partition and Poltiics of History' in Madhusree Dutta et al (ed.), *The Nation, the State and Indian Identity*, Calcutta: Samya (1996) pp. 1–26.

Rao, Mohan, 'Two Child Norm and Panchayats: Many Steps Back', *Economic and Political Weekly*, vol. XXXVIII, no. 33 (2003) p. 3452.

'Recommendations of the Lawyers Collective Bangalore Law School', *The Lawyers*, vol. III, no. 7 (1988) p. 20.

Saradamoni, K., 'Progressive Land Legislations and Subordination of Women' in Lotika Sarkar and B. Sivaramayya, *Women and Law: Contemporary Problems*, New Delhi: Vikas Publishing House (1994) pp155–67.

Sarkar, T., 'Rhetoric Against Age of Consent', *Economic and Political Weekly*, vol. XXVIII, no. 36 (1993) pp. 1869–78.

Sarkar, Tanika, 'Semiotics of Terror', *Economic and Political Weekly*, vol. XXXVII, no. 28 (2002) p. 2872.

Sathe, S.P., 'Uniform Civil Code Implications of the Supreme Court Judgment', *Economic and Political Weekly*, vol. XXX, no. 35 (1995) p. 2165.

Singh, K., 'Combating Communalism', *Seminar*, no.441 (1996) p.55

Sivaramayya, B., 'The Special Marriage Act, 1954 Goes Awry' in V. Bagga, (ed.) *Studies in the Hindu Marriage and the Special Marriage Acts*, Bombay: N.M Tripathi (1978).

Srivastava, Mihir, 'The Siege Within – Goes On', *Tehelka*, 2 September 2006.

Tiwari, B., 'Marriage Laws Revamped', *The Lawyers*, vol. X, no. 5 (1995) p.28.

Uberoi, P., 'Saving Custom or Promoting Incest? Post Indpendence Marriage Law and Dravidian Marriage Practices' in Archana Parashar and Amita Dhanda (ed.), *Redefining Family Law in India*, New Delhi: Routledge (2008) pp. 54–85.

Uberoi, P., 'When Is a Marriage not a Marriage? Sex, Sacrament and Contract in Hindu Marriage' in P. Uberoi, (ed.), *Social Reform, Sexuality and the State*, New Delhi: Sage Publicatons (1996) p. 319–46.

Upadhya, Carol Boyack, 'Dowry and Women's Property in Coastal Andhra Pradesh', *Contributions to Indian Sociology*, vol. 24, no. 1 (1990) pp.29–59.

Vargo, N. and R. Goldfaden, 'The Goa Uniform Civil Code: Alive and Kicking' *The Lawyers*, vol. X, no. 7 (1995) p.21.

Yadav, Bhupendra, 'Khap Panchayats: Stealing Freedom?', *Economic and Political Weekly*, vol. XLIV, no. 52 (2009–2010) pp.16–18.

Yuval-Davis, Nira, 'Women, Citizenship and Difference', *Feminist Review*, no.57 Autumn (1997) pp.4–27.

Official Documents

'Memorial addressed to the Education Commission' by J.G. Phooley (Phule) 19 October, 1882 in Education Commission Report (Bombay), Calcutta, (1884) pp.140–154.

Annual Report 2003–4 of the National Commission for Backward Classes.

Borradaile's Report of Civil Cases (SDA) 1820–24

Constituent Assembly Debates

Fourth Annual Report of the Minorities Commission (1983).

Gazette of India

Gazette of India, Extraordinary, Part II, S. 2, 22 June 1962.

Joint Select Committee Report, 'Evidence on Adoption Bill'.

Law Commission Reports

Lok Sabha Debates

Parliamentary Debates

Rajya Sabha Debates

Report of the Committee on Reforms of Criminal Justice System, Government of India, Ministry of Home Affairs (Malimath Committee Report) (March, 2003).

Report of the Committee on Status of Women, *Towards Equality* (1974).

Report of the Sub-Committee, 'Woman's Role in Planned Economy', 1947.

Sapru, Tej Bahadur (Sir) and Others, *Constitutional Proposals of the Sapru Committee*, the Sapru Report, (1945) p. 260.

Informal Publications

'A Study of Muslim Women in India' by Women's Research and Action Group, Bombay (WRAG) Vol. I/2 (September, 1994) Vol.II/1 (February, 1995) Vol. II/2–3 (August, 1995) and Vol. II/4 (October, 1995) (Informal Newsletter of the Organization).

'*Cross Border Movements and Human Rights*, Report of the International Seminar held on January 9–10 2004, New Delhi: Centre for Feminist Legal Research (2004).

Women's Initiative (1994), *Women's Testimonies from Kashmir: The Green of the Valley is Khaki*. New Delhi: Women's Initiative.

Agnes, F., *A Study of Family Courts*, Bangalore: National Law School of India University (2006) Unpublished.

Newspaper Articles

'A Strong Message', Editorial, *Times of India* (Mumbai), 26 September 2008.

'After MP, Jharkhand women paraded naked ', *Times of India*, 23 June 2006.

'Law Board makes it official: Shia women get divorce rights', *Indian Express* 27 November 2006.

'Nikahnama draft allows couples to opt for arbitration', *Times of India*, 27 September 2004.

'Rajya Sabha Passes Women's Reservation Bill', *Times of India*, 10 March 2010.

'Another Shah Bano in the Making', *Times of India*, 25 April 1994.

'Avadh Bar to Suspend Advocate General', *Times of India*, 19 May 1994.

'Divorced From Reality', *The Pioneer*, 25 April 1994.

'Fear Behind the Purdah', *Blitz*, 21 May 1994.

'Muslim women welcome court verdict on talaq', *The Statesman*, 22 April 1994.

'Muslims resent talaq verdict', *Times of India*, 18 April 1994.

'One Nation, One Law', *Sunday*, 1–7 May 1994.

'The practice is contrary to the spirit of Islam', *Indian Express*, 25 April 1994.

'Triple Talaq Again', *Times of India*, 19 April 1994.

'Understanding the Khairlanji Verdict', *The Hindu*, (Chennai), 5 October 2008.

Agnes, F., '*An Illusion of Equality*' *Asian Age*, (Bombay), 10 January 2006, p.10.

Agnes, F., 'In the Dock', *Humanscape*, August 1996, p.25.

Agnes, Flavia 'Vicious is the wrath of the state' *Asian Age*, (Edit) 1 November 2005.

Ashraf, A., 'A cap and a beard: Is that all to Muslims' *The Pioneer*, 1 May 1994.

Badshah, H., 'Uniform Civil Code - Chasing a Mirage' *The Hindu*, 24 December 1995.

Baig, T. A., 'Urgency of Adoption Law' *Mainstream*, 15 November 1980, pp.9–10.

Basu, A., 'Behind the Four Walls The Veil' *The Statesman*, 30 April 1994.

Chadha, K., 'The law that breaks the Constitution' *Hindustan Times*, 8 August 1993.

Hariharan, Gita 'A New Emergency' *The Telegraph*, (Kolkata) 24 August 2003.

Latifi, D. 'Verdict on talaq' *Hindustan Times*, 5 May 1994.

Mali, A, 'Uniformity among equals' *Hindustan Times*, 8 May 1994.

Sardar, Ziauddin, 'Change is coming to Islam', *Times of India*, 26 December 2004.

Sharma, Vrinda, 'Khap Panchayat Leaders Condemn Ruling', *The Hindu*, 14 April 2010.

Singh, Gajinder, 'Death for Honour Killling', *The Telegraph*, 31 March 2010.

Swamy, Kumara, V., 'Unfair Deal', *The Telegraph*, 20 May 2009.

Vyas, N., 'Much more at stake than triple talaq' *The Hindu*, 1 May 1994.

Internet Sources

'Gujarat rioters get life for rape, murder" in *Reuters Insider*', 21 January 2008, available at http://in.reuters.com/article/idINIndia-31509620080121, accessed on 16 June 2010

http://adaniel.tripod.com/cochin.htm, accessed on 30 May 2010

http://philtar.ucsm.ac.uk/encyclopedia/judaism/cochin.html, accessed on 2 June 2010

Index